The Big Fail

The Big Fail

WHAT THE PANDEMIC REVEALED ABOUT WHO AMERICA PROTECTS AND WHO IT LEAVES BEHIND

Joe Nocera and Bethany McLean

PORTFOLIO | PENGUIN

Portfolio / Penguin
An imprint of Penguin Random House LLC
penguinrandomhouse.com

Most Portfolio books are available at a discount when purchased in quantity for sales promotions or corporate use. Special editions, which include personalized covers, excerpts, and corporate imprints, can be created when purchased in large quantities. For more information, please call (212) 572-2232 or e-mail specialmarkets@penguinrandomhouse.com. Your local bookstore can also assist with discounted bulk purchases using the Penguin Random House corporate Business-to-Business program. For assistance in locating a participating retailer, e-mail B2B@penguinrandomhouse.com.

LIBRARY OF CONGRESS CATALOGING-IN-PUBLICATION DATA
Names: Nocera, Joseph, author. | McLean, Bethany, author.
Title: The big fail : what the pandemic revealed about who America protects
    and who it leaves behind / Joe Nocera and Bethany McLean.
Description: [New York, NY] : Portfolio/Penguin, [2023]
Identifiers: LCCN 2023019683 (print) | LCCN 2023019684 (ebook) |
    ISBN 9780593331026 (hardcover) | ISBN 9780593331033 (ebook)
Subjects: LCSH: COVID-19 Pandemic, 2020—United States. |
    COVID-19 Pandemic, 2020—Social aspects—United States. |
    COVID-19 Pandemic, 2020—Economic aspects—United States. | COVID-19 Pandemic,
    2020—Political aspects—United States. | Medical policy—United States—
    History—21st century. | Health services accessibility—United States.
Classification: LCC RA644.C67 N63 2023 (print) | LCC RA644.C67 (ebook) |
    DDC 362.1962/4144—dc23/eng/20230719
LC record available at https://lccn.loc.gov/2023019683
LC ebook record available at https://lccn.loc.gov/2023019684

Printed in the United States of America
1st Printing

Book design by Alissa Rose Theodor

For Dawn, and for Laine and Calla

Contents

Introduction

On February 21, 2023, three years after the United States first declared COVID a public health emergency, Bret Stephens of *The New York Times* published a column about one of the many hotly debated aspects of the country's response to the pandemic. The headline: THE MASK MANDATES DID NOTHING. WILL ANY LESSONS BE LEARNED?

Stephens cited a study about the efficacy of masking done by the Cochrane Library, a British nonprofit that is considered the gold standard of so-called meta-analysis—that is, gathering data from a collection of other studies to draw a conclusion. The masking study looked at seventy-eight randomized controlled trials, six of them during the pandemic, with a total of 610,872 participants in multiple countries. The authors of the study concluded that there was "little or no" evidence that masking reduced the incidence of COVID-19 in a population. In an interview with an independent science writer, Tom Jefferson, the Oxford epidemiologist who was the lead author of the study, was quite blunt in saying that there was no evidence masks worked. "We'd know if we had done trials," he said. But instead, governments behaved like "headless chickens."

The response was fast and vicious. The public health establishment, which had long stressed the importance of masking, was quick to dismiss the study, rather than wrestle with the questions it raised. Rochelle Walensky, the director of the Centers for Disease Control and Prevention—the CDC—questioned the reliance on studies done for respiratory viruses other than COVID-19 and said that her agency would continue to recommend masks in communities where COVID levels were high, including for toddlers in preschool. The sociologist Zeynep Tufekci, a *New York Times* contributing columnist who became a prominent voice during the pandemic, followed Stephens's column with one of her own, titled "Here's Why the Science Is Clear That Masks Work." She quoted Karla Soares-Weiser, the editor in chief of Cochrane, who said that Jefferson had gone too far, even though Soares-Weiser didn't actually say anything different. "Given the limitations in the primary evidence," she said in a statement, "the review is not able to address the question of whether mask wearing itself reduces people's risk of contracting or spreading respiratory viruses."

There were also personal attacks aimed at Jefferson. Kelsey Piper, a journalist at *Vox*, dismissed Jefferson as having "a number of eccentric and flatly nonsensical opinions about Covid-19."[1] Stephens, for his part, was lambasted. "He doesn't do his homework," sneered Michael Hiltzik, a *Los Angeles Times* columnist.

By the time the controversy faded, we were back where we started:

1 Jefferson no longer speaks to the media because he thinks his views have been badly misrepresented.

we still didn't know whether masks work. It might be, as Stephens pointed out, that the question of whether a well-fitting, properly worn mask protects an individual is different from the question of whether a mask mandate does any good. It could be true that a mask can protect an individual. It could also be true that if people are taking masks off to eat, or not wearing them properly, or contaminating them with their hands, or not wearing them in places where contagion runs rampant, like homes, that masks don't do much to limit community-wide transmission. *We just don't know.*

In so many ways, the mask controversy was a microcosm of the pandemic itself. During COVID-19, a mask wasn't just a mask; it was a symbol of one's politics. If you were a conservative, it was practically mandatory to scoff at masks as well as other mitigation measures like social distancing or lockdowns. If you were a liberal, you embraced them as lifesaving measures. Opinion and preexisting bias trumped fact-finding and scientific inquiry. Those who dissented from the liberal mainstream were silenced, rhetorically speaking, castigated for their supposed personal failings and for being "wrong"—even if it's the case (and it is) that there isn't a single person who called all of the pandemic accurately. Even when there could be common ground—in this case, an acknowledgment that there are things we simply do not know—we resorted instead to rhetoric that divides us further.

This debate over masks, coming three years in, shows why, even now, when most of us desperately want it all to be over, it's important to revisit the pandemic. One reason is that we understand so shockingly little, from the origins of COVID-19, to the reasons why it would crest and then disappear in particular geographies at particular times, to why it killed some people and treated others benignly. Some of that is the nature of the beast: viruses are tricksters. (Indeed, we still don't understand why the 1918 flu killed so many otherwise healthy young adults.)

But there's a darker truth, which is that as with masks we've refused to do the work necessary to get answers, and refused to listen to evidence that doesn't accord with our preexisting views. We've preferred to hunker down in ideological fortresses built with walls of unassailable virtue. As a result, we don't understand even those things that could be understood, like what mask mandates did or didn't accomplish, which mitigation efforts worked and which didn't, or even who should get how many shots of the vaccines.

That does not bode well for our ability to deal intelligently with the next pandemic when it arrives, as it surely will.

Despite its tremendous resources, America did not fare well during the pandemic. One of the simplest measures of how a country withstood the pandemic is the so-called excess death rate—that is, the number of dead above what was expected in a typical year. In the years since the pandemic started, the United States has seen about 1.3 million excess deaths, a damning number and a higher rate per 100,000 people than England, France, Germany, and Spain—and about the same as Brazil.[2]

In the fall of 2022, a time when most people were putting the pandemic behind them, an infectious disease doctor named Celine Gounder asked the question that had become a rallying cry among the public health establishment: "Couldn't America have done better?" If only we had masked up more and earlier. If only we had locked down harder and longer. If only Donald Trump hadn't been our president.

A central tenet of this book is that we could not have done better, and pretending differently is a dangerous fiction, one that prevents us from taking a much-needed look in the mirror. Consider: More Americans died during the first year of the Biden administration than in

---

2 According to an AI-powered daily estimate of excess deaths around the world created by *The Economist*.

2020, the last year of the Trump presidency. It turns out that stopping the carnage wasn't just a matter of replacing an erratic president.

The reasons why the virus hit our population so hard, and why our response was so inept, were deep-seated, decades in the making. Just as the virus feasted on people with comorbidities, it hit an America that was rife with its own preexisting illnesses. The illnesses weren't things that any politician, Democratic or Republican, could have fixed with a wave of a magic wand. The pandemic told us important, painful truths about who America helps and who it leaves behind, even as it left some people further behind than ever before. Both people and companies who looked like heroes one minute looked like villains the next, maybe because we both celebrate or dismiss too easily—or maybe because we can't tolerate complexity.

Part of the story we tell is how and why the pandemic intensified our divides. Another part of the story is the ways in which capitalism, as it's now practiced in the United States, left our economy unprepared for a crisis like the pandemic—and the ways in which the mores of capitalism have encroached upon the morals of society, most notably in caring for the sick and the elderly, whether in hospitals or nursing homes.

We tell one success story: that of Operation Warp Speed, which contains lessons—about leadership, about setting aside one's personal politics for the greater good, and about the need for cooperation between business and government—that are critically important to our future. Indeed, the core of the story we tell is the failure of government to set the right rules, whether for managing a pandemic or for establishing the boundaries of capitalism.

It is possible—barely possible, but still possible—to see a silver lining in the horror of the pandemic, if we care to see it. Easy truths evaporated in front of us. Maybe truths aren't easy. Experts said many things that proved to be untrue. Maybe experts don't have all the answers. The cost of polarization is that we don't learn anything. Maybe there's a lot to learn. And the problems with the business world aren't always just about business. They can also be about life and death.

We hope our book inspires that necessary look in the mirror.

PART I

Contagion

1

The Scapegoat

The first sighting of COVID-19 in the United States took place on January 19, 2020, when a man in his thirties who had just returned from Wuhan, China, showed up at a clinic in Snohomish County, Washington, with a mild cough and pneumonia-like symptoms. The clinic sent him home. But with a strange new virus already associated with Wuhan, the clinic staff took a nasal swab and notified state health officials.

Just over a week earlier, a virologist at the University of Sydney had tweeted that he, along with a consortium led by the prominent Chinese virologist Zhang Yongzhen, had sequenced this novel coronavirus. They posted its genetic sequence on virological.org, an open-access site. A week later, the Centers for Disease Control and Prevention—the CDC—had a test that could tell whether the sequence was present.

At this early stage of the pandemic, it was almost impossible to get tested for COVID-19. The illness didn't even have a name. The CDC was focused on testing people who had been in Hubei Province, of which Wuhan is the capital, and returned with a fever and respiratory issues. Which meant that if the disease were being transmitted more broadly, there was no way to know. It wasn't clear that the man in Snohomish qualified for a test. Nonetheless, worried state officials shipped his nasal swab to the CDC's Atlanta headquarters and requested that it be tested. It came back positive.

On January 21, Nancy Messonnier, a high-ranking CDC scientist, held a press conference in which she confirmed that the first case of COVID-19 had been recorded in Washington State. "Right now," she said, "testing for this virus must take place at CDC, but in the coming weeks, we anticipate sharing these tests with domestic and international partners." For his part, President Donald Trump was sanguine. "It's going to be just fine," he said. "It's one person coming in from China, and we have it under control."

But in Washington State, very little felt under control. Health officials wanted to know if the man had infected others, which would require testing. They even had the means to do so. Dr. Helen Chu, an infectious disease specialist at the University of Washington, had started something called the Seattle Flu Study, which included collecting nasal swabs from residents throughout the region. But she was told she couldn't test those swabs for COVID-19 until the CDC had manufactured its test. Chu's lab was also capable of developing its own test. But two of the government's chief health agencies, the CDC and the Food and Drug Administration (FDA), wouldn't allow that without almost insurmountable red tape.[1] Washington State would have to wait. If you

---

1 Washington State's odyssey was detailed in a *New York Times* article titled "'It's Just Everywhere Already': How Delays in Testing Set Back the U.S. Coronavirus Response."

think of the government's many pandemic mistakes as a series of cascading dominoes, here was the first domino. Early testing was the only way to find out if the coronavirus was spreading—and the most important tool if the country was to have any hope of containing it. But officials simply didn't view the new virus with any particular urgency.

One reason for that lack of urgency was that most pathogens in recent years had largely bypassed the United States. For instance, about eleven thousand people had died during the 2014 Ebola outbreak, but only four cases occurred in the United States. The lack of information coming out of China didn't help either. Wuhan was sealed off. The Chinese government was saying next to nothing about the virus. Western scientists didn't know how contagious it was, or how it spread, or what percentage of the population it was likely to kill. The pandemic's true fury wouldn't be felt outside China until it hit Italy in mid-February. That was still weeks away.

———

The way it's supposed to work is like this: when a country suspects that a deadly virus is circulating—a virus that might lead to a pandemic—it alerts the World Health Organization (WHO) and major governments so that the rest of the world can begin to take precautions. The process relies on transparency. China didn't live up to that responsibility.

Alex Azar, who was then Trump's secretary of health and human services, would later say that the first inkling the United States had about the Wuhan outbreak came not from China but from a notification from Taiwan's economic and cultural office in the United States.[2] That was December 30.

2 Azar said this in a speech he gave at the Heritage Foundation on January 14, 2021.

That same day, a document began circulating on the internet about an urgent notice issued by the Wuhan Municipal Health Commission citing a "pneumonia of unknown cause" and noting that patients had come from the seafood market. A reporter for a Chinese business news website called the Wuhan Municipal Health Commission's hotline and confirmed that the notice was true; just before midnight on December 30, ProMed, a low-tech list manned by part-time employees who try to confirm the truth of chatter like that in Wuhan, sent out a post. These early reports weren't filled with alarm, but some infectious disease specialists were immediately on high alert. "All of us who work in the field worry about the potential jump of a pathogen from an intermediate host to a human, so the live animal market was an obvious concern," says Dr. Kevin Messacar, a specialist in pediatric infectious diseases at Children's Hospital Colorado.

It took another three days—an astonishingly long time given the stakes—for a Chinese health official to contact Dr. Robert Redfield, the director of the CDC. Dr. George Fu Gao was his Chinese counterpart; he informed Redfield about the existence of the virus. Redfield then called Azar and said, "I think we have a problem." Azar alerted the National Security Council.

With a presidential election less than a year away, this was not welcome news at the White House. When Azar called Trump at his Mar-a-Lago estate, he had trouble getting the president to focus, he later complained to aides.

In a follow-up conversation, Gao told Redfield that there was no evidence of human-to-human transmission. But when China shared the initial data on the first twenty-seven human cases, not all of them could be traced back to the market, and some were clustered within families. Redfield would later say he was immediately suspicious, and he was right. According to the Independent Panel, established by the

WHO, Wuhan Hospital's chief of respiratory medicine told her superiors in late December that she was concerned about human-to-human transmission. On January 5, the Shanghai Public Health Clinical Center, which was led by Zhang Yongzhen, told authorities that it "should be contagious through respiratory passages," according to internal memos obtained by the Associated Press.

But no one seems to have shared this information with a team of researchers from the WHO, who went to China in mid-January to investigate the outbreak. On January 14 the WHO stated that "preliminary investigations conducted by the Chinese authorities have found no clear evidence of human-to-human transmission"—which the Chinese knew by then was at least highly debatable.

Redfield wasn't the only one who was suspicious. The deputy national security adviser, Matthew Pottinger, who had been a reporter in China for *The Wall Street Journal* in the late 1990s, was sure the situation was worse than China was admitting. "He was convinced a disaster was on the way. His Chinese sources were telling him that 'things were much, much worse in China than they were letting it out to be,'" recalls Anthony Fauci, the director of the National Institute of Allergy and Infectious Diseases (NIAID), who would become the public face of the pandemic response. Peter Navarro, Trump's irascible economic adviser whose distrust of China had helped spark a trade war, was even more strident. Navarro suggested a travel ban. "The lack of immune protection or an existing cure or vaccine would leave Americans defenseless in the case of a full-blown coronavirus outbreak on US soil," he wrote in a memo.[3] But other White House officials viewed him as something of a nutcase and ignored him.

3 This memo was first reported by *The New York Times* in an April 6, 2020, article titled "Trade Adviser Warned White House in January of Risks of a Pandemic."

What took place, in those early weeks, was a struggle between those who wanted to do everything and those who wanted to do nothing, a struggle exacerbated by the president's unwillingness—or inability—to choose a path. "There were people who were like, 'This is worse than the 1918 flu!' And then there were others who were like, 'This is no big deal,'" says one person familiar with events.

What's more, any possibility of teamwork was atomized by the many loyalties and feuds that had developed during Trump's three years in office—as well as by a Trump-fostered mentality that held that winning the game of public relations was the only victory that mattered. There were constant leaks as various factions tried to influence the president and knife their rivals. "It literally didn't matter who your direct supervisor was," says a former senior civil servant. "What mattered was who you could pick up the phone and call."

On January 29, the administration announced the formation of the new White House Coronavirus Task Force. Trump named Azar to lead it. That same day, Azar signed an order declaring a public health emergency. He did so alone in the Roosevelt Room, with his chief of staff taking pictures with an iPhone. The administration didn't have the official White House photographer taking pictures, whether because it was deliberately downplaying the virus, or because it still didn't seem like a noteworthy event. The experts "are on top of it," tweeted Trump.

On paper at least, Azar seemed well suited to lead the task force. A former law clerk for the Supreme Court justice Antonin Scalia, Azar worked at Health and Human Services (HHS) from 2001 to 2007, first as general counsel and then as deputy secretary. Those were years that saw the terrorist attack on 9/11, the anthrax scare, outbreaks of SARS and influenza, and, under the George W. Bush administration, the first real effort to come up with a plan in the event of a pandemic or a bioterrorist attack. Azar was in the middle of all of it.

Azar immediately began "marching through the pandemic playbook," as he'd later put it, that had been written in the Bush administration and updated by the Obama administration. But for all the man-hours that had been spent putting together the pandemic plans, the documents were essentially worthless. Reality was a lot different from a simulation or war-game exercise. "Nothing is self-executing," says someone close to the events. "It's not just like a bunch of switches you turn. If people in the administration and HHS and the Defense Department and the states haven't been working with this from the beginning, it's not going to happen."

For all his experience, Azar never seemed to be in control of the task force. Here is where all those rivalries between various agencies and officials came into play. Key people were left off the task force, whether purposefully or because it wasn't exactly clear what the task force was supposed to do. There was no coordination. "There were a lot of bad interpersonal interagency dynamics," says one senior official. "Nobody really knew what was going on."

Instead of focusing on broad pandemic planning, the task force was obsessed with trying to extract the Americans stuck in Hubei Province. They had quickly found that there was no real plan in place to accomplish such a thing. "You cannot overstate how much the repatriation . . . distracted the entire interagency process of the US government during this time period," Azar would later say. Dr. Anne Schuchat, then the CDC's principal deputy director, later told a committee investigating the COVID-19 response that federal leadership in February 2020 was so consumed with repatriating Americans that "key areas, like scaling up PPE [personal protective equipment] and getting our arms around the supply chain and protecting the healthcare system and so forth, didn't get sufficient attention."

The Chinese and the WHO both privately criticized the United

States in part for the efforts to evacuate people, according to several people who were involved. As a result, partly to placate the Chinese, the planes that collected the Americans in Wuhan dropped off almost eighteen tons of masks, gowns, and other PPE. The federal government still didn't comprehend that America wasn't going to be able to duck this virus.

But it wasn't just the U.S. government that lacked the foresight—or the imagination—to see what was coming. So did the WHO. On January 30, the WHO declared COVID-19 a "public-health emergency of international concern." There were by then 7,818 confirmed cases of the still unnamed virus, including 82 outside China's borders. But the agency was not ready to call it a pandemic.

"I said to officials at the WHO, 'When are you going to use the word "pandemic"?'" says a former administration official. "But there was tremendous pushback. The thought process was, 'If we use the word "pandemic," people are going to freak out.'"

There may be no better illustration of the schizophrenic, scattered nature of the response than that at the very same time the administration was debating taking dramatic action, Pottinger and several others had begun to argue that the United States needed to ban flights from China. Public health scientists had long known that travel bans didn't work. In 2006, for instance, a WHO working group had concluded that "screening and quarantining entering travelers at international borders did not substantially delay virus introduction in past pandemics . . . and will likely be even less effective in the modern era."

But then the husband of a Chicago woman who had been infected in China also came down with COVID-19. That settled it: human-to-human transmission had begun in the United States. Almost overnight, government scientists changed their minds about the efficacy of a travel ban. Azar would later tell people that he was shocked by their quick about-face.

Trump of course agreed immediately: a travel ban would allow him to appear to be taking action. On January 31, he announced that non-Americans who had been in China during the previous fourteen days could no longer come into the country. But it was already too late. At least 430,000 people had arrived in the United States on direct flights from China, thousands of them straight from Wuhan, since New Year's Eve, *The New York Times* would later calculate. And the ban was notoriously porous. Hong Kong and Macau were exempted. United States citizens, residents, and their family members were still free to enter. Did anyone really think that all returning Americans would be virus-free?

———

The day after the WHO tweeted that it saw no evidence of human-to-human transmission, Cheryl and Paul Molesky flew to Yokohama in Japan to board the *Diamond Princess*, a cruise ship owned by Carnival, the largest leisure travel company in the world. It was mid-January. The ship's itinerary called for it to sail from Hong Kong to Vietnam and Taiwan before returning to Japan. The Moleskys were among the 380 or so Americans on a ship with 2,664 other guests and 1,045 crew from fifty-six countries. Cheryl Molesky, a teacher, had just retired, and the couple had always wanted to go to Japan. Just before they left, Paul's brother told them, "Be careful. There's some kind of pneumonia in China."

Cheryl replied, "Well, we're not going to China."

On February 1, one of the travelers went to the doctor complaining of a fever and tested positive. The Moleskys had already begun to notice some oddities—at one port, officials took the temperatures of everyone leaving the ship—but it wasn't until the morning after the ship had returned to Yokohama, on February 4, that they were informed that passengers and staff would remain quarantined until those experiencing symptoms had all been tested for COVID-19.

It wasn't so bad at first. Passengers could still mingle. One of the entertainers did a Tina Turner revue. The *Diamond Princess* was anchored in the middle of a huge bay. The Moleskys' side of the ship faced out, and the views were sublime.

Then the results began to come back. There were ten positives on February 5, causing the ship's captain to announce that all guests would have to stay in their rooms for at least the next fourteen days. It was the first time China's approach—a forced quarantine, soon to be labeled a "lockdown"—had been used outside China. It wouldn't be the last.

It was also an early indication of how the virus would magnify socioeconomic divides. The passengers stayed in their cabins. The crew, meanwhile, delivered food and other supplies before returning to their cramped quarters. Sick passengers were tested. There wasn't the capacity to test everyone, and the policy requiring that passengers be tested didn't mention crew members.[4]

Every day, the infections multiplied, and the *Diamond Princess* soon became the largest COVID-19 cluster outside Wuhan. The Moleskys' side of the ship was now facing the dockside; the passengers with windows could see the ambulances.

On the morning of the fifteenth, the U.S. embassy in Japan emailed the Americans on the ship. Those who didn't have the virus could go

4 "Chronology of COVID-19 Cases on the Diamond Princess Cruise Ship and Ethical Considerations: A Report from Japan," published March 24, 2020, by Cambridge University Press.

home. "They kind of made it seem like we didn't have a whole lot of choice because there was going to be this one flight, and if we did not take the flight, they said we could not return to the United States for an undetermined amount of time," says Cheryl. So the next evening, close to midnight, the Moleskys got off the ship and boarded the bus taking them to the plane. "It was a fiasco," says Paul. "They collected our passports and didn't return them to the right bus. We sat for hours and people had to plead to go to the bathroom."

Only after everyone was ready to board the flight was it discovered that fourteen of them had tested positive. No one knew what to do. The CDC argued that sick passengers could not board the plane. The State Department said they had to be allowed to return home. The State Department won.

"The flight was really when things took a turn for the worse," says Cheryl. No one had told the uninfected passengers what was happening. Hours into the flight, the Moleskys realized that there was a slit in the plastic separating a section of the plane. Passengers had to walk by it to get food or water, or access the restrooms—but there were people in there. During the flight, when passengers, including the man seated directly behind the Moleskys, registered a fever or began to exhibit symptoms, they were moved behind the plastic, says Paul. "So here we felt we had been protected and isolated for twelve days, and without our consent or knowledge we were put in direct contact with people who were sick," says Cheryl.

After landing, they had to spend fifteen days in quarantine at Lackland Air Force Base in Texas before returning home. The Moleskys managed to avoid getting COVID-19, and there was no documented spread from any of the returning Americans. Still, at least 712 passengers and crew came down with COVID-19. Ten died. Alarmingly, almost 20 percent of the infected showed no symptoms. "An epidemic is not driven by asymptomatic carriers," Fauci had said at a press briefing in late January. That was true with an influenza virus, like the one that ravaged the world in 1918. But it wasn't true with this novel coronavirus; you could become infected, and infect others, without ever knowing you had contracted COVID-19. "When you have 50 to 60 percent of the transmissions occurring from someone who's without symptoms, that completely throws it in a different direction," Fauci says today.

For those seeking real-world data about the virus, the emerging facts from the *Diamond Princess* were terrifying. A small handful of scientists and policy types who had been involved in pandemic planning since the Bush administration created an email chain that they nicknamed "Red Dawn."[5] They all felt strongly that the government needed to wake up to the incipient disaster, and they saw the *Diamond Princess* as proof. "The spread, no doubt, involves those without symptoms," wrote Eva Lee, a researcher at the Georgia Institute of Technology, on February 10. "It shows why strategic (community) testing is a must." In other words, it wasn't enough to test only those with symptoms. The *Diamond Princess* showed that anyone could be infected and anyone could spread the disease.

Incredibly, in yet another telling example of how discordant the government response was, even though the *Diamond Princess* showed how vulnerable passengers and crew were, the major cruise lines were allowed to continue sailing. Vice President Mike Pence even flew to Florida—the epicenter of the cruise industry—for a sit-down with cruise industry executives on March 7. Seated next to Florida's governor, Ron DeSantis, Pence said, "I'm looking forward to hearing the industry's recommendations." It wasn't until March 14, after dozens of ships

5 The email chain was named after the 1984 film, starring Patrick Swayze and Charlie Sheen, about a small group of kids trying to save the world from an invasion.

stuck off America's shoreline kept requesting that the Coast Guard help evacuate the sick, that the CDC finally issued a no-sail order.

One participant in the Red Dawn group was Carter Mecher, a senior medical adviser at the Department of Veterans Affairs, who had worked on pandemic preparedness during most of the Bush administration. On February 20, he wrote, "The outbreak on the cruise ship should be the wake-up call for leaders in long term care (and I would think healthcare overall)." He added, "What has me worried is what happened on the cruise ship is a preview of what will happen when this virus makes its way to the U.S. healthcare system."

———

On February 4, the FDA approved the CDC's COVID-19 test, using a mechanism called an Emergency Use Authorization that allowed the agency to bypass some of its normal bureaucratic protocols in making tests and drugs available. By February 6, the CDC had sent test kits to thirty-three states and seventy labs in sixty-six countries.

The test was complicated, which in some ways was indicative of the CDC's culture: perfectionist and academic. It had three components. The first two involved reagents—the chemicals that react to substances—identifying genetic sequences unique to COVID-19; the third was supposed to detect any coronavirus, even ones that had never infected humans. It was meant as a fail-safe in case the virus mutated in a way that rendered the first two reagents useless.

For reasons that have never been explained, the CDC decided to manufacture its own test kits, instead of sending them out to a third-party manufacturer, even though the CDC lacked manufacturing expertise.

By February 8, the public health labs were sending frantic messages to the CDC: the tests didn't work. That third component was somehow creating faulty results. "When we received those kits, our first job was to validate them," says Dr. Kevin Messacar, the infectious disease specialist at Children's Hospital Colorado. "And they didn't validate. Very quickly, we all realized that this was a problem. The tests couldn't be used."

"There is likely a widespread issue that will need to be addressed immediately," a California official said in an email to the CDC.

Jennifer Rakeman, the assistant commissioner of the New York City Public Health Laboratory, later told NPR that the panicked emails from colleagues began to pour in. "It was very truly an 'oh, crap' moment," Rakeman said.

NPR also reported that at least some CDC officials knew the test was flawed but allowed it to go out anyway, though several people say the CDC head, Redfield, was not among those in the know.[6] "Bob made a couple of fundamental mistakes in trusting people underneath him," says a former administration official.

The deeper failing, though, is that the CDC's test should never have been the sun, moon, and stars upon which America's testing strategy hung. Even if the test had worked, other institutions would have to get involved. Yet there was no plan to have hospitals or academic labs make tests, or to engage testing companies, which can quickly manufacture them by the millions. Expecting the CDC to meet the entire country's demand was like expecting a local hardware store to become Amazon.

And bureaucratic roadblocks made it impossible for other labs to even try to make tests. Once Azar declared a public health emergency, a potential test maker had to jump through a series of complicated

6 "CDC Report: Officials Knew CDC Coronavirus Test Was Flawed but Released It Anyway," NPR, November 6, 2020.

hoops to get FDA approval. On top of that, the Centers for Medicare and Medicaid Services (CMS) is charged with deciding whether a facility constitutes a lab, meaning that a lab needs CMS certification before going to the FDA to get approval for a test. "You have this very intensive validation process that you have to go through to get permission to actually use your test," says Dr. Samuel Dominguez, another infectious disease specialist at Children's Hospital Colorado. "Most labs do not do it."

These bureaucratic hoops exist, of course, to protect the public from a faulty or fraudulent test. But the rigidity of the rules was counterproductive during the pandemic. "Lots of people around the country have the expertise to do this," Dominguez adds. "If you devote resources and time to it, you can get a test up and running relatively quickly." He always knew the CDC's test would go first to the public health labs, but, he says, "we thought, due to the urgency of what was going on, they would allow clinical microbiology laboratories to use their assay as well." But as February ticked away, nothing seemed to change.

Nor did anyone make a concerted effort to engage industry. No question, that would have required some serious persuading; companies that had built tests during the H1N1 and Zika crises had lost millions of dollars in unsold tests. "The private sector traditionally does not make big investments in these things unless they know demand is going to be big," says a person involved in the efforts to figure out testing. "As much as you want to wave the American flag and think about motherhood and apple pie, when it came down to actually making those investments, it's very hard to do that when you don't know when demand is going to drop off a cliff."

In mid-February, the FDA sent Timothy Stenzel, a veteran government scientist, to the CDC's Atlanta headquarters to find out why the test was failing. As if to underscore the Keystone Kops–like nature of the whole episode, when Stenzel arrived, he wasn't allowed past security because it was the weekend and the place was closed. When he did finally get in, he got only "vague answers" to his questions. "No one person could walk Tim through the whole process and tell him what was done," a lawyer later noted.[7]

By the end of February, by which time South Korea was conducting tens of thousands of tests each day, there was still almost no testing in the United States. The Government Accounting Office (GAO) would later report that as of February 29 only about 1,195 people had been tested in total. At which point, the FDA finally agreed to let academic hospital labs use their own tests and the CDC outsourced the manufacturing of the reagents. (A few days earlier, the FDA allowed labs to use the CDC test without the problematic third component.) The first private company to produce an authorized commercial coronavirus test was Roche Molecular Systems. It took all of two weeks.

At last, serious testing could begin in the United States.

Azar would later argue that the delays didn't really matter: cases were so few, and dispersed so widely geographically, that unearthing new cases of COVID-19 via testing would have been like "finding a needle in a haystack."[8] But he was wrong. Dr. Chu, the infectious disease specialist doing the flu study, began testing her nasal swab samples on February 25, unwilling to wait any longer for FDA approval. She and her team found the virus in 1.1 percent of the samples—a very large number. And some of the swabs dated back to early January.

"It must have been here this entire time," she told *The New York Times*. "It's just everywhere already."

---

7 *BuzzFeed News* obtained fifty pages of interviews conducted by two lawyers with the HHS Office of the General Counsel.
8 Azar's keynote address to the Foundation for Research on Equal Opportunity, January 15, 2021.

To Scott Gottlieb, who had stepped down as FDA commissioner in 2019, the inability to test for COVID-19 in January and February 2020 was a devastating blunder, "leaving the country dangerously blind to its spread." As he later wrote,[9]

> *We had lost control. Without a widely available diagnostic test, we missed the chance to use case-based interventions—the ability to diagnose the sick, trace their contacts, and place people who have been exposed into quarantine—as a way to limit spread. The window for preventing the virus from gaining a foothold had closed.*

———

It was in this time frame—late February and early March—that the evidence was inescapable: a pandemic was on the world's doorstep. Italy reported fifty-eight hundred cases and 233 deaths by early March. Prior to the Wuhan outbreak, no country in history had attempted to fight a pathogen by locking down its citizens for months at a time. Yet the Italian government decided to follow China's strategy and lock down northern Italy, the hardest-hit part of the country.

Every day, countries were reporting new cases, few of which could be traced back to Wuhan. In the United States a high school student who had no record of travel, no contact with anyone who had traveled, and no known contact with anyone else with the virus tested positive when he showed up at Everett Clinic in Washington State.

"We suspected that COVID-19 was circulating in our community

9 In 2021, Gottlieb published one of the best accounts of the first year of the pandemic, *Uncontrolled Spread: Why COVID-19 Crushed Us and How We Can Defeat the Next Pandemic.*

as our urgent care clinics were facing huge demands for testing from patients with respiratory virus symptoms who were testing negative for influenza," says Dr. Yuan-Po Tu, an infectious disease specialist at the clinic.

Back in 2009, Tu had also seen one of the first U.S. patients to be infected with the H1N1 virus (aka swine flu). In the wake of that scare, the clinic had stockpiled N95 respirators, surgical masks, and other necessary supplies. Tu and his colleagues thought they had more than enough. In the space of one weekend at the end of February, they'd used more than ten thousand surgical masks, many multiples of the normal burn rate. "I knew we were in trouble," Tu says.[10]

Already, there were shortages of the materials needed to conduct diagnostic tests, like swabs and reagents. "Those reagents disappeared," said Dominguez. "We had other reagents that could do similar things, but we were told we couldn't use those, because they weren't in the Emergency Use Authorization approval from the FDA.

"I understand why we do that," Dominguez continued. "I understand the need for regulatory oversight. And I fully support that. But this was an emergency."

By the first week in March, Washington State officials had put in two requests for additional protective gear from the Strategic National Stockpile, which is supposed to contain equipment, like N95 respirators, that can be used in an emergency. But it had been depleted during the H1N1 scare and had never been replenished. HHS officials told the state to ask for only one week's worth of equipment, reported *The Wall Street Journal*. When state officials objected, they were told that the

---

10 Work done by Dr. Tu with the support of UnitedHealth Group, which owns the Everett Clinic, led to the FDA approval of nasal swabs that patients could do themselves, which protected health-care workers, allowed for drive-up testing, and dramatically decreased the burn rate for PPE.

federal government wasn't prepared to provide the level of supplies they were going to need.

Dr. Jeff Duchin, the staff epidemiologist for the Seattle public health department, was a member of the Red Dawn group. On March 1, he sent them an email. "We are having a very serious challenge related to hospital exposures and impact on the healthcare system equipment," it read.

———

On February 25, Nancy Messonnier, the high-ranking CDC scientist, conducted another press briefing. Until that moment the Trump administration had continued to tiptoe around the increasing likelihood that the United States was going to experience a severe pandemic. Messonnier, however, did not mince words. "It's not a question of if this will happen but when this will happen and how many people in this country will have severe illnesses," she said. "Disruptions to everyday life may be severe, but people might want to start thinking about that now." She suggested that people would need to take social distancing measures, that schools might have to be closed, and that businesses might need to keep workers at home.

There were only fifty-seven recorded cases of COVID-19 in the United States when Messonnier gave that briefing. Forty of them were connected to the *Diamond Princess*. Her prediction came as a shock to most people, including White House officials, who felt blindsided because her remarks veered so sharply from the administration's position. Trump was particularly incensed because the stock market dropped 3 percent on the day of her press briefing.

White House aides quickly tried to reassure the public—and their boss. White House economic adviser Lawrence Kudlow told CNBC that the virus had been "contained" and that it would not be an "economic tragedy." From his plane, Trump called Azar to berate him. Messonnier later told the House Select Subcommittee on the Coronavirus Crisis that she got calls from both Azar and Trump that caused her to feel "upset," and that she learned her briefing "angered" the president. She never gave another press briefing. In 2021, she left her twenty-six-year career at the CDC to take a job running the Skoll Foundation, a $1 billion philanthropy in Palo Alto.

Shortly after Messonnier's press briefing, Trump demoted Azar as the head of the task force, replacing him with Vice President Mike Pence. His media appearances were canceled. Pence's press secretary told HHS officials that they were not permitted to issue any communication that raised concern among the public. "They took a very experienced cabinet member, someone who had been through 9/11, had been through Katrina, had been involved in pandemic planning during the Bush administration—they took the most seasoned person they had and benched him because of politics," says one former official who is supportive of Azar.

Azar had become Trump's COVID-19 scapegoat. His enemies leaked stories to *Politico* and other publications about his "failure to coordinate" a government response to the coronavirus. As the head of the federal agency that oversees the CDC, he was also blamed for the CDC's testing fiasco. Trump complained that his HHS secretary was an alarmist.

Whether it was fair or not, Azar was easy to scapegoat because he had become a deeply unpopular figure in the administration, someone who'd made plenty of enemies. Well before COVID-19, Azar had battled both the CMS head, Seema Verma, and the domestic policy adviser Joe Grogan on a variety of fronts. Admired in some quarters for his brilliance and his principles, Azar was detested and distrusted in others for his temper and what critics say was his propensity for pettiness and his fondness for the trappings and hierarchies of his office. Even Azar's fans say that he can be a difficult, demanding boss. When the virus hit, "the problems went from palace intrigue to policy decisions," says a former senior civil servant, who thinks that Azar's management style impeded the administration's functioning.

But Azar's biggest problem might have been that he didn't fit in. The cool-kid crowd—as they thought of themselves—who surrounded Trump saw him as a detail-oriented nerd and, perhaps even worse, an old-school Republican. Although Azar could be obstinate and persnickety, even some of his defenders say that there were also occasions when the pressure made him yield too much. "He's a political guy and he wanted to be accepted by the Trump administration," says one.

As Azar himself would tell people, "It's a tough crowd."

¹ Robert Redfield, the CDC head, suffered much the same fate. He appeared at a few more briefings, but eventually he stopped speaking publicly too. It would be June until anyone heard from him again—an unprecedented silence during a public health emergency. Schuchat later told the coronavirus subcommittee that "many of us" at the CDC felt "muzzled" by the White House.

For scientists who had always relied on the CDC, it was disconcerting. "We learned there was editing of scientific communication going on by people in the administration," says Dr. Kevin Messacar. "We started to have questions like, 'Is what I'm reading actually coming from the CDC, or is it politically motivated?' The integrity of something that we had always relied on and trusted had been deeply broken."

The newly reconfigured task force added Dr. Deborah Birx, a scientist who had directed the CDC's global AIDS project. She was supposed to be its coordinator. Birx was highly regarded, and she and Fauci, who had known each other for decades, both pushed to do more, faster.

Yet politics kept getting in the way. Birx had little or no power. "She's a well-intentioned scientist first and foremost," says a participant at some of the meetings Birx chaired. "Her assessment wasn't the rosy one, but it was correct, but she continually had her legs cut out from under her."

As for Pence, "He cared about the politics, not the virus itself," says one participant. "He was concerned that he would be hung out there as a fool on a fool's errand." On June 16, Pence wrote an op-ed in *The Wall Street Journal* declaring victory over COVID-19. The headline: THERE ISN'T A CORONAVIRUS "SECOND WAVE." Perhaps not surprisingly, the task force never accomplished anything notable.

———

On March 6, Trump fired his chief of staff, Mick Mulvaney, with whom he had grown disenchanted, and named Mark Meadows, a Republican congressman from North Carolina and a Trump true believer, as Mulvaney's replacement. Meadows was Trump's fourth chief of staff in three years. The timing could not have been worse. "Making a transition right then and there was a terrible mistake," says a former official. Meadows was supposed to bring greater cohesion to the White House, but if anything the factions only grew worse.

One indicator of those factions was the question of whether White House officials should wear masks. Before it was understood that the virus was transmitted via aerosols, most scientists didn't think that masks made a difference. Pottinger, however, was worried enough that he began wearing one in January. For this, he was ridiculed by many of his White House colleagues. Yet even after the CDC began urging people to mask up, few in the White House did. Trump simply refused, telling aides that "it would send the wrong message" and would make him look ridiculous.[11]

"It was a weakness walking through the West Wing wearing a mask, and it shouldn't have been," says a former senior civil servant. Learning that Hanes, the underwear company, was retrofitting some of its factories to make masks, Dr. Robert Kadlec, the assistant secretary for preparedness and response at HHS, devised a plan to have the company send a five-mask package to every American household. His plan went nowhere. Why? In part because of the disregard for masks, in part because of distrust of Kadlec, and in part because Kadlec was regarded as being part of Azar's camp, and Azar's enemies wouldn't support any initiative that might reflect well on the HHS secretary. "It became a joke," says another former official. "Because it was Hanes, people joked that the masks looked like underwear on your face. 'Dickhead,' we'd say. People wouldn't wear masks, because they didn't want to get mocked."

————

The one White House aide aside from Pottinger who was truly alarmed was Peter Navarro. A former business professor at the University of California, Irvine, Navarro was Trump's trade adviser. He and the president both harbored a deep suspicion of China; a few weeks after the Wuhan outbreak, he wrote a passionate memo warning that "the risk of a worst-case pandemic scenario should not be overlooked." Navarro's penchant for taking extreme positions—positions that he often expressed

11 "Trump Tells Allies His Wearing a Mask Would 'Send the Wrong Message,' Make Him Look Ridiculous," Associated Press, May 7, 2020.

by shouting over others in meetings—meant that he was never taken seriously by other White House aides. In this instance, he should have been.

At the end of February, Navarro received an email from Dr. Steven Hatfill, a bioweapons expert and virologist who, nearly two decades earlier, had been the subject of an intense government investigation, publicly fingered by Attorney General John Ashcroft as a "person of interest" in the anthrax attacks that put the country on edge after 9/11.[12] In 2019, Hatfill published a book titled *Three Seconds Until Midnight*, which laid out the likelihood of a major pandemic and the inadequacy of America's readiness. Since Wuhan, Hatfill had been appearing regularly on a podcast, hosted by the former Trump confidant Steve Bannon, called *War Room: Pandemic*. In a calm, almost drowsy voice, he made the case that this virus could be devastating. He was also highly critical of the White House's slow response.

Hatfill's email read in part,

> *The CDC has made a series of critical mistakes in implementing the most basic measure in infectious disease control, when it distributed defective test kits for coronavirus diagnosis. This served to limit our ability to screen individuals for COVID-19 infection and containment. In truth we do not have a clue how many are infected in the USA. We are expecting the first wave to spread in the US within the next 7 days. This will be accompanied by a massive loss of credibility and the Democratic accusations are just now beginning. From now on, the Government must be honest about the situation and show it is undertaking major decisive actions.*

12 Hatfill was eventually exonerated. He settled with the government for $5.8 million.

"What is your cell number?" Navarro replied.

The two men began a series of back-channel phone calls that led to Navarro asking Hatfill to become his unpaid COVID-19 adviser. Hatfill's email also led Navarro to write another memo to the president. Headlined MOVE IN "TRUMP TIME" TO STAY AHEAD OF VIRUS CURVE, it had a tone of pressing urgency. "Since the first news from China of a viral epidemic, I forecast a *significant* global pandemic," Navarro wrote. "Over the last month, I have presented the Task Force with action memos to combat the virus swiftly in 'Trump Time,' but movement has been slow. There is NO downside risk to taking swift actions as an insurance policy against what may be a very serious public health emergency. . . . If the covid-19 crisis quickly recedes, the only thing we will have been guilty of is prudence."

Navarro—and Hatfill—would go on to take a number of credibility-destroying positions on the pandemic, such as championing hydroxy-chloroquine as a miracle COVID-19 drug. But in suggesting that the administration try to get in front of a potential crisis, they were completely right.

Publicly, Trump continued to maintain that all was well. "We're prepared, and we're doing a great job with it," Trump told reporters on March 10—the day before the WHO finally declared COVID-19 a global pandemic. "Just stay calm. It will go away."

But privately he was worried. In interviews he gave at the time to Bob Woodward—interviews that came to light only months later when Woodward published his book *Rage*—Trump explained that he purposely played down the threat of a pandemic "because I didn't want people to panic." His actions also suggested he was taking the virus more seriously. For instance, with COVID-19 spreading throughout Europe, Fauci and Birx were advocating a European travel ban. Many of the economic advisers were opposed to it. To the surprise of many in the White House, Trump sided with the scientists and imposed a thirty-day travel ban.

Fauci and Birx had also begun to argue for a temporary nationwide shutdown, in which people would be encouraged to stay home—and away from restaurants, bars, and shops—while gatherings of more than small groups of people and nonessential travel would be discouraged. The damaging economic consequences of such a shutdown were not a significant concern for the scientists, but they were for officials like then Treasury Secretary Steven Mnuchin, who told people, "Every day that we're operating the economy at half speed, I'm losing billions in GDP."

"The economic forecast was maybe more frightening to me than anything else I heard," says a participant in the discussions. "They basically said, you are going to start the next Great Depression. There will be some parts of the economy, these smaller businesses, that will never recover."

But desperation was setting in. "By then, it was just, we need to do something," says one person who participated in the debate. "There were reports out of New York that hospitals were going to be overwhelmed and we were going to lose lives just because the health-care system would fail," says another.

What the White House did was announce on March 16 a series of federal guidelines, mostly the ones being advocated by Fauci and Birx. They included avoiding eating in restaurants, staying away from social gatherings of more than ten people, closing nursing homes to visitors, and moving children from classrooms to remote learning. The guidelines stopped short of a nationwide stay-at-home order in large part because the president didn't have that authority. Only the states could do that.

When the plans were presented to Trump, he was visibly relieved. "That's it?" he said. "I thought you were going to ask me to call in the military to get people to stay in their homes. We can't do this forever, but people will tolerate this for a few weeks."[13]

Trump himself announced the guidelines from the Rose Garden. "With several weeks of focused action, we can turn the corner and turn it quickly," he said. "If everyone makes this change, or these critical changes, and sacrifices now, we will rally together as one nation and we will defeat the virus."

For days afterward, Trump insisted that it would all be over by Easter, which was less than a month away, even as one state after another began imposing far tougher restrictions—restrictions that were mandatory, not voluntary. But on March 29, the president extended the guidelines to the end of April. His original timetable, he told the press, had been "aspirational."

When March began, there were 96 confirmed cases of COVID-19 in the United States and eight deaths, according to the COVID Tracking Project. By the time the month had ended, the number of known cases had risen to nearly 200,000, and with more than five thousand deaths. No one could question any longer whether the pandemic would hit the United States.

It was here.

---

13 Jared Kushner reported this exchange in his book, *Breaking History: A White House Memoir.*

2

Sealed City

On April 8, 2020, the Chinese government lifted its lockdown of Wuhan. It had lasted seventy-six days—two and a half months during which no one was allowed to leave this industrial city of eleven million people. Public transportation was shut down, as were the major highways. Parks were closed. People were expected to stay in their homes unless they had urgent business, such as grocery shopping or going to the hospital. When they did go outside, they were expected to keep their distance from others.[1] There had never been an event quite like the Wuhan lockdown, at least not for public health reasons; the WHO described it as "unprecedented in public health history."

---

1 The Chinese government also imposed lockdowns on a dozen or so other cities in Hubei Province where Wuhan is located. They ultimately affected some fifty million people during the early months of the pandemic.

The word the citizens of Wuhan used to describe their plight was *fengcheng*—"literally 'sealed city,'" as Peter Hessler would later write in *The New Yorker*.[2] But English speakers quickly started translating *fengcheng* as "lockdown." And why not? The word "lockdown" usually refers to prisoners confined to their cells after an altercation or security breakdown. For the citizens of Wuhan, their city had become a kind of prison—with no way to escape.

ʌUntil the Chinese government deployed this tactic, a strict batten-down-the-hatches lockdown had never been used before to combat a pandemic. There had been quarantines for centuries, of course, but those were different. During the Black Death in the fourteenth century, merchant ships had to anchor for forty days before being allowed to deliver their goods. For as long as there have been pandemics, infected people have been told to stay in their homes, where they would either recover or die, so they wouldn't infect others. During the Great Influenza of 1918, most of the major U.S. cities closed schools and businesses, but usually just for a matter of weeks.

In those early days of the pandemic, the people of Wuhan felt that locking down was a patriotic act. "Doing nothing but staying at home was viewed as an act of citizenship and quickly became a national norm," wrote Guobin Yang, a professor at the University of Pennsylvania whose parents lived in Wuhan. "Ordinary residents, including my eighty-year-old-plus parents . . . lived through COVID-19 and the lockdown with a silent courage that filled me with awe."[3]

To the Western media, however, the lockdown was a harsh, even cruel, strategy, the mark of an authoritarian government. "Only the Chinese government could implement draconian measures to such a

2 Hessler also reported that April 8 became known as *jiefeng*—"taking off the seal."
3 Yang wrote this in a book titled *The Wuhan Lockdown*.

large scale," Yanzhong Huang, a senior fellow at the Council on Foreign Relations, told *The Washington Post*. In *The Guardian* in London, Frances Eve, the deputy director of research at the Network of Chinese Human Rights Defenders, wrote, "That the Chinese government can lock millions of people into cities with almost no advance notice should not be considered anything other than terrifying."

Public health experts also criticized the Wuhan lockdown. "The truth is those kinds of lockdowns are very rare and never effective," Lawrence O. Gostin, a professor of global health law at Georgetown University, told *The Washington Post*. Howard Markel, a medical historian at the University of Michigan, wrote in *The New York Times* that the lockdown would likely not help end the crisis.[4] China "may now be overreacting . . . imposing an unjustifiable burden on the population."

China was unrepentant, convinced that the lockdown was saving lives. In mid-March, it recorded its first day since January with no domestic transmissions, which it offered as proof that its strategy was working. Over the next two years, lockdowns would be China's default strategy whenever a cluster of people were infected in a Chinese city. The attitude of the Chinese people, however, would change dramatically.

Here's the odd thing, though: lockdowns also became the default strategy for most of the rest of the world. Even though they had never been used before to fight a pandemic, even though their effectiveness had never been studied, and even though they were criticized as authoritarian overreach—despite all that, the entire world, with a few notable exceptions, was soon locking down its citizens with varying degrees of severity.

4 Markel is said to have invented the phrase "flatten the curve."

In the United States, lockdowns became equated with "following the science." It was anything but. Yes, there were computer models suggesting lockdowns would be effective, but there were never any actual scientific studies supporting the strategy. It was a giant experiment, one that would bring devastating social and economic consequences.

———

Despite the lack of scientific evidence, the lockdown strategy didn't come out of nowhere, at least not in the United States. It had been discussed—and argued over—by scientists and public health officials since 2005, when (as the story goes) President George W. Bush read John M. Barry's book *The Great Influenza* about the horrors of the 1918 pandemic. "Look," Bush is supposed to have said after finishing the book, "this happens every 100 years.[5] We need a national strategy."

In truth, there were people inside the administration actively engaged with the issue well before Bush read Barry's book. They had seen warning signs, and they were nervous. After 9/11, for instance, deadly anthrax spores had been mailed anonymously to several media outlets and Senate offices. Five people had died. In the fall of 2004, a plant in Liverpool, England, that manufactured influenza vaccine was shut down over contamination problems leading to a serious shortage. That caused several officials, including Alex Azar, who was then the general counsel for the Department of Health and Human Services, to realize that the United States was too dependent on too few manufacturers. He and

5 There had already been two pandemics in the post–World War II era, one in 1957 and another in 1968. But they had both been relatively mild.

others began pushing for money to fix that problem. That led, in 2006, to legislation that created the Biomedical Advanced Research and Development Authority (BARDA) with its mandate to develop vaccines and other medicines that could counter a pandemic or a bioterrorism attack.

Indeed, for decades there had been a small group of scientists who tried to warn the government about the potentially disastrous consequences of a pandemic. The leader of this ad hoc group was an epidemiologist named Donald Ainslie Henderson, or D. A. Henderson, as he was known to everyone, including his wife. In 1966, as a thirty-seven-year-old scientist working for the CDC, Henderson was lent to the World Health Organization to lead a program with a seemingly impossible task: eradicating smallpox, one of the world's great scourges. Henderson turned out to be a remarkable leader, and in the space of a decade he and his team pulled it off.

In Nigeria, William Foege, a doctor Henderson had recruited, realized that smallpox outbreaks could be contained using a technique he called ring vaccination. (We now call Foege's technique contact tracing.) Whenever there was a smallpox outbreak in Nigeria, Foege and two CDC staff members would race to the infected village, quarantine the infected person, and vaccinate anyone he or she had been in contact with. That strategy, along with improved vaccines and vaccination techniques, was so successful that in 1980 the WHO declared that smallpox had been eradicated. Richard Preston, the author of *The Hot Zone*, would later describe this feat as "arguably the greatest life-saving achievement in the history of medicine."

By the time Bush began pushing his administration to come up with a pandemic plan, Henderson was seventy-eight years old. He had spent a decade as the dean of the Johns Hopkins School of Hygiene and Public Health,[6] and had rotated in and out of government several times. He had never stopped thinking about smallpox. In 1995, he was invited to a series of secret government briefings with a Russian defector named Ken Alibek, who had been a high-ranking official in Russia's bioweapons program. Alibek explained that his department had been working on bioweapons that would use both anthrax spores and the smallpox virus. Henderson became so fearful of the possibility of a smallpox bioweapons attack that in 1998 he founded a research institute at Johns Hopkins called the Center for Civilian Biodefense Strategies.[7] Tara O'Toole, a longtime colleague who had recently stepped down as an assistant secretary at the Department of Energy, signed on as his deputy.

One of the center's original goals was to make government officials understand what a bioterrorism attack would be like and how much damage it could do. "What was very striking was that they were thinking about biological threats the same way they thought about other kinds of terrorism—something would go bang," recalls Margaret Hamburg, then an assistant secretary at HHS[8] and one of the few officials who understood pandemics. "I mean, an FBI agent literally said to me that if there was a biological attack, they would go in and diffuse the pathogens."

O'Toole has similar memories. "D.A. and I kept saying, 'But wait a minute, a bioterror attack is a pandemic, and that's a completely different beast from an explosion.' They weren't thinking clearly about what a bioterror attack would be like."

6 The school is now known as the Johns Hopkins Bloomberg School of Public Health.
7 It has since been renamed the Center for Health Security.
8 Hamburg was the head of the FDA during the Obama administration.

In June 2001, six months into Bush's presidency, O'Toole and several colleagues put together a now-famous war-game simulation, Dark Winter. It was an effort to show government officials what a smallpox attack on a midsize American city would be like. O'Toole would later describe the exercise as "unexpectedly dramatic." By the time it was stopped, after two days, the smallpox virus had spread (hypothetically) to twenty-five states and fifteen countries, and the United States had nowhere near enough smallpox vaccine. A few weeks later, the former Georgia senator Sam Nunn, who had played the part of the president in the exercise, testified to Congress about Dark Winter. "We'd have been much more comfortable with a terrorist bombing," he said.

Henderson was back at his Center for Health Security when Bush began agitating for a pandemic plan. But because of his stature, he was brought into some of the administration's discussions. He was not happy with what he was hearing.

The two men heading the planning team were Carter Mecher, the gadfly at the Department of Veterans Affairs, and Richard Hatchett, an oncologist who had been serving as Bush's biodefense adviser since 2002. They were smart and dedicated, but neither had any experience with epidemiology or pandemics. They wound up embracing a model built by a high school student, Laura Glass, for a science project. Her model, developed with the help of her father, Robert, a scientist at the Sandia National Laboratories in Albuquerque, purported to show that simply keeping people away from each other was as effective in preventing infection as a vaccine. Robert Glass, convinced that his daughter's model could save millions of lives, worked tirelessly to get it into the hands of someone in government who would take it seriously. He finally got it to Mecher, who took it very seriously indeed.

Henderson liked to say that there were two kinds of epidemiologists: those who used "shoe leather"—that is, they got out of the office and talked to people to learn about a disease and its spread—and those who used computer models. He was firmly in the shoe-leather camp. In meetings to hash out the plan, he made his position plain: he opposed creating policy based on hypothetical models—which, after all, were themselves based on hypothetical assumptions. "What computer models cannot incorporate is the effects that various mitigation strategies might have on the behavior of the population and the consequent course of the epidemic," he said. "There is simply too little experience to predict how a 21st century population would respond, for example, to the closure of all schools for periods of many weeks to months, or to the cancellation of all gatherings of more than 1,000 people."

Mecher and Hatchett were considering recommending travel restrictions. Henderson pointed out that measures such as airport closings and passenger screenings "have historically been ineffective." He was skeptical of home quarantining healthy people who had come into contact with someone who'd been infected, because it could "result in healthy, uninfected people being placed at risk of infection from sick household members." Most of all, he felt it was a mistake to overreact—to shut down society in the hope that extreme measures would put an end to the sickness and death. His experience led him to believe that they wouldn't.

In the end, Mecher and Hatchett stopped short of calling for lockdowns in the final document, which was issued by the CDC in February 2007. But they came as close as they dared, calling, for instance, for the use of "social distancing measures to reduce contact among adults in the community and workplace, including, for example, cancellation of large public gatherings and alteration of workplace environments and schedules to decrease social density."

Hatchett would later tell the author Michael Lewis[9] what he *really* believed: "One thing that's inarguably true is that if you got everyone and locked each of them in their own room and didn't let them talk to anyone, you would not have any disease. The question was can you do anything in the real world."

Henderson, who died in 2016, never stopped disagreeing. "D.A. kept saying, 'Look, you have to be practical about this,'" O'Toole recalls. "'And you have to be humble about what public health can actually do, especially over sustained periods. Society is complicated, and you don't get to control it.' There was also the fact that D.A. and I had been in government. We had a pretty clear sense of what government was, and wasn't, capable of."

Shortly before the final plan was issued, Henderson, O'Toole, and two other Johns Hopkins colleagues[10] wrote a paper outlining their problems with it. The last paragraph outlined what the authors called their "overriding principle":

> *Experience has shown that communities faced with epidemics or other adverse events respond best and with the least anxiety when the normal social functioning of the community is least disrupted. Strong political and public health leadership to provide reassurance*

9 The story of how Mecher, Hatchett, and a handful of others tried to get in front of the coronavirus pandemic is exuberantly told in Lewis's 2021 book, *The Premonition*. Lewis was a true believer in Mecher and Hatchett's approach and portrayed Henderson as a man whose time had passed.

10 The other two coauthors were Thomas Inglesby and Jennifer Nuzzo. At the time, both were affiliated with Henderson's center. Inglesby is now its director, while Nuzzo is the director of the Pandemic Center at the Brown University School of Public Health.

and to ensure that needed medical care services are provided are critical elements. If either is seen to be less than optimal, a manageable epidemic could move toward catastrophe.

———

After China came Italy, the second country to be hit hard by the coronavirus. How did the Italian government respond? With a lockdown almost as tough as China's, and one that lasted even longer—nearly three months. By the time it was lifted, in early June, 34,000 Italians had died of COVID-19, up from 463 when the lockdown was first imposed.

One might have concluded from those numbers that the lockdown had not been particularly effective. But Neil Ferguson, the head of the infectious disease department at Imperial College London and the cofounder of its center for global infectious disease analysis, saw a silver lining: it meant Western democracies would accept lockdowns! He had long assumed that lockdowns were politically impossible in democratic countries.

"And then Italy did it," he later told *The Sunday Times* of London. "And we realized we could."

There wasn't a more influential epidemiologist in the world than Ferguson. He had built his career on modeling disease; one of the things that drew him to pandemics, he once said, "was the way they behave mathematically." His modeler's mindset led him to believe in the value of lockdowns to squelch a virus.

Ferguson's center had published widely cited models of H5N1 (bird flu) in 2005 and H1N1 (swine flu) in 2009. Although the center's estimates were wildly off the mark—it predicted that 65,000 people might die from H1N1, when the actual number was 457—it remained one of the most respected sources of pandemic information in the world. (Whenever he was questioned about the disparity between the center's estimates and the actual numbers, Ferguson's standard reply was that the center's models represented a worst-case scenario—which had been averted thanks to the warnings emanating from his center.)

Ferguson and a small team within the center—they called themselves the COVID-19 Response Team—had been studying the virus since January. By March 16, they had completed a major report that included the center's first COVID model. The next day Ferguson laid out the team's dramatic findings at a press conference. Their model predicted that without serious countermeasures a staggering 81 percent of the population in the United States and Britain would become infected. It also estimated that 510,000 people in Britain and 2.2 million Americans would die of COVID. In addition, the authors wrote, "we predict critical care bed capacity would be exceeded as early as the second week in April, with an eventual peak in ICU or critical care bed demand that is over 30 times greater than the maximum supply in both countries."

For Ferguson, the purpose of the report wasn't just to release their shocking estimates; it was also to push the American and British governments to adopt lockdowns. It worked. The scientific establishment in both countries, including Anthony Fauci in the United States, quickly embraced lockdowns. The British prime minister, Boris Johnson, had been contemplating a so-called herd immunity strategy—that is, waiting for enough people to become infected until the population achieved immunity from the virus. Instead, within a week of Ferguson's press conference, Johnson ordered Great Britain to lock down.

In the United States, Tomas Pueyo, a middle manager at an education company, published a lengthy cri de coeur on Medium, an online publishing platform, arguing that China had gotten it right and that the rest of the world needed to do the same. Within a few weeks, it had received forty million hits. At the White House, Trump himself was reported to be shaken up by Ferguson's estimates. The report, along with urging from Fauci and others, helped push him to issue his administration's COVID guidelines.

Looking back now, one of 2020's enduring mysteries is why Fauci was such an early and unyielding supporter of lockdowns. He was seventy-nine when the pandemic arrived on U.S. shores. He had spent his entire career at the National Institutes of Health (NIH), including, for the previous thirty-six years, as the director of the National Institute of Allergy and Infectious Diseases, a division of NIH. He had more experience with disease outbreaks than anyone else in the country. He had done a great deal of important science during his career. He had to know that lockdowns as a mitigation measure had no basis in science.

Fauci first became a well-known figure in the 1980s, when he headed up the effort to stop the spread of AIDS. As the government's point man, he was vilified by AIDS activists who demanded that the FDA move faster to approve potential lifesaving drugs.[11] He came to agree with the activists, and the government did eventually make it possible for AIDS drugs to be approved quickly. Fauci also discovered that he enjoyed being in front of the cameras. When the SARS pandemic hit and later the Ebola pandemic, Fauci was again one of the government's chief spokesmen.

During the Trump administration, of course, no one in the federal government could be perceived as being a more important spokesman

---

11 That activism would eventually lead the government to establish its Emergency Use Authorization designation that the FDA used to get COVID-19 vaccines approved quickly.

than Donald Trump himself. But during White House briefings, many Democrats would look to Fauci to see if he was expressing subtle disagreement, by pursing his lips or lowering his head. When he took the lectern, or gave one of his frequent television interviews, they saw him as the government's *true* voice of authority—the man who represented science.

Others who had assumed authority were eventually sidelined by Trump, or at least kept away from the press. But that only happened once to Fauci, and it wasn't long before he was giving interviews again. "Ultimately, it was the administration's decision in terms of how they wanted to position him," says a former senior civil servant. "It would have been very easy to say, 'Thanks, now go back and run your institute, you're not permitted to speak to media.' And as a government employee, he would have had to obey that." Why didn't that happen? "Trump was a man of the media, and how many hits you got was a way of determining dick size," says this person. "Fauci generated a lot of hits."

One significant problem for the public health officials trying to combat COVID-19 was that it was a different kind of virus. All of the government's planning had been done in anticipation of an influenza pandemic. There was much less known, especially in the early months, about how the coronavirus spread and how deadly it was. And Fauci was never willing to acknowledge that uncertainty. For instance, on March 8, he told an interviewer, "There's no reason to be walking around with a mask." A month later, the CDC did an about-face and recommended that people wear masks. No one in government—including Fauci—gave a clear reason for the shift. (Fauci says now that the policy changed as scientists learned more about how the virus spread.)

As for lockdowns, Fauci brooked no dissent. Just as Neil Ferguson used his stature in England to equate lockdowns with science, so did

Fauci in the United States. "If you look at the data," he said in June on an HHS podcast, "the fact that we shut down when we did and the rest of the world did has saved hundreds of millions of infections and millions of lives." The data he was referring to was derived from a University of California, Berkeley, computer model that estimated the lockdowns had prevented sixty million infections in the United States.

Fauci continued: "One of the problems we face in the United States is that unfortunately, there is a combination of an antiscience bias that people are—for reasons that sometimes are, you know, inconceivable and not understandable—they just don't believe science and they don't believe authority. So when they see someone up in the White House, which has an air of authority to it, who's talking about science, that there are some people who just don't believe that—and that's unfortunate because, you know, science is truth."

———

Gavin Newsom, the governor of California, didn't need either Neil Ferguson's estimates or Anthony Fauci's certainty to push him toward a statewide lockdown. That's because he had Charity Dean advising him. Newsom, a successful entrepreneur turned Democratic politician, had served as the mayor of San Francisco and California lieutenant governor before winning the 2018 gubernatorial race with 62 percent of the vote. He'd been in office fourteen months when the pandemic hit California.

Charity Dean[12] was the state's assistant director of public health, an unknown bureaucrat who was an early member of the Red Dawn email

12 Dean is another central character in *The Premonition*.

group. By March, emails between members of the group had taken on a tone of near despair. *Why weren't government officials doing anything?* Why wasn't the United States responding to the coronavirus the way South Korea was—with massive testing—or like China, with its lockdowns? "I believe there is a contingency plan . . . where we will quarantine everyone inside a city if there's a severe disease spread," wrote Eva Lee, a researcher at the Georgia Institute of Technology. "It is like what China did for Wuhan." (In fact, there was no such contingency.) Lee's email contained two graphs charting the number of people in Santa Clara, California, likely to be infected, depending on when certain non-pharmaceutical interventions (or NPIs), such as masking, closing businesses, and maintaining social distances, were put in place. According to Lee's model, the earlier these non-pharmaceutical interventions were put in place, the fewer people would get COVID-19.

This insight—the earlier the intervention, the better the result—had become conventional wisdom among the Red Dawn group. Back in the 2006–7 time frame, three groups of scholars had published studies about the 1918 pandemic, comparing U.S. cities that were early to adopt NPIs with U.S. cities that were late to take action. One of the research teams was led by Mecher, while another was led by Howard Markel under the auspices of the CDC. Their favorite example was St. Louis versus Philadelphia. In St. Louis, the city's health commissioner ordered that the sick be quarantined and that schools, movie theaters, bars, and sporting events be shut down. This was in October 1918. By mid-November, most businesses were closed as well. The rules were lifted on November 18, but reimposed when the number of sick and dying rose again. In all, fewer than three thousand people died during the last three months of the year, giving St. Louis the lowest death rate among the ten largest cities.

Philadelphia officials, meanwhile, downplayed the epidemic, even allowing a huge parade intended to sell Liberty Bonds to take place. (The United States had entered World War I the year before.) Philadelphia's death rate wound up being twice that of St. Louis.

As Markel later wrote,

Our research successfully demonstrated how cities that acted early *(before the virus had a chance to spread widely in a community),* in a layered manner *(the use of more than one NPI at a time), and* for long durations *(because NPIs do not prevent cases, they merely delay viral spread and buy time) enjoyed* far lower morbidity and mortality (cases and deaths) *than those cities that did not act in such a manner.*

In addition to her involvement with the Red Dawn group, Charity Dean had been the one California official who saw what was coming and tried to sound the alarm. As Michael Lewis tells the story, she'd had very little success, held back by a boss who refused to let her brief local health officials and who wanted her to say as little as possible about the coming pandemic.

That all changed on March 6, when Dean was asked to fill in for her boss and brief Newsom and his top aides. She laid out for them how the virus would spread exponentially, with one infected person giving it to two or three others, each of whom would give it two or three others, until there were so many sick people that the hospital system would collapse. Compounding the matter, many of those infected were likely to be asymptomatic, spreading the virus without even knowing they had it.

The meeting shook up the governor and his aides. Newsom's economic adviser brought in some technologists who tapped into Dean's expertise. Their collaboration soon gave rise to (of course) a model that showed that if California did nothing, 56 percent of the population would become infected; in a state of forty million, that translated to a staggering twenty-two million COVID-19 patients. It also showed that even though only eighteen Californians had died of COVID-19 up to that point, the exponential rise in cases would leave the California hospital system some ten thousand beds short of what it needed to handle a tidal wave of patients.

Newsom pulled the trigger on March 19, making California the first state to impose a full-fledged lockdown. The state had already shut down the schools, closed theaters, bars, parks, and gyms, and restricted restaurants to takeout only. It had ended prison visits and kept visitors out of nursing homes. The advice Newsom was getting from Dean was that a lockdown was the logical next step. In the space of two months, lockdowns had gone from being unthinkable to being an unquestioned tool in the NPI toolbox.

When Newsom announced the state's "stay at home" order, he stressed that its purpose was to "bend the curve." He explained that without the lockdown the hospital system would become overwhelmed and that if people stayed at home, the disease curve would rise more gradually. "If we change our behaviors," the governor said, "we can truly bend the curve to reduce the need to surge." "Bending the curve"—aka "flattening the curve"—became common parlance among epidemiologists, government officials, and, eventually, the general public.

But there were questions that no one advocating for lockdowns addressed, maybe because in the urgency of the moment the questions didn't occur to them. How long was the lockdown going to last? Was flattening the curve supposed to mean staying indoors just long enough to give hospitals some breathing room, or was it actually supposed to wipe out COVID? Even if the lockdown did slow the disease's progression, what would happen when the lockdown was lifted? In other words, what was the endgame? In 1918, even St. Louis didn't close down for more than a month at the most. Store closures upset the business community. School closures angered parents. What 1918 had also shown was that people weren't willing to put up with lengthy lockdowns, even knowing they were risking illness and possibly death by abandoning them.

———

Like Newsom in California, Governor Ron DeSantis in Florida had been in office fourteen months when the pandemic hit, though his path was strikingly different. Newsom was a liberal governor in a liberal state. DeSantis was a pugnacious Trump supporter who once ran a campaign ad showing his children learning to say "build the wall" and "Make America Great Again." A graduate of Yale and Harvard Law School, DeSantis spent six years as a navy lawyer (including a stint at Guantánamo), and three terms in Congress as a Tea Party Republican, where he became known as an unyielding Trump defender. Soon after he decided to run for governor, at age thirty-nine, Trump endorsed him, which helped DeSantis steamroll a better-financed primary opponent. In the general election, the president's backing again carried the day as he defeated Andrew Gillum, the Black mayor of Tallahassee, by 32,000 votes.

Given the country's polarized politics and the strong antiestablishment sentiment among those on the right, it was perhaps inevitable that Trump and his supporters would eventually oppose the establishment-supported lockdowns. And given DeSantis's political ambition, it was also probably inevitable that he would become one of the movement's standard-bearers. Even as one state after another followed California in ordering lockdowns—New Jersey on March 21; New York on the twenty-second; Ohio on the twenty-third; thirty-eight states in all by April 1—DeSantis held back. But his reasoning in those early days was not ideological. It was practical.

Florida has no state income tax; some 75 percent of the state's revenue comes from sales taxes. And a great deal of those taxes are paid by tourists who come to Florida to visit Disney World, or to take a cruise, or to attend a convention. The Walt Disney Company shut down Disney World on March 15. The CDC had finally issued its no-sail order for cruise ships. DeSantis and his aides feared that a lengthy lockdown would level the economy.

DeSantis was also worried about the psychological effect of a long lockdown. "You simply cannot lock down our society with no end in sight," he told a group of local television reporters. "Floridians are willing to do what it takes," he added, but "I don't think it's going to be stay in your house for nine months. That's just not going to work."

For his stance, DeSantis was pummeled, both by public health officials and by the news media. An editorial in the *Miami Herald* called him "a timid leader in the face of the growing scourge" and urged him to follow the example of Newsom and other governors who had locked down their states. The editorial was titled "Coronavirus Is Killing Us in Florida, Gov. DeSantis. Act Like You Give a Damn." Almost daily, the state's top Democrat, the agriculture commissioner, Nikki Fried, called for DeSantis to lock down the state.

Despite his Ivy League education, DeSantis had developed many of the same resentments toward the country's elites that Trump harbored. In his view, he was trying to balance the state's economy with the need to keep the greatest number of people safe. And he found the constant criticism from the media and establishment scientists infuriating. So he pushed back. He could often act like the playground bully, and so it was here. In late March, for instance, when a reporter asked that social distancing be practiced at his news conferences, he responded by banning her from his meetings with the press.

Trump's announcement that he was extending the voluntary stay-at-home guidelines through the end of April shifted the ground under DeSantis. He called the White House and spoke to the president. Although he says that Trump agreed with his approach, the result of the phone call was that DeSantis decided that he had to issue a statewide lockdown order for Florida. As the *Tampa Bay Times* put it, "When Trump's coronavirus task force ordered the nation to practice social distancing, work and school from home, avoid discretionary travel, stay away from nursing homes and limit social gatherings to 10 people for another 30 days, DeSantis had little choice but to follow."

At the same time, however, DeSantis set up a task force of his own. Its purpose was to figure out how—and how quickly—he could reopen Florida.

———

If there is one thing New York state and city public health officials knew, it was that any pandemic that reached U.S. shores would hit New York City early and hard. How could it be otherwise? No other city was a busier port of entry to the United States; if a respiratory pathogen was going to make the jump from overseas, it would likely do so in New York. Even after Trump's ban on travel from China, some eight thousand Chinese nationals managed to make their way to the city.

The other thing New York state and city public health officials knew—and took pride in—was that they had two of the best public health departments in the country. Both the city and the state public health departments had their own pandemic plans. They were capable of developing tests for the virus—and would have, if the FDA had allowed it. They had experience dealing with everything from HIV to H1N1. The city had something it called "syndromic surveillance" that could serve as an early warning system for viruses and other contagious diseases by tracking the complaints of patients being admitted to participating hospitals. They had more pandemic experience than any other department in the country. What the two public health departments did not have, inexplicably, was the trust of the city's mayor and the state's governor. Making matters worse, the two men, Mayor Bill de Blasio and Governor Andrew Cuomo, loathed each other. At a time when all hands desperately needed to be on deck, their rivalry was every bit as problematic as faulty tests or bureaucratic sluggishness.

De Blasio's distrust of the city's public health department was the result of an outbreak of Legionnaires' disease in July 2015, during his first term as mayor. Dozens of people in the South Bronx came down with the illness, which turned out to be caused by several contaminated cooling towers. By early August the outbreak was contained. Public health experts around the country praised New York's response, but de Blasio was furious. He had been hammered in the press for taking too long to speak publicly about the outbreak. Cuomo had gleefully piled on, describing the South Bronx during a press briefing as "almost like a bad science fiction movie." When the pandemic hit, de Blasio decided that he would bring in someone he trusted, someone who would have an office in city hall rather than the health department and whom he could consult without having to deal with the city's public health officials. He chose Jay Varma, a former deputy commissioner of the city's health department who had just returned from a three-year stint advising Africa's CDC.

As for Cuomo, who was in his third term as governor, he had developed a reputation in Albany for believing that his own intellect towered over those of mere government bureaucrats, even when they were highly experienced scientists. He was also, to put it bluntly, a bully, who had created in the governor's office "a culture that favored dominance over competence," as Ross Barkan put it in *The Prince*, his 2021 book about Cuomo's handling of the pandemic. Finally, Cuomo surrounded himself with loyalists, people who were going to carry out his orders no matter what. Howard Zucker, the head of the New York State Department of Health, was one such person who would play a prominent role in the coming months. Cuomo also had an outside adviser in Michael Dowling, the CEO of Northwell Health, a New York–based hospital chain. Dowling wasn't a scientist, but that made no difference to Cuomo. In addition to being Northwell's CEO, Dowling was a board member of the Greater New York Hospital Association, which poured $1 million into Cuomo's reelection campaign.

The experts in both the city and the state health departments were urging de Blasio and Cuomo to impose NPIs well before the number of deaths and hospitalizations became grim. But the two leaders resisted.

One high-level public official remembers a meeting with Cuomo in late February. Cuomo, this man says, "basically went on a tirade that we had people coming in from China and they weren't under lock and key. He seemed to have this notion that when someone was in quarantine, there would be a guard on their porch to make sure they didn't leave the house." After an hour or so of this, one of the scientists in the meeting explained to the governor that the virus was probably spreading quickly and the time would soon come when he would have to make a decision about whether to close restaurants, and schools, and maybe shut down the entire city. He even went through the comparison of St. Louis and Philadelphia in 1918 to drive home the point that the earlier NPIs were put in place, the better the outcome. Cuomo nodded. "But now's too soon, right?" he asked.

And so it went for the next three weeks, with public health officials putting together plans to impose NPIs, and Cuomo—and de Blasio—ignoring them. Here was Cuomo in late February: "It's like looking at the weather map when they have different tracks for a hurricane. The hurricane could hit Florida or could hit Washington or could hit New York or could miss everybody and go out to sea, right?" And here was de Blasio on March 2 as the virus was ripping through Italy. "I'm encouraging New Yorkers to go on with your lives + get out on the town despite the Coronavirus," he tweeted.

On March 7, with seventy-six confirmed cases in New York state, Cuomo declared a state of emergency. That's as far as he would go. In New York City, public health officials wanted to take advantage of its syndromic surveillance to better gauge how quickly the virus was spreading. De Blasio blocked the effort.

A week later, March 13, with more than ninety confirmed cases in New York City, de Blasio declared a citywide state of emergency, which included reducing restaurant and bar capacity by 50 percent, eliminating after-school activities, canceling concerts and sporting events, and requesting that at least 10 percent of the city's workforce start working from home. Strangely enough, he also said, "If you love your neighborhood bar, go there now."

Cuomo couldn't resist the chance to one-up the mayor. On Monday morning, with the number of confirmed cases in the city closing in on five hundred, the governor announced his own set of statewide NPIs: restaurants and bars would be closed (except for takeout), along with gyms, casinos, and movie theaters. These closures would begin that evening—twelve hours before de Blasio's measures were supposed to take effect.

The same day Cuomo's NPIs went into effect, de Blasio took the next step: he called for the city to lock down, or, as he called it, "shelter in place." His rationale was the one the city's public health experts had been trying to convince him of: it was the only way to flatten the curve. How did Cuomo respond? By pointing out that the mayor lacked the authority to order a lockdown; that power resided with the governor.

"We hear New York City is going to quarantine itself. That is not true. That cannot happen. It cannot happen legally," Cuomo quickly declared after hearing what de Blasio had proposed. "No city in the state can quarantine itself without state approval."

On March 19, with cases statewide well over five thousand, Cuomo insisted to the press that "the fear and panic is, if anything, worse than the virus." The next day, however, he ordered a statewide lockdown. He called it his PAUSE program: Policies Assure Uniform Safety for Everyone. One of its rules was that everyone over seventy needed to be confined to their home or nursing home, except for solitary exercise. He called this Matilda's Law, after his own mother.

"Among de Blasio's aides," wrote Ross Barkan in *The Prince*, "there was the widespread belief that Cuomo had delayed a shelter-in-place order because de Blasio, his perpetual political nemesis, had suggested it first."

Five days after ordering the lockdown, Cuomo and his health commissioner, Zucker, took one more consequential action—one that would only be noticed several months later. The Department of Health issued an order that nursing home residents who had been hospitalized should be returned to their residence, even if they still had COVID-19.

———

On March 30, a week after Boris Johnson ordered the country into lockdown, Neil Ferguson went on a BBC radio show to implore people to abide by the new rules and stay at home. It would help keep everyone safe, he said. Later that same day, he was visited by a climate activist named Antonia Staats, a married woman he was sleeping with.[13] She paid a second visit on April 8.

A month later—with London still in lockdown—the *Telegraph* newspaper broke the news of their trysts. The paper framed the story exactly as you would expect: "Prof. Ferguson allowed the woman to visit him at home during the lockdown while lecturing the public on the need for strict social distancing." In other words, he was a hypocrite.

The outcry was enormous. Some members of Parliament called on Scotland Yard to get involved. (It declined.) Commentators blasted Ferguson for acting as though he were above the rules he was forcing on others. Though Ferguson held on to his Imperial College job, he resigned from a government scientific advisory post. "I accept that I made an error of judgement," he told *The Telegraph*.

He also said this: "I deeply regret any undermining of the clear messages around the continuing need for social distancing to control this devastating epidemic." But that is exactly what he had done. By acting as if the government's mandate didn't apply to him, he had bred resentment—the same kind of resentment toward all the we-know-

---

13 Staats would later say that she was in an open marriage, and bridled at being labeled Ferguson's mistress.

what's-good-for-you elites that gave Britain Brexit and America Donald Trump. That resentment would continue to grow over the ensuing months.

For while Ferguson might have been the first member of the establishment to be caught breaking the COVID-19 rules they had imposed on everyone else, he wouldn't be the last.

3

Black Market

On April 12, 2020, Marc Schessel wrote a memorandum that he hoped would find its way to someone in the federal government who would not only read it but act on it.

Schessel was one of the few people who understood the complexities of hospital supply chains; his small company, SCWorx, leased software that helped hospitals keep track of the thirteen million or so items that medical supply distributors sell them. By the time Schessel wrote his memo, more than half a million Americans had been infected with the virus, and more than twenty-two thousand had died. Around one hundred thousand were in the hospital. The pandemic was raging in New York, Boston, Chicago, and a handful of other big cities.

And as COVID-19 patients streamed into hospitals, the personal protective equipment that helped keep health-care workers safe—N95 respirators, surgical masks, hospital gowns, nitrile gloves, and so on—

was in desperately short supply. The big distributors, like McKesson and Cardinal Health, had their customers on allocation, sending them maybe—maybe—a tenth of what they ordered. A hospital gown shortage was exacerbated when Cardinal Health had to recall almost ten million gowns that had been improperly sterilized by a Chinese subcontractor. Nitrile gloves were running low. Surgical masks, when they could be found, were selling for ten times what they had cost just a few months earlier. The supply chain for personal protective equipment had completely broken down.

But the item that had become, in Schessel's words, "the poster child" for the PPE shortage was the N95 respirator.[1] The N95 had been invented in the 1970s by 3M, the same company that gave the world Post-it Notes, Thinsulate, Scotch tape, and hundreds of other useful products. It was called an N95 because the electrostatic charge that ran through its microfibers blocked 95 percent of airborne particles, making it by far the safest option for hospital workers.

Prior to the pandemic, says Schessel, a hospital wouldn't use more than a few hundred N95s a month. In fact, only 10 percent of 3M's annual run rate of nineteen million N95s went to hospitals; the rest were sold to industrial companies that worked with substances like asbestos. In April 2020, now that hospitals were filled with COVID-19 patients, health-care workers were sometimes using hundreds of them a day. Even if 3M diverted all its manufacturing capacity to serve hospitals—even if it doubled its run rate, which it was trying to do—the company still wouldn't come close to filling the demand. The situation with surgical masks, hospital gowns, nitrile gloves, and other PPE was even worse: virtually all of it was imported. Once the pandemic hit, the countries

---

1 "Respirator" is the proper term for an N95, although many health-care workers use "respirator" and "mask" interchangeably.

that manufactured the equipment, starting with China, halted exports of PPE so that the equipment could be used by their own hospitals. You could scarcely blame them. But you also had to ask the obvious question: Why hadn't anyone in the United States prepared for this possibility?

Schessel had seen these situations before, and he'd helped his hospital clients cope. There had been shortages during earlier pandemics like H1N1 and Ebola; each time, his hospital customers asked him if he could find alternate supplies, and each time he had succeeded. But this time, as he went looking for supplies for his clients, he discovered that the dynamic was very different. As Schessel explained in his memo,

I quickly came to understand that something in the marketplace had dramatically changed as not only could I find no distributor that had any of these [N95] masks—an entirely new type of seller emerged in the marketplace that changed the landscape seemingly overnight. These new sellers seemed to be investors, not distributors, and the market they created more resembled that of the gas and petroleum trading floor rather than the basically stable market that existed prior to Covid-19.

He continued:

Since January I have been chasing the sun around the globe in search of these masks. I have tried to make deals in Malaysia, Turkey, Poland, Qatar, Saudi Arabia and the Emirates. I would have stopped a hundred times—as this has been the most singularly humbling experience that I have been part of—and having to let hospitals know each time I have failed—knowing that my failure caused more deaths, more sickness . . . to the point of being unbearable—

however for the hospitals failure was not an option—for them this wasn't going away and there was no one coming to help them.

Schessel went on to describe what it was like to search for PPE. He would first make contact with someone claiming to be a PPE "dealer" who said he had access to a huge number of N95s—50 million to 100 million, maybe, which he was selling for, say, $4 a mask. Although the dealer did not hold title to the masks, he assured Schessel that they were OTG—"on the ground"—in a warehouse somewhere near a U.S. port. Schessel was never given the name of the manufacturer, and this utter lack of transparency meant that neither side trusted the other. Sometimes there was a daisy chain of dealers—three or four or even more of them sitting between the buyer and the seller, each hoping to take a cut of the proceeds. Understanding who was doing what was like trying to tackle air. A dealer would sometimes ask for a deposit, but Schessel—and the hospitals—had learned the hard way that handing over money before any masks were delivered was a very bad idea. Theft was more the rule than the exception. Eventually, after the buyer had proven that he had the money in escrow, it came time for the seller to offer "proof of life"—"a term up to now I had never heard of when it came to medical supplies," wrote Schessel—to show that he truly had access to the masks. At that point, he wrote, "the inventory vaporized and the deal was never consummated." It was infuriating; Schessel eventually decided that the brokers must have been trying to get banking information from him to use to insinuate themselves into other deals. He couldn't think of another reason that might explain such behavior. Three months in, he had yet to complete a single deal. Dozens of people just like him, trying to land PPE for a health-care institution or state government, were in the same frustrating position.

⁂ The purpose of Schessel's memo—along with a letter he sent to

President Trump and Mike Roman, the CEO of 3M—was twofold. First, Schessel wanted the government to understand that his clients, which included the Yale New Haven Health System, Northwell Health, a New York hospital chain, and Providence Health and Services, a Catholic hospital system on the west coast, were desperate for PPE. They had formed a consortium, putting close to $300 million into a third-party escrow fund, giving the hospitals serious buying power—enough to compete with wealthy hedge funds that were also said to be searching for PPE. (It was generally thought that the hedge funds' strategy was to flip the PPE for a quick profit, though no one had been able to prove it.) Schessel was convinced that shortages could be at least ameliorated with a well-thought-out public-private partnership. If certain arms of the federal government, like the Defense Logistics Agency, worked with companies that had insight into hospital supply chains, they could perhaps find and direct PPE to those hospitals that needed it the most. They would at least have a better chance than Schessel operating on his own.

The second purpose of the memo was to plead with the Trump administration to let the hospital consortium he had put together buy twenty-five million N95 masks for which it had contracted in China. "We want to pay the purchase price and pick up the masks today, and then to immediately begin distributing them to the hospitals where they are needed—today," wrote Schessel. His biggest fear—incredibly—was that the federal government was going to steal them. He had begun to hear rumors that the N95s his consortium was planning to buy were going to be snatched up by FEMA—the Federal Emergency Management Agency—instead. Who could say where they would wind up if FEMA got them?

"The entire reason that hospitals are relying on us to provide these face masks is that the federal government has been challenged to do so on its own," Schessel wrote.

> If the hospitals run out of these masks—as is happening now—then the situation spirals out of control rapidly. Frontline medical workers, who are interacting face to face with infected patients, become infected—and they become very infected because they are being exposed over and over to high viral loads. When our doctors and nurses become sick, they can no longer care for patients—who become much sicker.

Schessel concluded his memo with this promise: "We will make sure the masks get to the hospitals that need them. Today. We will not hoard them so that they get stuck in a bureaucratic abyss or doled out for political purposes."

Months later, reflecting on his effort to get the government more involved in finding and distributing PPE, a disgusted Schessel said, "It was a complete waste of time. FEMA took the masks. We never saw them again. The government never had the slightest interest in helping hospitals get PPE."

———

There was one man who had long predicted this PPE crisis. His name was Mike Bowen, and he was one of the only Americans who was making surgical masks in the United States. Early in his career, he had worked at Tecnol, a Texas company that in the 1990s was the dominant surgical mask maker, with close to 90 percent of the market. In 1997, Kimberly-Clark, the paper goods company, bought Tecnol; sure enough, seven years later, it shut down its U.S. factory and moved its mask operation to China.

In 2005, one of Bowen's former Tecnol colleagues, Dan Reese, started a new mask company, which he called Prestige Ameritech. Bowen signed on as the company's chief marketer.

"How are we going to sell these masks?" Reese asked Bowen. Bowen replied, "We make them in the U.S. so we can't compete on price. Our products aren't that different, so we can't say ours are better. The one thing we have is national security. The entire U.S. mask supply is under foreign control. If there's a pandemic, we're going to be in trouble."

For years, Bowen's sales pitch got them nowhere. Prestige Ameritech survived by making specialty and private-label masks, which were less price sensitive. All the while, Bowen kept talking about the trouble he saw lurking. In the fall of 2008, for instance, he told a trade publication,

> *In the event of a pandemic, mask-producing countries will divert mask supplies to their own people, removing up to 90 percent of America's ongoing supply. . . . Hospitals would be out of masks in days or weeks at the most. When the masks run out, there would be no protection for America's HCWs [health-care workers].*

Which is exactly what happened in 2009, when the H1N1 virus hit. Sure enough, masks were suddenly impossible to obtain. HHS officials, who'd had many conversations over the years with Bowen about a possible PPE shortage, asked Prestige Ameritech to help the country get through the emergency. Reese and Bowen agreed to gin up the company's mask production.

"We went from 80 employees to 250," says Bowen. "We bought Kimberly-Clark's old mask factory—220,000 square feet. We built new machines. The phones were ringing off the hook. We thought, 'People finally get it. We're going to fix this problem.'"

But no sooner had the H1N1 virus receded than all the new mask customers went right back to buying foreign masks. "The cost savings was like crack cocaine for America's hospitals," Bowen says.

"I knew the mask supply would fail," he adds. "I knew people would die unnecessarily. I thought that if I told the story long enough, I would finally convince someone in authority. I was wrong."

———

If the people of Wuhan believed it was their patriotic duty to stay locked in their homes to fight the pandemic, some entrepreneurial Americans had a different way of expressing their patriotism. They would start companies that would manufacture PPE, primarily surgical masks, which were the easiest to mass produce. Not having done this before, they plunged in without really thinking about what would happen when the crisis was over.

The company that gained the most prominence during the pandemic was DemeTech in Miami. It was a family-run company with a long history of manufacturing surgical supplies, primarily sutures. The family patriarch, Luis Arguello, had retired, and his son, Luis Jr., who was in his thirties, had taken over. "We started hearing from state and local officials who were asking us if we could help with the shortage," Luis Jr. said. "So we decided to take a risk as a family." His father came back to help, and his sister left her job in the music industry to join her brother and father. She was put in charge of the company's small HR operation—an important position because DemeTech planned to hire a lot of people. The Arguellos leased a large empty industrial space, built dozens of mask machines, and hired two thousand workers in all.

When it started churning out surgical masks, it was instantly the largest mask manufacturer in the United States. By June, it was making 150 million masks a month. Its core customers were the Veterans Affairs hospitals.

In Houston, Diego Olmos, a manufacturing expert who had recently left a multinational company, used his severance to help start a mask-making company called Texas Medplast. "My business partner and I said, 'This is the right thing to do,'" he said. In Lindon, Utah, an entrepreneur named Paul Hickey helped found PuraVita Medical to make KN95 respirators. (KN95s are a version of N95s.) In South Carolina, Lance Brown, a former Wells Fargo executive, started a small PPE distributor, which he named Rhino Medical Supply. Its goal? To work only with domestic manufacturers. In time, there were at least forty American companies either making or distributing PPE, all of them assuming the same thing Bowen once assumed—that once the pandemic ended, they would have customers who would stick with them because of the help they had given during the crisis.

"They're all screwed," said Bowen, as he watched these companies race to build their mask-making businesses. Yet Prestige Ameritech was also doing its part, though with a twist.

Bowen had one ally inside the Trump administration: Rick Bright, the head of the Biomedical Advanced Research and Development Authority. Created as part of a 2006 law that gave vaccine makers protection from lawsuits, BARDA's role was to develop medical countermeasures—like vaccines—in the event of a bioterrorism attack, pandemic, or other public health emergency.

Bright, Bowen says, was one of the few people in the administration who felt the same urgency he felt about the PPE shortage. Bright wanted Prestige Ameritech to start making respirators that the government would buy. Bowen told Bright that the government would have to agree to keep buying his respirators after the pandemic ended. He wasn't going to do what he had to do last time: shut down the assembly lines, lay off the 150 workers he had hired, and take a significant financial hit. "The hard landing after H1N1 nearly put us out of business," he emailed Bright at four o'clock one morning. Still, he peppered Bright with emails and warnings, which Bright tried to put in front of the White House. At one point, Bowen, who had come to loathe Trump despite voting for him, even went on Steve Bannon's podcast to sound the alarm, hoping that the president might hear him.

"Mike," Bright eventually had to admit to Bowen, "they're not listening to me."

Just like in 2009, however, Bowen was getting hundreds of calls every day from desperate hospital administrators and others seeking N95s. Letters and emails would pour in from citizens asking if they could buy masks from Prestige Ameritech. The need was overwhelming. So he went to certain hospitals where he had developed relationships— MD Anderson in Houston was one—and had them sign long-term contracts so that the company would retain the business even when the pandemic was over. Prestige Ameritech built seven respirator machines, and before long the company was making between five million and seven million respirators a month. Bowen priced them at 76 cents a mask, the same as the company's pre-pandemic price, earning his new customers' gratitude. He was happy to be doing his patriotic duty, but this time he wasn't going to get screwed.

———

In late March, a handful of high-profile CEOs came to the White House for a meeting. They were seeking guidance from the administration: What could their companies do to help ease the shortage of protective equipment? "There was a real opportunity for a coordinated response," said one person who attended the meeting, according to *Vanity Fair*. Their companies had the ability to manufacture and innovate, but the government had buying power, political clout, and logistics expertise that few other entities could match.

Jared Kushner, the president's son-in-law and top aide, quickly put a damper on their hopes. "The federal government is not going to lead this response," he said.

Several of the CEOs pointed out that because the response wasn't being coordinated by the federal government, states and health-care institutions were bidding against one another, driving up the price needlessly. Kushner didn't care. "Free markets will solve this," he replied. "This is not the role of government."

Once again, the one White House official who was pushing for the administration to get involved was Peter Navarro. Working with Rick Bright, Navarro drafted a memo for the Coronavirus Task Force that included as one of its three major points that the government use its authority to force U.S. companies to begin making masks. The White House wasn't interested.

During the Clinton administration, the government had built a national PPE stockpile, but as much as three-quarters of it had been emptied out during the H1N1 pandemic. Some of the remaining PPE was so old its expiration date had come and gone. Trump would later say that the stockpile shortfall was Obama's fault, but that wasn't exactly true. A few years after the H1N1 crisis, the Obama administration requested $655 million for the stockpile, an increase of $59 million. That would have allowed the government to begin restocking it. Instead, Congress cut its budget by 10 percent. Its budget would continue to be cut in ensuing years.

In the earliest days of the pandemic, Washington State and Massachusetts were able to get some PPE from the stockpile. But by the time Veterans Affairs put in an order for 200 million N95s in mid-March—saying it would be out of masks within a week—the cupboard was bare.

At which point, chaos descended as states frantically sought PPE for their hospitals, where patients were dying and doctors and nurses were getting infected. And all the while, the Trump administration stood by, seemingly amused at their distress. A video clip of a conference call between Trump and a group of governors on March 19 summed up the prevailing attitude. Trump is seen sitting at the head of a conference table at FEMA headquarters, surrounded by aides and FEMA officials. Charlie Baker, the moderate Republican governor of Massachusetts, is on speakerphone.

"We took very seriously the push that you made previously on one of these calls that we should not just rely on the stockpile and that we should go out and buy stuff and put in orders," says Baker.

"Right," says Trump, nodding.

"And I gotta tell you," Baker continues, "on three big orders, we lost to the feds. . . . I got a feeling that if somebody has a chance to sell to you or sell to me, I'm gonna lose every one of them."

Trump laughs—yes, laughs!—at Baker's dilemma. "Well, Charlie," he says. "We do like you going out and seeing what you can get. If you can get it faster, and price is always a component of that also, and maybe that's why you lost to the feds," he adds with a self-satisfied smirk.

There is a second video that offers an even more shocking illustration of the administration's laissez-faire attitude. It's early April, and Kushner is at the lectern during a COVID-19 briefing. He wants to clarify an issue concerning the national stockpile. The states may think they should have access to the PPE in the stockpile, but they're wrong, says Kushner. "The notion of the federal stockpile . . . that's supposed to be our stockpile. It is not supposed to be state stockpiles that they then use," he insists. But what other purpose would a federal stockpile have if not to make PPE available to the states in a health-care emergency? Time and again during the first year of the pandemic, one or another arm of the federal government walked off with PPE that a state or a hospital had managed to track down and import. Though there have long been rumors that the PPE wound up hidden away on military bases, the truth is that nobody knows where it went.

Kushner did realize that the PPE shortage was a serious problem, and eventually he decided to take matters into his own hands. He recruited a handful of his MBA friends, starting with Adam Boehler, his old college roommate—and a former health-care executive—who was already in the administration. Boehler would later tell friends he didn't want to be dragged into Kushner's operation because he was happy in his current job. (He was the head of the U.S. International Development Finance Corporation.) But in a meeting with Kushner and Matthew Pottinger, he learned that the stockpile was low on ventilators and almost out of N95s. "It was clear that this was worse than they had expected," he later told friends. So he signed on.

Boehler and Kushner's answer to the PPE shortage was to create a highly irregular off-the-books "task force" to land PPE deals. They brought in a group of twentysomething volunteers who would take to their laptops to hunt for PPE—in effect, doing the same thing Marc Schessel was doing, without his years of supply chain experience. This effort was chronicled in Alex Gibney's biting documentary *Totally Under Control*. One of the volunteers was Max Kennedy Jr., Robert F. Kennedy's grandson. He told Gibney that he and nine other volunteers—all equally ignorant about hospital supply chains—were put in a windowless conference room at FEMA filled with televisions tuned to Fox

News. "One representative from FEMA and one representative from the military gave a quick pep talk," he said. He continued:

> *They kept saying "the stuff," and by that they meant PPE. And they kept saying there's stuff all around the world, there's stuff in the U.S. and we need to get it to hospitals as fast as possible. . . . We thought we would be auxiliary support for an existing procurement team. . . . And instead we were the team. So we started cold-emailing people we knew who had business relationships in China, looking for factories online, and emailing them from our personal Gmail accounts. Because we had never done this before, there were all these really basic questions about how a federal procurement operation should work. We would call factories and say, "We think the federal government can send you a check in sixty days." And they would say, "There is someone with a briefcase of cash, and they are offering to pay me right now."*

According to Kennedy, Kushner's PPE "task force" didn't land a single deal.

As for Bright, his constant agitating about PPE and other pandemic issues inside the administration caused him to become persona non grata at the White House. In late April, he was suddenly transferred to a different department inside HHS. A government spokesperson characterized the transfer as offering him a new challenge. But Bright didn't see it that way. As he put it in a whistleblower complaint he filed a few weeks later, "Dr. Bright was removed as BARDA Director and Deputy Assistant Secretary for Preparedness and Response in the midst of the deadly COVID-19 pandemic because his efforts to prioritize science and safety over political expediency and to expose practices that posed a substantial risk to public health and safety, especially as it applied to

chloroquine and hydroxychloroquine, rankled those in the Administration who wished to continue to push this false narrative."

In October 2020, saying that he was being given no meaningful
work, he resigned from the government.

———

The media, of course, soon picked up on the dire situation. There were
newspaper photographs of nurses wearing garbage bags because they
were out of gowns. Hospitals rationed disposable surgical masks—one
per shift for each doctor and nurse. Most of all, though, health-care
workers needed N95s.

"I started chasing lead after lead," recalled Lisa Lattanza, the head
of the orthopedic department at the Yale School of Medicine, who had
somehow become "the PPE person" at the Yale New Haven Hospital.
"Time after time we would march down the road, place an order, and
then watch it disappear. Then we would be told it was confiscated." She
added, "I've placed orders for 1.5 million masks and gotten 100,000.
And I felt lucky for getting the 100,000."

Many of the purported sellers of PPE were, to put it bluntly, crooks.
Early in the pandemic, plenty of hospitals and state purchasing departments, not realizing how prevalent fraud was in this new black market, made down payments for big orders from a factory in China or
Vietnam, only to see the "seller" walk off with the money, never to be
heard from again. So many people were selling counterfeit 3M respirators that the company put together a team to track them down and sue
them. 3M also got the FBI involved.

"3M does not—and will not—tolerate price gouging, fraud, decep-
tion, or other activities that unlawfully exploit the demand for critical 3M products during a pandemic," said Denise Rutherford, 3M's

senior vice president of corporate affairs. "3M will not stop here. We continue . . . to investigate and track down those who are illegally taking advantage of this situation for their own gain." The company filed its first lawsuit against a man who was trying to hoodwink New York City's procurement office.

There were other kinds of fraud as well. Some sellers sent boxes that were filled with soiled or contaminated PPE. Others tried to lure brokers into turning over bank information that could be used to con a different party in a different deal. Some brokers would promise to deliver masks or gloves or gowns before they had access to the PPE—access they almost never got. ("Joker-brokers," these people were sometimes called.) Fraudsters in China went to PPE factories and siphoned off supplies that were supposed to be part of the supply chain, planning to sell them at a much higher price. LinkedIn became the most popular platform for both alleged buyers and alleged sellers. "It is a gruesome marketplace," Schessel said. Another person involved in this PPE black market put it this way: "It was like putting your tongue on the battery of capitalism."

Oil traders were among the first to jump into the PPE black market. That was understandable: after all, N95s were standard equipment on an oil rig. Oil industry insiders realized there was likely to be a shortage when 3M suddenly stopped selling to industry and diverted all its respirators to hospitals. The thing about oil traders, though, is that the last thing they want is to actually take hold of a tankerful of oil. They want to trade that oil. The same was true of PPE: their goal was not to take receipt of PPE but rather to flip it to another buyer while it was still crossing the ocean. Their trading was one factor in driving up the price of PPE.

After the oil traders, in came the retired businesspeople, the day traders, the small hedge fund operators, the ex–FBI agents, the people with connections to China, and more—all believing they could make a once-in-a-lifetime score. A Dallas banker was said to be trying to broker PPE. A big British hedge fund was searching for PPE. So, reportedly, was Sammy Sosa, the former Chicago Cub slugger. A New Jersey lawyer who said he was representing the Saudis. A woman affiliated with the Vatican. The thirty-year-old CEO of Delco Medical, a company that, upon further inspection, turned out to have been formed two months earlier and was "headquartered" in Broken Arrow, Oklahoma.

"Everyone who is out of work is trying to sell PPE," said Schessel.

One such person was Brian Kolfage, the decorated air force veteran who was indicted (along with Steve Bannon) in August 2020 for allegedly defrauding people who donated to a campaign to help build Donald Trump's wall on the Mexican border. Kolfage and several partners started a company called America First Medical. They sent out emails claiming to have "exclusive North American rights" to fifty million COVID-19 test kits from South Korea. They also said they had access to masks made in South Korea, for which they were planning to charge $4 apiece—more than four times their cost pre-pandemic.

"All we need is the proof of funds to validate the ability to purchase the 20 million units," wrote a Kolfage associate. "The first 5 million will be at the bonded warehouse in Seoul Korea tomorrow. The remaining 15 million will follow over the next three days. if we miss tomorrow's pickup we will not be able to get future production from this distributor."

Then the kicker: "The entire deal will disappear in the next couple hours if we don't deliver proof of funds."

A few days later, Kolfage was back with a different offer. "We have an 800 million unit seller in USA," he wrote. "Proof of funds gets you in the door and first in line to inspect and in person and buy." And so it went.

"It was a Wild West mentality," says one of Kolfage's former partners. But his group never had any masks—or anything else. "If you weren't a hedge fund with a lot of money, you couldn't get any product," the former partner added.

The PPE black market was a reminder of how important trust and the rule of law were to business transactions. In this market, there was neither. One side was essentially saying, "Show me the PPE and I'll show you the money." The other side was saying, "Show me the money and I'll show you the PPE." More often than not, the seller didn't have the PPE and the buyer didn't have the money. Just about everybody who got into the game eventually dropped out. The amount of time and work and energy required to put a deal together was exhausting, and the payoff almost never came. There was no pot of gold at the end of the rainbow after all.

"We spent a lot of our time vetting people," said a supply chain executive at a major hospital. "We were trying to figure out who was not trying to price gouge, who was actually trying to help. We wanted to work with people who were fair in the situation versus those who were only in it to make a quick buck."

Were there people who were trying to source PPE because they genuinely wanted to help in the crisis? Of course. But the PPE black market didn't distinguish those whose motives were pure from those whose weren't. Robert Kraft, the owner of the New England Patriots, sent a plane to China to retrieve an order for 1.2 million N95s that Kraft and the State of Massachusetts had bought together. When the Patriots' plane landed in Boston in early April, Governor Baker hailed it as "a significant step in our work to get our front-line workers the equipment they needed." Except that the masks, while useful, were not real N95s and didn't offer the same protection as a 3M product.

On LinkedIn, a former pharmaceutical executive, writing anonymously, laid out his "guide for making successful PPE deals."

"The market is completely unregulated, fraudulent, and nowadays it seems that everyone knows billion-dollar hedge funds, presidents and of course my all-time favorite: members of the 3M board of directors. And the real sellers and buyers are having a hard time concluding real business when they are constantly surrounded by scammers." He then offered advice to the various parties trying to make money in the PPE game.

Do you know the seller? "I cannot stress this enough . . . you must know exactly who the other party is, what financial capabilities they have, etc. If you fail to acquire this information you are essentially gambling."

Can the offer be real? "For example, it is highly suspicious if the seller claims to have quantities above 1 billion on the ground (OTG)."

How long has the seller company existed? What was their core business before getting into the PPE industry? "Most scammers use newly founded companies so you cannot make proper background checks."

Do not fall for everything on the internet. "I receive lots of messages from different sources claiming to have access to astronomically big quantities of products. These are usually other intermediaries fishing for your buyer's information. Do not engage especially if you do not know them."

Do not lie. Ever. "A lot of intermediaries lie. And lots of them lie because they either do not know something or want to pose as professionals with several successful deals behind them. Do not do this. You will be exposed and a laughingstock."

The anonymous PPE dealer had one final tip: "If something seems shady, it probably is."

———

In May 2020, Bowen testified before Congress about the PPE shortage. At one point, in talking about his inability to convince people over the years that a PPE shortage was inevitable, he choked up.

"I'm a salesman telling a story nobody believes, the story that the U.S. mask supply is gonna collapse, and people are gonna die, and it doesn't cost much to fix. That's the story."

He continued: "I'm getting 500 to 1,000 emails a day. I'm getting email from people, not businesses. I'm getting emails from moms. I'm getting emails from old people, 'Please send me masks'"—he stopped for a moment to compose himself—"and I can't.

"I can't help all these people."

4

Safety Net

In February 2020, Kealey Neuville was midway through her residency in general dentistry at Brookdale, a hospital in Brooklyn, New York. Brookdale is what's known as a safety net hospital—meaning that many of its patients are either on Medicaid or uninsured.

Brookdale had merged four years earlier with two nearby hospitals, Kingsbrook Jewish and Interfaith Medical, to create a new system known as One Brooklyn. The goal was to reduce the bed count by two hundred. Even before the pandemic hit, the hospital was always overcrowded. "We called it battlefield dentistry even before the pandemic hit," Neuville says. "The ER was always full."

In March, Governor Andrew Cuomo shut down elective surgeries to free up more beds in New York hospitals for COVID-19 patients. Dental surgery was considered an elective, so dental residents like Neuville were pressed into service in the emergency room. Brookdale was quickly overwhelmed, with patients sleeping on chairs in hallways. There was almost no PPE, and the dental residents were last in line to get what little there was. "The explanation was, we just can't," Neuville says. "There isn't any. We tried to work with other hospitals, but those who had PPE didn't want to give it to us, either. There was a lot of fear. Nobody wanted to do any patient interaction without it, but you also feel horrible because you know your job is to take care of people."

To enter a COVID-19 floor, Neuville had to walk through a big plastic barricade. She was lucky, she says—the medical residents asked her what she was comfortable doing and not doing—but other dentistry residents were pressed into doing work that was normally handled by doctors. "It felt so crazy, but it was like wartime, you do what you're supposed to do," she says. Seeing people die, including a Brookdale nurse, "I realized how big it was, and that no one was untouchable."

Dr. Alex Andreev, a critical care resident at Brookdale, says that even before COVID-19 the hospital was in a precarious state. "COVID was a trigger that pushed everything over the edge," he says. "All the problems that existed before, they just became even more noticeable, even uglier." The understaffing was chronic. And Brookdale lacked equipment that the wealthy hospitals had as a matter of course. For instance, it had only a few CT scanners for the entire five-hundred-bed hospital. (CT scanners create images from various angles in a patient's body.)

Andreev remembers his first patient who died from COVID-19. "She was around sixty," he says. "No major medical problems, maybe some hypertension, but nothing crazy. She was fully functional. Everything seemed stable." But within three or four hours, she had deteriorated badly. "She developed low blood pressure, and multi-organ failure, and required intubation, and was sent to the ICU," says Andreev. Within twenty-four hours, she was dead.

Soon there were well over a hundred patients in the emergency room. All the PPE was gone. There weren't enough monitors to check patients' oxygen levels. There were shortages of critical medicines. A heart-lung machine called ECMO—which sends oxygen-filled blood back to the body and cut the risk of dying from COVID by half—Brookdale didn't even have one of them. The flood of new patients continued. At least five patients would die each night, Andreev recalls, and because the New York City morgues were overwhelmed, the bodies were dumped in the hospital's backyard. The windows were covered, he says. But everybody knew what was there.[1]

Kelley Cabrera, whose parents immigrated to Peekskill, a New York exurb, from Ecuador, always wanted to be a nurse. By the time the pandemic hit, she was working at Jacobi Medical Center in the Bronx, another of New York's eleven public hospitals. "It was always clear to me that we have a two-tiered health-care system," she says. "One for people with 'good' insurance, and the other for people without it. COVID played out exactly as a lot of us would have predicted it would. Of course it was going to hit the people with limited income, immigrants without insurance. It was very clear to us. Because the care beforehand is one of the biggest keys to health."

New Rochelle, fifteen minutes away from Jacobi, was the scene of one of the first outbreaks. "We knew we were screwed," Cabrera says. "Ambulances were backed up because we could only triage people so fast. I was triaging one patient in the ambulance bay. They told me she had been calling since midnight the night before. She got to me at 9:00 a.m. She had shortness of breath and abdominal pain. She needed oxygen. She was talking to me. I said, 'The doctors are coming.' By noon she was dead. That kept happening over and over again."

---

1 Brookdale has denied any problems with staffing or equipment during the pandemic.

Both Andreev and Cabrera say that one of the most frustrating things for them was their inability to transfer their patients to other hospitals that had empty beds. Many of the wealthy hospitals could have taken more patients, and under federal law they are supposed to accept so-called transfer patients. But taking patients who have Medicaid or are uninsured cuts into their profit, so they've long found ways to duck that responsibility. "In COVID," says Andreev, "it got even worse." New York eventually built emergency facilities that were supposed to provide extra beds for COVID-19 patients, including at the Javits Center and the Billie Jean King National Tennis Center. Incredibly, Jacobi couldn't send its patients there. "The requirements were ridiculous," says Cabrera. Patients had to only be on a certain amount of oxygen and had to be continent. "I thought, 'Ummm, how is this going to help me? None of my patients fit these criteria. Where are the healthy COVID patients? Because I don't have them.'" Even the government, it seemed, was putting the lives of the health-care haves over those of the health-care have-nots.

That spring Andreev told *The New York Times*, "Out of 10 deaths, I think at least two or three could have been saved."

The scenes from inside New York's hospitals were the stuff of nightmares. "Especially in the early months, we witnessed death on a level we had never experienced, and many nurses lost patients, colleagues, family members, and other loved ones," says Nancy Hagans, who has been a nurse for more than thirty years and works at Maimonides Medical Center in Brooklyn. "COVID exposed and exacerbated the existing problems in our profit-driven health-care system—from bare bones staffing to lack of access to health care, which led to a disproportionate number of Black and Brown patients dying."

Nor was there any incentive, beyond the moral one, for hospitals to help each other—or any way to enforce or coordinate that help. In

New York, city and state officials pointed fingers at one another for their failure to establish a centralized hub to coordinate the transfer of patients from hospitals that were overwhelmed to ones with empty beds, reported *The Wall Street Journal*. *The New York Times* reported that the elite hospital systems generally wouldn't share their precious PPE with the harder-hit safety net hospitals. The *Times* also found that even within the same hospital system the death rate was far higher at the less well-off institutions. It was as low as one in ten at prestigious medical centers, and as high as one in three at community hospitals like Brookdale.[2]

Yet another reason the pandemic disproportionately affected the disadvantaged was that the virus feasted on those with preexisting conditions like diabetes and kidney disease and poor people were more likely to have such conditions.[3] COVID-19 didn't just shine a spotlight on the problems in our health-care system; it stacked multiple inequities on top of one another. "That population is disproportionately represented at a safety net hospital, so safety net hospitals are at least doubly challenged," says Greg Martin, an ER doctor in Atlanta. "It's not just the scarcer resources, but also that they're dealing with a very different population than would have sought care in some of the other more highly resourced hospitals." Martin says he sees the disparities every day, because he splits his time between a university hospital and a safety net hospital. "Me as a physician, I'm the same," he says. "I'm not the one who is changing from place to place, but the other resources and the policies and particularly the patients can vary dramatically from one

---

2 "Why Surviving the Virus Might Come Down to Which Hospital Admits You," *New York Times*, July 1, 2020.

3 According to researchers at the CDC, rates of chronic obstructive pulmonary disease, kidney disease, and diabetes, for example, among the poorest 10 percent of New Yorkers are estimated to be more than 40 percent higher than the median rate.

place to another. COVID made the disparities in both patient needs and hospital resources much, much worse."

As the pandemic spread beyond New York, to Michigan, to California, to rural areas, that same pattern played out again and again. Those with lower incomes had worse COVID-19 outcomes. Maybe they were so-called essential workers, who, unlike the white-collar workers able to stay at home, had to brave the virus to earn their living. Or maybe they were people afraid to seek medical care early for fear of being bankrupted. Or maybe they lived in multigenerational housing, where asymptomatic grandchildren might infect their grandparents. A study done by CMS at the end of 2021 found that for Medicare beneficiaries of every racial, ethnic, and age group, the rate of infection among those with incomes low enough to be on Medicaid was far higher than for everyone else in the study. Americans living in poorer counties, especially in the rural South, died during the pandemic at almost twice the rate of those in rich counties, a study by the Poor People's Campaign found. A study published by a University of South Florida epidemiologist found that in 2020, COVID-19 mortality was five times higher for adults who had a low socioeconomic position, as measured by educational achievement, versus a high one. And on, and on, and on.

And that's just the start of the issues that the pandemic would expose and exacerbate.

—

The disparate outcomes between white and Black, rich and poor, insured and uninsured, weren't a surprise to David Ansell, a doctor at Rush University Medical Center in Chicago who wrote about health inequities in his 2017 book, *The Death Gap*. "When people are like,

'Oh my gosh, why are Black and brown communities being hit so hard by [COVID-19]?' David and I would look at each other and say, 'Because that's what happens in under-resourced neighborhoods,'" says Darlene Hightower, who at the time ran the Office of Community Health and Engagement at Rush. "The shock is that people were shocked," says Ansell.

Thanks in no small part to Ansell, Rush saw itself as a catalyst for health equity on Chicago's West Side; in fact, after a decade as the hospital's chief medical officer, Ansell had been named Rush's senior vice president for community health equity in 2016. As part of Rush's commitment to health equity, it became, in the pandemic, the rare well-off hospital that accepted transfer patients from safety net hospitals.

When Rush realized that the COVID tsunami was coming, its staff began reaching out to Chicago's safety net hospitals to make them aware that Rush, with its advanced technology, including ECMO, and its capacity for 170 ICU beds, would be available to accept transfer patients. "We'd hold daily COVID huddles with them," says Dr. Airica Steed, who at the time was the CEO of Sinai Health, a Chicago safety net hospital. "It was almost like Rush was becoming an extension of us."

From a moral standpoint, it was obvious that this was the right thing to do. But from a financial standpoint, it was a losing proposition. Rush decided it would ignore the economics during the pandemic and act the way hospitals used to act before the hospital industry became obsessed with maximizing profits, a trend that began with the founding of the Hospital Corporation of America in 1968. (The company is now known as HCA Healthcare.) "The very clear instruction from our leadership was that we are not going to care about insurance," says Helen Park, the nurse who handled most incoming calls. "The reason was that people were going to die if they couldn't get to us."

The calls poured in. "I think Helen's name and number are pasted on bathroom stalls all over Chicago," jokes Edward Ward, the vice-chairman of Rush's ER department. "For a transfer, call Helen!"

In order to handle both transfers and its own patients, Rush expanded its capacity by converting other wings of the hospital into COVID-19 areas, expanding its ICU beds, and doubling its ECMO capacity. "Going from six to twelve ECMO, that's rooms and staff that's required twenty-four hours a day," says Jane Krivickas, a nurse who oversees the transfer center at Rush. "The human cost to our own staff was considerable. Things got really, really tough here."

The sheer amount of work wasn't the worst of it. "The effect it would have on our staff when we didn't have capacity, it was horrible," says Ward. "We'd hear, for instance, this is a forty-year-old guy, and we can't do anything more, and if you don't take him, he's going to die. But we couldn't."

"There were times when we had no beds," says Ansell. "And so people died. It was heartbreaking."

Park says the call that crushed her most came from a Rush ICU nurse who was showing up day after day to work and whose sister was being treated at a safety net hospital. Staff there were telling the nurse that her sister had to be put on a ventilator. "She called me and cried and begged," Park says. "She said, 'Please, I'm caring for these dying patients in other people's families. Please get my sister here.' But we had a triage scale—we had to have one—she wasn't sick enough to transfer. It was a terribly hard conversation. It was moments like that that you feel so helpless. There's nothing you can say that's going to make that situation better. It was a gut punch."

But there were uplifting moments too. "We were their last hope," Park says of the safety net hospitals that would call hoping to transfer patients. "When we said we were accepting the transfer, we'd sometimes hear people shout back out at their co-workers, 'Rush is taking them. Rush is taking them!'"

From the start of that terrible spring of 2020 through January 2022, Rush accepted nearly five hundred transfers and estimates that it took a few hundred patients that otherwise might have died. Accepting transfers cost the hospital financially; by the spring of 2021, Rush was estimating that it would lose a quarter of a billion dollars. But the city was grateful. In the spring of 2021, Chicago's mayor, Lori Lightfoot, awarded Rush a Medal of Honor for the "tremendous resources" it mobilized during the first wave of the pandemic, including "accepting transfers of some of the most acutely ill patients in Chicago." Rush was the only hospital honored.

In Los Angeles, Dr. Elaine Batchlor, the head of MLK Community Hospital, and her staff were, like most safety net hospital staff, working the phones to transfer patients. They rarely succeeded. Batchlor knew that the patients' lack of money was the issue, but she couldn't prove it. "What they say is that they don't have a bed available," she says. "And if they don't have a bed, they don't have to take the patient."

In California, the public health authorities tried to facilitate moving people around, but they didn't have any more success than New York officials. Batchlor says it wasn't until the end of 2021, when she finally got government data showing the number of COVID-19 patients in each hospital—versus the number of licensed beds—that she got her proof. "I was shocked because what I saw was that some of the biggest, most well-resourced hospitals in L.A. had the fewest COVID patients," she says. "We had more COVID patients than hospitals three to four times our size."

She'd already sent a letter to Governor Gavin Newsom, which essentially said, as she puts it, "Let me tell you what's happening in South L.A." The day after Christmas 2020, he sent a team to MLK Community Hospital to see what was happening, and the day after that he sent the National Guard to help, including some medical strike teams. "They gave us access to travel nurses and respiratory therapists. I was really pleased," Batchlor says.

Still, there was nothing anyone could do about transfers. "At one point," she says, "the local public health department, which was trying to help, called us up and said, 'Hey, there are five open beds at X hospital.'" (She won't divulge the name because she hopes to be able to transfer future patients there.) So her team spent all day talking to the staff at that hospital. But it was all for naught; not a single patient was transferred. "I later called the CEO of that hospital and I said, 'We couldn't get a single patient transferred.' And you know what he said to me? 'Oh, I guess those beds were full.'"[4]

Rural hospitals fared no better than the urban safety net hospitals. Pre-pandemic, rural Americans had a 20 percent higher overall death rate than those who lived in urban areas. Almost two-thirds of rural hospitals have no ICU beds, according to the Chartis Center for Rural Health. In the decade before the pandemic, 119 rural hospitals had closed. Alan Morgan, the head of the National Rural Health Association, says that the closure of a hospital results in a 10 percent increase in mortality in the community.

Just as in urban areas, the ability to transfer patients relied on personal networks and in some cases email lists. All of that broke down as the system became overwhelmed. FEMA eventually began to help manage transfers, but there were multiple accounts of both COVID-19 and non-COVID patients who died awaiting transfers. Morgan said he

---

4 On October 19, 2020, *The Wall Street Journal* published an article titled "Some California Hospitals Refused Covid-19 Transfers for Financial Reasons, State Emails Show." The article noted that the California Hospital Association was averaging forty phone calls to place just one patient.

can't count how many rural hospital CEOs complained to him about the transfer problem. "It's unacceptable," he says.

"I think the epidemiologists and the data people will show you that the communities that did not have ready access to health care before the pandemic suffered in two ways. I think they suffered because a lot of their chronic diseases were less controlled," says Tim Putnam, who at the time was the CEO of Margaret Mary Health hospital in Batesville, Indiana. "And I think the ability for patients to get treated, understand what's going on, or even communicate about the disease without a local health-care authority put them at a disadvantage." Data shows that he's right. An analysis by STAT, an online health-care news site, found that for most rural counties—those with fewer than fifty thousand residents and at least fifty miles from a major city—the death rates were 66 percent higher than the rest of their state.

———

There was another group that was especially vulnerable to the coronavirus: the elderly. The influenza pandemic of 1918 had been an indiscriminate killer: children, adults, the old—the virus made little distinction between them. But this pandemic wasn't like that. According to the CDC, people between the ages of sixty-five and seventy-four were 60 times more likely to die of COVID-19 than people between eighteen and twenty-nine. A person eighty-five or older was *360 times* more likely to die of COVID-19 than a young adult. Children, though hardly immune from the virus, were the least likely to be infected (or to infect others) and *by far* the least likely to die from COVID-19.

This was clear to public health officials early on. "The data coming out of China continues to say that the people who are at higher risk for severe disease and death are those who are older and with underlying health conditions," said the CDC's Nancy Messonnier during a press briefing in early February, before she was muzzled by the Trump administration. By October 2020, the CDC was reporting that 80 percent of COVID-19 deaths were among people sixty-five or over.

One obvious reason for this is that the elderly are more likely to have comorbidities or weakened immune systems. But another reason is that the institutions the United States relies on to care for millions of older people were pathetically unprepared to do so. Although there were some publicly traded nursing home companies, the dominant players in the industry were private equity, or PE, funds. In theory, private equity funds buy struggling companies—using debt that is loaded onto the acquired companies—and then use their business smarts to improve the operations while cutting costs. In reality, it hadn't worked that way in a very long time—if it ever did. One knowledgeable critic was Dan Rasmussen, who had worked at the private equity firm Bain Capital before starting his own business. In 2018, he wrote a scathing paper based on an analysis of 390 PE deals. He found that more than half the time a company's revenue growth slowed and capital spending fell following a PE firm's takeover. The reason was simple: most of the time, all the private equity firm did was add debt. "The industry mythology of savvy and efficient managers streamlining operations and directing strategy to increase growth just isn't supported by data," he wrote. The title of his paper was "Private Equity: Overvalued and Overrated?"

Nursing homes were treated no differently. These financiers had loaded their nursing homes with debt they could ill afford while sucking out millions of dollars for themselves. Their nursing homes could hardly care for their residents in normal times, much less during a pandemic. As *The New York Times* put it in May 2020, "When the pandemic struck, the majority of the nation's nursing homes were losing money, some were falling into disrepair, and others were struggling to attract new occupants, leaving many of them ill equipped to protect workers and residents as the coronavirus raged through their properties."

An early tragedy that took place in Holyoke, Massachusetts, set the tone. Just weeks after the coronavirus hit Massachusetts, thirteen residents died of COVID-19 at the Holyoke Soldiers' Home, a state-run nursing home for veterans. Investigators quickly realized that the superintendent of the facility—a political appointee with no nursing home experience—had put COVID-19 patients in the same areas as uninfected residents. The superintendent was replaced, but the damage was done; ultimately, seventy-six residents died due in part to his incompetence.

Every state, it seemed, had a similar story.

In Minnesota, North Ridge Health and Rehab in New Hope, a Minneapolis suburb, saw 495 cases of COVID-19—despite having only 320 beds. The disease ravaged not just the residents but the staff; by December 2020, ninety-four people who either worked or lived at North Ridge had died. According to an investigation by the *Star Tribune* in Minneapolis, it got so bad that employees were calling the facility "Death Ridge." One resident, a seventy-year-old retired surgical technician, told the paper, "This place is a giant petri dish."

North Ridge was part of Mission Health Communities, a large health-care chain owned by Windward Health Partners, a Tampa, Florida–based private equity firm. In its investigation, the *Star Tribune* documented a chronic pattern of neglect as the firm continually cut back on services and staff. "Pressure sores were left to fester untreated for so long that they bled," wrote the *Star Tribune*. "Emergency call buttons were so poorly staffed that residents often had to wait hours or call 911 for help. Bedridden patients went weeks without being bathed because of inadequate staffing. Rooms smelled of urine and mildew, and outdated food was left in the facility's kitchen, according to state and federal inspection reports." And that was *before* the pandemic.

Once COVID-19 arrived, North Ridge never had a chance. Nurses treated both COVID-19 patients and uninfected residents, spreading infection as they did. There wasn't enough PPE, so many employees went without. Nurses who felt sick were still told to come to work. Employees stopped showing up—sometimes because they were dying of COVID-19 themselves. The state health department reported that the facility was in a "staffing crisis," because it tried to get by with only 80 percent of its normal staff. Meanwhile, North Ridge was also accepting COVID-19 patients—171 in all—from hospitals. Why? Because empty beds don't generate cash.[5]

In Vermont, by the end of 2020, one out of every six COVID-19 deaths could be traced to a single nursing home, run by Genesis Health-Care, the country's largest nursing home chain. In New Hampshire, one out of every five COVID-19 deaths took place in three nursing homes owned by Genesis. (Overall, an astonishing two-thirds of the state's COVID-19 fatalities were nursing home residents or staff.) "A New Jersey analysis of Covid-19 deaths found that facilities owned by private equity firms . . . had a higher rate of both deaths and cases than facilities that were not owned by private equity," wrote Bill Barclay in the magazine *Dollars & Sense*.

As of June 1, 2021,[6] according to *The New York Times*, nursing home residents accounted for 4 percent of all COVID-19 cases, but 31 percent of all deaths. The *Times* compiled data showing the percentage of

5 A North Ridge executive offered this response to the *Star Tribune*: "From day one, North Ridge has been vigilant and proactive in containing the virus spread within our community—because we understand the stakes, and we take seriously our responsibility to those we serve and to our community."
6 The *Times* stopped tracking nursing home deaths on that date.

nursing home deaths in each state: Pennsylvania, 49 percent; Tennessee, 22 percent; Rhode Island, 61 percent; Minnesota, 59 percent; New York, 30 percent; and so on.[7]

Most astonishing of all, perhaps, despite this data, neither the companies nor government officials seemed either able or willing to do anything to protect nursing home residents. On the contrary: many of them made it worse.

———

If the simple measure of life or death was the most profound measure of the functioning of our health-care system, there were other ways the coronavirus both exacerbated and highlighted the strains on the system.

Nurses at both hospitals and nursing homes, pushed to the brink long before the pandemic, were at the breaking point. Over the years, as hospitals focused on continually increasing profits, most had cut back on staff and taken other steps in the name of efficiency. "The just-in-time staffing model is the equivalent of the just-in-time supply chain," says Dana Simon, the director of strategic campaigns at the Massachusetts Nurses Association. "For years, this was our greatest fight with the hospital industry. We're constantly telling them that they are so short-staffed that there are negative patient outcomes. By the time the pandemic hit, the hospitals were already so deliberately short-staffed that it was impossible to meet the crisis."

Labor is typically the largest expense at any hospital, and nurses make up around 43 percent of hospital payrolls, according to federal

---

7 New Hampshire had the highest percentage of nursing home deaths—66 percent. Alabama, with 12 percent, had the lowest.

labor department data.[8] So it's no surprise that a hospital company would look to shrink that payroll—even when it meant increasing the burden on the staff that remained. "Nurses have long been the shock absorbers, the human shock absorbers, of hospitals," says Alan Sager, a professor of health law, policy, and management at the Boston University School of Public Health.

"I've been a nurse for seventeen years," says Ralaya Allen, who works at HCA Sunrise, an eight-hundred-bed hospital in Las Vegas, and is a member leader of SEIU Local 1107. "We've had staffing issues the entire time."

Over the years, the resentment built up. "The attitude is, the nurses can always do more," says Cabrera. "There's a lot of, how can we staff a unit to the minimum, what's the fewest amount of staff possible and still meet the needs?" says Calah Raab, who was a bedside nurse for five years and then got her doctorate in nursing studies. "We'd be sent home early if we had too many staff and not enough patients." She's no longer a bedside nurse, but still feels strongly that staffing needs fixing. "I'm just one nurse, but it seems like this is a pretty prevalent feeling among us," she adds.

When nurses were asked to work without proper PPE, it added insult to already existing insult. A study done by the American Nurses Association found that 87 percent of nurses were afraid to go to work and 36 percent reported having to care for an infectious patient without proper PPE. Allen says that at her hospital nurses were assigned a single mask per shift and the rest of the PPE was kept in a collective depot under lock and key. Prior to the pandemic, she says, every nurse had their own "PAPR hood," an all-in-one respirator that provides far more

8 This data was cited in a September 17, 2020, *Wall Street Journal* article titled "Why Did COVID Overwhelm Hospitals? A Yearslong Drive for Efficiency."

protection than a mask. But just before COVID-19 hit, the PAPRs seemingly disappeared after there had been a move, and so in the pandemic they had to share PAPRs—meaning nurses had to try their best to disinfect a PAPR that had been worn by a previous nurse caring for COVID patients. Eventually, Allen says, she learned from the county commission that they had a warehouse full of PPE. "They were hoarding it, because they were worried they wouldn't get more," she says. "What it came down to was fear. When you're afraid, you hunker down. You get as frugal as you can. But you're putting people's lives at risk."[9]

She saw colleagues die, including a close friend, a nurse practitioner who worked at another hospital. He'd purchased his own mask that he named Air Dog, but she says that after he'd worn it for a few months, his hospital stopped letting him use it because it wasn't FDA approved. The hospital said that he didn't get infected through work, but that's not what anyone close to the situation believes. "He helped to stabilize a super, super sick patient," she says. "There was one physician and two nurse practitioners. All three of them contracted COVID."

Inevitably, nurses began to quit. "After showing nursing & ancillary staff how much they cared for their well-being by denying them N95s, limiting access to PPE & asking staff to reuse PPE for days to weeks, we're supposed to be SHOCKED they left in droves?" tweeted a nurse who goes by the moniker @shesinscrubs. This nurse, who asked not to be named, works for a hospital in Florida. "We have begged them to listen, begged them to witness the abhorrent lack of standards in their facilities directly related to unsafe staffing. Directly related to decades of deprioritizing nursing staff," she said. "At the very beginning of the pandemic, the faux praise, the free food, the banners, it all

---

9 HCA categorically denies that there were any problems with PPE at Sunrise, and blames the complaints on the ongoing efforts by the SEIU to unionize HCA hospitals.

made us think, maybe they do care," she continued. But when the spotlight went away, so did the support and the hazard pay. By the time the delta variant hit Florida in 2021, and her hospital was once again overwhelmed, she says the nurses in her facility were hanging disposable gowns outside patient rooms to reuse. "That is unheard of in terms of infection control," she says.

———

There was yet another way the pandemic exposed a preexisting problem: the way hospitals made their money. Hospital profits come almost entirely from expensive cancer care and elective surgeries, like hip and knee replacements, not from routine care. "A system that allows those who can pay to have whatever they want, with very few boundaries, while not reimbursing for basic health care, turns out not to be a resilient system in a crisis," says Dr. David Asch, a professor at the Perelman School of Medicine and the Wharton School at the University of Pennsylvania.

When the pandemic first hit, elective surgeries and nonessential procedures were canceled at hospitals across the country. So while hospitals were busier than they'd ever been, their revenue plummeted. "You kind of knew that the financial engine behind health-care organizations generally was around procedures, but I never realized the degree to which that's true," says Ansell. "It became really difficult to reconcile how we can be asking everyone to work so incredibly hard and yet we're losing $40 million a month. Doing the right thing and taking care of patients and serving your community does not do the right thing by the bottom line."

As a result of the drop in revenue, many hospitals asked workers to take furloughs—*during the ongoing pandemic.* According to *Becker's*

Hospital Review, more than 260 hospitals and health systems furloughed workers in 2020, and dozens of others implemented layoffs. Even while ER doctors were reeling under the weight of COVID-19 care, new medical school graduates were having trouble finding jobs, because hospitals didn't want to pay them. "I work at a teaching hospital, so our residents who graduated in the spring of 2020 were looking for jobs," says Cabrera. "But there were none. That's just the biggest slap in the face to doctors who worked through hell. For hospitals not to be hiring because they aren't making money?"

At the hospital where @shesinscrubs works, health-care benefits for the staff were reduced, people were asked to retire early, and some staff were even terminated. "I tried to explain to them that they were going to lose nurses if they cut our pay," she says. "They told me it would take $2 million to give the entire staff a $1 per hour raise. What that told me is that I wasn't worth a dollar." She continues, "That was the biggest slap in the face, because you're not just messing with us, but with our children and the people who depend on us."

In late March 2020, Congress passed the CARES Act, a $2.2 trillion bill to help the country get through the pandemic. It included $175 billion for hospitals. Without question, that money made a big difference, especially for the deeply troubled rural hospitals. "At that point, you have to understand that half of our members only had thirty days' cash on hand," says Morgan. "I was having our members call, saying, 'I'm not going to be able to make payroll.' It was just crazy how close we were to really bad things happening. It [the CARES Act] was just such a lifeboat."

But—no big surprise—most of the money benefited the big and prosperous hospitals, not the small and struggling. The payout formula was essentially based on past revenues. That meant that hospitals with a high percentage of patients with private insurance—the very hospitals that were likely to have the fewest COVID-19 patients—got far more money than poor hospitals that treated Medicaid patients and the uninsured. The payments didn't take into account *need*, or even how many COVID-19 patients a hospital treated. "Institutions representing the top 10% of hospitals based on share of private insurance revenue received $44,321 in coronavirus relief per hospital bed. That was more than double the $20,710 per hospital bed for those in the bottom 10% based on private insurance revenue," reported a Kaiser Family Foundation study. While he is sympathetic to the need to get money to hospitals and thinks the government was well intentioned, Zack Cooper, an associate professor of public health and economics at Yale, still says, "It was literally the dumbest way you could have designed it."

According to *The New York Times*, which analyzed the tax and securities filings of the country's largest hospital chains, the sixty biggest hospital companies got more than $15 billion in stimulus. At least thirty-six of those hospital chains laid off, furloughed, or reduced the pay of employees to save money during the pandemic.[10]

The juxtapositions laid bare more unpleasant realities. Saint Vincent is a hospital in Worcester, Massachusetts, owned by Tenet Healthcare, a large, publicly traded hospital chain. By that summer, as the initial coronavirus surge was winding down, Saint Vincent resumed elective surgeries, but told its staff that it was furloughing nurses and would rely more heavily on its flex system, in which nurses worked as needed. More than seven hundred nurses eventually went on strike. "Most of

10 Pushback from public health experts and others led to reforms in how relief funds were distributed. The next two funding phases directed money to hospitals that were most affected by COVID-19.

us felt like we went from heroes to zeroes quickly," Dominique Muldoon, who had worked as a nurse at Saint Vincent for more than twenty years, told *The Guardian*.

Overall, in April 2020—*April*—Tenet furloughed more than 10 percent of its workforce and suspended a retirement benefit for its employees.[11]

Tenet itself, though, did just fine. Rosemary Batt of Cornell University and Eileen Appelbaum, the co-director of the Center for Economic and Policy Research, calculated that in total Tenet received more than $2.8 billion in loans and grants and other funding from the federal government. The day after the strike was announced, Tenet reported that with the infusion of taxpayer funds it had made $400 million in profits during that first pandemic year, compared with a loss of $243 million in 2019.

The biggest hospital chain in the country was HCA Healthcare. For years, its business model had been to develop quasi-monopolies in well-off, growing communities where most people had commercial insurance. For the most part, HCA's hospitals were not overtaxed, and they were mostly located in states that quickly allowed hospitals to return to performing elective procedures. And so, by some measures, HCA came out of the pandemic stronger than ever. The company ended 2020 with a profit of $3.8 billion on revenue of $51.5 billion. It was the only hospital chain to give back the approximately $6 billion it had gotten from the government in the pandemic. The profits made it politically impossible not to do so.

But that year, some of the seeds of several problems that could eventually make even the mighty HCA stumble began to emerge. HCA's nurses began to revolt. Medical workers at some nineteen HCA hospi-

11 Tenet did not respond to a request for comment.

tals filed complaints with the Occupational Safety and Health Administration (OSHA) about the lack of respirators like N95s and having to reuse disposable gowns, according to *The New York Times*. HCA tried to fight it, telling union officials that the company would lay off up to 10 percent of its members unless the unionized workers amended their contracts to include wage freezes and the elimination of company contributions to workers' retirement plans, among other concessions. "You buckled down, and you took from your employees, and you profited more than you had during any other period of time," says Ralaya Allen, the Sunrise nurse. "To me that just leaves my stomach feeling sour. Instead of building an empire, you're tearing down the army you have."[12]

In the past, HCA's tactics might have worked. People needed their jobs. As the United States careened toward a possible recession, it was unclear how the balance of power between corporations and workers would shake out. What was clear was that the more the stress to the system, the larger the cracks. And the cracks in nursing were becoming very, very large.

12 HCA said that the company had "provided appropriate PPE." HCA also told the *Times* that it had "not laid off or furloughed a single caregiver due to the pandemic, that it had paid medical workers 70 percent of their base pay, even if they were not working, and that executives had taken pay cuts, while the union had refused.

5

QEternity

Like the rest of the United States, Wall Street took a long time to realize that a health catastrophe was on the way. The World Economic Forum in Davos, the annual retreat of the world's elite, was taking place in Switzerland when the Chinese closed Wuhan. News of the shutdown barely created a stir. There was a panel called "The Next Super Bug," but it was about antibiotic resistance, not coronavirus. In mid-February, just before the Italian government ordered almost a dozen municipalities to lock down, the stock market was hitting new records.

The handful who did sense trouble tended to have China experience. Justin Simon runs a hedge fund that among other things looks for frauds among Chinese companies. In early February, the China-based investigators he talks to told him they couldn't leave their homes. "I was getting calls from guys in Guangdong and they're like, 'I can't work for you anymore,' and it was like, 'Oh my God, did you get arrested?'" he says. "They're like, 'No, no, no, no. My universe has collapsed to two blocks.'"

At J.P.Morgan, Troy Rohrbaugh, who oversees trading, had spent part of his early career working in Asia. When the news crossed the tape that Chinese authorities had locked down Wuhan ahead of the Lunar New Year, he was stunned. He told colleagues, "This is like closing the tristate area over Thanksgiving." He and his colleagues began to activate J. P. Morgan's backup sales and trading facilities in New Jersey, on the theory that people might need somewhere else to work. And Rohrbaugh sent his wife to buy toilet paper "like a never-ending blizzard was coming," he says.

The Federal Reserve chairman, Jerome Powell, would later recall being at the G20 meeting for finance ministers in Saudi Arabia in late February. "Everybody had a model of the problem in their head at that point," he'd later say. "If you're in China, it will be a pain in the neck. If you're in one of the peripheral countries, it won't be anything serious. And if you're in the United States, it's not a first-order kind of thing." But after a meeting where his Italian counterparts were present, he remembers thinking, "There's nothing between Italy and the shores of New York."

That evening, he called a few senior people at the Fed and said, "This is going to be a huge deal." But no one outside the Fed was talking about any role for the central bank. "The thinking was, 'Interest rates don't cure pandemics,'" Powell would later say.

What Powell was starting to see was that a deadly virus could wreak havoc not just on people's health but on a country's economy. Pandemics instill panic. And panic distorts behavior. Soon, you'd see this in the health system, with the collapse of the PPE supply chain and the lurch to lockdowns despite the lack of scientific backing.

But you could also see it in the market. It's largely forgotten now, given how well stocks ultimately performed in 2020, but there was a moment when the United States appeared to be headed for a crash even more devastating than the 1987 market crash or the bursting of the dotcom bubble in 2000, or even the 2008 financial crisis. The S&P 500 index peaked on February 20. Then, with the realization finally dawning on investors that the coronavirus was not going to spare the United States, the index began falling. By the time it stopped dropping on March 23, it had lost 34 percent of its value. And that was just the visible panic. Behind the scenes, there was a bigger crash brewing—one that was the result of some of the same systemic issues that had gone unsolved since the 2008 financial crisis.

As it turns out, the Federal Reserve *did* have a role to play in the pandemic. Racing to prevent disaster, the Fed took actions that prevented the crashes while also creating staggering wealth and profits for those lucky enough to be on the receiving end: hedge fund managers, tech company CEOs, and others of that ilk. At the same time, however, the measures the Fed took dramatically increased wealth inequality, a consequence that was all the worse for its actions over the previous decade, and contributed to the onset of inflation—a consequence that could have been at least blunted.

———

To understand the Federal Reserve's mindset, one has to go back to 2008, to that scary time when Lehman Brothers went bankrupt and the world's financial system appeared to be on the verge of collapse. Under the then chairman, Ben Bernanke, the Fed took a series of steps that helped rescue the markets. Bernanke had been a Princeton economist before joining the Fed; one of his most important insights was that the Great Depression might have been avoided if the Federal Reserve in the 1930s had taken more aggressive action.

As Fed chairman facing a crisis, he practiced what he had long preached. Among other critical measures, the Fed cut interest rates to near zero and instituted an emergency bond-buying program that was labeled "quantitative easing," the idea being that buying a specific quantity of assets would "ease" long-term interest rates.[1] "The Fed has used QE when it has already lowered interest rates to near zero and additional monetary stimulus is needed," as the Congressional Budget Office put it.

It's well understood in financial circles that low interest rates encourage the use of debt and increase the value of riskier assets, such as stocks, which is why quantitative easing was applauded by many investors. The Fed, however, also believed that the stock buying spurred by quantitative easing would help the broader economy. As Bernanke put it in 2010, "Higher stock prices will boost consumer wealth and help increase confidence, which can also spur spending. Increased spending will lead to higher incomes and profits that, in a virtuous circle, will further support economic expansion."

Originally, quantitative easing was expected to wind down within two years. But in early November 2010, the Fed announced that it was extending the policy for another eighteen months. Traders quickly dubbed the extension QE2. The first round of quantitative easing had seen the Fed buy $1.7 trillion worth of treasuries and securities backed by mortgages. With QE2, it planned to purchase another $600 billion.

Bernanke argued that quantitative easing had to be extended because unemployment was still high and economic growth still sluggish.

---

1 The Fed, which doesn't like the term "quantitative easing," prefers the phrase "long-term asset purchases."

It was too early to end the program. "We could hardly be satisfied," he wrote in a *Washington Post* article defending the decision. "The job market remains quite weak; the national unemployment rate is nearly 10 percent, a large number of people can find only part-time work." By that time, Congress was mired in the austerity mindset of the Tea Party, so the economic problems weren't going to be addressed via legislation. The Fed felt that it had no choice but to try to provide a solution. Yet even after the $600 billion worth of bonds had been bought—and the unemployment rate was close to 4 percent—the policy was mostly continued. And it kept on being renewed year after year; just before the pandemic hit, the Fed's balance sheet stood at an astounding $4 trillion, up from less than $1 trillion before the 2008 financial crisis.[2] Traders took to calling the policy "QE Forever" or "QEternity."

Critics had three core complaints about the Fed's insistence on maintaining ultralow interest rates. The first was that by inflating asset values and encouraging a build-up of debt, risk increased in ways both obvious and nonobvious. While reforms to the financial system after the 2008 crisis made banks much safer, the reforms didn't really touch what's loosely known as the shadow banking system—the network of hedge funds, money market funds, and other institutions that in some ways mimic banks but are lightly regulated by the government, if at all. The interplay of these institutions—the dealings they have with one another and with regulated banks that most people never see—and the liquidity they create allow the modern financial markets to function. That plumbing is pretty much invisible to those who don't live in the guts of the markets. But it has become as important to their functioning and to the economy as the electricity grid is to your everyday life.

The lifeblood of the financial system is debt, and so the low-interest

2 According to the Richmond Fed.

environment fostered by the Fed, plus the tighter regulations limiting what banks could do, led to enormous growth in the shadow banking sector in the twelve years following the financial crisis. That helped make the financial system surprisingly fragile. In fact, just months earlier—in September 2019—a critical part of the Treasury market known as the repo market, which financial firms use to fund themselves, had broken down, requiring the Fed to step in once again to get the system to function. "It demonstrated to anyone who was paying attention that this market was fragile in ways we didn't really understand," says Andrew Metrick, a professor at the Yale School of Management.

The second complaint was that low interest rates exacerbated wealth inequality. Karen Petrou, the highly respected cofounder of Federal Financial Analytics, points out that inequality had dramatically worsened after the 2008 financial crisis, yet "the only thing that changed so much so fast in 2010 and thereafter is monetary and regulatory policy."[3]

Did quantitative easing in particular help create jobs, as Bernanke claimed? Unlikely, she believed. Companies were using the cheap capital available to them to buy back their own stock[4] —$6 *trillion* worth between 2010 and 2019, according to the Bank for International Settlements—instead of expanding their businesses and hiring more workers.[5] In addition, cheap capital increased *relative* inequality, because the rich, not the poor, benefit from rising asset prices: By 2016, the wealthiest 10 percent of Americans owned 84 percent of stock

3 In 2021, Petrou published a book making her case. Its title is *Engine of Inequality: The Fed and the Future of Wealth in America*.

4 It is widely believed on Wall Street and in executive suites that buying back a company's stock—thus shrinking the number of shares—will cause the stock price to rise.

5 Many companies would prefer to use the capital to grow. But in postindustrial America, they may not see opportunities to do so.

market wealth, a number that has grown dramatically over the years. As for the notion that low interest rates make it easier for poor households to pay off debt, Petrou pointed out that the poor don't have access to those ultralow rates. "They rely on high-cost payday, installment, and other lenders as well as their credit cards," she said. "These rates are remarkably inelastic to market rates."

The third criticism was that the Fed was normalizing what was always intended to be a crisis-era tool. Why was this a problem? Because in so doing, the Fed was becoming a captive to the markets.

"I saw central banks getting pulled in more and more by inherently self-interested financial markets, going from what were supposed to be emergency measures into market-comforting ones, fueling a very unhealthy codependency between the markets and the Fed," says Mohamed El-Erian,[6] the former CEO and co-CIO at bond giant Pimco and now the president of Queens' College at Cambridge University, and one of the country's most respected economists and market observers. "The Fed can floor interest rates and buy assets and do all sorts of things without going to Congress," he says. "But pretty soon the central bank will discover that the exit is challenging to navigate."

That's exactly what happened in 2018, after President Trump named Jerome Powell[7] to be the new Fed chairman—to the relief of the financial community. ("Powell is perfectly normal," says Metrick. "Any Republican would have made him chair.") Powell, who had been a member of the Fed's board of governors, came into the office as someone who had expressed worries about the side effects of very low interest rates at in-

6 In 2016, El-Erian published a book about the Fed titled *The Only Game in Town: Central Banks, Instability, and Avoiding the Next Collapse.*
7 Powell replaced Janet Yellen, who would later become President Joe Biden's Treasury secretary. *The Washington Post* reported that in choosing Powell over Yellen, Trump complained that the five-foot-three Yellen was "too short" to be a Fed chair.

ternal Fed meetings. With unemployment down to 4.1 percent, there was no ostensible reason to keep the bond-buying program going.

The Fed slowly hiked interest rates throughout 2018 while signaling that it would continue to do so for the foreseeable future. It also finally began reducing its enormous balance sheet by selling the bonds it had purchased during the years of QE and signaled that this would be its course for the next several years.

Trump, who viewed the performance of the stock market as a scorecard for his presidency, was irate. With each increase, Trump would have a fit, taking to Twitter, the airwaves, and the press to hurl childish insults at Powell, whom he called "loco" and "crazy." He argued that the Fed's interest rate increases were the "biggest threat" to the U.S. economy, and he'd regularly scream obscenities at his Treasury secretary, Steven Mnuchin, for recommending Powell, *The New York Times* later reported.

The Fed has always prided itself on its independence, and Powell could probably have withstood Trump's public tantrums if that was all he had to endure. But it wasn't. Upon learning that quantitative easing was coming to an end, the market had its own tantrum. On Christmas Eve, the Dow Jones Industrial Average fell 653 points, nearly 3 percent, breaking 1918's record for the worst Christmas Eve performance ever. Stocks ended the year down about 6 percent. Bonds and other asset classes fell too. Reports surfaced that Trump was asking his advisers if he could legally fire Powell.

And though Powell tried to hold firm at first, he soon capitulated. As 2019 began, he announced that the Fed would stop shrinking its balance sheet. Six months later, Powell said that the Fed would start cutting rates again—even though the unemployment rate was now down to 3.7 percent and wages were rising. Powell has always insisted that the Fed did not reverse course because of the markets. He argues that the change happened because of the risk to the economy from a trade war with China as Trump slapped tariffs on Chinese goods. But the truth almost doesn't matter. Market psychology has a life of its own, and the market believed the Fed was at its mercy.

And then came the pandemic.

———

On Monday, March 9, the S&P 500 declined by 7 percent within five minutes of the opening bell. Oil prices cratered in anticipation of a global recession. The repo market was freezing up again. When Wall Street institutions can't fund their operations, disaster looms. To prevent that, the Fed announced on Thursday, March 12—the same day the National Basketball Association became the first sports league to shut down—that it would buy up to $1.5 trillion in securities held by Wall Street firms and provide cash in return. In other words, the Fed would supply the money Wall Street needed.

On Sunday afternoon, March 15, Powell held an impromptu press conference in which he announced that the Fed had again cut rates to near zero and that it was buying bonds in previously unheard-of quantities. The Fed would buy $80 billion worth before the following Tuesday, meaning that it would push as much money into the banking system in forty-eight hours as it had done in a month during earlier rounds of quantitative easing, noted author Christopher Leonard.[8]

"We moved unbelievably quickly, much faster than any other central bank," Powell would later say. "We upped our purchases, and upped our purchases, and finally said, we're just going to keep buying until

8 His book is *The Lords of Easy Money: How the Federal Reserve Broke the American Economy.*

this works"—meaning until the market was functioning normally again. "And it didn't help."

Indeed, the shock and awe did nothing to quell the panic. "It's like the on switch flipped to off, globally," says the head trader at a big bank. "Markets were getting destroyed." Traders were stunned by the ferocity and the speed of the collapse.

One trader remembers the financial crisis, as frightening as it was, being somewhat exhilarating because of the intense need to focus on the trades that had to be done. This was different. Because of COVID-19, "people were afraid for their families," he says. "It was really hard to say, just focus on trading."

And stocks were the least of it. The real carnage, the carnage that terrified those who understood the market best, was taking place in the Treasury market. U.S. government bonds—Treasury bonds—were supposed to be the world's safest securities. Institutions buy them because they know they can be exchanged for cash at a moment's notice. Traders are accustomed to buying and selling Treasuries in split seconds. Now, however, there were moments when there was "literally no bid" for Treasury bonds, recalls Rohrbaugh.

"The then–$17 trillion market for U.S. government bonds . . . was brought to the brink of failure," wrote Yesha Yadav, a professor at Vanderbilt Law School, in the *Columbia Law Review*. If institutions were no longer willing to buy Treasuries—if the world's safest asset was no longer liquid—then even the mighty U.S. government might have trouble financing itself, because investors would hesitate to buy an asset that they could no longer sell on demand. "The potential collapse of Treasuries presented an unthinkable doomsday scenario for global markets and the U.S. economy," Yadav wrote.

The near collapse in the Treasury market was in large part caused by the shadow banking system. Big players like money market funds, which were critical to the system's plumbing because they provide financing for so many activities, seized up as nervous investors yanked money from these funds. Hedge funds that had found ways to profit from small discrepancies in pricing in Treasuries had to dump their Treasuries as the market seized up, causing it to seize up even more. A potential death spiral set in.

"There were moments in Treasury markets, bond markets, commercial paper markets, there were moments of real peril where the markets just wouldn't work," says the former Treasury secretary Jack Lew. "And if markets don't work, then the system shuts down."

Ironically, the one set of institutions that weren't in trouble, at least not at first, were the big banks. In that sense, the reforms from the financial crisis had worked. But those very reforms also prevented the banks from stepping in and providing liquidity. As the shadow banking system fell apart, and companies couldn't sell their debt to money market funds, they began to draw down their credit lines with the banks. Southwest Airlines drew down a $1 billion revolving credit facility. Hilton drew down $1.8 billion. General Motors drew down $16 billion. If this vicious circle wasn't stopped, it would eventually crater the banks too. Not surprisingly, the stock value of the big banks fell 48 percent between the stock market's peak in February and March 23.

It would take an extraordinary intervention, unlike anything the Fed had ever done, to prevent disaster. Among the Wall Street cognoscenti, the Fed got huge plaudits for the scale and swiftness of its response. "But for the very quick action of the Fed, we would all be probably sifting through the ashes of what used to be our economy," says Lew.

That's true. But just as the pandemic was exposing other shortcomings of modern American capitalism, the enormity of the Fed's rescue also revealed how the financial system had devolved into a flawed and fragile thing. Even a shock like the pandemic shouldn't cause the whole financial system to cease to function. But it did. Which should tell you that something is wrong.

———

What did the Federal Reserve do when its first round of bond buying didn't quell the panic? It doubled down.

"You're just fighting and you're not entertaining the thought of losing," Powell said. "You're doing everything you can think of, but it looks like giant American corporations are going to get downgraded and there's going to be a mass selling of their paper and half of industrial America is going to be in Chapter 11 in, like, ninety days. But you can't think, 'Oh my God, I'm going to lose,' because you just have to keep going and thinking of things to do and doing them really quickly. It was incredibly stressful and horrible, but you haven't got time to think about that."

"I had never seen a government organization operate at that level of urgency," says one trader.

Unlike in the financial crisis, there was little prevaricating. The Fed acted fast, and there was no opposition—partly because people had seen the Fed take extreme measures before, in 2008, and partly because the pandemic, which was sweeping through New York, was scaring Wall Street traders and government officials alike. "Physical isolation kept conversations shorter than they otherwise would have been," says one person who was present in many discussions.

The Fed quickly set up a slew of additional programs, most of them intended to shore up the shadow banking system, such as agreeing to lend to money market funds. "There were a lot of late-night hours with the CEOs of banks and funds trying to determine what measures would be responsive to the stresses," says Randal Quarles, who at the time was the vice chair of the Federal Reserve. "We knew if we didn't get it right, you could have people losing confidence in our ability to get it right. There were white knuckles, because everyone understood what was at stake."

The programs were all humongous beyond comprehension. A week after the Fed announced its support for money market funds, they had offloaded over $50 billion of assets to the Fed.[9]

Another part of the shadow banking system is the debt that is denominated in dollars but consists of loans made in foreign countries; it amounts to a staggering $13 trillion, according to the Bank for International Settlements.[10] In a crisis, when funding dries up for these borrowers, they turn to their own country's banks to get money—which try to raise the necessary cash by selling Treasuries. Which adds to the panic in Treasuries.

Just as had happened in the financial crisis, the Fed needed to solve this too. By the end of March, 14 central banks were able to borrow directly from the Fed, while another 170 central banks around the world were able to borrow dollars by pledging their holdings of Treasuries as collateral. "The U.S. government is the liquidity provider to the world," said one longtime Washington lobbyist.

And even *then*, the carnage didn't end. Powell knew the Fed would have to do even more.

For all the ire that Trump had directed at him, Powell had a very well-placed supporter: Treasury Secretary Steven Mnuchin. The controversial cabinet member was a former Goldman Sachs partner and

9 "Liquidity Restrictions, Runs and Central Bank Interventions: Evidence from Money Market Funds," from *The Review of Financial Studies*'s November 2021 issue.
10 The BIS figure is cited by David Beckworth, a senior research fellow at the Mercatus Center, who notes that the Fed's interventions in this market in 2008 and 2020 "have created expectations of an FDIC-like backstop" for such debt. "The more the dependent the world economy becomes on the Fed backstop, the more the Fed is forced to intervene in times of financial stress," he says.

hedge fund manager who had gotten more press for his marriage to actress Louise Linton than for any important policy views when Trump named him to the cabinet. Larry Summers, a former Treasury secretary himself, famously called Mnuchin "the greatest sycophant in the cabinet" after he defended President Trump's attacks on NFL players kneeling during the national anthem. Liberals detested his great wealth, while conservatives suspected he was secretly a Democrat. But he was a "fundamentally normal creature of the financial sector in a fundamentally abnormal administration," as *The New York Times* memorably put it. By 2020, he was also a survivor from Trump's original cabinet. And his moment to shine had come.

When the pandemic hit, Powell and Mnuchin began talking constantly, often up to a dozen times a day, Mnuchin from Treasury's nearly deserted offices and Powell from home. By law, the Fed is not supposed to take the risk of loss on any loan it might extend. As a result, to do more, Powell needed money that could absorb losses. Mnuchin assured Powell that Congress would provide that money.

That money would ultimately come from the $2.2 trillion CARES Act, which Trump signed into law in late March. The CARES Act, the biggest economic stimulus act in American history, was the administration's response to the havoc the pandemic was already wreaking on the economy. It included $454 billion to absorb any losses on various Fed programs. Another $500 billion went to buy the bonds of large corporations, while $150 billion went to state, local, and Tribal governments. But unlike the money used to bail out the financial system in 2008, the CARES Act didn't just rescue big institutions. A chunk of the money, $292 billion, went directly to people in the form of onetime tax rebates, with another $250 billion boosting unemployment benefits. The CARES Act also allocated $349 billion to a loan program called the Paycheck Protection Program, or PPP. Under this program, companies that agreed to maintain their payroll at 75 percent of prepandemic levels for eight weeks after getting the loan could have the loan forgiven. This would soon become a flash point for small businesses scrambling to stay afloat.

There are many, including Powell, who say that without Mnuchin the CARES Act would not have passed. Mnuchin set up a temporary office in the historic Lyndon Baines Johnson Room in the Capitol and spent his days shuttling back and forth between the offices of the Senate minority leader, Chuck Schumer, and the Senate majority leader, Mitch McConnell. "People believed that he could say honestly, 'This is what the president will do and this is what he won't do,'" says one person familiar with events. "Nor was he running in there with a bunch of Republican talking points. He was trying to get a deal done."

Even before the bill was signed into law, the Fed had begun buying Treasuries and mortgage bonds, and would continue to do so in previously unimaginable quantities. Between March 16 and April 8, for instance, the Fed purchased $1.1 trillion in Treasury securities, according to the General Accounting Office (GAO). It would purchase another $1 trillion through the end of the year, for a total of $2.1 trillion.

But even those vast sums weren't the shocking part. The various programs the Fed announced would take it into uncharted territory while showing that the central bank had far more power than most people had ever realized.[11] Among them: purchasing existing corporate bonds

---

11 Lev Menand, a former Treasury official, argues that some of the Fed's programs ran counter to laws passed in the wake of the financial crisis limiting the Fed to "providing liquidity to the financial system." But, he notes, language in the CARES Act effectively overrode the earlier laws, which he calls a "sub silento overruling of other legal restrictions." "Congress likely acted not just out of expediency but also to avoid drawing attention to the fact that it was asking the Fed to take on an enlarged economic role," he writes.

directly, buying exchange-traded funds that invested in bonds, and announcing they'd purchase securities backed by assets like credit card receivables and car loans, including subprime auto loans. The Fed also started something called the Main Street Lending Program, which was supposed to buy loans made to small and midsize businesses. "We're convinced that its policy response was truly historic, wholly debunking the incorrect notion that the central bank's policy tool kit is finite," tweeted Rick Rieder, the global fixed income chief at the money management giant BlackRock (whose money market funds were among those bailed out by the Fed).

"I would not be able to explain to people if we fail why we didn't use our tools to the fullest extent of our authority," Powell would later say. "If you think about it, it was Boeing, it was General Motors, it was household names that were shut out of the capital markets. There were no capital markets. They weren't working. I mean, it was millions, millions, millions of jobs."

The Fed began announcing these programs on Monday morning, March 23, based on Mnuchin's reassurances that the CARES Act would pass and the money would be there. "It's incredible how complicated these are and how long it takes to get them set up and organized and legal," Powell would later say. "So I said, 'We're going to announce them when they're not ready, because it's the announcement effect that matters. No one is going to care when you do it, because they're going to know that you're going to do it.'"

He was right. With the promise of unprecedented Fed support for the markets, the S&P 500 index stabilized, and the lending spigot turned back on. Perhaps no company better illustrates the abrupt change than the heavily indebted cruise ship operator Carnival, which had seen its business collapse as COVID-19 turned cruise ships into floating incubators of disease, and whose bonds were plunging to levels that suggested bankruptcy was inevitable. Just over a week after the Fed's announcement, Carnival was able to issue over $6 billion in stock and debt.

As J.P.Morgan's chief economist, Michael Feroli, put it, "The Fed has effectively shifted from lender of last resort for banks to a commercial banker of last resort for the broader economy."

Perhaps because the threat of the virus was so all-encompassing, or perhaps because so much money was being directed to helping individuals and small businesses, no one asked questions about why the markets had become so fragile. What's also true is that the Fed moved so quickly, and with so much firepower, that most people simply never noticed how close the system came to collapsing.

"At least in 2008 our government had the decency to say there's moral hazard here and we need to do something so the crisis doesn't repeat," says John Cochrane, an economist at Stanford University. "This time no one even mentioned moral hazard or all the incentives there were to take risks. It was just, thank you for another big bailout, Fed. The reason markets are so fragile is that no one keeps cash around to buy bargains. They'd be silly to do so, because every time the market goes down, the Fed props it up again."

Indeed, Congress seemed utterly uninterested in investigating what had happened, other than making sure their states had gotten some of the bounty. Quarles recalls testifying before Congress in May. "At least three-quarters of the questions were, why not my town, why not my jurisdiction, why hasn't the Fed supported my city," he recalls.

But perhaps the most important reason everyone seemed to forget about the huge sums of money the Fed was laying out, and its unprecedented actions, was that it did what it was meant to do: it ended the crisis.

"They stopped the panic, so most people forgot there was a panic," says Lev Menand, a former Treasury official who is now a professor at

Columbia University Law School and the author of *The Fed Unbound: Central Banking in a Time of Crisis*. Investors were euphoric. "If you had asked me beforehand, I would have said the Fed would step in," says one trader. "If you had asked me the size in which they would step in, I never would have gotten that right. I would have thought, much, much smaller." He continues, "By April 15, it was crystal clear that every asset was a screaming buy. It was one of the most unbelievable trading opportunities the world has ever seen."

"We almost didn't stay down long enough for anyone to get freaked out," says another trader. "It's like going over a huge bump in a car. You feel the jolt, but it's over before you can process how scary it was."

Sure, a few hedge funds went under, and there were a handful of corporate bankruptcies, mainly heavily indebted companies that had been owned by private equity firms, like Hertz, J.Crew, and Neiman Marcus. But the real shock was not that some companies filed for bankruptcy or that some hedge funds folded; rather, it was that so few of them did. No one even found out which funds or companies were the most distressed, or how distressed they were. "There were bazillion-dollar major funds [meaning hedge funds and other asset management firms] that were down 20, 30 percent in March," one well-placed hedge fund manager says. "But by the end of the month, they printed numbers that were up 10 percent. Because of the Fed intervention. Never have so many financial oligarchs been bailed out at the expense of the U.S. taxpayer."

Corporations were saved too. It wasn't just Carnival. According to an analysis by the Swiss bank UBS, markets in late March were signaling that investors expected corporations to default on as much as 35 percent of high-yield debt; by July, that number had dropped to about 12 percent. "The reality is they saved a lot of those firms," Matt Mish, the head of credit strategy at UBS, told *Politico*.

By April, companies had begun to borrow again. In June, sales of U.S. junk bonds hit an all-time high. "You get an invitation to a party from the Federal Reserve, Treasury and Congress—they offer to pick you up, take you home, and bring you breakfast in bed the next morning," Bill Zox, a portfolio manager at Diamond Hill Capital Management, told *Bloomberg.* "You know it's going to be a party like no other."

El-Erian says he remains mystified that the Fed didn't stop its programs once it was clear that the markets had turned a corner. "This was no longer about liquidity risk. This wasn't about fixing malfunctioning markets. This was about a willingness to re-encourage the system to take on credit risk," he says.

The extraordinary measures taken by the Fed saved the financial system and created a bull market in all kinds of asset classes. Junk bond issuance for 2020 was $450 billion, up 57 percent from 2019 and well above the prior record set in 2013, according to Oaktree Capital Management. Investment-grade debt issuance totaled $1.9 trillion, up 58 percent from the previous high.

"Because the Fed's tools are financial in nature, its leaders are unelected, and its procedures are relatively insulated from democratic participation and public disclosure, this sort of state banking by the Fed is likely to disproportionately favor asset owners," Menand wrote in a subsequent paper.

And the fix, in some ways, was an illusion, a short-term injection of sugar. Critics argue that it did nothing to fix the problems that had made the system so fragile.

"The Fed's interventions in March and April of 2020 were almost 100 percent about the shadow banking system," says Menand. "It was not about trying to respond to the economic crisis that existed independently of the financial crisis. When the Fed then switched gears, if you look at the Main Street and municipal programs, you're talking less than $40 billion, compared to the trillions that were committed to deal with the panic. Is this surprising? No. The Fed is set up to ensure monetary functioning. Since the Fed is not set up to do that in a system where shadow banks are as important as banks, it takes a lot of ad hoc backstopping to hold the system together."

Instead, in some ways, it exacerbated those problems. If the interest on all our debt wasn't going to crush us, then interest rates had to stay ultralow. Inflation, which low interest rates can arouse, had to stay away. And the country couldn't afford a malfunction in the Treasury market, because the United States had to be able to sell debt. As for the markets, they were more dependent on the Fed than ever. Or was it the other way around? "The market feels very strongly that it basically is holding the Fed hostage," El-Erian told CNBC in June 2020.

The rescue from the pandemic-induced crisis would soon accelerate some of the worst trends in American life: the widening of wealth inequality, the inflation of asset prices, and the big getting bigger at the expense of the small.

PART II

A Broken System

6

The Folly of Efficiency

The various health-care crises the country was confronting due to the pandemic—the collapse of medical supply chains; the enormous pressure placed on have-not hospitals when wealthy hospitals had empty beds; the rising death toll in nursing homes—were all predictable. They, and much else, were the result of trends in American capitalism that had been in vogue for forty years or more—trends that were so taken for granted that most people had no memory of a time when it hadn't been thus.

One such trend was globalization, heralded by establishment economists and other elites since at least the 1960s and the dominant industrial philosophy in most of the world by the late 1980s. In China, globalization meant transforming itself into a manufacturing powerhouse, building everything from Apple iPhones to Nike shoes to solar panels, leading to a rising standard of living for hundreds of millions of Chinese citizens.

In the United States, globalization meant cheaper goods, sure. But it also meant closing domestic factories, throwing people out of work, and moving manufacturing to countries with lower labor costs, like China and Mexico. It also meant crafting complex just-in-time global supply chains, which reduced inventory and lowered costs. The shortages of medical supplies—and the rise of the PPE black market—were direct results of the embrace of globalization by America's elites and businesses.

The second trend was the growing belief that the "free market" was the right mechanism for determining every aspect of human life. One mark of its manifestation was the economist Milton Friedman's famous dictum that the only purpose of a corporation was shareholder value. As stock options became a key component of CEO compensation, those at the top were essentially paid for ignoring other considerations.

But that was just the tip of it. The more extreme and insidious idea was that everything in American life should be measured by its ability to make money. If it made money, it was good. If it didn't make money, it was unworthy. Few bothered to look at whether the money being made was really a measure of the value being created. If the rules set by the government determined the ability to make money, then wasn't it important to make sure the rules were the right ones? And if favors granted by the government enabled the existence of a particular industry, didn't that industry owe something to society in return?

Hospitals, and health care overall, marked the spot where these ideas were most problematic. The right choice for a patient, let alone for a country, is not always the profitable one. As hospitals were bought up by companies that issued stock and employed financially minded executives, the lure of the stock market inevitably put shareholder wealth first. Bigger was better, because bigger meant more money. That belief spread to nonprofit hospitals. Getting bigger and making more money became what "the best" did to survive and thrive. But did it mean better care at a lower cost? Demonstrably, no. Over the ensuing decades, Americans have gotten less and less healthy, while hospital costs have soared.

Meanwhile, the hospitals that provided care to patients without insurance or with Medicaid were increasingly left behind, or put out of business, because they struggled to make money. But the very ability to make money was predetermined by government or private insurance reimbursement rules. It had very little to do with who provided the best care at the lowest price. "One of the things that often goes unnoticed is that we have socially constructed who makes money by how we've negotiated who gets paid for what," says David Asch, the University of Pennsylvania professor. And it all made a mockery of the notion of a "health-care system," which presupposes a goal of making people healthier, not creating a Darwinian world in which your value—indeed your very life—is determined by your ability to pay.

The third trend was the rise of the private equity industry. Private equity firms had once been a cottage industry. In 1980, there were just 24 firms, according to research firm Preqin; by 2015, there were more than 6,000 firms, with 620 founded just that year. By 2021, the industry globally had $7.4 trillion in assets. When the industry was in its infancy, it described its deals as "leveraged buyouts"—meaning that the money it used to buy companies was largely borrowed and put on the balance sheet of the acquired company. Though the unappealing term "leveraged buyout" faded from use and was replaced by the more innocuous sounding "private equity," the business model became, if anything, more dependent on debt. Private equity's primary strategy—aided enormously by the Fed's low interest rate policy—was now financial engineering: adding debt—which often led to layoffs and even bankruptcy—while rewarding itself with various fees and dividends.

The private equity machine was, ironically enough, fed by pension funds—some representing the very workers who lost their jobs as a result of private equity buyouts. The reason was sheer desperation. Underfunded plans needed surefire returns, and the PE industry sold itself as offering exactly that. Or as a top executive of the country's biggest pension fund, CalPERS, told his board in 2019, "If I could give you a one-line summary of this entire presentation [it] would be we need private equity, we need more of it, and we need it now."

Once private firms began buying up nursing homes and nursing home companies—and sucking money out of them while ladling on debt—it was inevitable that nursing homes would start laying off nurses, skimping on care, and accepting avoidable deaths. They also owned hospitals and emergency room staffing companies, with equally disastrous results. Private equity firms "look at health care the way they used to look at supermarkets," says Eileen Appelbaum, the private equity critic. "They said, 'People have to eat, so this is a safe investment.' Now they are saying that about health care."

No one ever seemed to understand, or even think about, the havoc these trends would cause if there was a crisis like, well, a pandemic. The policymakers and business leaders who embraced globalization never thought about how America's dependence on foreign manufacturers—and the lack of resiliency it caused—would virtually guarantee shortages of badly needed equipment. The hospital industry created plenty of "shareholder value" in the form of stock price appreciation fueled by acquisitions, dividend payments, and of course private equity buyouts, but few cared to notice that as the billions were extracted, costs spiraled and the country got sicker. Even fewer asked what vulnerabilities might be created by an increasingly unhealthy population. Back in 1987, when U.S. corporations were beset with threats from so-called corporate raiders, a hospital executive named Tommy Frist Jr. testified before

Congress as the industry sought legislation that would keep the raiders at bay. "The purpose of the company is to generate measurable benefits to the company, the medical staff, the employee, the investor, and most importantly, the patient," he said. "It [the company's mission statement] does not say: most importantly, the investor." The fact that this sentiment was uttered by Frist Jr. is rich with irony, as shall soon become evident.

And what of the government officials and legislators who were supposed to oversee the country's nursing homes? From time to time they would hold hearings to bemoan the sorry state of affairs, and they even levied the occasional fine for negligence. But they never tried to impose broad reforms that would force the industry to take proper care of the residents entrusted to them.

Once the pandemic arrived, it was too late.

———

It's an exaggeration to say that *no one* saw it coming. There's always someone who sees it coming—some prophet without honor, someone whistling in the wind until a traumatic event causes others to finally see what he or she saw all along.

With globalization, that role was played by Clyde Prestowitz, a former government official who spent most of his career trying to convince Americans that free trade, which was the cornerstone of globalization, was doing far more harm than good. He came to this view in the 1980s while working for the Commerce Department. His job was to negotiate trade deals with Japan, then the dominant Asian exporter to the United States.

The central idea behind globalization went all the way back to 1817, when David Ricardo, a British economist and politician, published his famous theory of comparative advantage. Its central tenet held that countries should export products where they had an advantage and import goods where they were at a disadvantage. In the words of the Harvard economist Dani Rodrik, "Comparative advantage and free trade became the crown jewels of the economics profession."

Comparative advantage is not what Prestowitz saw as he tangled with the Japanese, however. "Every time we completed a trade negotiation, some economist at a Washington think tank would turn out a model to show that the deal was going to create x number of American jobs, and would reduce the trade deficit by y," Prestowitz says. "And it never happened."

As a government negotiator, Prestowitz pushed for Japan to open its markets, as the rules of international free trade dictated. Eventually, he realized that it wasn't so much that the Japanese weren't playing by the rules of international trade; it was that they had a different set of rules. Unlike the United States, Japan had an industrial policy, with powerful government ministers dictating which companies and industries should be protected and to what extent. "And it wasn't just Japan," Prestowitz says. "It was Korea, it was Taiwan, it was Singapore, it was Germany. It was Switzerland. All of them had very effective industrial policies that we just completely ignored."

Prestowitz eventually concluded that the United States was going about it all wrong. "Either we have to play their game, or we have to take measures to ameliorate the problems that arise from the interaction of two different games," he says. "And the conventional response among economists was that it didn't matter." After all, even if Japan was keeping certain U.S. products out of its market, the United States still benefited from the lower prices of Japanese imports. Prestowitz recalls Herbert Stein, who had been President Richard Nixon's chief economist, telling him, "The Japanese will sell us cars, and we'll sell them poetry." To Prestowitz, this remark summed up the establishment's attitude toward trade.

"It became a movement," says David Rothkopf, a political scientist who was a trade official in the Commerce Department under President Bill Clinton. "I remember we would go out and give speeches saying, 'We're not losing jobs to emerging countries; we're losing them to progress.' It was sort of quasi-theological, and the high priests of free trade were the Wall Streeters who were active in the global economy." It was no coincidence that Clinton's Treasury secretary was Robert Rubin, the former cochairman of Goldman Sachs.

It wasn't easy for Prestowitz to buck the tide. After leaving the government, he set up a small think tank and began churning out antiglobalization books. Mostly, he was ignored by mainstream economists. The few who paid him any attention could be withering in their scorn. "I was a Japan-basher, a protectionist, and so on," Prestowitz said. "And worst of all, I was not an economist! I got called a lot of names," he added.

In 2005, Prestowitz published a book about China and trade, titled *Three Billion New Capitalists*. In it, he wrote, "In many respects, [globalization] resembles the *Titanic*, a magnificent machine with serious and largely unrecognized internal flaws heading at full speed for icebergs, armed with knowledge and assumptions significantly at odds with reality."

A year later, in 2006, Dr. Michael Osterholm, a prominent infectious disease specialist at the University of Minnesota, appeared on Oprah Winfrey's popular talk show. He told her that pandemics had arisen throughout history, and sooner or later the world would face another one. It was just a matter of when. Then he added,

One of the problems we know we're going to be confronted with is, during a pandemic when we will obviously shut borders . . . we will

basically see, I believe, a collapse of the global economy as we know it. Which means we're going to run out of those things. Things like medical supplies, drugs, masks, whatever. . . . I don't have any belief that much of this will be available during a pandemic.

What had caused Osterholm—who would become a frequent talking head during the pandemic—to make this prediction? "It was obvious," he would say years later. "The whole world had gotten so dependent on just-in-time delivery and offshore production. They never basically thought about an insurance policy for supply chain integrity. What they thought about was how much more can they squeeze out of the cost."

For decades, one industry after another had moved its production overseas. After Clinton signed the North American Free Trade Agreement in 1992, U.S. auto companies closed numerous factories and moved that work to the new maquiladoras on the Mexican side of the Rio Grande. Japan had long ago decimated the U.S. consumer electronics industry. China had become the world's largest producer of steel, cement, chemical fertilizer, and dozens of other critical products. And in the early years of the twenty-first century, China decided to enter the personal protective equipment business. One by one, American manufacturers either moved their production abroad or went out of business. Like Prestowitz, Osterholm could envision what that might someday mean.

Like so many of the products that gravitated to China, Mexico, and other low-cost countries, most personal protective equipment had been invented by American companies. Scientists at 3M had patented the N95 respirator, using a new 3M material called "nonwoven fabrics," which is now standard in hundreds of products as varied as car mats and insulation. Although Tecnol hadn't invented the surgical mask, it had refined it and dominated its manufacture.

A third important piece of protective equipment, the nitrile glove, was the creation of Neil Tillotson, a New Englander and the founder of Tillotson Rubber. As a young man in the early 1930s, Tillotson had been one of the first people to experiment with latex. Having invented the hospital latex glove in the 1960s, he went back to the lab during the AIDS crisis, when he was ninety-two years old, after the government mandated that doctors and nurses wear gloves and some people discovered they were allergic to latex. "I invented the latex glove, and now I'm gonna kill the latex glove," Tillotson is supposed to have said. The new glove he emerged with—the nitrile glove—was not only superior to the latex glove but nonallergenic.[1]

It was the 2003 SARS[2] virus that drove the Chinese to get serious about manufacturing PPE. Although the SARS threat didn't last long, China was by far the hardest-hit country, with 5,300 cases and 349 deaths.

During SARS, the government decreed that hospital workers had to wear N95 masks, and the state-controlled television station, CCTV, said that everyone else should do likewise. But there were very few mask makers in China. Most health-care workers wound up using ineffective cloth masks.[3]

---

1 When Tillotson died in 2001, at the age of 102, his obituaries focused less on his advances in protective gloves than on the fact that, having bought the Balsams Grand Resort in Dixville Notch, New Hampshire—and having maneuvered to have the resort used as a polling place on Election Day—Tillotson was the first person to vote for president every four years.

2 SARS stands for "severe acute respiratory syndrome." It was the result of a novel coronavirus.

3 Ironically, the biggest mask maker in China was 3M, which had built its first Chinese factory in Shanghai in the mid-1980s, with the goal of making 3M products for the Chinese market. Because it was one of the few companies making N95 respirators during SARS, "the image of people wearing 3M N95 masks became a collective memory," as one Hong Kong newspaper put it much later.

No sooner had the SARS threat faded than dozens of homegrown companies set up mask-manufacturing facilities, both for N95s and for surgical masks. They had names like Lanfan Medical, Shenzhen Glory Medical, XinXing JiHua International, and Shanghai Dasheng Sanitary Products Manufacturing. If a mask met the standards set by the U.S. government, it was approved and exported.

The U.S. medical supply distributors were soon sourcing from China. It was the logic of globalization: Chinese masks were a lot cheaper than U.S. masks, which meant more profit for the distributors and lower costs for hospitals. By the late aughts, the only N95s still being made in the United States were 3M's, which remained the gold standard. Soon, every medical products distributor had its own supply chain in China and was delivering masks and respirators to hospitals and other institutions on a just-in-time basis. That meant they bought masks only as needed and kept very little in reserve.

It was the same story with nitrile gloves. As nitrile gloves became more popular, factories cropped up in Thailand, Vietnam, and especially Malaysia, which had an undeniable comparative advantage: its rubber trees were the source of much of the world's latex and nitrile. United States distributors inevitably gravitated to the Asian manufacturers. By 2007, Malaysian manufacturers controlled 60 percent of the nitrile glove market. That same year, Tillotson's company was acquired by Showa Gloves from Japan.

———

It's easy to point to the moment when the financialization of the hospital industry began. It was June 25, 1968. Before that date, there was no such thing as a hospital industry; there were only hospitals. But on that day, Tommy Frist Sr., a Nashville internist, announced the formation of a new company, Hospital Corporation of America, which he founded with two partners, one of whom was his son Tommy Frist Jr. (Yes, the same Tommy Frist Jr. who piously told Congress that investors were low on his company's list of priorities. But that was when hospitals were trying to fend off corporate raiders.) In announcing the company, Frist Sr. said, "The founders of our corporation believe that private enterprise can build and operate hospitals with an efficiency which will combat the spiraling cost of hospitalization." In all likelihood he believed this to be true; unlike most modern-day hospital CEOs, Frist Sr. was always a doctor first and an executive second.[4]

The idea actually came from Frist Jr. Although he had a medical degree, his primary ambition was to get rich, a fact that he made no attempt to hide. At a time when franchises and chains were all the rage in corporate America, Frist Jr. believed that a hospital company could be built on the same model as, say, Holiday Inn or Kentucky Fried Chicken. "Banks are together, filling stations are together, grocery stores are together," he told his father. "Why can't we put hospitals together?"[5]

The Frists wasted no time in doing so. By the end of 1969, HCA Healthcare, as it is now known, had bought nineteen hospitals and sold stock to the public. The shares rose from $18 to $46 on the first day of trading. It was now a for-profit, publicly traded health-care company— the kind of company that would have to generate steady earnings increases or face the wrath of Wall Street. Other for-profit hospital companies would soon follow in its wake.

HCA would go on to become the largest hospital company in the

4 Frist Sr. died in 1998 at the age of eighty-seven. Another of his sons, Bill Frist, was a senator from Tennessee from 1995 to 2007 and majority leader for the last four years of his tenure.
5 This quotation can be found in an oral history project maintained by the American Hospital Association.

United States; with 2022 revenue close to $60 billion, and 185 hospitals, it is roughly twice the size of the next-largest hospital chain. But Frist Sr.'s insistence that private enterprise would tame spiraling health-care costs was laughably naive. On the contrary, for-profit hospitals have brought neither efficiency nor lower costs. As a percentage of America's gross domestic product, health-care spending is over three times as a percentage of GDP what it was when HCA Healthcare was founded. It currently consumes 20 percent of the country's GDP. "It's not just that the U.S. health care sector is expensive," wrote authors Charles Silver and David Hyman in their book, *Overcharged: Why Americans Pay Too Much for Health Care.* "The payment system behaves as though its *purpose* is to move as much money as possible into the pockets of health care providers."

Indeed, the flaws in the payment system—and the government's failure to fix them—essentially encouraged hospitals to extort the government. The foundational issue was that hospitals were historically paid by performing procedures, and the more procedures they performed, the more money they made. The 1965 law that created Medicare and Medicaid did nothing to change that; on the contrary, instead of capping what it would pay for a procedure, the government agreed to pay hospitals on a cost-plus basis. Not surprisingly, in Medicare's first year of operation, the average hospital service charge increased by more than 20 percent.

In addition, the new law rewarded hospital chains for making acquisitions by reimbursing them for the cost of borrowed funds and allowing generous depreciation schedules whenever they bought a new hospital. "The reimbursement environment from the late 1960s until the early 1980s made it difficult *not* to make money operating hospitals," wrote the scholar Bradford Gray in his 1991 book, *The Profit Motive and Patient Care.*

In 1981, HCA bought Hospital Affiliates International (HAI), a smaller hospital company. As usual after an acquisition, its Medicare costs shot up. Bill Gradison, a Republican congressman from Ohio, asked the General Accounting Office to investigate. In examining the HCA-HAI deal, the GAO concluded that the reimbursed costs for the former HAI hospitals had increased by about $55 million in the first year alone. Its report concluded, "HCA used a number of methods that GAO questioned under Medicare reimbursement principles . . . these methods generally increased the amount claimed for reimbursement under Medicare and Medicaid."

Hoping to control Medicare costs, Congress changed the rules in 1984, clamping down on reimbursable costs. But HCA was hardly done gaming the federal government.[6]

———

In 1994, after HCA merged with its biggest competitor, Columbia Hospital Corporation in Fort Worth, Texas, Rick Scott, the cofounder of Columbia, took over as CEO of the combined company, now known as Columbia/HCA. Medicare rules had gotten increasingly complicated, and while the newer ones were meant to impose controls on healthcare spending, their sheer complexity meant that smart executives could find loopholes—or simply violate the law and hope the government wouldn't notice.

And, in fact, the government might never have noticed what was taking place at Columbia/HCA. But in 1997, a junior accountant named John Schilling, seeing that the company was consistently requesting

6 As Frist Jr. would later put it, "We could write a book about various other times when the federal government's actions have created opportunities for HCA."

reimbursements that were unallowable, became a whistleblower. "They didn't think of it as stealing," Schilling later told the *Sarasota Herald-Tribune*. "They called it 'maximizing reimbursements.' As a company, they were always looking for ways to book more profits," he says today.

That June, the FBI executed what is still the largest coordinated raid on a business in agency history, with five hundred agents in six states seizing fourteen thousand boxes' worth of evidence from thirty-six Columbia/HCA offices. Five years later, HCA agreed to pay $1.7 billion in fines for what the Justice Department called a "'systemic' conspiracy to defraud the government." Four executives went to trial; two were not convicted and the two found guilty had their convictions overturned on appeal. Scott was forced out—replaced as CEO by Frist Jr.—but he left with $300 million in stock, some of which he later spent getting elected governor of Florida in 2011.[7] (In an email, HCA said it has "evolved as an organization and today has an award-winning ethics and compliance program.")

Frist Jr. took over as CEO, a job he'd had before Scott's arrival. In 2004, *Fortune* magazine said that he had "applied the right medicine." And what was that medicine? Selling off half the company's hospitals to focus the business "on the nation's biggest and fastest-growing markets." The magazine added, "In major metropolitan areas from Denver to Las Vegas to Kansas City, HCA has oligopoly-like status, controlling 25% to 40% of the market for hospital services."

By then there was a handful of big, publicly traded hospital companies. Many of them had played the same reimbursement games as HCA—and had gone on to have their own, very similar scandals. They then all tried to shift their business model the same way HCA did, by building quasi-monopolies in upscale cities and communities. This al-

---

7 Scott is now Florida's junior senator.

lowed them to take advantage of insurance companies, rather than the government. Patients covered by private insurance were where the money *really* was.

Consider the example of Sutter Health, a California-based hospital chain. Sutter was a not-for-profit chain, though that was a meaningless term, because it had become every bit as financially aggressive as the for-profits. Indeed, it's almost an industry cliché to say that a "not-for-profit is just a for-profit in disguise," as Engy Ziedan, a health-care economist at Tulane University, notes.[8]

The core of Sutter's strategy was to own or control what are known in industry parlance as "must-have" hospitals. These are hospitals that an insurance company must cover if it hopes to offer a compelling package to its customers. Once it gained control of a must-have hospital, Sutter would tell insurers that if they didn't accept the rates it was demanding across its entire network, they couldn't have the must-have hospital either.

A hospital chain with enough must-have hospitals can raise prices almost at will, because it controls the market. In May 2014, Dr. Greg Duncan, an orthopedic surgeon who served on a Sutter hospital board, sent a letter to the Federal Trade Commission (FTC) alleging that a Sutter health executive boasted at board meetings that Sutter's large market share allowed its affiliated hospitals to charge 30 to 40 percent more than competing hospitals.[9] Sutter also inserted "gag clauses" into its

8 A January 25, 2023, *New York Times* investigation titled "How Nonprofit Hospitals Put Profits Over Patients" found that "many of these institutions are abandoning patients and straying from their charitable missions."
9 In 2018, California began an investigation into Sutter's pricing practices. In October 2019, on the eve of trial, Sutter Health agreed to pay $575 million in damages to settle the claims against it. Sutter denied engaging in "all-or-nothing negotiations"; in 2022, a federal jury ruled in the company's favor in a similar class action case.

contracts with insurers, forbidding them to disclose the pricing, meaning there was no ability for anyone to compare the pricing across hospitals.

"American health-care markets are more consolidated than at any point in history," says Jaime King, a professor of law at the University of Auckland and the executive editor of The Source, which tracks the drivers of health-care costs. According to King, hospital prices increase between 20 and 44 percent after a merger, and rising hospital prices are now a major driver of rising U.S. health-care costs. Indeed, a comprehensive study published in the *The American Journal of Medicine* in early 2023 found that consolidated systems have led to "marginally better care at significantly higher costs."

To investors and the business press, HCA has not been shy in explaining that the market power that comes from consolidation is core to its strategy. "HCA's aggressive pricing, enabled by its market share and patient volume, is a major factor in its financial success," wrote *Modern Healthcare* in a 2018 piece celebrating HCA's fifty years in business.

The great irony is that HCA itself, when trying to prevent a competitor's acquisition, has complained to state regulators that monopolies are bad for everyone except, well, HCA. "Not only do patients suffer from a lack of access to care in their communities, but they also have little to no healthcare provider choice," HCA argued. "This type of monopolistic environment within the healthcare market stifles innovation and breeds a culture that negatively impacts the cost and quality of care."

Johns Hopkins University research shows that in 2018, nine hospitals in the United States billed patients more than ten times the actual cost of their care. Seven of the nine, including the top five, belonged to HCA.[10]

---

10 Johns Hopkins did not cite HCA's ownership of the hospitals. We looked at the ownership of the hospitals they listed. HCA says that the study is referring to charges, not the actual amount patients were billed, and can be misleading as patients "rarely" pay the full charge.

And what of the safety net hospitals, the ones that dealt with so many dead bodies in the early days of the pandemic that they had to bring in refrigeration trucks to hold them all? The unintended consequence of the financialization of the hospital business is that these have-not institutions wound up with the task of providing health care for patients who were either on Medicaid or uninsured. A large study published by the National Bureau of Economic Research in 2023, which looked at the effects of the last two decades of privatization in the hospital industry, found that while privatization did increase profits, it did so because Medicaid patients lost access to care—particularly in concentrated markets.

For-profit hospitals didn't want these patients for an obvious reason: they lost hospitals money. "I remember going to Jefferson Parish, Louisiana, and seeing the public hospital across the park from the private hospital," says Dr. Paul Keckley, a highly respected hospital industry analyst who writes a newsletter called *The Keckley Report*. "They explained to me that the doctors put the paying patients in one and the nonpaying patients in the other."

According to Dr. Elaine Batchlor, the MLK Community Hospital head, Medicaid, which serves the bulk of MLK's patients, pays only $150 for an emergency room visit. Private insurance, meanwhile, pays on average $2,000. (Medicare, says Batchlor, pays $650.)

Batchlor, who graduated from Harvard and became board certified in both internal medicine and rheumatology, was the child of activists. She grew up as one of the few people of color in her community. Because she felt like an outsider, "I spent a lot of my time in the public library, reading," she says. "One of the books I read was about Saint Luke, who was a physician. I just fell in love with the story of this scientist, who was contributing to new knowledge about health and medicine as a healer and who was a public health and social advocate." Saint Luke's story motivated her to get a master's degree in public health.

Batchlor spent her career working with underserved communities in Los Angeles before coming to MLK Community Hospital, and she refers to the area of Los Angeles where the hospital is located as the hole in a donut. "All around us are communities that have more than they need, and in the middle of the donut hole is our community that is lacking everything," she says. "We have the lowest number of hospital beds per 100,000 people in the entire county. Any type of health-care infrastructure you can think of is missing here."

———

Because of its lack of beds and services, her hospital is dependent on other hospitals to take patients who can't be treated at Martin Luther King. But, says Batchlor, "no other hospital wants them." And they find ways to avoid taking them in.

"Structural racism sounds abstract," Batchlor adds. "These are the concrete examples of what structural racism looks like."

Prior to joining Rush University Medical Center, David Ansell worked at two safety net hospitals. In *The Death Gap*, the book he authored about that experience, he wrote, "I learned from my practice . . . something that I was not taught in medical school. Inequality itself is a cause of death."

One example among many: The safety net hospitals where Ansell worked have busy trauma units, and the patients who die there often have their organs donated to save patients in the wealthy transplant centers across the city. "Yet," he noted, "in my twenty-seven years at those institutions, not one of my patients—or those of my colleagues—ever received a lifesaving organ transplant."

The second reason the poor and the uninsured wind up in safety net hospitals is a series of public policy decisions that sound logical in theory but are both callous and misguided in practice. Take, for instance, the decision by many states to reduce the number of hospital beds. They did so believing that fewer beds would help control spiraling Medicare and Medicaid costs. Theoretically, that makes sense. But the game was rigged: the closure of hospitals was determined by their profitability, which had already been determined by government reimbursement policies.

So, notes Alan Sager, the Boston University health-care management expert, the primary consequence of eliminating beds by closing entire hospitals was to further separate the wealthy hospitals, which were rarely affected, from the poor hospitals, which bore the brunt of the reductions. It was a classic example of a policy being handed down by elites who would never be affected by it and imposed on people who had no say in the decision.

Nowhere was this policy carried out with more vigor than New York. And nowhere were its flaws more glaring.

In 2005, when New York State first began reducing hospital beds, there were about 3.3 hospital beds per 1,000 New Yorkers, considerably higher than the national average. A commission chaired by Stephen Berger, an investment banker and longtime New York political player, targeted five safety net hospitals in New York City for closure, along with four upstate hospitals, and recommended that forty-eight others be "restructured," either by merging with nearby facilities or by converting hospital beds to other uses.

And so, since 2003, forty-one hospitals have closed in New York

State, including eighteen in New York City alone. That created tremendous hardships for patients, who often had to travel long distances to find an emergency room that would take them. The number of hospital beds has plummeted—but it hasn't plummeted equally. Wealthy Manhattan has six beds for every thousand residents, according to the Community Service Society of New York. Queens has only one and a half beds.

Today, there are five wealthy hospital chains in New York, where people come from all over the world to get top-of-the-line care, often in settings as lovely as a five-star hotel room. Those five, NewYork-Presbyterian, NYU Langone, the Mount Sinai Health System, Northwell Health, and the Montefiore Medical Center, collectively spend $150 million a year on advertising and pay their chief executives as much as $30 million, according to *The New York Times*.[11]

In the run-up to the pandemic, local newspapers published pieces about the "arms race" between expensive hospitals competing for high-end patients. Montefiore, for instance, invested $272 million in a gleaming new hospital in the city of White Plains in Westchester County, featuring a two-story lobby with expensive boutiques, good food, and "floor-to-ceiling windows, dark wood, gray sofas, and vibrant blue-butterfly sculptures gracing the walls [that] evoke the lobby of an upscale hotel." Meanwhile, Montefiore was trying to shut down another Westchester hospital, this one in Mount Vernon, which serves predominantly people of color, many of them either on Medicaid or uninsured. Many of those patients would be forced to use Montefiore's Moses Campus in the Bronx. Nurses working at the Moses Campus complained to the *Daily News* in 2018 that sick patients are "packed into rooms like

11 "Why Surviving the Virus Might Come Down to Which Hospital Admits You" is the title of a July 1, 2020, *New York Times* article.

sardines" and the emergency rooms are "often dangerously overcrowded and unruly."

Overall, the safety net system in New York City, called NYC Health + Hospitals (H+H), accounts for roughly half of all uninsured hospital stays and emergency department visits and 80 percent of uninsured nonemergency hospital visits. Nearly 70 percent of its hospital stays are for Medicaid and uninsured patients, as compared to less than 40 percent of stays for other New York City hospitals.[12] As the pandemic hit, the system was projected to lose $1.3 billion that year.

Yet New York *still* had the second-highest Medicaid payments in the country on a per capita basis. In fact, Medicare spending actually increased.

What had happened? The answer was pretty simple: the kind of hospital that could be closed easily—one with little or no power and prestige—was not the kind of hospital that was likely to save the government money. The same number of people were still going to need to visit a hospital; they would just have to visit one that was still open. Back in 2006, Sager wrote a report predicting that "shifting more hospital care into fewer, larger, and more specialized hospitals would speed New York State toward an increasingly costly and unequal pattern of hospital services." Which is exactly what happened.

And it wasn't just New York. The same pattern played out across the country; hundreds of hospitals in disadvantaged neighborhoods were closed, ostensibly to save money, yet neither hospital costs nor overall health costs went down. All that was really accomplished was a massive reduction in hospital beds in neighborhoods that needed them.

Many health-care economists did, and do, argue that hospital beds

12 These statistics are from a 2017 report titled "Sustaining the Safety Net: Recommendations on NYC Health + Hospitals' Transformation."

are expensive places to provide care. But if hospital beds could have been reduced in an intelligent way, the United States didn't do that. Instead, the country allowed a perverted version of free-market economics to dictate where beds were cut and which hospitals were closed. "Many governments—obsessed by the persistent hope of saving money by closing hospitals—have paid insufficient attention to assessing which hospitals, of what types, and in what locations are actually needed to protect the health of the public," Sager wrote. He says that he's found that hospitals located in the Black neighborhoods of the fifty-two cities he's studied over the decades from 1936 to 2020 have been more likely to close, even after controlling for all relevant factors.

Overall, the United States has about 2.9 beds per 1,000 people, compared to an average of 4.6 for many other wealthy countries, according to the Peterson-KFF Health System Tracker. The United States does have more intensive care beds per capita than many other countries. But in 2010, *The Journal of the American Medical Association* published a study concluding that the beds weren't where they needed to be. As a result, the study concluded, "a pandemic or disaster affecting a small proportion of the population could quickly exceed critical care capacity in some areas while leaving resources idle in others. This reflects the limitations of a private health system in which planning occurs primarily from the hospital perspective."

———

And then there's private equity.

Long before private equity firms started buying up nursing home companies, their operators were notorious for cutting corners. Nursing home companies were constantly being investigated by state attorneys general and federal regulators for shoddy care and financial fraud. Fines were legion. At one point, Henry Waxman, then a powerful California congressman, commissioned a report showing that between 1996 and 2000 reports of serious abuse by nursing home staff members had more than doubled and that fully a third of the country's nursing homes had been accused of at least one incident.

The fines and investigations changed nothing, for the simplest of reasons. The entrepreneurs who started gobbling up America's fifteen thousand nursing homes in the 1960s and 1970s and turning them into publicly traded nursing home chains were convinced the profits would roll in. So was Wall Street, which led to a nursing home stock bubble. After all, as the need for nursing homes grew in the 1960s, the federal government was dangling financial incentives to get operators to expand, leading one Wall Street wag to tell *Barron's*, "Nobody can lose money in this business. There's just no way." Needless to say, this expectation was wrong.

There were three issues. First, the government eventually got rid of those incentives. Second, the industry grew too fast, going from 460,000 nursing home beds to 1.1 million in the space of just eight years. That growth was unsustainable, and by 1973 the bubble had burst. And third, the federal government had concluded that Medicare should not be used to cover nursing home residents. The reason was that Medicare was intended only for "acute" patients—people who expected to get better and move on—rather than residents who had moved permanently to a nursing home. Instead, operators had to rely on Medicaid payments, which weren't enough to cover the cost of care. The only way an operator could make any real money was by scrimping on care or defrauding the government. Or both.

It wasn't until the mid-1980s that someone figured out a work-around for the Medicare problem. That someone was Michael Walker, the thirty-seven-year-old CEO of Genesis HealthCare,[13] a Pennsylvania company he cofounded. "Walker's philosophy," the *Philadelphia Business Journal* wrote years later, "was nursing homes should be proactive centers of health care, rather than centers focused solely on custodial care." Walker himself famously said, "No one wants to end up in a nursing home."

That may seem like an odd thing for a nursing home executive to say, but consider: if nursing homes really were "proactive centers of health care," that meant they were (supposedly) populated by sick patients hoping to (eventually) move to a less intensive care environment. Which also meant the patient could be covered by Medicare. If the patient needed regular rehab, that too would be covered by Medicare. And who owned the rehab facility? Genesis. When they needed to fill prescriptions? Genesis owned the pharmacy. Visit the doctor? Genesis had its own primary care physicians. Yes, Genesis still had a large number of Medicaid patients, but its ancillary services overcame that deficit.

By 1998, the company's revenue had risen to $2.4 billion. In addition to billing Medicare at least double that of other nursing home companies, it boosted revenue by establishing its own real estate investment trust, or REIT; when it needed a revenue bump to impress Wall Street, the company would sell off some of its real estate to its REIT and book the sale. And it went on an expansion tear, which required mountains of debt—more than $2 billion by the late 1990s.

The timing was spectacularly bad. A new Medicare payment system aimed at lowering reimbursements to nursing homes became the law of

13 Its original name was Genesis Health Ventures. Portions of this description of Genesis's early years come from an excellent article titled "Caring by the Dollar: Nursing Homes, Private Equity, and Covid-19," by Bill Barclay. It appeared in the March/April 2021 edition of the magazine *Dollars & Sense*.

the land in 1997. Genesis and the rest of the industry should have seen this coming; Congress had passed the law three years earlier. But they overlooked it somehow. The result was that by the end of 2000 most of the big nursing home companies were bankrupt—including Genesis.

Enter private equity.

Private equity firms have long been known for jumping into an industry when other investors turn against it. The theory is that by buying companies when they're cheap, the firms can make changes that will allow them to profitably bring these companies back to the public market. At which point, they usually cash out.

Some private equity executives were so convinced that nursing homes would become a major source of profits that they started new firms to focus solely on eldercare. The most influential of these firms was Formation Capital, which was founded in 1999 by Arnold Whitman and Steven Fishman.[14] Whitman,[15] the CEO, had been in the nursing home business for nearly two decades before starting Formation. His particular expertise was REITs. In 2005, with Formation up and running, Whitman bought fifty-three nursing homes in Florida at a cost of $165 million, almost all of it debt. Florida nursing homes were then drowning in class-action lawsuits, causing companies to spend millions on lawyers, insurance, and settlements. Most of the big chains wanted out of the state. Not Whitman. When he talked about the deal years later, he bragged that the first thing his new firm did was separate "the real estate and the operations."

In 2007, Whitman gave an interview with *The New York Times* in

---

14 Fishman, who had been Formation's president and cochairman, was forced out of the firm in 2018 when the Securities and Exchange Commission accused him of hiding the fact that other investors were secretly funding his financial obligations to Formation's funds.

15 Whitman did not respond to interview requests for this book.

which he explained his rationale: "Lawyers were suing nursing homes because they knew the companies were worth billions of dollars." By stripping out the real estate, he said, "we made the companies smaller and poorer." Within months of buying the Florida facilities, Formation Capital cut the number of registered nurses it employed in half. "Regulators repeatedly warned that staff levels were below mandatory minimums. When regulators visited, they found malfunctioning fire doors, unhygienic kitchens and a resident using a leg brace that was broken," the *Times* reported.

For the next few years, Formation Capital continued to scoop up Florida nursing homes at bargain prices; within two years, it was the largest owner of nursing homes in the state. Then it branched out, buying nursing homes in a number of states, including Maryland and North Carolina. Meanwhile, with the threat of lawsuits receding in Florida, Formation sold its original fifty-three nursing homes for more than double its purchase price.

Formation Capital soon gained a reputation for financially engineering its way to big profits, at least for its partners. It not only sold off real estate assets but also recapitalized companies, using financial engineering to ensure that the deals included "fees" and "dividends" that went directly to the firm.

Genesis had emerged from bankruptcy by then. George Hager, who had been the chief financial officer under Walker, became the CEO. Hager wanted to borrow $1.5 billion to take the company private, which would have made the top executives very wealthy. The board, however, decided to solicit other bids, and Formation came away with the prize, paying more than $1.7 billion, virtually all of it debt that was put on the Genesis balance sheet. Four years later, Formation sold Genesis's real estate for $2.4 billion, and three years after that Genesis became a public company again (although Formation continued to control the board until 2018). Here's how journalist Maureen Tkacik[16] described the result:

> *Having financed all the deals with debt, and having used more than $700 million of the proceeds to pay Formation a dividend, Genesis went public with 531 homes, virtually no real estate and $17.6 billion in long-term financing obligations, on which it was paying interest rates as high as 22.2 percent. The company was glaringly insolvent, and it had sold most things of value it had owned.*

Not surprisingly, patient care did not improve. In 2017, Genesis paid a $53 million fine for submitting "false claims to government health care programs . . . and [for] grossly substandard nursing care," according to a Justice Department release. The company ignored state staffing requirements. According to Tkacik, a whistleblower told the government how "bosses gave cash bonuses to nurses for bringing their average reimbursement levels up, while patients' open wounds went undressed for days at a time, a patient's leg brace went missing for a month, and one resident subsisted on a liquid diet for a full year because a nurse couldn't be bothered to retrieve his dentures from a dresser drawer."

And it wasn't just Genesis. Between 2010 and 2018, private equity's investment in the nursing home sector increased from $5 billion to $100 billion. After the 2008 financial crisis, when the Federal Reserve lowered interest rates to near zero, private equity deal making revved into overdrive as money became almost absurdly easy to borrow. With

---

16 Tkacik writes frequently about the excesses of private equity for the left-leaning *American Prospect*.

nursing home companies, that meant there were even fewer that could afford minimally adequate care, or even maintenance. Their debt load was a noose around their neck. Often, nursing home companies were sold from one private equity firm to another, with each new owner finding ways to move money from the companies to themselves.

In March 2020, shortly before the pandemic descended on the United States, four researchers[17] published a paper examining the effect of private equity ownership on nursing home patients. The researchers studied 118 private equity transactions that took place between 2000 and 2017. "The quality of care declines after the private equity buyout, which seems to reflect staffing cuts," said Sabrina T. Howell, one of the study's authors. The study found that after a private equity firm bought a nursing home, staff hours per patient fell 2.4 percent, while quality of care, as measured by the federal government, fell 3.6 percent. It documented one other telling statistic: that "short-term" mortality increased by 10 percent, which implies twenty-one thousand lives lost "due to private equity ownership over the sample period."

———

Did private equity's ownership of other parts of the health-care system have a better track record? Well, no, not in the case of hospitals. The lure of more taxpayer subsidies in the wake of the passage of the Affordable Care Act led to a barrage of deals that put a huge amount of the hospital industry in the hands of private equity. "PE ownership of hospitals reached its high-water mark in 2011, when seven of the twelve

17 The four authors of the paper were Atul Gupta of the University of Pennsylvania, Sabrina T. Howell of the Leonard N. Stern School of Business at New York University, Constantine Yannelis of the University of Chicago, and Abhinav Gupta of NYU.

largest for-profit chains were owned by private equity firms," report Eileen Applebaum and Rosemary Batt, two of the most knowledgeable critics of the PE industry's effects on health care. By the time the pandemic hit, it had become obvious who the winners and losers were. The winners were the investors who had used financial engineering to get money out of struggling hospitals. The losers were, well, everyone else. It's true that many hospitals would have struggled in any event. But what private equity left in its wake was a bastardization of capitalism: not an improvement in the underlying businesses that justified the money they'd made, but rather a deeply indebted system just waiting for a catalyst to tip it into crisis. As Eileen O'Grady, who is the research and campaign director for health care at the Private Equity Stakeholder Project and is another prescient critic of private equity in health care, says, "By definition, debt makes companies less resilient because they have less cash available. So in the case of health care, that leaves more money going toward debt service than to patient care."

Steward Health Care, a money-losing chain of not-for-profit New England community hospitals, offers a typical case study. In 2010, Cerberus Capital Management paid $246 million to purchase a struggling six-hospital chain in Massachusetts called Caritas Christi Healthcare, which was renamed Steward. Cerberus, which has a reputation for being one of the more ruthless firms on Wall Street, is run by Stephen Feinberg,[18] a billionaire Trump donor. The firm was vilified after Adam

18 Feinberg loathes publicity and almost never gives interviews. "If anyone at Cerberus has his picture in the paper and a picture of his apartment, we will do more than fire that person," he once said at a meeting of his investors. "We will kill him." Neither Cerberus nor Steward returned messages requesting comment for this book.

Lanza killed twenty children and six adults at the Sandy Hook Elementary School in 2012 using a semiautomatic weapon manufactured by a Cerberus-owned company.

As an owner of hospitals, Cerberus has excelled at pulling money out for itself and its investors. One of the techniques private equity firms use is a "dividend recapitalization," in which the company raises new debt that is not for its own uses, but rather is paid to the private equity investors. When Cerberus bought Steward, however, it had promised not to do a dividend recap for five years. And it didn't. Instead, Steward did a $1.2 billion "sale leaseback" transaction, selling its real estate to Medical Properties Trust, or MPT, a REIT that specialized in health-care properties. That put Steward in the position of paying rent on properties it had once owned. But the MPT deal allowed Cerberus to pay itself a $484 million dividend, according to *Bloomberg*. (In a press release, Steward described the deal as allowing the hospital company to "return" Cerberus's investment.)

As for MPT, it became a key tool for private equity firms wanting to pull money out of the hospital chains they owned—and thereby a critical, if little known and even less well understood, part of America's health-care infrastructure. The REIT, which was founded in 2003 and is headquartered in Alabama, is now the second-largest owner of hospital beds in the United States, with 444 properties and more than forty-five thousand beds. And it has a business model Wall Street loved, at least for a time; once it purchases a hospital's real estate, MPT gets a stream of never-ending lease payments—payments that increase every year and usually require hospitals to bear the majority of the expenses for any maintenance or improvements. That is, as long as the hospital can pay. Skeptics, however, long wondered whether it could last. MPT has a "concentrated tenant base of poorly performing, highly-levered hospital roll-ups which have been stripped of assets, milked for fees and starved of capital reinvestment by private equity owners," wrote Richard Mortell, the founder of investment firm Third Coast Real Estate Capital in a piece he first published for Value Investors Club.[19]

Just as the pandemic was heating up, Cerberus made another move. Easton Hospital in Pennsylvania's Lehigh Valley was a Steward facility that had seen its services cut dramatically over the years as it attempted to achieve profitability. But on March 22, 2020, three days after Governor Tom Wolf ordered a statewide lockdown, Steward went one step further: it announced the hospital would close unless it got money from the state. "I cannot stress enough the importance of keeping Easton Hospital open," the state representative Robert L. Freeman wrote to the governor's office. "They are a critical hospital in the Easton area for providing medical care in the face of the Covid-19 pandemic." Pennsylvania wound up giving Steward $8 million in aid to keep the hospital open for the duration of the pandemic. What choice did it have?

Overall, *Bloomberg* calculated that Cerberus made an $800 million profit on its investment in Steward, roughly quadrupling its money—certainly far better than Steward has fared. There are allegations of unsafe staffing by nurses, and lawsuits alleging that Steward is having trouble paying its bills. "Cerberus is exiting with its profits and just in time to distance itself from the remaining shell of the Caritas health system before the long term impact of its action is fully felt," wrote one lawsuit.[20]

———

It wasn't just hospitals private equity firms coveted. Among the other health-care businesses they gravitated toward was emergency room

19 MPT did not return requests for comment for this book.
20 Steward has previously argued that its finances are perfectly healthy.

practices. In fact, they had come to control swaths of that sector of the health-care industry. By the time the pandemic hit, private-equity-controlled companies, including two named Envision and TeamHealth, controlled a quarter to a third of the medical practices that provide staffing for hospital emergency rooms. There were allegations that they had found ways to maximize revenue that could be devastating to both the system as a whole and to patients. Patients who visited the ER might not generate much money, but if they were admitted to the hospital, the reimbursement rates skyrocketed. If a doctor—rather than a nurse— saw a patient, the reimbursement was higher. If the underlying medical problem was given a more severe rating—"upcoding," it's called—then reimbursements rise. And so on. Of course, that contributed to America's rising health-care costs. But there was another aspect, one that could destroy patients financially too. When people go to the ER, they often don't realize that the doctor treating them may not be a hospital employee, and therefore may not take their insurance. In that case, patients might get an enormous bill. Even if an insurer did pay, the patient might get the unpaid balance of the bill, which could also be enormous. These controversial practices became known as "surprise billing" or "balance billing," and while private equity firms may not have invented these tactics, the aggressive use of them certainly seems to be correlated with private equity ownership.

Envision Healthcare in particular was a creature of private equity. Its ER staffing business, called EmCare, was partly owned in quick succession by two private equity firms even before 2011, when the company was sold to Clayton Dubilier & Rice, another private equity firm, for $3.2 billion. Only about $900 million was cash. The rest was debt. The next year, Clayton put another $450 million of debt onto Envision's balance sheet to pay itself a hefty dividend. And the year after that, Clayton took Envision public, tripling its original investment. In two years, meanwhile, the company's debt had grown from $421 million to almost $3 billion. Making money became imperative.

For the health-care system and for patients, there were problems from the start. In 2005, EmCare took over the staffing for five emergency rooms at hospitals owned by Health Management Associates, an HCA wannabe, in North Carolina. The physicians who had previously staffed the ERs had refused to go along with some of HMA's demands, like, say, ordering a battery of diagnostic tests for anyone over sixty-five, regardless of whether they were medically necessary. So they were replaced with EmCare.

The Service Employees International Union (SEIU), which is the largest health-care union in the country, keeps track of numbers like emergency room admissions rates to try to suss out which hospitals are playing games. "Their rates were way above what you'd expect," says Joseph Lyons, a researcher with SEIU. "Workers started coming forward saying, we're getting told we have to do this, or we're going to lose our jobs."

Eventually, almost a dozen whistleblowers filed cases against HMA and EmCare. Prosecutors stepped in, and both companies eventually settled with the Justice Department. As part of its settlement, HMA admitted that it had "instituted a formal and aggressive plan to improperly increase overall emergency department inpatient admissions at all HMA hospitals." Prosecutors noted that EmCare's retention of the contracts was tied to increased admissions, and that EmCare was getting "remuneration" from HMA for this.

The scandal didn't stop hospitals from doing business with EmCare. In 2012, EmCare and HCA entered into a joint venture, in which HCA was to get a fifty-fifty split with EmCare once their business together had achieved a 13 percent profit margin, according to a Deutsche Bank report.[21] In 2021, an ER physician who had complained that he was terminated after raising concerns about staffing in an HCA-owned ER run by EmCare was awarded $26 million.

In 2017, Yale researchers led by economist and public health professor Zack Cooper published a study analyzing nearly nine million emergency room visits between 2011 and 2015. They found that after EmCare took over, the likelihood that a patient was treated by an out-of-network doctor almost doubled. At the same time, the out-of-network charges climbed more than 80 percent. In other words, not only were EmCare patients far more likely to get an out-of-network bill, but the total amount billed was likely to be far greater.[22]

"They built a machine that was incredibly effective at collecting huge amounts of money," says Mark Reiter, the past president of the American Academy of Emergency Medicine. "They did it through very aggressive increases in fee schedules, very aggressive negotiations with insurers, and by making threats that they would often carry out, that if you do not agree with this, then we will go out of network and balance bill your patients."

In 2017 and 2018—after Cooper's work was public—Envision and TeamHealth were taken private by KKR and Blackstone, respectively. KKR, for its part, funded its purchase with an additional $7 billion of debt. It's not clear whether they were clueless about the bad publicity that was on the way, or just cynical. In an article in *The American Pros-*

---

21 Batt and Appelbaum cite the HCA deal with EmCare in a 2019 article titled "Private Equity and Surprise Medical Billing."

22 TeamHealth says it has long eschewed so-called surprise billing as a matter of policy. But in a letter to Congress first obtained by Axios, the company acknowledged it used balance billing because it is "our only available source of contract negotiating leverage," meaning that it was a way to get insurers to agree to higher reimbursements. Envision says it ended the practice after a new chief executive, Jim Rechtin, joined in 2020.

pect, Appelbaum and Batt wrote that "loading patients who sought emergency care with often unpayable debt was KKR's secret sauce. It was as simple as that." ("We wholeheartedly disagree" with this characterization, says KKR.)

By the end of 2019, insurer United Healthcare had stopped paying the rates demanded by TeamHealth. (United also eventually cut Envision from its network for the same reason.) Multiple lawsuits in venues around the country sprang up, with TeamHealth arguing that United was trying to underpay them.[23] Stories about both companies' practices appeared across various media outlets. The then Missouri senator Claire McCaskill launched a congressional investigation. A bill that was meant to end surprise billing called the No Surprises Act began to gain momentum.

As the bill wended its way through Congress, the price of both Envision and TeamHealth's debt began to slide, reflecting the market's belief that if the companies couldn't continue to charge patients and insurers exorbitant rates, profits would suffer. But at the end of 2019, headlines blamed the Massachusetts congressman Richard Neal, then the ranking member of the powerful House Ways and Means Committee, who had gotten a $29,000 campaign contribution from Blackstone Group, for effectively killing the bill. *The New York Times* found that a shadowy group called Doctor Patient Unity was pouring millions into opposing the legislation. Its two largest backers? TeamHealth and Envision. A watered-down version of the bill finally passed in 2020.[24]

23 Both Envision and TeamHealth allege that United underpays their doctors, and both have scored some wins in court against United. United, for its part, has previously noted publicly that the rates charged by TeamHealth and Envision can be far above market rates.

24 KKR says that under its ownership, Envision advocated for an end to balance billing, and that Envision was the first national physician company to adopt a corporate policy prohibiting balance billing even before the No Surprises Act passed.

"We have this very strong belief that health-care institutions should be following the Hippocratic oath," says hedge fund manager Justin Simon. "But when private equity gets involved, the reality is that that is not the number one priority. Their number one priority is their fiduciary duty to their investors."

———

"There's no incentive whatsoever for an investor-owned hospital to do anything around public health," said Paul Keckley. Nor is it any different for the big nonprofits: even though they get tax breaks partly in return for committing to provide community-wide health care, in many places there is very little enforcement. In fact, a study published in *Health Affairs* in 2021 found that nonprofits provided less charity care per dollar of expenses than did for-profit and government-run hospitals.

At the same time, general public health spending has been a casualty of federal budget cutters. Officially, the coordination of local and national public health is the responsibility of the CDC, but adjusted for inflation, the CDC's core budget was essentially flat from 2007 to 2017. The Affordable Care Act—aka Obamacare—established a fund that was supposed to be dedicated to prevention and public health, but money has been cut and diverted from it repeatedly to pay for non–public health legislative proposals. Overall, from 2002 to 2019, according to *The Lancet*, public health funding in the United States fell from 3.21 percent to 2.45 percent of national health spending. Some fifty thousand jobs were lost.

"We don't have system of health and human services," Keckley says. "We have system of health *or* human services. Think about how much money we've spent on electronic health records, on digital connectivity, on fighting the battle to make sure hospital A and clinic B can share data," he says. "Instead, we should have stepped back and recognized that the real foundation of a health system is disease surveillance, such as how many people are in an emergency room? Why are they there? Because they don't have a place to live? Because they are drug dependent? Because they are morbidly obese?"

Much of what has taken place in health care has been in the name of efficiency, the same impulse that led America to outsource its supply chains to China. But that illusion of efficiency would come at an enormous cost.

In 2016, a commission on global health risk established by the National Academy of Medicine released a report titled *The Neglected Dimension of Global Security: A Framework to Counter Infectious Disease Crises*. "A primary health care system without the support of strong public health capabilities will lack the ability to monitor disease patterns and be unable to plan and mobilize the scale of response required to contain an outbreak," the commission wrote. "A public health system without strong primary care capabilities will lack both the 'radar screen' to pick up the initial cases of an outbreak and the delivery system to execute an effective response strategy."

The report went on to point out something that should have been obvious all along: any savings resulting from a lack of investment would disappear in a poof if a pandemic hit. The influenza pandemics of 1958 and 1968, while far milder than the Great Influenza of 1918, were estimated to have cost 3.1 percent and 0.7 percent of global GDP, respectively; the commission calculated that the expected annualized loss from future potential pandemics was on the order of $60 billion. They proposed spending $4.5 billion annually to strengthen national public health systems. "If we overinvest, we will have upgraded primary health care and public health systems more than merited by the pandemic threat alone and spent more on vaccine and diagnostic research than strictly necessary," they wrote. "Yet it is hard to see this as wasted money. The core capabilities of primary care and public health systems are crucial to achieving many other health objectives."

And while $4.5 billion in annual spending sounded like a lot, it was a "fraction of what we spend on other risks to humankind," they wrote. "Framed as a risk to human security, this is a compelling investment. Framed as a risk to economic growth and stability, it is equally convincing."

The commission's advice was ignored.

PART III

Advice and Dissent

7

The Zoom Class

In the parlance of Silicon Valley, Eric Yuan was "a grown-up" when he founded Zoom Video Communications in 2011. In a tech industry where founders are often twenty-five or younger, Yuan was forty-one, a Chinese immigrant who had moved to the United States fourteen years earlier and become a charismatic, much-admired leader and engineer first at WebEx and then at Cisco Systems after it bought WebEx in 2007. WebEx was one of the first videoconferencing companies, and thanks in no small part to Yuan it controlled some two-thirds of the market at one point. At Cisco, he was in charge of the company's videoconferencing division.

By 2011, however, WebEx had lots of competition, including Skype, GoTo Meeting, and others. "The video conferencing market was seen as ossified," Bill Tai, a venture capitalist, told one reporter. It was a B2B product, that is, a business selling to other businesses, with scarcely a thought given to the consumer market. What's more, there hadn't been any significant technological advances in years. Every company's software was glitchy and difficult to use; the apps would regularly crash in the middle of meetings. Yuan would later tell CNBC that when he talked to customers about the WebEx app, he "did not see a single happy customer." But when he asked Cisco for the resources to create a better version, the company turned him down. So Yuan left, determined to build a product that would make customers happy. When he started Zoom, some three dozen Cisco engineers joined him.

In Zoom's first four years, its employees were almost all engineers, obsessively focused on writing code that would make videoconferencing simple and glitch-free. And its early customers were nearby tech companies, like Uber and Oracle. But even after Zoom had sales and marketing teams, it still focused on the corporate market; Yuan viewed Zoom as a superior product serving traditional users, which were businesses, rather than a revolutionary product that could create new users.

And then came the pandemic, and as millions of people became aware of Zoom—how easy it was to use, how little it cost,[1] how rarely it crashed—it became the product that made the lockdown bearable, at least for white-collar workers. With Zoom, you could attend meetings and earn your salary, even though your office had shut down. Your kids' school was likely shut down as well, but thanks to Zoom they could attend remote classes. You could stay connected to your parents, whose assisted living residence was off-limits because of the virus. After work, you could even wind down with Zoom cocktails with friends. Between

---

1 Zoom calls less than forty minutes were (and still are) free; many people who wanted to talk longer would simply wait for Zoom to shut down the connection and then start a new one.

December 2019 and April 2020, Zoom's usage increased thirtyfold. One can't help wondering whether lockdown would have been so readily agreed to had Zoom not existed.

And what if you didn't have a white-collar desk job? What if you still had to leave the house every day to go to work even though your children's school was closed? What if you weren't a member of the educated elite, for whom—thanks to Zoom and Amazon and Uber Eats and a raft of other apps—a lockdown was not much more than a nuisance?

Early in the pandemic, Madonna released a video. Sitting in a bathtub surrounded by red roses, with dramatic music playing in the background, she said, "It doesn't care about how rich you are, how famous you are, how funny you are, how smart you are, where you live, how old you are, what amazing stories you can tell. [The pandemic is] the great equalizer, and what's terrible about it is what's great about it."

She could not have been more wrong.

———

The first real inkling that lockdowns were going to create new layers of economic inequality were the stories that emerged early about the nation's meatpackers. At both the state and the federal levels, certain industries were designated "essential"—too important to the economy to shut down. Which of course meant that the employees in those industries were essential workers. They included truckers, health-care personnel, postal workers, grocers, "merchant wholesalers" (that is, Amazon warehouse workers), and meatpackers. Essential workers were overwhelmingly blue collar and poorly paid.

Of all these jobs, few put workers in as much proximity to their colleagues as meatpackers, who stood shoulder to shoulder as they processed meat along lengthy tables. Although they would all deny it, three of the major meatpacking companies, Tyson Foods, Smithfield Foods, and JBS USA, seemed far more interested in profits than their workers' health. *The Washington Post* published the results of an investigation just a few months into the pandemic; it found that the companies ignored federal guidelines about using PPE. At some plants, workers told the *Post*, they were encouraged to come to work even when they felt sick. "If you're not in a casket, they want you there," said a former Smithfield worker. In thirty of the companies' plants, 3,300 workers had been infected, and seventeen had died. Of that number, an astonishing 890 COVID-19 cases came from one Smithfield plant in Sioux Falls, South Dakota. In another plant, owned by Tyson Foods in Amarillo, Texas, half the workforce came down with COVID-19. A report by the Agriculture Department concluded that the culprit was "the physical proximity of workers."

The government did not exactly ride to the rescue. Although the companies would be forced to temporarily shut down a handful of plants—and install flimsy plastic dividers between workers—Trump signed an executive order, largely drafted by industry lobbyists, forcing the meat-packers to get back to work without requiring the companies to take any further safety measures. That same order was also supposed to indemnify the companies from lawsuits by employees.

The results were horrifying. According to the House Select Subcommittee on the Coronavirus Crisis, a staggering fifty-nine thousand meatpackers were infected during the first year of the pandemic, and 269 died. Rural counties with meatpacking plants often had infection rates ten times that of rural counties without meatpacking plants. During a subcommittee hearing, the former OSHA official Debbie Berkowitz said, "More workers have died from COVID-19 in the last 18 months in the meat and poultry industry than died from all work-related causes in the industry in the last 15 years."

Nor were meatpackers the only vulnerable workers. Amazon warehouse workers were also hit hard by the virus even as the company reported record profits. Although Amazon was mum about the COVID-19 cases at its warehouses—not even informing employees at first—workers began speaking up about what they said was a lack of PPE, and a rise in infections. At a Staten Island warehouse, workers walked out to protest conditions.[2] In a statement, Amazon described the allegations of worker neglect as "unfounded" and described its employees as "heroes." It also fired several of the employees who were protesting conditions. But seven months later, under pressure from labor groups and legislators, Amazon revealed that close to twenty thousand employees had been infected. It insisted this number was lower than the infection rate for the overall population.

The *Houston Chronicle* surveyed workers at local FedEx and UPS shipping centers, as well as an Amazon warehouse. "I don't want to miss work because I'm a single parent, but I'm afraid I'm gonna catch something," a FedEx driver told the paper. He added, "We're panicking." A second FedEx employee said, "It makes me feel like I'm less than a human being, that we're expendable and that our lives don't matter." Two UPS employees complained of the impossibility of staying six feet away from others—the CDC's recommendation for social distancing—in the company's warehouse. Amazon workers reported that large numbers of employees simply weren't coming to work because they feared the virus was spreading inside the warehouses. (Amazon

2 In 2022, the workers in this warehouse became the first Amazon employees to unionize.

sent out a memo saying that employees would not be penalized for virus-related absences. All three companies insisted the health and safety of their workers was paramount.) When you got right down to it, the working class was putting their health—and potentially their lives—at risk to serve those who were lucky enough to lock down.

Unlike the financial crisis of 2008, the government did try to help middle-class and working-class families. In addition to the money that came from the CARES Act, the government raised unemployment compensation by $600 a week. It placed a moratorium on evictions, allowing tenants to stay in their apartments even if they couldn't pay the rent.

This infusion of federal cash was important. For twenty straight weeks, new unemployment claims topped one million—a number that far exceeded anything in the past. The money the unemployed received from the government was deeply meaningful. Even so, it paled in comparison to the largesse doled out to the wealthy, both to individuals and to large corporations. After all, they had the Federal Reserve on their side, where the nonstop asset purchases and ultralow interest rates guaranteed that the rich would get richer.

For investors, the pandemic was financial nirvana. Sure, stocks tumbled in March with the first pandemic tremors, but by April the market was rising again and kept rising month after month. "If you had told me that a year later, stock prices would have been at an all-time high, I would have said you were crazy," Mnuchin told a friend. In fact, it didn't even take a full year. By August, U.S. stock indexes were at all-time highs. The S&P 500 ended the year with a total return of 18.4 percent—and up 68 percent from its late March low.

An extraordinary disconnect was unfolding. In April, a record 20.5 million people lost their jobs. Unemployment soared to 14.7 percent, a level not seen since the government began tracking that data in 1939. In the second quarter, the United States experienced the worst quarterly drop in real GDP ever, an annualized decline of 33 percent, worse than the Great Depression, the Great Recession, and more than three dozen economic slumps over the past two centuries, noted CNBC. "So we had a health emergency, an ailing economy, the most generous capital market of all time, and strong stock and bond markets," wrote Howard Marks, a longtime fund manager, in a letter to clients. "The seemingly anomalous relationship between the pandemic and recession on one hand and the strong capital and stock markets on the other can be explained by the Fed's and the U.S. Treasury's aggressive actions."

Shares of companies whose businesses were badly damaged by the pandemic—airlines, for instance, or cruise lines—fell far less than one might have expected, while shares of companies that the pandemic aided—tech companies most of all—saw their shares soar. Apple's market value went from just under $1 trillion in mid-March 2020 to $2.2 trillion by the end of the year. Amazon's shares were up 76 percent in 2020. Facebook's stock nearly doubled in just the first five months of the pandemic. Elon Musk's Tesla—the hottest stock of them all—was up an astonishing 740 percent in 2020. With so much of their wealth in stock and stock options, the big-name tech CEOs saw their wealth increase by staggering amounts. Amazon's Jeff Bezos: $58 billion. Mark Zuckerberg of Facebook: $29 billion. Elon Musk: $118 billion. In total, the wealth of the top nine tech barons increased by more than $360 billion over the pandemic's first year, reported *The Washington Post* in the spring of 2021. Eric Yuan, whose product became so ubiquitous its users were sometimes called the "Zoom class," saw his net worth hit almost $20 billion by the end of 2020. Zoom's stock, which had begun 2020 at $73 a share, stood over $560 a share by October.

And it wasn't just the titans of tech; according to a group called the Patriotic Millionaires, America's 740 billionaires became $2 trillion richer during the pandemic. The Fed itself reported that the top 10 percent of households captured 70 percent of wealth created in 2020, wrote *Bloomberg.* The bottom half? They got just 4 percent.

———

The government also stepped in to try to save small businesses. They badly needed the help; a report by J.P.Morgan showed that in the typical community nearly half the small businesses had less than two weeks' worth of cash on hand. "We started talking to members who were completely panicked, because they were running through their savings," says Holly Wade, the research director at the National Federation of Independent Business. "For so many small business owners, the profits from their business are their income and their primary financing resource."

Prodded by Mnuchin, who told legislators that unemployment could reach 25 percent if the government did nothing, Congress had passed that $349 billion Paycheck Protection Program. The agency in charge of disbursing the money was the Small Business Administration. Its primary task was to serve as the guarantor of bank loans to small businesses. In 2019, it had guaranteed $28 billion worth of small business loans. With the PPP, the SBA was being asked to handle thirteen times more money. And to do it in a matter of weeks.

Nor were banks set up to handle the flood of calls from desperate small business owners. Their job was to accept applications from businesses, forward them to the SBA, and make the loans (while keeping a not-so-small percentage, ranging from 5 percent for loans under $350,000 to 1 percent for loans over $2 million). But there was such a rush to get money out the door—and such furious anxiety on the part of business owners—that the program quickly devolved into "chaos and confusion," as *The New York Times* later put it.

Eric Terrell, the senior manager at the SBA office in Memphis, told *The Washington Post* that he was getting 120 calls a day, many from panicked entrepreneurs who hadn't heard from their banks after applying. "You get phone calls from business owners who are crying, all the savings they had have run out," Terrell said. "You get other people, they're so upset they use profanity. And I understand." C. J. Castro, who ran the SBA office in Tampa, said his cell phone "started ringing at seven in the morning and it didn't stop till 10 o'clock at night" for weeks afterward.

The rules had been cobbled together so quickly that the SBA wound up handing money to dozens of big companies that should never have been part of the program. And although the maximum loan amount was supposed to be $10 million, companies with more than one location could get a separate loan for each location. AutoNation, for instance, received $77 million in loans. Hospitality companies affiliated with a Dallas-based Trump donor named Monty Bennett applied for over $126 million in loans—while paying preferred shareholders over $10 million, including $2 million to Bennett and his father. "I won't apologize for being a capitalist in America, or being reasonably successful at it," Bennett wrote in a blog post.[3]

National restaurant chains like Applebee's, P. F. Chang's, Ruby Tuesday, and TGI Fridays all got between $5 million and $10 million, NPR reported. Shake Shack, the popular burger chain, got $10 million. Some four hundred golf clubs got loans. The Los Angeles Lakers applied for a $4.6 million loan and got it.

As the news of these well-off recipients emerged, there was a huge outcry. "I'm a big fan of the team," Mnuchin told CNBC, "but I'm not

3 Bennett's dealings were detailed in an April 22, 2020, *Wall Street Journal* article titled "Dallas Hotel Owner Is Biggest Beneficiary of Coronavirus Loan Program."

a fan of the fact they took a $4.6 million loan." Small business owners were equally irate that their applications had been passed over while much bigger companies seemed to be getting all the loans.

By April 16—after just thirteen days—the SBA had approved more than 1.6 million loans. The first $349 billion was gone. "I mean, it was just all gone," says Wade. "Hundreds of billions out the door. And we kept hearing from our desperate members, who didn't get a loan."

In late April, Mnuchin warned that any company that had taken more than $2 million could expect an audit, and perhaps criminal prosecution. But that's not really what changed things. Some big companies, like Shake Shack and AutoNation, embarrassed by the bad publicity, gave the money back. Bennett, who blamed the media for forcing the SBA to rewrite the rules and require applicants to prove they had no other way to raise the money, gave the money back too. In addition, the Treasury Department clarified that the money was supposed to go to small companies, and when a second round of PPP was distributed in late April, the banks did a much better job of getting it to genuinely small businesses that needed it most. Ultimately, many small businesses were able to survive because of their PPP loans.

Still, the SBA would later release data (because a court ordered them to do so) showing that more than half of all the PPP money went to just 5 percent of recipients. And a quarter of the money went to just 1 percent of the companies.

In contrast to the chaos of the PPP, the government made sure big companies were taken care of. The airlines received $25 billion from Congress "to preserve aviation jobs and compensate air carrier industry workers"—but by early 2021, about 400,000 airline workers had been fired, furloughed, or told they might lose their jobs, according to *Bloomberg*. And the Fed's policies meant that big business could get low-interest credit; even the riskiest companies could sell copious amounts of debt. Junk bond issuance soared to record levels in 2020 and again in 2021.

The Fed insisted that the purpose of its actions was to help workers and avoid layoffs. But there was no way to ensure that, because the money came with no strings attached. The Select Subcommittee on the Coronavirus Pandemic would later report that of the roughly 500 companies that issued debt purchased by the Fed, nearly a third furloughed or laid off workers, affecting more than one million employees. Among them: Boeing, which sold a massive $25 billion in bonds and then, a month later, laid off 10 percent of its workforce; Raytheon, which laid off fifteen thousand workers despite being part of the Fed's bond-buying program; and the energy services giant Schlumberger, which cut roughly twenty-one thousand jobs. Another 383 of the companies sent money to shareholders in the form of dividends.[4] *The Washington Post* reported that the 50 biggest U.S. companies collectively distributed more than $240 billion to shareholders through buybacks and dividends between April and September, representing about 79 percent of the profits they generated in that period. More than half of them laid employees off. Even in the middle of a pandemic, most corporations simply could not shed their now-ingrained habit of putting shareholders above employees.

The pandemic, at least initially, stripped away progress that had been made on many fronts. While overall unemployment skyrocketed, it was particularly severe for Black and Hispanic workers, and for those without a college degree. The unemployment rate for those with a four-year degree hit 8.4 percent in April—compared with 17.3 percent for those who had just a high school degree, according to the Congressional

---

4 Powell said that he didn't think the report reflected the Fed's actions accurately, because "none of those companies see themselves as having gotten a loan from the Fed."

Research Service. And Black and Hispanic workers were also dying at much higher rates than college educated whites. Women left the workforce in droves—two million in 2020 alone, according to the United Nations—because the demands of caring for children during a lockdown made it impossible to hold down a job. IN THE COVID-19 ECONOMY, read a *New York Times* headline, YOU CAN HAVE A KID OR A JOB. YOU CAN'T HAVE BOTH. The phenomenon became known as a "shecession."

In August 2020, just a few days after the then candidate Joe Biden selected Kamala Harris as his running mate, the two got a video briefing from Raj Chetty, an economics professor at Harvard and one of the foremost experts on inequality. By April, he told them, the bottom quarter of wage earners, those making less than $27,000 a year, had lost almost eleven million jobs. That was more than three times the number lost by those earning more than $60,000 annually. By June, that top segment had recovered. "The recession has essentially ended for high-income individuals," Chetty told Biden and Harris.

———

And then there were restaurants.

Prior to the pandemic, there were 500,000 independent restaurants—that is, restaurants that are not part of a national chain. Restaurants and their suppliers employed more than sixteen million people—more than four times the number of airline employees. Restaurants were the anchor of many neighborhoods and a defining element of many cities. They were also an enormous source of jobs; the industry estimated that 60 percent of Americans have had a restaurant job at some point in their lives. "These are the places where you want your kid to get their first job because you know the owners, and they're going to learn about the basics of work," says Rick Bayless, the Chicago restaurant impresario. "They are the fabric of culture in our society." People go to restaurants not just for the food but because "we're social animals," said Ken Aretsky, the owner of the New York restaurant Aretsky's Patroon.

But restaurants have always been a precarious business, a cash-in, cash-out industry with paper-thin margins even in the best of times. So, given their centrality, one might have expected state and federal governments to rush to their aid. Instead, the opposite happened: for most of the pandemic, restaurants were abandoned. "The government said to us, 'Hey, guys, here you go,'" says Kevin Boehm, the cofounder of the Boka Restaurant Group in Chicago. "'Here's a boat with fifteen holes in it. We're going to drop you in the middle of the ocean with no paddles. Good luck.'"

Aretsky recalls going to a big industry fundraiser at the beginning of March. "Everyone was in a great mood," he said. But as the pandemic began to take hold in New York, the city's restaurateurs became worried. "We talked about shutting down," he says of Patroon's executive team. "Our private party business, which is very important to us, dwindled to nothing, almost overnight." On March 13, a Friday, whispers started that Mayor Bill de Blasio was going to reduce restaurant capacity to 50 percent. That day, Danny Meyer, one of the most respected restaurateurs in the city,[5] shut his nineteen New York restaurants. Other restaurants soon followed, including Patroon. On Tuesday, March 17, de Blasio handed down his order, and it went well beyond a reduction in capacity. All restaurants and bars were to close except for takeout and delivery. "It was one of the most heartbreaking days of my life," says Aretsky. "We had people who worked for us for twenty years. You're letting people go and you're crying. These people are my family."

5 Meyer is also the founder of Shake Shack.

In Greenwich Village, a few miles from Patroon, Gabe Stulman was going through a similarly wrenching ordeal. His small company, Happy Cooking Hospitality, owned nine restaurants, buzzy neighborhood spots popular with locals. He had put himself through college working in restaurants, and in 2005, at the age of twenty-five, he opened his first New York City spot. "What's great about restaurants is that you don't need a high school or college degree in order to be a great cook, server, or bartender. It opens our industry to so many amazing people who get shut out of other occupations. If you're passionate and willing to work hard, you can make a path for yourself," he says. His restaurants employed some three hundred people.

When Stulman heard the de Blasio rumor, he found it hard to believe. But as the horror from Italy blared on TVs and across newspaper headlines, the unimaginable became the inevitable. On Sunday morning, March 15, two days ahead of the mayor's decree, Stulman gathered his employees and told them they were closing. In the face of a clearly contagious virus that no one understood, it seemed to be the right thing—the only thing—to do.

Stulman couldn't conceive of a shutdown that would last a long time. "Weeks, right?" he says. Like many restaurateurs, his first thought was how he could help his employees. By utilizing his relationships with distributors—whose business had suddenly gone away too—he could get food and supplies at wholesale prices, give the groceries to his employees, and make his limited cash stretch further than if he simply gave people money. "By day three we were planning it, and by day six we were executing," he says. Employees could come every Thursday and get a forty-pound bag filled with groceries and staples, including what became hard-to-get household needs like paper towels and toilet paper.

Stulman funded this effort by using his long history with vendors and landlords to hold off on paying those invoices in order to redirect his money to getting the groceries. "At the onset, the government was scrambling," he says. "Nobody had answers to anything. It was everyone for themselves." He managed for sixteen weeks, eventually supplementing the company's resources by setting up a GoFundMe, where loyal customers could help provide for his team.

It was a similar story for Bayless in Chicago, where the close-knit chef-owner community met on March 15. "Everybody said, basically, we can't continue," says Bayless. "We can't pay our rent, because business has fallen off so much. When the mayor [Lori Lightfoot] came on a few hours later and said she was closing everything, we gave a sigh of relief. Because we couldn't continue."

Kevin Boehm and his partner, Rob Katz, shut down their twenty-three Chicago restaurants and laid off more than eighteen hundred employees. "We immediately set up weekly grocery giveaways for everyone, extended everyone's health care through the summer, and Rob and I then put $100,000 in an employee fund to seed a GoFundMe campaign for our team." Within three months, the two men were $4 million in the hole.

And where was the government? Nowhere. The first round of CARES Act money wasn't designed to help independent restaurants. To start with, the size of the PPP loan was based purely on payroll. A loan was supposed to be two and a half times average annual payroll, so the more employees you had—and the more they made—the more money your business got. The loan would be forgiven only if 75 percent was used to maintain payroll at pre-crisis levels. That didn't leave much for rent—or anything else.

But restaurant employees made a lot of their money on tips, and rent was often a restaurant's biggest cost. And if a restaurant couldn't establish a take-out business, there was no point in keeping employees on payroll because there was no work for them to do. "The first PPP was set up so that we had to take our employees off unemployment and just pay them what they would normally have been paid," says Bayless. "And we didn't have any work for them, so we were paying them to stay home, which is exactly what unemployment was doing."

This might not have sat so poorly with many restaurant owners if there hadn't been such specific bailouts for industries like the airlines. "So certain industries have unique circumstances that require unique solutions," says Stulman. "We've seen this with government bailouts for airlines, the automotive industry, banks, and on and on."

When Congress replenished the PPP funds in June 2020 legislators made a number of changes to the rules, including reducing the amount that had to go to payroll so that businesses could use more of it for rent. And many cities made one concession to the industry: they allowed restaurants to sell take-out drinks. But for many independent restaurants in the costliest cities, like New York, it still wasn't enough.

Stulman, for instance, had nine rents to pay each month. Even with the PPP loans he finally got, he had no way to cover all those rents. Absent any government guidance, he needed his landlords to make accommodations that would allow him to stay in business. Some were compassionate and understanding—"mensches." "They said, 'I'm hurting, you're hurting. I understand that I cannot expect you to pay me rent when you're not allowed to use your space. I don't know how we're going to do this, but we'll do this together.'"

But others weren't so forgiving. In New York, owners of restaurants and other small businesses usually must sign personal guarantees, meaning that if the business can't cover the rent, they are on the hook personally. Obviously, the rental agreements did not foresee a pandemic in which commerce was stopped but rent was still due. "Imagine if somebody said, 'You're not allowed to live in your home, but you still owe your rent or your mortgage,'" Stulman says. "There would have been riots. I do not understand why we view this differently for commercial spaces. I think they should also have said, 'You are not responsible for your rent.'"

Nonetheless, that was the situation he was faced with. If he stopped paying the rent, the landlord had the right to sue him personally, and several threatened to do just that. "You can threaten to take my home, my savings account, everything," Stulman says, referring to some of the landlords. "Why? Because of a contract I signed before a pandemic, because never in my generation or my parents' generation has something like COVID happened."

Restaurants did succeed in marshaling their combined forces to get the New York City Council, in May, to cancel personal guarantees on commercial leases if the failure to pay rent was due to the pandemic. But Stulman believed the law would be challenged and wasn't sure it would hold up in court.[6] So rather than roll the dice, he handed over large sums of cash in exchange for ending his leases and liability. That resulted in the bitter decision to close five of his restaurants.

This same set of stark choices faced restaurateurs all over the city and the country. In New York City alone, almost 1,300 restaurants, each one a fixture of a neighborhood, closed between March 1 and July 10, according to a report by the comptroller's office. Overall, in 2020, 110,000 American restaurants closed, about 17 percent of the nation's total, and two and a half million restaurant workers lost their jobs permanently, according to the National Restaurant Association.

Months later, the lobbying group organized by the independent restaurateurs got a bill passed through the House that would have sent

---

6 In April 2023, it was overturned, opening the floodgates for landlords to sue tenants over missed rents during the pandemic.

money to restaurants based on 2019 revenue rather than payroll. It passed the House in the fall as part of a larger relief package. But when the bill was signed by President Trump in December, the restaurant provisions had been stripped out.

"It's hard not to feel like we're the last kids picked on the kickball team," said an angry Kevin Boehm. "I talk to people every single day who are just barely hanging on."

8

A Very Expensive Lunch

O n April 17, 2020, at 5:00 p.m., the city of Jacksonville, Florida, reopened its beaches. They had been closed since mid-March, and the locals were so eager to feel the sand under their feet they made a mad dash for the beach as soon as the police removed the barriers at the entrances. Jacksonville's mayor, Lenny Curry, a Republican, limited the hours the beaches would be open—six to eleven in the morning and five to eight in the evening. And he asked beachgoers to practice social distancing and forgo the use of beach chairs, umbrellas, grills, and anything else that would encourage group gatherings that might spread the virus.

Nobody paid the mayor any attention. CNN interviewed several happy beachgoers who laughingly acknowledged that no one was practicing social distancing. The *Miami Herald*, however, was irate. "You know what Florida really needs right now?" asked the editorial page, in reference to Governor Ron DeSantis. "A governor." And when photos of the Jacksonville beaches were posted on social media, many people, especially those in blue states who were adhering to their state's lockdowns and other non-pharmaceutical interventions, reacted with fury. Their anger was not due to envy that Floridians were lucky enough to have their beaches back; it was that they, the blue staters, were "following the science" by remaining in lockdown and Floridians were not. The Twittersphere quickly created a hashtag: *#FloridaMorons*. Thousands of people chimed in, their tweets dripping with scorn and condemnation. One tweet showed a photo of DeSantis with the caption "#FloridaMan dooms thousands to die in the state by reopening public beaches during a pandemic. #FloridaMorons." Another, which showed people walking on a Jacksonville beach, read, "#FloridaMorons. They aren't wearing masks. They are a threat to the public health & might travel to your state!" And a third, with pictures depicting people playing on the beach, read, "@GovRonDeSantis is a criminal ghoul for allowing this. #FloridaMorons." They also came up with a hashtag for the governor: #Deathsantis.

Two weeks later, DeSantis stood at the entrance of a Jacksonville state park, flanked by local officials. A kayak and a bicycle had been artfully placed by the lectern. With temperatures in the eighties, it was the kind of day, pre-pandemic, that would have caused people to flock to their local park. Though DeSantis had imposed his statewide lockdown less than a month earlier, he was already in the process of lifting it. Even during the lockdown, he had never closed churches and synagogues, and had allowed the construction industry to continue operating.

The parks were part of his reopening. Was DeSantis easing restrictions because the president who had helped him get elected now opposed lockdowns? No doubt that played a part. A few weeks earlier,

Trump had sent out three tweets: "LIBERATE MINNESOTA!" followed by "LIBERATE MICHIGAN!" and "LIBERATE VIRGINIA!" In all three states Democratic governors had mandated lockdowns. Shortly after that, DeSantis visited Trump in the White House, in a calculated gesture to show that his approach—the "red state approach"—was superior to the approach being taken by blue states like New York and California.

By late April, the numbers appeared to be bearing him out. Florida, with a population of twenty-two million, had suffered fewer than thirteen hundred COVID-19 deaths, compared with New York's twenty-seven thousand deaths. Massachusetts, with a population a third of Florida's, had triple the COVID-19 deaths. An alliance of science organizations had published a statistical model predicting that 465,699 Floridians—a weirdly precise number—would be hospitalized with COVID-19 by late April unless the state took quick action to flatten the curve. Marc Lipsitch, a Harvard epidemiologist, was quoted in the *Miami Herald* saying that Florida was quickly running out of time to slow transmission of the virus. DeSantis mocked the model. "I think what I've found on these models is that they have assumptions that are totally unreasonable," he said.

But there was more to it than just a Trumpian governor trying to align himself with Trump. He simply didn't believe lockdowns were effective. "DeSantis is extremely data-driven," said Charles Lockwood, the head of the Morsani College of Medicine at the University of South Florida. "He actually read much of the COVID literature himself." When he saw that in Italy it was largely the elderly who were dying of COVID-19, he quickly focused on nursing homes. He put together working groups to grapple with how to fight the pandemic. The groups debated the best approach while DeSantis listened. Although he was insistent that it made no sense to lock the state down for months at a time, he said he would either lift or impose measures according to how a county or a city was faring at any given moment. For instance, even as the parks were opening, DeSantis did not try to stop the counties that included Miami and West Palm Beach from continuing their local lockdowns, because they had the highest numbers of deaths and hospitalizations. He liked to say that Florida wasn't taking a "one-size-fits-all" approach to pandemic mitigation.

DeSantis's purpose in visiting Jacksonville was to explain why reopening parks was sound public policy and not a red state stunt, as his critics would undoubtedly charge. Even in a pandemic, DeSantis said, open spaces were necessary for peace of mind. The evidence showed that the risk of contracting the virus was much lower outdoors than indoors, he added. And maintaining social distancing in parks was not terribly difficult. All of which was true.

Florida, he continued, would maintain social distancing even after the lockdown was lifted; for instance, restaurants would be held to 50 percent capacity. He reiterated the importance of protecting the elderly; Florida's prohibition against nursing home visits was ironclad. But, he added, the virus posed much less risk to anyone under fifty. Florida, he said again and again, was being guided by "data, facts, and science."

There was something else he needed to get off his chest. The abuse heaped on Floridians when the beaches had opened infuriated him. And he wasn't the kind of politician who turned the other cheek.

A lot of people—"from between D.C. and New York," he said, taking a jab at the East Coast elites—made it sound as if opening the beach were akin to a death warrant. DeSantis continued:

They did misleading pictures, acting like it was Lollapalooza on the beach or something like that. And this is what they were focused on. Not dirty subway cars . . . And people here were mocked. . . . Has there been some type of major outbreak? No. In fact cases have declined. . . . Two weeks ago, [Duval County][1] *reported 29 new cases. Out of a county of a million people, that is extremely low.*

"That's like lunchtime in Queens," DeSantis concluded, unable to resist one last poke at New York.

———

Two of the scientists DeSantis was relying on were Martin Kulldorff and Jay Bhattacharya. Kulldorff was a highly regarded, Swedish-born Harvard epidemiologist who had developed vital tools the CDC used to evaluate vaccine health and safety risks. Bhattacharya was the director of Stanford University's Center on the Demography and Economics of Health and Aging. Both men were fierce opponents of lockdowns.

Researching how the coronavirus affected various populations, Kulldorff and Bhattacharya came to conclusions that were at odds with the scientific establishment. For instance, the government's pandemic plans had always called for schools to close. That was because the kind of severe influenza America's pandemic plans were predicated on was devastating to children. With the coronavirus, however, very few children became seriously ill. (By the fall of 2021, seven hundred children had died, out of seventy-four million nationwide, which amounts to .001 percent.) Yet even after this evidence became clear, most mainstream public health officials stuck to the view that schools should remain closed.

To Kulldorff and Bhattacharya, this made no sense. "With COVID, there's a thousandfold difference in the risk of mortality between the

1 Jacksonville is located in Duval County.

old and the young," Kulldorff says. "So in my view it is a no-brainer that you do everything you can to protect that older, higher-risk population." He continued: "There was this idea that if you just close down society as a whole, that will protect everyone. But if you try to shut down a society very harshly, it has enormous collateral damage." With school closings, millions of students had fallen behind, many of whom would never catch up. Most school districts instituted remote learning, but parents soon realized it was a poor substitute for classroom instruction. According to the nonprofit Bellwether Education Partners, some three million of the "most educationally marginalized students in the country" had been "missing" from school since the pandemic began. By the fall of 2022, test scores in reading had fallen to 1992 levels, while 40 percent of eighth graders failed to grasp basic math concepts. Closed schools also meant it was harder to access the school lunches many disadvantaged families depended on. It deprived children living in difficult circumstances of a safe space during the day. Indeed, the CDC reported that adolescent suicide attempts soared during the pandemic. "I just can't overstress how harmful these lockdowns were to the public at large, from a public health point of view," Bhattacharya told one interviewer. "Forget about the economics, just in terms of health outcomes."

Lockdowns had other unintended consequences. People died because hospitals stopped performing surgeries and shut down departments to focus on COVID-19 patients. Millions of small business people lost their livelihoods. There was a big jump in domestic violence. And on and on. "One of the huge mistakes people like Fauci made was failing to consider these impacts," Kulldorff said. His strong belief was that while protecting the immunocompromised and the elderly was critically important, it was equally important to let everyone else go about their lives. He was aligned with D. A. Henderson's principle that "communities faced with epidemics or other adverse events respond best and with the least anxiety when the normal social functioning of the community is least disrupted."

Kulldorff had his own series of public health principles that grew out of COVID-19—twelve of them, which he listed in a series of tweets in late 2020. "Public health is about all health outcomes, not just a single disease like Covid-19" read one principle. "Public health is about everyone" began another. "It should not be used to shift the burden from the affluent to the less affluent." A third: "It is important for public health scientists and officials to listen to the public, who are living the public health consequences. This pandemic has proved that many non-epidemiologists understand public health better than some epidemiologists."

And then there was this, the eleventh of Kulldorff's twelve principles: "In public health, open civilized debate is profoundly critical. Censoring, silencing and smearing leads to fear of speaking, herd thinking and distrust." Winston Churchill, Kulldorff liked to point out, "was famous for having different people in the room, different generals who had different views. And he encouraged different views to be expressed because that is how you think things through and come to reasonable conclusions." When it came to the pandemic, most American politicians weren't doing that, even though some of the mitigation measures the country was using were far from settled science.

Take social distancing. Were people safe standing three feet apart, or did they need to stand six feet apart? As the chief of the infectious diseases division at Massachusetts General Hospital, Rochelle Walensky advocated for three feet when a local school district asked her advice. But after she became President Joe Biden's CDC director in 2021, she began saying that six feet was necessary, which was the agency's position. Or how about travel bans? Did they save lives, or were they pointless?

Masking was another example. In April 2020, the CDC, in reversing its original position that no one needed a mask, said that Americans should immediately start wearing masks, including cloth masks. Overnight, tens of millions of American began wearing them, and hundreds of entrepreneurs began churning them out, many pivoting from their normal business, which had been shut down. But as more was learned about the coronavirus, some experts began to realize that cloth masks didn't do much good. "We have known for many months that COVID-19 is airborne and therefore a simple cloth mask is not going to cut it," said Leana Wen, a public health professor at George Washington University. Finally—*finally*—in early 2022, nearly two years into the pandemic, the CDC acknowledged that "loosely woven cloth products offered the least protection" from the virus. That kind of grudging change didn't inspire confidence.

Perhaps most important, did lockdowns save lives, or merely delay the inevitable? The problem with "following the science" is that science, particularly in the early stages of discovery, is not an immutable thing. It rarely offers certainties. It offers theories and models and probabilities, which are then supposed to be tested against real-world evidence. But self-righteousness does not easily acknowledge uncertainty.

Politics also intruded. Some red state governors were ignoring all mitigation measures because that's what Trump favored. Some (including DeSantis) were even touting hydroxychloroquine, a malaria treatment that did nothing for COVID-19 patients but that Trump had extolled. In blue states, measures like lockdowns, school closings, and mandatory mask wearing took on a patina of virtue, giving people in those states a sense of moral superiority over the #FloridaMorons. Besides, for many liberals, if Trump was against something, they had to be for it. In New York, joggers were sometimes loudly chastised for failing to wear a mask while running alone in a park. In Texas, where the hard-line conservative Greg Abbott was governor, people were sometimes scorned for putting on a mask in a crowded Walmart.

Kulldorff and Bhattacharya were not the only outliers in the scientific community, but they were among the few who were willing to express their views openly. For most scientists who disagreed with the mainstream consensus, there wasn't much upside in speaking out. Dissident scientists sometimes had their tweets removed from Twitter and their videos taken down by YouTube. Early on, Kulldorff posted to LinkedIn a lengthy article criticizing the country's pandemic response—the first serious dissent by an important epidemiologist. Not only did the article disappear from LinkedIn, but so did Kulldorff: his profile was removed.[2]

And when their views were given air, their critics often went after them personally instead of their scientific views. Once, after Kulldorff had posted a tweet saying that measures to fight COVID-19 needed to be age specific, one respondent replied, "You still don't understand how epidemics work, do you?" Michael Osterholm, the prominent University of Minnesota scientist, described the theories espoused by Kulldorff and Bhattacharya as little more than "pixie dust and pseudo science." And on and on.

"What is surprising," said Kulldorff, "is that scientists resort to personal attacks with slander and so on. I think that's very damaging to science because that means that if I'm a scientist, I'm not going to dare to speak up. That's been very much the case here. A lot of scientists see

2 The article and profile were revived after a conservative media site criticized LinkedIn for deleting them.

what happens if you speak up against the accepted media narrative. So it's better to keep quiet," he concluded.

———

By the summer of 2020, DeSantis had lifted most of Florida's mitigation measures. Small businesses had reopened, as had gyms, movie theaters, bars, and restaurants, though the latter at 50 percent capacity. SeaWorld, the Universal Studios theme park, and Disney World were all open for business. (Cruise ships were still docked, but that was due to an order by the CDC.[3]) Nursing home residents were allowed to see a limited number of visitors. Arguing that the COVID-19 risk to children was low, and that education was too important to be halted, DeSantis mandated that the state's public schools reopen in August, when the Florida school year starts.

Although some of Florida's big-city mayors imposed local mask mandates, DeSantis refused to issue one statewide. "Your refusal to impose a mask order . . . is out-of-touch with the mainstream," wrote the *Sun Sentinel* of Orlando in a scathing editorial. In his regular public briefings, DeSantis would often encourage people to wear masks, but rarely wore one himself. He insisted that a state mandate would backfire because people would resist, police in many jurisdictions would refuse to enforce it, and in any case there were lots of counties with low COVID-19 numbers where masks were unnecessary.

No sooner had DeSantis eased restrictions than the state was awash in new cases. In May, the average number of new daily cases had been about six hundred; two months later, it was closer to ten thousand. The

———

3 In April 2021, DeSantis sued the CDC to get the cruise lines reopened.

infection rate reached a staggering 17 percent in July, meaning that out of every one hundred Floridians tested for COVID-19, seventeen were positive. In the big Florida cities like Miami, hospitals were overwhelmed. The reproduction rate—an important statistic that registers how many people are likely to get the virus from someone already infected—was 1.42. Until that number fell below 1, it meant that Florida's infected population would continue to rise. It was as if the coronavirus, having wintered in the north, decided to summer in Florida and other southern states.

Not surprisingly, DeSantis's many critics leaped on the new numbers as proof that his pandemic policies were killing Floridians. One critic wrote, "When you look at the states that are facing surges right now—Florida, Texas, Arizona, Mississippi, Nevada, and others—they follow the same pattern. They saw very little of the virus when the Northeast was getting crushed. They let their guard down—even bragged about their success. Then, when it turned out that the virus had simply taken its sweet time making its way south and west, it took them too long to awaken to the threat."[4]

The *Sun Sentinel* chimed in: "If coronavirus were a hurricane, it seemed to reach category 5 status over the weekend. More than ever, Florida needs decisive, resolute guidance to get through this storm. Instead, Ron DeSantis continues to muddle and spin his way through."

In response to the upsurge, a visibly peeved DeSantis closed down the bars again, essentially blaming the problem on young people who

---

4 Full disclosure: that critic was the coauthor Nocera, who wrote a series of columns about DeSantis's response to the pandemic for Bloomberg Opinion in 2020. As Nocera learned the hard way, criticizing or praising any state's approach based on a rapid upsurge or a decline in cases was a fool's errand—one that far too many journalists fell for.

had swarmed back into clubs and bars. "I mean, they're young people," he said at a press conference. "They're going to do what they are going to do."

As usual, DeSantis also punched back at his critics with ferocity. The most important statistic was not the number of COVID-19 cases, he insisted, but the number of deaths, and on this count Florida was still doing well: its 380,000 positive cases had yielded fewer than fifty-five hundred deaths. There were lots of theories about why this might be so—the weather, maybe, or the lack of density in many Florida cities. DeSantis's many critics attributed it to sheer dumb luck, while the governor said it was the result of his "tailored and measured approach that not only helped our numbers be way below what anybody predicted, but also did less damage to our state going forward." In truth, however, nobody really knew the answer; to this day, the reasons the virus took the paths it did, as well as the reasons it would crest in an enormous wave and then dissipate, remain a scientific mystery.

DeSantis also gave his critics ammunition in the way he informed the public about the pandemic. At one point, his office promised to post data on hospitalizations, which it had been holding back. But when reporters asked him a week later why it hadn't happened, he wouldn't give a straight answer. His health department ordered the Florida Medical Examiners Commission to stop releasing its comprehensive list of COVID-19 deaths. He would rattle off COVID-19 statistics but never acknowledge when they indicated that things were going south. When he ruled that the schools had to open, he offered no advice or aid that would help teachers and students feel safe. He was brusque and lacked empathy. And he often treated the media as if they were children who didn't understand the pandemic the way he did.

A few months earlier, a thirty-year-old Department of Health employee, Rebekah Jones, was fired for insubordination; she had refused orders, she alleged, to manipulate the state's COVID-19 data. Jones had helped build the state's COVID-19 online dashboard, and as she later told *Cosmopolitan* magazine, her superiors wanted her to do things like lie about positivity numbers. She says she became so stressed that she threw up. "Knowing how many people were going to get killed and that any model we did would undercount them and it not mattering to the people in charge," she said. After her firing, she put together her own COVID-19 dashboard—one that would contain the accurate numbers Florida was trying to hide, she claimed. At first DeSantis mocked her credentials and described her firing as a nonissue. When she began to get glowing press coverage, he became so furious that he resorted to some truly ugly tactics. He charged, for instance, that she was under "active criminal charges in the state of Florida" for cyberstalking and cyber sexual harassment. Jones filed a whistleblower complaint against the health department.

The media instinctively assumed that Jones was a legitimate whistleblower calling out a governor who hid the truth. Her allegation seemed to confirm the suspicion of blue state liberals and the press that Florida's COVID-19 numbers had been doctored to make DeSantis look better. Jones was sympathetically interviewed by Chris Cuomo on CNN, by Joy Reid on MSNBC, by Rachel Martin on NPR, and many others.

Then, toward the end of 2020, a team of heavily armed police raided her home and took her computer and phone. Someone had hacked the health department's email system to download confidential information and post an agency-wide message telling employees to "speak up before another 17,000 people are dead." The health department suspected Jones was the leaker. She denied it.

The raid generated a whole new round of publicity portraying Jones as a courageous truth teller being harassed by a vengeful governor. "They claimed it was about a security breach," she tweeted. "This was DeSantis. He sent the gestapo." By then, her initial allegation—that the Florida health department wanted her to manipulate data—was simply assumed to be true by DeSantis's critics. In 2021, she ran for Congress and described herself as the "scientist, whistleblower and mother who risked it all to fight corrupt government."[5]

Except that as time went on, her story started to crumble. After her dashboard went live, it became clear that the difference between her numbers and the state's was negligible. When a young Florida mathematician, after trying to collaborate with her, developed a thesis that the state was overstating—rather than understating—its COVID-19 cases, Jones responded by accusing him of sexually harassing her. (She backed off when the police got involved.) She was charged criminally for hacking the health department's computers—which caused prosecutors to yank a plea deal her lawyer had negotiated in the misdemeanor stalking case that DeSantis had referred to. Finally, in the spring of 2022, two years after her original allegations, the Florida health department's inspector general issued a lengthy report that found no evidence of wrongdoing by the department. For her part, Jones accepted a guilty plea on the hacking charge in December 2022. She was fined $20,000 and was granted a deferred prosecution.

Most Floridians didn't care that DeSantis was treated like a piñata by most of the mainstream media. They viewed his hands-off approach as a big success. During the fall, cases ranged from an average of two thousand a day in September to more than ten thousand a day by Christmas. Deaths sometimes reached two hundred a day, but mostly ranged in the mid-double digits. And it was difficult to know if Florida's big-city hospitals had run out of beds for COVID-19 patients; the federal

5 Jones lost to the MAGA congressman Matt Gaetz by a 2–1 margin.

government said they had, while DeSantis insisted that the hospitals were fine and were "showing great results."

Florida's numbers were higher than either New York or California, but Floridians had come to the conclusion that the risk was acceptable. They were willing to live with 60 or 80 or 150 deaths a day; the risk of dying of COVID-19 was small enough that they would go about their lives. And it wasn't just Floridians. Entrepreneurs and executives from New York, Silicon Valley, and elsewhere flocked to Miami. Jeff Zalaznick, the cofounder of the Major Food Group, a high-end New York restaurant company, went to Miami for vacation shortly before New York shut down. He never returned. The company had long planned to open a restaurant in Miami, but the pandemic accelerated those plans. "Being in Miami caused me to understand how much opportunity there was here, between the obvious demand for great food and great hospitality and the migration that was taking place," Zalaznick said. When asked whether Florida's openness during the pandemic also played a role, he laughed. "Of course," he said. "We opened Carbone on January 23." Carbone was the company's first Miami restaurant; its New York flagship had the same name. "On January 23 in New York, you couldn't eat inside a restaurant." He added, "We're really thinking about Miami and South Florida as our second home base and we're planning to build out a footprint similar to the one we have in New York City."

The Silicon Valley executives who gravitated to South Florida were often motivated by ideology. Keith Rabois, a well-known venture capitalist—and Peter Thiel business partner—moved from Silicon Valley to Miami and soon became a proselytizer for Florida. "Lots of people are moving from the Bay Area and escaping jail," he told one interviewer. "Lots of people are moving from New York and improving their lives." Florida, he added, "is capitalist"—in contrast to his former home, California. (He didn't mention the absence of a state income tax in Florida, though that surely played a role in the state's newfound popularity.)

Bill Carmody, the head of the New York office for the law firm Susman Godfrey, came to Miami in January. "I came down here to get access to the same people I had access to in New York," he said. "I love the energy down here, and the atmosphere—it's as if the pandemic never happened." In truth, the percentage increase in Florida's population wasn't terribly different from what it had been in previous years. But in Miami especially, it felt like an invasion of companies and executives and economic energy. Spotify opened an office. So did Elliott Management, a big New York hedge fund. THE FLOODGATES HAVE OPENED read a *Miami Herald* headline. And of those executive transplants, Democrats were almost as likely to praise DeSantis as Republicans. When the pandemic first struck, one such person said, he was convinced the governor's strategy was crazy. "Now it looks like he's the one who got it right."

DeSantis heard what people were saying, of course. His job approval fell when he announced that schools would open in August, but began rising when parents discovered their children were not coming home with COVID-19. His pandemic response had gained him a great deal of attention and millions of fans among conservatives. He began building a significant war chest, ostensibly for his 2022 reelection bid. But it was obvious that he now had his eye on 2024. COVID-19 had made Ron DeSantis a star, and maybe—just maybe—a potential presidential candidate.

———

June 2020 was the month when the #BlackLivesMatter protesters took to the streets. In blue states—and in blue cities within red states—

hundreds of thousands of people, men and women, Black and white, marched to demand an end to needless killings like that of George Floyd, who died when a Minneapolis police office pressed his knee hard on Floyd's neck for nine minutes. The wrenching video, showing Floyd's life slipping away, contrasted with the indifference of the police on the scene, sparked the protests, which went on for weeks and in several cities turned violent.

For scientists who considered themselves liberals, the protests put them in an awful bind. For months, the scientific establishment had been saying that large gatherings spread COVID-19. Yet *these* large gatherings were in support of something they believed was important: an end to police killing Black people, and more broadly an end to racism in America. Government scientists like Fauci tried to walk a fine line. "It's a delicate balance because the reasons for demonstrating are valid, but the demonstration puts one at additional risk," he said.

Yet some of the same scientists who had condemned religious or right-wing gatherings now said that these demonstrations were justified, no matter what the COVID consequences. "While everyone is concerned about the risk of Covid, there are risks with just being black in this country that almost outweigh that sometimes," Abby Hussein, an infectious disease fellow at the University of Washington, told CNN. More than a thousand public health experts signed an open letter making the case that, as *Politico* put it in a headline, "social justice matters more than social distance." Written by scientists from the University of Washington, it contrasted protests against racism with protests against lockdowns. It read in part,

> *As public health advocates, we do not condemn these gatherings as risky for COVID-19 transmission. We support them as vital to the national public health and to the threatened health specifically of*

Black people in the United States. . . . This should not be confused
with a permissive stance on all gatherings, particularly protests against
stay-home orders. Those actions not only oppose public health inter-
ventions, but are also rooted in white nationalism and run contrary
to respect for Black lives.

Conservatives, of course, reveled in pointing out the seeming hypocrisy: How could anyone say that a right-wing gathering was dangerous because of COVID-19 but a progressive demonstration was okay
despite COVID-19? This was "following the science"?

The #BlackLivesMatter protests also created problems for some blue
state governments, starting with California. The downtown areas of
several major California cities were looted during nightly protests. Some
of the more radical protesters defended the looting, saying that it was a
form of "reparations." But Governor Gavin Newsom, while expressing
solidarity with the protesters, wasn't willing to look the other way. After several nights of looting, he called up the National Guard to put a
stop to it.

Newsom's longer-term problem was that California's COVID-19
numbers were going up. The governor had instituted a process to gradually lift the COVID-19 restrictions; in announcing it, he used language
remarkably similar to DeSantis's. "We have to recognize you can't be
in a permanent state where people are locked away—for months and
months on end—to see lives and livelihoods completely destroyed, without considering the health impact of those decisions as well," he said.
That impact was considerable: five and a half million Californians had
applied for unemployment insurance, and while the big California tech
companies were thriving, thousands of small businesses had been forced
to shut down—nineteen thousand by September 2020, according to a
report compiled by Yelp.

Was it the #BlackLivesMatter protests that were bringing about all these new cases? Or the lifting of restrictions? Or was it another one of those pandemic mysteries? Many of Newsom's conservative critics pointed to the protests as the reason for the growing number of cases. But several studies, while not definitive, seemed to indicate that the protests were not super-spreaders, perhaps because they were outdoors. But if hospitals started to fill up again because California wasn't "bending the curve" any longer—for whatever reason—there wasn't much doubt how Newsom was likely to respond, no matter what he said about not locking people away for months at a time.

In early July, with cases creeping up again, he took the first step toward new restrictions, issuing guidelines for nineteen counties to close restaurants, movie theaters, and several other businesses—most of which had only reopened two weeks earlier. "We bent the curve in the state of California once, and we'll bend the curve again," Newsom said in a press release. "But we're going to have to be tougher and that's why we are taking this action today."

On July 13, Newsom closed bars, restaurants, zoos, and museums statewide. That same day, five of California's biggest counties closed gyms, churches, hair salons, malls, and offices with nonessential workers. Various state and county restrictions continued to be added for the rest of July.

At the end of August, Newsom unveiled a new color-coded system for evaluating how open—or closed—a county could be, depending on the prevalence of COVID-19. He called it the "Blueprint for a Safer Economy." "COVID-19 will be with us for a long time and we all need to adapt," he said. "We need to live differently. And we need to minimize exposure for our health, for our families and for our communities."

For the California public health officials who put together the color-coded plan, living differently meant being willing to close down businesses that had reopened—and do it again and again, if necessary—no matter what the cost to the owners of those businesses.

Over the next few months, counties loosened restrictions as their COVID-19 numbers dropped. In early September, Los Angeles County opened indoor salons and barbershops; shortly afterward, Santa Clara County allowed indoor religious services and movie theaters. Later that month, the state allowed all hair salons to open (though at 25 percent capacity) and reopened playgrounds. In October, the state said that up to three households could gather together outdoors, and established guidelines for reopening theme parks and stadiums. And it lifted the ban on nursing home visits in most of the state.

Then came November. On November 10, the City of San Francisco announced that the number of COVID-19 cases had risen by 250 percent. As a result, city officials said, restaurants would have to halt indoor dining. The Zoom class—and the press—found much to praise in the state's willingness to reimpose restrictions. It showed that California was putting people's health above mere economics—or so it was said. But restaurateurs were furious; they had only been open—at 25 percent capacity—for six weeks. They could still serve takeout, but that was scant solace. In a statement, the Golden Gate Restaurant Association pointed out the obvious. "With winter on the way, limited indoor dining represented the only real hope for many restaurants to survive the next three months," it said, because "the majority of restaurants simply cannot make it financially on takeout alone." Nevertheless:

November 14: San Diego County closes restaurants, gyms, churches, and movie theaters. Retailers must keep stores at 25 percent capacity.

November 16: Newsom orders all nonessential businesses to close or severely restrict their hours. He also issues a mandatory mask mandate.

November 19: California issues a 10:00 p.m. to 5:00 a.m. curfew. Newsom says the curfew will last a month.

November 27: With Los Angeles County averaging forty-five hundred cases, and twenty deaths a day, county officials impose a new lockdown. "We know we are asking a lot," says Dr. Barbara Ferrer, the director of the county's public health department. But, she adds, "acting with collective urgency right now is essential if we want to put a stop to this surge."

December 3: Newsom orders a "conditional" lockdown that will be triggered whenever a region's available intensive care beds drop below 15 percent.

December 9: The state decides to reopen playgrounds, despite the rise in COVID-19 cases, because parents are so angry.

December 20: Newsom says he is quarantining himself after being exposed to a staff member who tested positive.

December 24: On Christmas Eve, California becomes the first state to record more than two million COVID-19 cases. Its nearly twenty-four thousand deaths put it behind only New York.

Whatever else you could say about these numbers, they hardly inspired faith in the power of restrictions to reduce COVID-19 cases.

———

In early November, at the same time Newsom and California's public health officials were shutting down the state, the governor attended a luncheon to celebrate the birthday of a friend who was a political adviser and lobbyist. It was held at the French Laundry, one of the most exclusive restaurants in the country, where the celebrated chef Thomas Keller serves nine-course meals that start at $350 a head. There were twelve people at the lunch, and none of them wore a mask. And unbeknownst to the diners, someone was taking pictures.

A week later, news of the luncheon broke. In response, Newsom claimed that he and his wife, who had also attended, "had followed public health guidelines," which included eating outdoors. But it wasn't true. Four days later, a local Fox station got ahold of the photographs and spoke to the woman who had taken them. They clearly showed Newsom's party, maskless, sitting close together around a large table, indoors.

Newsom apologized—what else could he do?—calling it "a bad mistake" and acknowledging that in attending the luncheon he had ignored his own dictates and undercut his moral authority. California Republicans, of course, jumped on the obvious hypocrisy. But it wasn't just Republicans. People all across the political spectrum were furious. They saw it as the worst kind of do-as-I-say-not-as-I-do elitism. It also didn't help that Newsom's children were in a private school with in-person learning and that a winery the governor owned remained open while many businesses were shut.

California restaurateurs, irate over the repeated orders to close, began to stage small protests. One of the leaders of the protest movement was Angela Marsden, who owned the Pineapple Hill Saloon and Grill in Sherman Oaks, a Los Angeles suburb. She was forty-eight and had owned the popular eatery for ten years. She liked to compare her place to *Cheers*. "Everyone in the neighborhood and community comes here, all different ages, and plenty of regulars. There are people who have met here and gotten married," she said.

In July, after the county shut down the restaurants—but still allowed outdoor dining—Marsden persuaded her landlord to let her turn her parking lot into an outdoor patio so that she would still be able to serve food. The work cost her thousands of dollars, but it allowed her to hold on to her employees—and her customers—in September and October. In late November, with Thanksgiving approaching, she spent $10,000 on food, in the expectation that the holiday would be a big revenue day for the Pineapple Hill Saloon. But then the county struck again: two days before Thanksgiving, it banned outdoor dining. Marsden had to let go of her staff. "I remember calling my mom and saying, 'We're done. We're done.' It was devastating," Marsden said.

The day after Thanksgiving, Marsden, still bereft, found herself wandering around one of Sherman Oaks' two huge indoor malls. And that's where it hit her. "I'm in the mall on Black Friday and they are open, and my outdoor patio is closed," she said. "After I try on clothes, I put them back on the rack for someone else to try. But I have to throw my menus away if they get touched?" She left the mall and called her mother, who had suggested she come back to Indiana, where she had grown up, and decompress. She decided at that moment to stay in California. "I said if I'm going to go down, I'm going to go down fighting."

Marsden learned of a rally that would soon be taking place in front of Barbara Ferrer's home. She joined it. The protesters were composed almost entirely of small business owners and restaurateurs. There were police around Ferrer's house, and her neighbors had gathered on her porch. "They kept calling us losers," she recalled.

Marsden then decided to organize a second rally, this one made up solely of restaurant owners. On December 4, a Friday, she went to her restaurant, where she planned to give her employees their final paychecks and hand out whatever food was still on hand. She also planned to make some protest signs. But when she drove up to her restaurant, she saw, no more than fifty feet away, a long row of huge, white, open-air tents covering picnic-style tables. They had been put there by a movie crew. The movie-crew tables were much closer together than Pineapple Hill's socially distanced open-air tables. It was clear that the tables had been set up for the crew to eat their meals.

"I lost it," Marsden would later recall. One of her employees tried to calm her down. "It's going to be okay," he said. "No," she replied, "this is not okay, and it's never going to be okay." She handed her phone to a friend sitting at the bar and asked her to follow her outside. With the friend recording her, Marsden pointed to the huge movie-crew area and then her own, smaller outdoor patio. "I'm losing everything," she said to the camera. "They have not given us money and they have shut us down. We cannot survive. My staff cannot survive." She couldn't hold back her tears—or her anger. "Look at this," she said, pointing to her patio. "Tell me that this is dangerous, but right next to me, as a slap in my face"—she paused to collect herself as the video moved to the movie-crew tables—"*this* is safe. Fifty feet away. Mayor [Eric] Garcetti and Gavin Newsom are responsible for every single person . . . who does not have a job, and all the businesses that are going under. And we need your help." There was desperation in her voice. "We need somebody to do something about this." Still weeping, she walked away from the camera.

Marsden posted her video on Facebook. It instantly went viral. Journalists all over California flocked to Sherman Oaks to interview her. Other restaurateurs echoed her anger in interviews. She raised more than $100,000 in what had been a dormant GoFundMe campaign.

On the east side of Los Angeles, about half an hour from the Pineapple Hill Saloon and Grill, one man took special notice of Marsden's viral video. Mike Netter was a sixty-five-year-old retired salesman who loathed Newsom and had been trying to gin up a petition to recall him for practically the entire time the governor had been in office.

Maybe, he thought, the anger so many people were feeling about Newsom's pandemic rules—and the elites who both wrote the rules and felt free to ignore them—might cause more people to warm to the idea of a recall. Maybe he could rally small business people to the cause. Maybe a recall vote was finally within reach.

He picked up the phone and called Angela Marsden.

9

Cuomosexuals

By the summer of 2020, Governor Andrew Cuomo of New York was the most popular politician in his state, with a favorability rating of 77 percent. *Rolling Stone* and *Vanity Fair* put him on their covers. Some of his most ardent fans, including the talk show host and comedian Ellen DeGeneres, began describing themselves as "Cuomosexuals." Even as the mainstream media was savaging DeSantis's approach to the pandemic, it swooned over Cuomo's. HELP, I THINK I'M IN LOVE WITH ANDREW CUOMO??? read the headline of an article by the journalist Rebecca Fishbein. In *Vogue*, Molly Jong-Fast wrote an article titled "Why We Are Crushing on Andrew Cuomo Right Now." The *New York Times* editorial writer Mara Gay declared in a tweet, "This may prove to be the finest moment of Andrew Cuomo's public life."

What caused all this swooning was Cuomo's daily pandemic press briefings, which began in early March and ended in mid-June. Reporters attended them, seated (of course) six feet apart from one another. But they were not the primary audience. Seated at a raised table, Cuomo looked out over the heads of the journalists directly at the New York electorate, intent on showing them that he was leading them out of this awful crisis. He had slides, updated each day, to illustrate the progress the state was making against the virus—and the markers counties had to meet to have some restrictions eased. He had a slogan: "New York Tough." On most days, Howard Zucker, the head of the Department of Health, sat next to him, thus implicitly—and sometimes explicitly—conveying the message that New York was "following the science." Most of all, though, it was Cuomo's manner during those briefings that people were "crushing on"—the way he conveyed steadiness, empathy, and competence all at once, along with dollops of humor. Quite simply, he exuded leadership.

"Mr. Cuomo has emerged as the executive best suited for the coronavirus crisis, as President Trump flails and New York City Mayor Bill de Blasio wrestles haltingly with a crucial decision and then heads to the gym," wrote Ben Smith, then *The New York Times*'s media critic.

"As the pandemic rages, and my city is decimated and I watch the empty streets from my window," wrote Jong-Fast, "I'm comforted by Andrew Cuomo's 11:00 a.m. press conferences. . . . It's nice to know that someone is governing . . . and keeping the pressure on the federal government."

Millions of people saw Cuomo's daily briefings. Sometimes, Cuomo would end his workday by appearing on the CNN show hosted by his younger brother, Chris[1] —where their loving, antagonistic, brotherly

1 Chris Cuomo was fired by CNN in December 2021, after an investigation showed that he had been involved in helping his brother defend against sexual harassment allegations.

chitchat made the governor seem even more endearing. "All of it, from a distance, could make a degree of sense," wrote Ross Barkan, in his account of Cuomo's handling of the pandemic. "During natural or man-made disasters, executives often win praise for presenting a cool exterior and attempting to comfort the populace."

Except it was a lie.

Far from following the advice of New York's public health officials, some of whom had spent their careers preparing to deal with a deadly pandemic, Cuomo sneered at them. "When I say 'experts' in air quotes, it sounds like I'm saying I don't really trust the experts," Cuomo said. "Because I don't." When pushed by reporters about whether he was listening to any scientists at all, he would mention Michael Osterholm, the University of Minnesota expert. But when reporters asked Osterholm about his work with Cuomo, the scientist was taken aback: he'd spoken to the governor only once, he replied. Public health officials complained that they often found out about changes in the state's COVID-19 policies when Cuomo announced them during his briefings. By the fall of 2020, scientists were quitting in droves at the New York State Department of Health.

Cuomo persuaded the federal government to lend New York a naval hospital ship, the USNS *Comfort*, with a crew of twelve hundred and a thousand beds—and trumpeted its arrival. But because of onerous naval regulations, the ship never had more than a few dozen patients at a time, even as hospitals in New York City were overwhelmed. (The state had more success transforming the city's primary convention hall, the Jacob K. Javits Convention Center, into a temporary hospital for COVID-19 patients.) Cuomo's efforts to acquire PPE mostly ended in failure; when several nursing homes pleaded with the health department for more protective equipment, Cuomo responded that it wasn't the state's responsibility.

The praise for Cuomo's briefings also obscured two key failings. The first was his unconscionable delay in taking the pandemic seriously. His second big mistake—one he might have avoided had he been willing to listen to his own public health experts—was his disastrous decision to send infected nursing home patients who had been hospitalized back to their residence *even if they still tested positive.* This resulted in thousands of preventable deaths when the returning patients spread the virus to other residents. It would also turn out to be disastrous to Cuomo's political career.

———

At the end of June, with the number of cases—and deaths—in New York finally declining, Cuomo declared victory. ("We got smart. New Yorkers stepped up. We wore masks.") He said the time had come to end the daily briefings. But that didn't mean the Cuomosexuals were ready to move on. Many Democrats were openly urging him to run for the presidency, believing he would be a more dynamic candidate than Joe Biden. And in July, Penguin Random House, the giant publisher,[2] offered Cuomo $5.2 million to write a book about his pandemic leadership. It was a staggering amount of money for a politician who had never been president.

The book, titled *American Crisis: Leadership Lessons from the COVID-19 Pandemic,* was published in October. In the preceding months, Republicans in the state legislature—along with the relatives of many of the nursing home residents who had died—had turned up the heat on the question of nursing home deaths in New York. In June, the health department prepared a report that put the number of nursing home

2 Portfolio, the publisher of this book, is an imprint of Penguin Random House.

deaths at 9,250—by far the highest of any state. Cuomo administration officials not only took that number out but pushed the writers of the report to say that nursing home staffers—rather than Cuomo's policy—were responsible for spreading the virus.

Two months later, the health commissioner, Howard Zucker, testified before the New York Senate health committee. In addition to the issue of sending COVID-19-positive residents back to their nursing homes, there was a second question that related to Cuomo's handling of nursing home numbers. Early on, the Cuomo administration had quietly changed the way nursing home deaths were counted in New York. If someone died in a nursing home, that would count as a nursing home death. But if an infected nursing home resident died while in the hospital, that person's death would not be included in the nursing home count. No other state did it this way. This certainly seemed to be another way Cuomo and his top aides were trying to suppress the true number of nursing home deaths.

At the hearing, according to Ross Barkan, who covered it for *The Nation*, Zucker couldn't answer a simple question: "Why does New York have such a strange way of counting nursing home deaths from Covid-19?"

"It seems, sir, that you are trying to do it one way so you can look better," said Gustavo Rivera, the committee chairman.

The Democratic senator James Skoufis was incredulous that Zucker wouldn't even attempt to estimate a number. "You don't have a ballpark you can give?" he asked. "So the total official number is 6,500. So is the total deaths, with hospitals included, 8,000, 10,000, 15,000?"

"I am not prepared to give you a specific number," Zucker responded.

Needless to say, Cuomo's book doesn't spend much time on the nursing home controversy. He portrayed it as a Republican plot aimed at blaming Democratic governors—starting with him—for nursing home deaths. "It was an orchestrated strategy and a Fox News drumbeat," he wrote. According to Cuomo, he had ordered hospitalized COVID-19 patients back to their nursing homes because that's what the federal government told him to do. The Centers for Medicare and Medicaid Services, he said, called for nursing homes not to reject patients solely based on their COVID-19 status. There wasn't a single other state that read this particular recommendation the way New York did. It was the flimsiest of excuses.

It would be another six months before the truth came out—that the actual number of nursing home deaths was twice what New York State was reporting and that the Cuomo administration had buried the true numbers, fearing they would tarnish the governor's story of triumph, and his $5.2 million book. The truth was uncovered by Letitia James, the New York attorney general, and a former ally of Cuomo's, who in late January 2021 issued a report showing that nursing home deaths had been undercounted by as much as 50 percent. In other words, the number of nursing home residents who had died of COVID-19 in New York was closer to twelve thousand than the sixty-five hundred the state reported.

Months earlier, as Cuomo was ending his briefings, Jesse McKinley, the then Albany bureau chief for *The New York Times*, wrote a story that asked a prescient question: "Can a state with more than 30,000 deaths claim success?" The answer was starting to become clear.

———

By the time Mike Netter began his latest recall petition drive against Governor Gavin Newsom of California in June 2020, he had already been involved in several previous attempts. To get a recall petition on the ballot, the organizers need the signatures of 12 percent of the voters in the previous gubernatorial election. That amounted to around one and a half million signatures. Two quixotic earlier efforts, with Newsom's approval rating around 70 percent, didn't get very far. Republican politicos viewed the recall drives as the work of right-wing crackpots. The press, which largely applauded Newsom's lockdowns and business closures, barely noticed them.

This latest recall effort, however, was different. In the early days of the pandemic, most Californians had locked down without complaint. Over the summer, as the number of cases dropped, most restrictions were lifted. When California reimposed them in November, many people in the state were no longer so willing to go along. They were angry, and there were nearly as many angry Democrats as there were angry Republicans. When news of Newsom's French Laundry luncheon broke in November, well, that was the final twist of the knife.

As the recall gained momentum that fall, Newsom's defenders began claiming it was a dirty trick being played by the Republicans. A political strategist for the governor told *The New York Times* that "state and national GOP partisans" were behind the recall because they hoped to create "an expensive, distracting and destructive circus." Democrats also pointed out that far-right fringe groups like the Proud Boys and QAnon believers were involved.

But both the extremists and the Republican Party regulars were really just grabbing onto the coattails of furious small business people. According to Yelp data, by the fall of 2020, the number of closed California businesses had more than doubled from the early summer, from nineteen thousand to forty thousand. Half of those closures were permanent. No other state came close to those numbers. And it was the owners of those businesses, their anger stoked by the lack of help—and empathy—from the state, who were most responsible for turning the

recall into a cause. It was yet another example of elites failing to understand the effect their edicts had on the larger population.

Netter didn't consider himself a MAGA conservative. He liked to
say that what he fought against was dictatorial power, which is what he
believed the Democrats wielded in California. "If the Republicans
had a supermajority, I'd probably be fighting against the Republicans,"
he said.

Newsom represented everything he loathed about California's Democratic establishment. Newsom had wealth; he had connections (he
was close to the Gettys); he exuded arrogance; and he had unrepentant
liberal views, which he had no qualms about imposing on everybody
else. He even looked the part of a coastal elite, with his slicked-back
hair, expensive suits, and trim athletic build. Less than two months
after he'd been sworn in as governor, he placed a moratorium on the
death penalty, "overruling the will of the people," as the recall petition
put it. His critics charged that he signed a bill that let shoplifters off
if they stole less than $950 worth of merchandise. (Actually, the law,
which was passed in 2021, downgrades small-time shoplifting to a misdemeanor that can still result in six months in prison.) "It just seemed
like nothing in California was getting better," said Netter in an anti-
Newsom documentary he helped produce. In Netter's opinion, all Newsom had done in his three years in office was make everything worse.

Orrin Heatlie, Netter's partrner in the recall effort, and Randy
Economy, a consultant they hired, believed that as well. Heatlie, a former sheriff's sergeant in his early fifties, met Netter during an earlier
recall effort. He first decided to attempt a recall after watching a video
of the governor telling undocumented immigrants not to talk to the
border patrol if the officers didn't have a warrant. Heatlie was profoundly
anti-immigrant. He once wrote a Facebook post suggesting that "illegal aliens" should be implanted with microchips. ("It Works" read the

headline. "Just Ask Animal Control.") After *Politico* asked him about the post, Heatlie said, "It was an inflammatory statement and I regret saying it."

Economy was the only one of the three who could be called a Republican politico—he'd worked on campaigns over the years—but he also enjoyed being a provocateur. A grassroots petition drive, organized by a bunch of nobodies, was right in his wheelhouse. Economy was the one who had the French Laundry episode and had leaked the story to Fox News.

Netter and Economy both point out that the recall petition never mentioned any of Newsom's pandemic mandates. It was focused instead on long-standing complaints conservatives had about life in California. What the pandemic did, they would later say, was wake up hundreds of thousands of their fellow citizens—many of whom had never been especially political—to Newsom's "I know what's best" approach.

But no matter what the petition said, it was California's pandemic policies—and the way they seemed almost intentionally designed to hurt small businesses—that were causing people to add their signatures. For example, Andrew Gruel, the owner of Slapfish Restaurant Group, complained to *The New York Times* that while his restaurants were forced to close during the lockdown, a Walmart just up the road from his Huntington Beach place had a Burger King that remained open. "It's like WWE[3] in there," he said. "People cross-blocking each other for a BK Delight." When Los Angeles locked down for a second time, Gruel defiantly kept his restaurants open. By then, he had lost $100,000 and was in more debt than he was comfortable with to stay in business. He became a volunteer in the recall drive.

---

3 That's World Wrestling Entertainment, in case you were wondering.

April Gallegos, who owned a small Mexican restaurant in Whittier, California, had kept her place alive through two closings by shifting to low-priced take-out platters designed to help families. "My big concern was how people who were out of work were going to eat," she said. She had been able to stay in business because California had put in a rule that landlords could not evict small businesses even if they stopped paying the rent. When that rule was lifted, Gallegos's landlord demanded all the back rent immediately, which she couldn't afford. She went out of business at the end of September 2020. She got involved in the recall drive.

In the San Francisco Bay Area, Marguerite Pavsidis ran two businesses, a specialty merchandise company that sold items to big hotels, and several stores in the San Francisco airport. When lockdowns closed the hotels, her first business was wiped out. And with few people flying, her airport stores suffered too. She was also a landlord of a small building. But of course the rent moratorium meant that it didn't generate any income either. Her revenue dropped between 80 and 85 percent, she said.

A former Democrat, she had become highly critical of the way Newsom was handling the pandemic. "I resent the fact that we have such corrupt leadership in this state," she said. "And that one person rules on everything. We are seeing the destruction of California." She became a volunteer in the recall drive.

The on-again, off-again nature of the mandates was another grievance small business owners had. To them, it seemed heartless. Belinda and Joe Lyons, who owned two bars in the San Fernando Valley, had used their retirement money to survive the first California lockdown. "When we were told we could open last June by Gavin Newson, I put full insurance back with the intention of reopening, only to be told that we could not," Belinda told *The New York Times*. "That cost me over $8,000 that I'm still paying, as the insurance company would not cancel." The Lyonses joined the recall drive.

And of course there was Angela Marsden, the restaurant owner whose wrenching video—the one that showed her crying as she pointed to the movie crew's outdoor lunch area next door—had gone viral. "Angela's video was a pivotal moment for us," said Economy, "and we worked hard to get her story out there. She was expressing the pure emotion that everybody was feeling, and she was smart to pull out her phone and make a statement with tears coming down her cheeks." Marsden became the public face of the small business community. She made speeches and gave interviews. She helped lead protests. When a congressional candidate, Joe Collins,[4] went on a fifteen-city road trip to promote the recall and gather signatures, she was one of the featured speakers. "The accidental spokeswoman for her pandemic-ravaged industry," *The Washington Post* called her. Dan Crenshaw, a conservative congressman from Texas, said "she represents millions of Americans suffering."

Netter, Heatlie, and Economy decided that these angry small business people could do more than just sign the petition; they could also help gather signatures. They found some twelve hundred business owners who agreed to put the recall petition in their stores and encourage customers to sign it. Even some churches handed out the petition. Early on, Newsom had ordered churches to close, and though the courts had reversed his edict, state guidelines still ordered them to end "singing and chanting activities," which of course infuriated many conservative churchgoers. Netter later said that the small businesses collected some 300,000 signatures.

---

4 He lost badly to Maxine Waters, 72 percent to 28 percent.

The recall leaders used Facebook and other social media platforms to organize volunteers to go door-to-door; according to Netter, they had between sixty thousand and seventy thousand volunteers. They sent out blast emails that stressed the idea that here was an action they could take that could change how California was handling the pandemic. By April 2021, when they submitted the petition signatures to the secretary of state, they turned in more than 2.1 million. Of that number, 1.7 million were deemed valid, more than enough to meet the threshold. The recall vote was set for September 14, 2021.

Still, the signatures notwithstanding, Newsom remained favored to retain his office. In this bluest of blue states, there were millions of Californians who strongly believed that lockdowns, mask mandates, school closings, and other non-pharmaceutical interventions were saving lives. The titans of Silicon Valley, who had seen their wealth grow substantially thanks to the run-up in stock prices, lined up behind Newsom. Netflix's CEO, Reed Hastings, donated $3 million to Newsom's "Stop the Recall" committee. (The most prominent tech billionaire to back the recall drive was Chamath Palihapitiya, an outspoken libertarian who had worked at Facebook before becoming a venture capitalist. He briefly toyed with running for governor himself.)

There were two things that especially helped Newsom. The first was that by the spring of 2021, the number of COVID-19 cases was dropping fast, so much so that in mid-June the state ended its indoor mask mandate (though only for people who had been vaccinated), and finally allowed restaurants to open at 100 percent capacity. The end of the mandates took a good deal of steam out of the recall movement. And Newsom doubled down by insisting that his "health first focus" would allow the state to "come roaring back."

The second thing that helped was that the leading contender to replace Newsom was a longtime Black conservative talk show host named

Larry Elder. Under California's rules, if a governor was recalled, he would have to immediately cede his office to the top vote getter among those running to replace him. (Their campaigns run parallel to the recall drive.) In 2003, for instance, when California's governor, Gray Davis, was recalled,[5] Arnold Schwarzenegger became the new governor, having accumulated 48.6 percent of the vote. Elder was late in getting into the race, but once he was in, he was the front-runner.[6]

Most Californians knew who Elder was. He had his first talk show on a local Los Angeles station in 1993, and he had been on the air in some iteration or other ever since. He had written books, done podcasts, and from time to time said things that generated controversy. One example came in 2000, when his book *The Ten Things You Can't Say in America* was published; the first among those ten things was that "blacks are more racist than whites." He wanted to abolish the Internal Revenue Service, eliminate corporate taxes, and reduce government by 80 percent. He described climate change as "a crock."

All of which meant that he was exactly the kind of Trump-supporting, right-wing front-runner the Democrats needed—"the absolutely perfect foil for Newsom's strategy of frightening supporters to the polls," Dan Schnur, a former spokesman for California's governor Pete Wilson, told Bloomberg News. "Imagine waking up on the morning of September 15th to find out Gavin Newsom has been recalled and Larry Elder will be the next governor of California" read one fundraising appeal. "It is terrifying to consider." Newsom's mantra in fighting the recall was that Elder wasn't just another Trump; he was *worse* than Trump. The specter of Elder allowed Newsom to avoid talking about

---

5 Davis was the only governor ever recalled in California history.
6 In all, there were forty-six candidates, including Caitlyn Jenner.

California's pandemic efforts, which is what most of the recall supporters cared about.

Two weeks before the vote, Bloomberg News cited a CBS/YouGov poll showing that 82 percent of conservative voters were "very motivated" to vote, compared with 64 percent of liberal voters. But of course, California had many more liberal voters than conservatives. During the last few weeks of the campaign, as more of Elder's views were aired— he wanted judges who were explicitly pro-life, and he said the ideal minimum wage should be zero—a tight race began to widen. By September 14, the day of the vote, it had become a blowout: two-thirds of the voters rejected the recall petition.

In his victory speech, Newsom gave no quarter. The vote meant that Californians had said "yes to science," he said. "We said yes to vaccines. We said yes to ending this pandemic." There was no acknowledgment that the state's on-again, off-again pandemic measures were causing a great deal of economic harm to California's small business community. He seemed not to care that many people had been hurt by state and local pandemic mandates. Simply acknowledging that people were suffering would have made a difference. But Newsom never did.

On the contrary: Newsom ordered that by the end of September all California health-care workers had to be vaccinated or face the prospect of being fired. California was the first state in the nation to institute such a mandate. Following the governor's lead, Los Angeles County gave local government employees a week to get vaccinated, while employees of the school district had three weeks to get their jabs. And indoor mask and vaccine mandates—including for schoolchildren— remained in force. California officials would later insist that their tough measures saved lives. But evidence would soon emerge to cast doubt on the efficacy of such mandates.

10

The Dissidents

Jay Bhattacharya had long been an admirer of D. A. Henderson's and of a book the great epidemiologist wrote in 2009 about the eradication of smallpox. The book, he said, was "a master class" in an extremely important—and too often overlooked—part of public health: "convincing a population to cooperate so that they actually want to participate in the mitigation effort." It was equally important, he believed, that "when you design a program you have to understand how people are going to react to it. There are going to be knock-on effects or consequences that you may not necessarily know about or think about that can undermine the effectiveness of the program or cause unexpected problems."

Although these were hardly new concepts, the federal government had done neither during the pandemic. Instead, it had given conflicting advice or made recommendations that were simply illogical. When you had to wear a mask into a restaurant but could take it off while eating—how in the world did that keep COVID-19 at bay? And it had imposed the most drastic non-pharmaceutical interventions, such as closing businesses and schools and ordering lockdowns, from above, regardless of the severity of the pandemic in particular regions and without proper explanations or attempts to rally widespread support. Throw in the fact that when a Walmart or a Home Depot managed to be labeled "essential" while mom-and-pop hardware stores were forced to close, who could possibly be surprised that there was so much resentment toward lockdowns in all those red states that were already suspicious of government? Without apps like Zoom and Uber Eats, Bhattacharya believed, there would never have been lockdowns, because the "lockdown class" would never have put up with them. Where the public health experts had failed most of all was what Henderson had always understood: they couldn't control human behavior.

As a point of comparison, Bhattacharya liked to use the example of Sweden. Sweden was controversial because it eschewed lockdowns and kept its society running. But when vaccines became available, "Sweden got 97 percent of adults to take the vaccine without any mandates," Bhattacharya said. "Why? Because people trusted the government. And the reason they trusted the government was that officials were honest with what they knew and what they didn't know. And they didn't force people to do things that were outside their capacity to manage."

By contrast, he recalled an article he had seen in the San Jose *Mercury News* during the early months of the pandemic. There was a photograph of two children, seven or eight years old. "Their parents had dropped them outside a Taco Bell with what looked like Google Chromebooks," he said. "They were sitting on the sidewalk doing schoolwork because that was the only place they could get free Wi-Fi. Their parents weren't there, because they had to go to work. I mean, that should have ended the lockdown right then and there. It should have at least ended school closures."

Bhattacharya got his first taste of the blowback reserved for scientists who strayed from the establishment position early. He coauthored an article for *The Wall Street Journal* questioning the validity of the scary 2 to 4 percent fatality rate that the early models like Neil Ferguson's were estimating—and that were causing governments to panic. He believed (correctly, as it turns out) that the true fatality rate was much lower,[1] and that the United States should conduct widespread antibody testing to get a more accurate count of infected Americans and come up with a more accurate fatality rate, which would then help the country devise sound mitigation strategies. The penultimate sentence of his article read, "A universal quarantine may not be worth the costs it imposes on the economy, community and individual mental and physical health."

"All hell broke loose," Bhattacharya recalled. "It was amazing. We weren't saying it wasn't a deadly disease. We were just saying we don't know how widespread it is. Some of my colleagues at Stanford wrote me letters basically disowning me. Other people unfriended me on Facebook. It really got nasty," he said.

Inevitably, Bhattacharya and Martin Kulldorff, the Harvard epidemiologist who also dissented from the party line, became close colleagues. They met for the first time in the White House, when they were brought in—much to the concern of Fauci and Deborah Birx, who didn't want their outsider views to be legitimized—to explain their views to some of Trump's aides. They connected again in late September,

---

1 As of August 2021, the fatality rate for the United States was 1.1 percent, according to Johns Hopkins. Even that number is likely overstated, because it fails to count infected people who were asymptomatic and were never tested.

when DeSantis held a virtual roundtable, asking the two of them, along with another Stanford scientist, the Nobel laureate Michael Levitt, a series of scientific questions designed to reinforce his no-lockdown policy for Florida. ("What can we say about the efficacy of these lockdowns?" asked DeSantis in a typical question. "I notice Peru had one of the most severe lockdowns, and I think they're number one in the world for per-capita mortality.")

And they met a third time in Great Barrington, a city of fewer than eight thousand people in the bucolic Berkshire Mountains of western Massachusetts. A resort town, Great Barrington is also home to a small think tank, the American Institute for Economic Research. Its purpose, it says on its website, is to support "the fundamental values of personal freedom, free markets, private property, sound money and private governance."

Not surprisingly, AIER's writers and economists opposed lockdowns from the start. "A sadistic social experiment in the name of virus mitigation," wrote Jeffrey Tucker, the group's editorial director, in one of his many jeremiads. An AIER researcher was the first to unearth—and link to—D. A. Henderson's 2006 paper. And AIER openly mocked the idea that a high school science project was the basis for the belief that lockdowns would stop a pathogen from spreading.

Their anti-lockdown position only grew more strident as the evidence began to pile up that lockdowns not only created economic and social havoc but also didn't save many lives. Could they delay a virus from sweeping through a community and overwhelming the hospitals? No doubt—that's what "bending the curve" had always meant. But they couldn't make the virus disappear. "Full lockdowns and wide-spread COVID-19 testing were not associated with reductions in the number of critical cases or overall mortality," concluded a study published in *The Lancet*, a prestigious British medical journal, in August 2020. An

October 2020 study conducted by scientists from the University of Edinburgh concluded, "Prompt interventions were shown to be highly effective at reducing peak demand for intensive care unit (ICU) beds but also prolonged the epidemic, in some cases resulting in more deaths long term." In March 2021, Christian Bjørnskov, an economist at Aarhus University in Denmark, compared weekly mortality rates in twenty-four European countries that had varying degrees of non-pharmaceutical interventions. "The findings in this paper suggest that more severe lockdown policies have not been associated with lower mortality," the economist wrote. "In other words," he added, "the lockdowns have not worked as intended." There were ultimately more than fifty studies reaching the same conclusion.

Were there countries where lockdowns seemed to make a difference? Yes. Lockdown proponents could point to the island nations of Australia and New Zealand as examples of strictly enforced lockdowns—much tougher than anything in the West—and low numbers of COVID-19 cases. On the other hand, you could also cite countries like South Korea and Sweden, which never accepted the lockdown thesis yet whose COVID-19 cases weren't all that different from countries that embraced lockdowns.

Kulldorff lived in Connecticut, just a few hours from Great Barrington. Sometime that summer, he and AIER connected; the think tank was happy to publish his work, which most mainstream outlets viewed as disinformation. His first article for AIER, published in April, laid out his view about how to minimize COVID-19 deaths. "Among the individuals exposed to Covid-19," he wrote, "people aged in their 70s have roughly twice the mortality of those in their 60s, 10 times the mortality of those in their 50s, 40 times that of those in their 40s, 100 times that of those in their 30s, and 300 times that of those in their 20s." Kulldorff continued:

Considering these numbers, people above 60 must be better pro-
tected, while restrictions should be loosened on those below 50. Older
people who are vulnerable should stay at home. . . . Younger people
should go back to work and school without older coworkers and
teachers at their sides.

He called this policy "focused protection."

In early October, AIER held a small, impromptu conference to discuss pandemic strategies. The think tank asked Kulldorff, Bhattacharya,
and a third anti-lockdown epidemiologist, Sunetra Gupta from Oxford
University, to come to Great Barrington and speak to a group composed
of AIER economists and a few freelance journalists. Over the course of
a weekend, they discussed various COVID-19 mitigation strategies, with
each of them reaffirming their view that the best way to deal with the
coronavirus—at least until a vaccine came along—was to protect the
elderly and let those at less risk go about their lives, minimizing the economic and social disruptions. Focused protection, in other words.

On the Sunday morning the conference ended, "the idea came up
that we ought to do a statement of principles to summarize everything
that had been discussed over the weekend," recalls Phil Magness, a senior research fellow at AIER. "It was basically an afterthought." The
three scientists sat around a laptop and banged out a short, one-page
statement. When they had finished, they signed it with a flourish and
sipped champagne as onlookers cheered. An AIER tech staffer threw
together a web page, posted a few photographs from the conference,
and invited readers to add their signatures to the document, which by
then had a name: the Great Barrington Declaration.[2]

2 Bhattacharya: "I came up with the name because on the way in, I asked the driver,
'What's the name of this town again?'"

In many ways, it was a reiteration of Kulldorff's earlier article. "Current lockdown policies are producing devastating effects on short and long-term public health," the three scientists wrote. They continued:

> *The results (to name a few) include lower childhood vaccination rates, worsening cardiovascular disease outcomes, fewer cancer screenings and deteriorating mental health—leading to greater excess mortality in years to come, with the working class and younger members of society carrying the heaviest burden. Keeping students out of school is a grave injustice. Keeping these measures in place until a vaccine is available will cause irreparable damage, with the underprivileged disproportionately harmed.*

"Our goal," they continued, "should be to minimize mortality and social harm until we reach herd immunity"—that is, immunity that would come about either because most of the population had been infected and now had antibodies or because a vaccine had been introduced. "By way of example," they wrote,

> *nursing homes should use staff with acquired immunity and perform frequent testing of other staff and all visitors. Staff rotation should be minimized. Retired people living at home should have groceries and other essentials delivered to their home. When possible, they should meet family members outside rather than inside. A comprehensive and detailed list of measures, including approaches to multi-generational households . . . is well within the scope and capability of public health professionals.*

As for younger, less vulnerable people, the Great Barrington Declaration called for the immediate resumption of normal life:

Schools and universities should be open for in-person teaching. Extracurricular activities, such as sports, should be resumed. Young low-risk adults should work normally, rather than from home. Restaurants and other businesses should open. Arts, music, sport and other cultural activities should resume. People who are more at risk may participate if they wish, while society as a whole enjoys the protection conferred upon the vulnerable by those who have built up herd immunity.

To the amazement of all involved, the declaration went viral. Within a few days, close to 200,000 people had signed it. Some were fake signatures, but most were not, and many of the signatories were scientists. (By mid-2022, the number of signatures was well over 900,000.) "There was enormous support for it," says Kulldorff. "People would translate it on their own and then send us the translation." AIER would then post the translation to the website. "It's now in forty-four languages."

Still, supporters of the Great Barrington Declaration were largely drowned out by its critics, who argued that counting on herd immunity to stop the spread was unethical. Besides, was it really possible to protect the elderly and the immunocompromised, who make up some 30 percent of the population?

Kulldorff scoffed at these objections. "The claim that it is not possible to protect older vulnerable people is nonsense," he said. "That's basic public health. If they don't know how to do it they should listen to those of us who do." Properly staffed nursing homes, for instance, would have staff living for extended periods with the residents so that they didn't bring the virus in when they came to work. When other nurses arrived to take a shift (which could last several weeks), they had to test negative before they could enter. Younger people with immunity problems would be allowed to work from home, or take paid leave if they didn't have a desk job. The kind of focused protection the Great Barrington Declaration envisioned required money and dedication, but it was far from impossible.

Yet in *The Lancet*, eighty researchers wrote an open letter calling the declaration's strategy "a dangerous fallacy unsupported by scientific evidence." Trying to isolate such a large percentage of the population, they added, was "practically impossible and highly unethical." (The title of their letter was "Scientific Consensus on the COVID-19 Pandemic.") Thomas File and Judith Feinberg,[3] the heads of two important medical associations, issued a statement describing the herd immunity approach as "inappropriate, irresponsible and ill-informed." *The New York Times*, *The Washington Post*, and many other outlets published articles criticizing the declaration. Facebook removed most mentions of it. A Yale professor, Gregg Gonsalves, tweeted, "This f*****g Great Barrington Declaration is like a bad rash that won't go away."

Inside HHS, the response to the Great Barrington Declaration was, if anything, even more heated. In a series of emails,[4] Fauci and the National Institutes of Health director, Francis Collins, sought ways to discredit the declaration and its authors.

"This proposal from the three fringe epidemiologists . . . seems to be getting a lot of attention—even a co-signature from Nobel Prize winner Mike Leavitt [*sic*]," wrote Collins four days after the declaration was posted. "There needs to be a quick and devastating published take down of its premises." He gave an interview with *The Washington Post* in which he said of the Great Barrington Declaration, "This is not mainstream science. It's dangerous."

3 File is the president of the Infectious Diseases Society of America. Feinberg is chair of the HIV Medicine Association.
4 The emails were unearthed by AIER, which obtained them under the Freedom of Information Act.

As for Fauci, he even compared the three authors to the scientists in the 1980s who denied that HIV caused AIDS. Even with the passage of time, as the issue became less heated, Fauci never backed away from his view that the authors of the Great Barrington Declaration were spreading disinformation.

———

A few days after the declaration was issued, however, its premise gained support from someone who unquestionably represented mainstream science. David Nabarro, the World Health Organization's special envoy on COVID-19, was interviewed by Andrew Neil, the chairman of the *Spectator* magazine in London.

The WHO had implicitly supported lockdowns as a worthwhile mitigation tool. Now, he made clear, the WHO had had a change of heart.

"We in the World Health Organization do not advocate lockdowns as a primary means of control of this virus," he said emphatically. The only time lockdowns are justified, he added, is when hospitals are being overwhelmed and need to buy some time. Mostly, they did far more damage than good. Thanks to lockdowns, "we may have a doubling of poverty," he said.

"Remember," Nabarro added, "lockdowns just have one consequence that you must never, ever belittle, and that is making poor people an awful lot poorer."

———

Of all the consequences of lockdowns, the most damaging, surely, was the closure of public schools in big cities all across the country.

When the pandemic first hit, schools of every kind, from elementary schools to universities, from large public schools to small private ones, shut their doors and switched to remote learning, which wasn't easy, because few teachers had ever taught remotely on such a scale and few school systems had the technology in place. Given how little was known about the coronavirus, it only made sense to close schools temporarily. Children were highly vulnerable to the influenza virus; maybe the same would be true of this virus. Indeed, there were those who believed that remote learning would be *better* than classroom learning. "Research suggests that online learning has been shown to increase retention, and take less time, meaning the changes coronavirus have caused might be here to stay," wrote the authors of an April 2020 paper for the World Economic Forum—that is, the business elite's annual shindig in Davos—thus showing zero understanding of what home life was like for most people.

By the time school started up again in the fall, most of the children of the privileged were back in the classrooms of their private schools. During the summer months, many private schools had built new ventilation systems, installed plastic barriers on desks, and revised schedules so that no grade would come into contact with any other grade. (That limited the spread should someone in a class become infected.) They also consulted with public health experts to come up with protocols for mask wearing, testing, recess, lunch, and the inevitability of positive cases. In the big cities, the public schools, with their limited resources, did none of these things. Instead, public school systems stuck with remote learning, which they would continue to do, with some notable exceptions like Florida and Rhode Island, for most of the 2020–21 school year. (Rhode Island was the rare blue state that pushed to keep schools open.)

This was so even though it had become obvious in the interim that remote learning was a disaster. One of the first groups to call for children to return to the classroom was the American Academy of Pediatrics. "Lengthy time away from school," it wrote in a position paper,

> *often results in social isolation, making it difficult for schools to identify and address important learning deficits as well as child and adolescent physical or sexual abuse, substance use, depression, and suicidal ideation. . . . Beyond the educational impact and social impact of school closures, there has been substantial impact on food security and physical activity for children and families.*

Around the same time, Jennifer Nuzzo, a highly regarded epidemiologist who was then at Johns Hopkins, and one of Henderson's coauthors in that now-famous 2006 paper, began advocating for schools to be opened. In the early phase of the pandemic, Nuzzo had favored lockdowns to keep hospitals from being overwhelmed. But she was rare among establishment experts for consistently calling on public health officials to weigh the benefits of interventions like lockdowns against the potential harms. A Johns Hopkins study she oversaw in the fall of 2019, months before the pandemic began, included this recommendation: "Nonpharmaceutical interventions (NPIs) have a greater likelihood of being implemented effectively if well analyzed ahead of time than if considered ad hoc during a crisis. Countries and international organizations need to . . . determine in which contexts, if any, a particular NPI would be effective; and conclude in which contexts they are likely to do more harm than good." That, of course, never happened.

Nuzzo took to the op-ed page of *The New York Times* to make the case for reopening schools. She and a coauthor, the pediatrician Joshua M. Sharfstein, pointed out how absurd it was that states were reopening restaurants and bars but keeping schools shut. Research, they wrote, was already showing that "the sudden switch to online learning was costing some students a full year of academic progress." This was especially true of disadvantaged students who lacked computers or reliable internet access. "The disruption of learning can have lifetime effects on students' income and health," they concluded.

In *The New Yorker*,[5] the journalist Alec MacGillis vividly described what was happening on the ground, with a powerful—and tragic—portrait of Baltimore's school system. With no classrooms to go to, thousands of students simply abandoned school. "I don't care if I fail," one student told his teacher. "I'm fourteen, in seventh grade—I don't think they're going to fail me again." The school system made free laptops available, but few students took the trouble to get one. Teachers gave up trying to prod those who didn't log on to their remote classes; all that did was annoy the parents. Even the students who wanted to learn found it difficult because both students and teachers were new to remote learning platforms and there were constant screwups. Plus, teachers had kids of their own to take care of, which made it difficult for them to teach. Many teachers conducted their remote classes for a few hours at best. "The cost of this is going to be huge," Christopher Morphew, the dean of the Johns Hopkins School of Education, told MacGillis.

As critical as classes were, public schools had an importance that went beyond education. It's where kids made friends and where many of the rituals of childhood and young adulthood took place. For children who lived in unstable homes, their public school offered some stability during the day. Without open schools, domestic abuse was likely to rise. (It did.) Public schools offered hot meals to students who were unlikely to get one at home. And they were places where parents knew

5 The article was co-published by ProPublica, where MacGillis works.

their kids were safe when they were at work. One consequence of the pandemic was that millions of children were left to fend for themselves because their parents couldn't afford to leave their jobs to take care of them. Not everybody could Zoom to work.

There was a second reason advocates were calling for schools to reopen: surprisingly, the coronavirus didn't seem to spread nearly as much in schools as it did in homes or "essential" workplaces. Or maybe that wasn't such a surprise, given that the coronavirus seemed to focus far more on the elderly than on kids. By midsummer 2020, when cities were trying to decide whether to reopen their public schools, 146,000 Americans had died of COVID-19. Exactly sixteen of them were children between the ages of five and fourteen. More schoolchildren died from mass shootings.

That fall, Emily Oster, a Brown University economist and parenting expert, published an article in *The Atlantic* titled "Schools Aren't Super-spreaders." It was a relatively short article, but it packed a punch. Frustrated that the U.S. Education Department didn't seem interested in collecting COVID-19 data for schools, Oster decided to do it herself. She surveyed schools where students were in classrooms in states like Florida, Georgia, Indiana, and Rhode Island. Her survey encompassed about 200,000 children. The infection rate, she discovered, was 0.13 percent among students and 0.24 percent among teachers. "That's about 1.3 infections over two weeks in a group of 1,000 kids, and 2.2 infections over two weeks in a group of 1,000 staff," she wrote. Oster then set up what she called the COVID-19 School Response Dashboard, which eventually tracked twelve million kids in both public and private schools and continued to collect infection rate data over the next nine months. Not once did the student rate hit 1 percent during any two-week span; in fact, it rarely got above 0.20 percent.

"Democratic governors who love to flaunt their pro-science bona fides in comparison with the anti-science Trump administration don't seem to be aware of this growing body of evidence," she concluded. "We do not want to be cavalier or put people at risk. But by not opening, we are putting people at risk, too."

In their *New York Times* article, Nuzzo and Sharfstein also noted the extremely low incidence of childhood hospitalizations—0.01 percent per 100,000—and the relative safety of schools. "Austria, Denmark, Germany and Norway have reopened schools without major outbreaks," they pointed out. Not only did children largely avoid serious illness from the virus; they also didn't seem to be major spreaders of COVID-19. Nuzzo and Sharfstein offered a number of examples, including a survey conducted by the Pasteur Institute in France, which found just three probable cases of COVID-19 in school-age children among 510 students in a town that experienced a major outbreak. The children did not pass the infection to teachers or other students.

———

Over the entirety of the pandemic, the essential facts about schools never changed. Their relative safety was irrefutable, confirmed again and again in studies. The infection rate for teachers in Sweden, where schools never closed, was no higher than the infection rate for teachers in Finland, which had closed its public schools. In Mississippi, "gatherings and social functions outside the home . . . [were] associated with increased risk of infection; however, in-person school attendance during the 14 days prior to diagnosis was not." In Norway, "transmission of SARS-CoV-2 from children under 14 years of age was minimal." In England, "prevalence of infection among pupils sampled in school was consistently lower than prevalence of infection among children in the wider community across all time periods." In early 2021, three CDC scientists acknowledged in an article in *The Journal of the American Medical Association* that "as many schools have reopened for in-person instruction in some parts of the US . . . there has been little evidence that schools have contributed meaningfully to increased community transmission."

———

You might think that this accumulation of evidence would cause officials in blue states to sit up and take notice. But with the exception of Rhode Island's Gina Raimondo,[6] most ignored the data. Raimondo was able to force the schools open because the state had control of the school system in Providence, Rhode Island's capital, and the state could provide funding to help the schools pay for preventive measures. But many of the state's other cities kept their schools closed, much to Raimondo's frustration. At one point, she told *The New York Times*, she announced that if disgruntled parents in the Providence suburb of Warwick, which had not opened its schools, wanted to sue the school district, the state would join in. Warwick soon capitulated.

"This is how I analyzed it, right, wrong or indifferent," Raimondo told Susan Dominus, the author of the *Times* story. "If you look at the risk that children who go virtual will be left behind—get behind academically, suffer from severe mental-health issues, suffer from food insecurity, suffer from abuse and neglect—it's 100 percent. One-hundred percent certainty. . . . So, yeah," she added, "I came out aggressively."

Her analysis was irrefutable and supported by reams of data. So why were so many other blue state governors—not to mention mayors,

6 After Joe Biden was elected president, Raimondo joined the administration as commerce secretary.

public health officials, and Democrats both in and out of government—unwilling to reopen schools? There were three reasons. The first, and most understandable, was fear. No matter how small the chance, no parent wanted his or her child to be the rare one to die from COVID-19. And no teacher wanted to become infected while in school and bring COVID-19 home. Because kids often brought colds and flus to school—which then spread to others—both parents and teachers had a hard time accepting that that was not how the virus spread. Here, for instance, was a typical comment from a teacher in Westchester, New York, reacting to a series of *New York Times* articles about reopening schools:

> *Tell me how to get a 6-year-old to not sneeze on his friends let alone play and work from a distance (mucus, saliva, pee, poop, this is all part of our day at the lower levels of education). Tell me how each child is going to have her own supplies for the day as shared supplies are no longer an option. No more Legos, no more books. Tell me how to comfort a hysterical child from a distance of six feet. Tell me how to have a socially distanced active shooter drill. Seriously, tell me. Because no one wants to go back to school more than I do.*

The fact that the airborne COVID-19 virus was not spread though saliva or urine, or by sharing books and supplies—and that this had been well established—seemed not to matter. To put it bluntly, the drastic measures the society had taken to mitigate the spread of the virus, especially lockdowns, had panicked the country, just as D. A. Henderson had predicted. Too many people were simply unable, or unwilling, to judge risk rationally. In 2021, for instance, COVID-19 ranked well below suicide, cancer, accidents, homicide, and even heart disease as a cause of death for children under the age of fifteen, according to CDC data. Yet public health experts did not stress any of this; on the contrary, the CDC and other public health agencies only fueled parents' fear by emphasizing the possibility that children could get COVID-19 without explaining how minuscule the risk was. Is it any wonder, then, that COVID-19 seemed to be the only thing parents and teachers focused on?

There were people—supposed experts, many of them—who actively sought to undermine those who encouraged schools reopening. The person who bore the brunt of this blowback was Emily Oster, who had become a lightning rod for those opposed to opening schools. She was mocked for being a parent expert who was wading into an area in which she had no expertise. Her data was said to be untrustworthy because her COVID-19 dashboard was funded by right-wing sources like Peter Thiel and the Koch family. "On social media," wrote Dana Goldstein in *The New York Times*, she was labeled "a 'charlatan' and 'monster' pushing 'morally reprehensible' positions that 'endangered many lives needlessly.'"

The criticism stung, Oster acknowledged. But as the evidence grew that she was right, she not only stuck to her views but doubled down. As did her opponents, who were never willing to concede that they had been wrong about schools. A year after her *Atlantic* article ran, one of her many critics tweeted, "Happy one-year anniversary to the most entitled, thoughtless and careless article written by @ProfEmilyOster."

The second factor was Donald Trump. On July 6, he posted another of his incendiary all-cap tweets. "SCHOOLS MUST REOPEN IN THE FALL!!" it read. The next day, at a White House event, the president said, "We're very much going to put pressure on governors and everybody else to open the schools. It's very important for our country. It's very important for the well-being of the student and the parents."

Trump was right; it *was* important. But by this late stage in his presidency, just about every Democrat assumed that anything he said was a lie. That was especially true with his pandemic statements. This, after all, was a man who suggested that ingesting disinfectant might deter the virus. If Trump thought schools should be opened, all the more reason to fight to keep them closed.

The strong reaction against anything that came out of Trump's mouth was understandable on one level. But on another level, it was inexcusable. Long before vaccine hesitancy became an issue, the fight over schools was an early sign of how stupidly polarized the country had become, and in this case it wasn't the red states refusing to follow the science. It was blue state Democrats who valued their political affiliation over common sense—and even over their pre-pandemic pretensions about protecting the underprivileged.

"The effect of Trump's declaration [that schools should reopen] was instantaneous," wrote Alec MacGillis in his *New Yorker* article. "Teachers who had been responsive to the idea of returning to the classroom suddenly regarded the prospect much more warily. 'Our teachers were ready to go back as long as it was safe,'" Randi Weingarten, the president of the American Federation of Teachers (AFT), told MacGillis. "Then Trump and [the education secretary Betsy] DeVos played their political bullshit." In the major American cities, most teachers were Democrats, and their reaction echoed Weingarten's.

Weingarten was a critical player in the third reason it was so difficult to move away from remote learning to in-person classrooms: the nation's teachers' unions. Unlike meatpackers or Amazon warehouse workers, big-city teachers had never been declared essential workers. They were unionized, and their unions—Weingarten's American Federation of Teachers and the larger National Education Association—were allies of, and contributors to, the Democratic Party, which dominated most major urban areas. With 75 percent of the nation's one and a half million urban public school teachers unionized, they held enormous sway over big-city school systems.

No one can doubt that teachers were afraid of dying of COVID-19. They truly believed they were putting themselves in harm's way if they went back into a classroom full of children. They complained that most big-city school districts lacked the funds to put in better air ventilation systems or plastic barriers between desks, the way private schools had. They felt vulnerable. But instead of helping their members see how small the risk truly was, the teachers' unions fought to keep teachers away from the classroom.

By the time September 2020 rolled around, at least a dozen of America's biggest cities had announced that they would start the school year remotely. They included Los Angeles, San Francisco, New York, Chicago, and Houston—all cities with the kinds of large, disadvantaged communities that would suffer the most if schools were closed. In most cases, city officials said they were trying to move from remote learning to at least a hybrid model—in which students would spend several days a week in classrooms and the rest of the week online. But with COVID-19 cases rising that fall, most of them said they would move slowly and cautiously.

That wasn't good enough for the unions. "It is time to take a stand against Trump's dangerous, anti-science agenda that puts the lives of our members, our students, and our families at risk," said a union leader in Los Angeles.

In New York, where Mayor Bill de Blasio was hoping to begin a hybrid system in September, hundreds of teachers marched to the Department of Education's headquarters carrying coffins, body bags, and a mock guillotine with a blade that read "DOE."

In Chicago, the Chicago Teachers Union filed a lawsuit to prevent the city from implementing a phased-in reopening. They claimed that

Chicago schools weren't yet safe enough, even though the school district had spent $100 million updating ventilation systems, adding hand sanitizer, and taking other mitigation measures.

In school districts that did open their schools in 2020, the results were remarkably aligned with the data Emily Oster had been compiling. De Blasio was finally able to get the schools open in late September; between Thanksgiving and the end of the year the city's positivity rate rose from 3 to 6 percent. The positivity rate in the public schools also rose—from 0.28 to 0.67 percent. "The safest place in New York City is, of course, our public schools," said de Blasio. To the holdout unions, those numbers didn't matter. Ultimately, only 15 percent of school districts offered full-time classroom instruction during the fall 2020 semester. Everywhere else, the teachers' unions held the upper hand.

———

Joe Biden had just become president when *The Journal of the American Medical Association* published the article by three CDC scientists saying that schools had not "contributed meaningfully" to the spread of the virus. Proponents of in-person learning quickly began citing it as proof that it was time to reopen America's schools. The new president, meanwhile, told the country that he wanted to get children back into their classrooms within a hundred days, and vowed that the federal government would spend $130 billion to fortify the nation's classrooms against the virus. (It was largely forgotten that $67 billion in school aid had been authorized by Congress during the Trump administration.)

With Trump no longer in the White House, union leaders agreed— so long as the classrooms were safe, of course. "Hallelujah!" said Weingarten in a press release. "Unlike Trump, . . . Biden understands that if we secure the resources and put the public health safeguards in place, we can open schools safely in the second semester." She added, "Between this, a vaccine and a Centers for Disease Control and Prevention director who is ready to give national guidance free of political interference, we see a path forward for safe school buildings reopening."

"Freedom from political interference" was one of the watch phrases of the new administration. Wasn't political interference a sin of the Trump administration, and one that was now solidly in the past?

Maybe not. The new CDC director was Dr. Rochelle Walensky.[7] She had run the infectious disease department at Massachusetts General Hospital and taught at Harvard Medical School. One of her first tasks was to come up with guidance for reopening schools. Weingarten, a longtime Democratic ally, wasn't about to let this happen "free of political interference." In an email[8] sent on February 1 to a Walensky aide, Kelly Trautner, the AFT's senior director for health issues, wrote, "Thank you again for Friday's rich discussion about forthcoming CDC guidance and to your openness to the suggestions made by our president, Randi Weingarten, and the AFT. We are hopeful that lines of communication will remain open, and that we can serve as a true thought partner as you continue the important work towards safe reopening of schools." Trautner then offered "suggested language" regarding accommodations for "high-risk individuals."

The next week, Weingarten and Walensky had a second conversation, the contents of which are unknown. And on February 11, just before the guidance was issued, Trautner sent an email to Walensky

7 Walensky held the position for a little less than two and a half years. She announced her resignation in May 2023.

8 The emails were obtained by Americans for Public Trust, a conservative group that seeks, as it puts it, to hold "politicians and political groups accountable for corrupt and unethical behavior."

and other CDC officials complaining that the guidance didn't contain "provisions providing for when schools should close." She added—with no intended irony—"We really want to lend our efforts to helping restore faith in the CDC."

The fundamental fact about the guidance the CDC published is that it showed the Biden administration had no intention of crossing the teachers' unions. It was designed primarily to assuage the fears of the teachers, even though most of those fears were already known to be unfounded. It called for (among other things) mask wearing, social distancing of six feet between students, and sticking with remote learning in high-transmission communities. It also included the language Trautner had suggested virtually word for word. Weingarten praised the agency for relying on "facts and evidence."

And *still* there was pushback from some big-city locals. In March, the Chicago Teachers Union finally agreed to return to the classroom. But even then, high school students had to continue with remote learning. By the time they returned, the school year was nearly over.

In San Francisco, the city sued its own school district for failing to come up with a reopening plan, in violation of a state requirement. It took months for the school board to first devise a plan and then cut a deal with the teachers' union. Primary schools opened April 12; incredibly, middle and high schools remained remote until the following school year.

———

By 2022, journalists, academics, and even some public health officials were finally coming to grips with the enormous damage done to children—especially disadvantaged children—because of remote learning. A lengthy analysis by two education professors[9] in *The Atlantic* totted up some of the issues. First, millions of kids simply gave up on learning. For instance, during that first pandemic semester, 40 percent of Los Angeles public school students didn't participate in remote learning. Many other big-city school systems reported similar numbers. In New York, even after schools had reopened, the chronic absentee rate was 40 percent—up from 26 percent before the pandemic. With fewer high school graduates, community college enrollment fell 12 percent. Studies showed that public school children got less exercise (no recess) and ate more junk food (no free hot meals) during the pandemic. According to a CDC survey, during the first six months of 2021, nearly half the high school students surveyed "felt persistently sad and helpless," a 20 percent increase from 2019. One out of every five "thought seriously about suicide," a 5 percent jump. Parental emotional abuse was four times higher than in 2013, and parental physical abuse nearly doubled, *The Atlantic* reported.

A study by three major research institutions, including Harvard's Center for Education Policy Research, showed that the longer a school relied on remote learning, the further behind its students were. "In high-poverty schools that were remote for more than half of 2021, the loss was about half of a school year's worth of typical achievement growth," said Thomas Kane, the director of the Harvard center.

Although test scores in 2022 would suggest that students were slowly catching up, those scores didn't take into account the hundreds of thousands, perhaps millions, of kids who had dropped out entirely.

9 The authors were Meira Levinson, a professor of education and society at the Harvard Graduate School of Education, and Daniel Markovits, a professor at Yale Law School.

A subsequent analysis by the Associated Press, Stanford University's Big Local News project, and the Stanford professor Thomas Dee found an estimated 230,000 students in twenty-one states whose absences could not be accounted for. They had simply gone missing.

"The pandemic has amounted to a comprehensive assault on the American public school," concluded the authors of the *Atlantic* article. Yet as late as the fall of 2022, there were still those who refused to acknowledge the damage done by lengthy school closings. One such person was Anthony Fauci, who made several appearances in which he was asked whether he regretted his forceful advocacy of lockdowns, especially given their effect on children. At one forum, he said, "Sometimes when you do draconian things, it has collateral negative consequences . . . on the economy, on the schoolchildren." But, he added, "the only way to stop something cold in its track is to try and shut things down."

What he didn't acknowledge was that shutting things down didn't stop the virus, and that keeping schools closed didn't save kids' lives. To understand that, you had to be willing to follow the science.

11

"The Most Corrupt
Market of All"

The mask shortage gradually eased through the summer and fall of 2020. Hospitals learned to re-sterilize and reuse disposable masks. There was also a big increase in output. 3M was ramping up production of its coveted N95 respirators as quickly as it could, going from twenty-two million a month in January 2020 to ninety-five million a month by October. Chinese manufacturers had pivoted to mask making; there were well over a thousand mask manufacturers in China by the fall of 2020, many of them making KN95s, China's version of the N95. (Unlike an N95, the Chinese counterpart was not approved by the FDA for hospital use.) And of course there were those small American companies manufacturing masks because they felt it was their patriotic duty. Supply remained tight but manageable.

Sure enough, this spelled disaster for the three dozen or so homegrown mask makers that had sprung up because, as one of them put it, "this is the right thing to do." Determined to gain back lost market share, the Chinese manufacturers were selling masks for less than a penny. And the hospitals that had pleaded with the American companies for masks just months earlier simply could not resist the lure of rock-bottom prices. "All the hospitals and government agencies and retailers that had been begging for American products suddenly said, 'We're good,'" said Paul Hickey, whose PuraVita Medical had been making KN95 respirators. "We're on the verge of losing it all." The companies had banded together to form an association and hire a lobbyist, who pleaded with the Biden administration to purchase American-made masks to replenish the federal stockpile, which had long since been emptied out. And though the White House said encouraging things—Biden even said in his State of the Union address that the government would be more rigorous about buying American goods—nothing ever happened. One by one, the companies went out of business, or reverted to their original business.

"Hospitals drive the mask market," wrote Mike Bowen in a letter to the White House. Bowen, you'll recall, was the Prestige Ameritech executive who had predicted precisely this outcome. "Any plan that allows imported masks to cost less than U.S.-made masks will result in a foreign government-controlled U.S. mask supply—as currently exists."

DemeTech, the family-owned surgical supply company based in Miami, was in the latter category. At the height of the mask shortage, it hired some fifteen hundred workers to make masks and respirators. It had rented a large factory just for its mask operation and bought several million dollars' worth of equipment. Customers had promised to stay with DemeTech once the mask crisis ended. But they didn't. By the end of 2020, the company had laid off almost all the new workers, and its factory was stocked with some 170 million unsold masks—and enough raw material to make 200 million more.

And Luis Arguello Jr., the company's young president who had led it into the mask business, was bitter. "The Chinese are flooding the market for the sole reason of putting an end to the American production," he said. To make matters worse, hospitals were using money they had gotten from the CARES Act—money the government had given them—to purchase foreign-made masks, he said. Laying off workers didn't just mean the loss of a job; it also meant the loss of expertise, since these employees now knew how to make masks. "Isn't it worth paying a little more for American products if it creates jobs and expertise?" he asked.

Arguello was among those asking the Biden administration to buy American-made masks for the stockpile; it was the only way companies like his could continue in the business until some kind of legislation was passed—legislation that would create incentives for hospitals to buy American PPE. But realistically, he knew that wasn't going to happen. "If anyone asked me to scale up, I'd have to think twice about it," he said.

———

Though masks had become easier to acquire, that lack of resilience in the supply chain was still taking a severe toll. The worst of the shortages was in nitrile gloves. Unlike masks, however, U.S. companies were not racing to get into the nitrile glove business. The manufacturing process was not something you could gin up at a moment's notice: it was expensive, and the essential ingredient—rubber—still had to be purchased from a foreign supplier. And nitrile glove manufacturing had environmental issues. Glove manufacturers tended to be in countries that had lots of rubber trees, most prominently Malaysia. It didn't help matters that Malaysian industry had been shut down from mid-March until early May, as part of a wider lockdown, and that employees of Top Glove, the country's leading manufacturer, suffered a series of COVID-19 outbreaks in the latter half of 2020. The company was also accused of using child labor, causing the U.S. government to block Top Glove imports for six months.

Just as with masks, the need for gloves rose geometrically once the pandemic hit. Just as with masks, the supply chain for gloves evaporated, leading to a free-for-all, with prices that could be as much as ten times what they had been pre-pandemic. And just as with masks, the amount of fraud was staggering. With their normal distribution channels gone, hospital supply chain experts spent their days making frantic phone calls as they tried to suss out which companies were for real and then put together deals to land some of their nitrile gloves. It was a nearly impossible task.

Sometimes, a hospital would buy tens of thousands of gloves from some Malaysian or Thai company, only to discover that the shipment contained used gloves, stuffed carelessly in boxes. In New York City, two young entrepreneurs, Robert Murtfeld[1] and Martin Steinbauer, "got sucked into the personal protective equipment environment," as Murtfeld put it. Over time, they had collected an array of fake PPE samples that they had held on to and were happy to show anyone who asked. They had counterfeit 3M N95s. They had torn gloves. ("These are terrible, terrible gloves," said Murtfeld, laughing in spite of himself. "Terrible gloves.") They had gowns that shredded the minute you tried to put them on; bogus test kits; and masks with phony government certificates. And they had videos of their team showing up at a ware-

---

1 Murtfeld had been a commercial salesman with Cambridge Analytica, the data firm that became embroiled in an election scandal involving Facebook. He left the company when it imploded in 2018. "I just had to have a clean break with all that dodgy data stuff," he later said.

house, only to discover that the promised PPE was nowhere to be found. "There is always a fraudster in every discussion of a PPE deal," Steinbauer said.

Still, they were having more success than most other PPE brokers. There were two reasons for this. The first was that they had two employees living in China. The employees could visit manufacturers and see whether the protective equipment was good or not. Just as important, they could use cold, hard cash to pay for the PPE, instead of trying to transact business from half a world away. A buyer with cash was going to win every time.

The second reason is that unlike most newbies in the business, they didn't view the PPE black market as a once-in-a-lifetime chance to get rich. Murtfeld had worked for a hospitality company prior to the pandemic and had been laid off, like most workers in that industry. "I'm basically doing this to make a living since I don't have another job," he said. He and Steinbauer looked for small lots that rarely cost more than $1 million and were far more likely to be real than the elusive $10 billion worth of PPE that was OTG (on the ground) waiting for POL (proof of life). They were also less likely to be scammed.

"Nitrile gloves are the most corrupt market of all," said Murtfeld, who stayed away from it at first. CNN later conducted a months-long investigation into the nitrile glove black market and concluded that tens of millions of "filthy, used medical gloves"—as well as counterfeit gloves—were being imported into the United States. It quoted a PPE expert, Douglas Stein, saying that nitrile gloves were "the most dangerous product on earth right now" because some of those gloves were undoubtedly being used by doctors and nurses caring for COVID-19 patients. "There is an enormous amount of bad product coming into the U.S. of which federal authorities, it seems, are only now beginning to understand the enormous scale," he said.

One of the companies CNN focused on was Skymed, a Bangkok-based distributor of nitrile gloves and other PPE. As it happens, Murtfeld and Steinbauer had also had some experience dealing with Skymed; in their minds, it was the quintessential example of pandemic corruption.

Skymed was started in 2020, not long after the World Health Organization declared COVID-19 a pandemic. It was a subsidiary of Sufficiency Economy City Co. Ltd., a Bangkok-based company that, pre-pandemic, traded in airplane parts. Sufficiency Economy's CEO was a former air force captain, Kampee Kampeerayannon, whose father had been the deputy commander of Thailand's air force. Over the years, Kampee had built a reputation as a philanthropist and a patriot. He often participated in national events and was a conspicuous presence whenever there was a natural disaster, making donations and finding other ways to provide high-profile aid. He was said to be close to the king. A few months after Skymed was formed, with rumors already beginning to circulate in Thailand that it was shipping fraudulent goods, Kampee issued a statement insisting that his intentions were honorable. The company's purpose, he wrote, was "to continue the royal philosophy of improving the quality of life of the Thai people . . . in order to improve the public health during hardship times of the coronavirus pandemic."

Murtfeld first learned of Skymed in the summer of 2020 when he met a woman in New York who said she was Kampee's niece. According to Murtfeld, she tried to interest him in Skymed and introduced him and Steinbauer to other members of the family who worked for the company in Thailand. Skymed's business model—so it claimed—was to sell allocations for Skymed-branded gloves, which the buyers would then have to wait for, because the company was still in the process of acquiring gloves from various manufacturers. As the nitrile glove shortage became more severe, Skymed was suddenly on the lips of everyone trying to nab PPE—even though no one had seen a single glove. Those who bought allocations, mostly hedge funds, says Murtfeld, momentarily felt as if they'd won the lottery. Of course they had to put money down—40 percent of the purchase price—to hold their allocation.

Murtfeld and Steinbauer stayed in regular contact[2] with the company—even getting Kampee on the phone at one point—but they never bought an allocation. "It always seemed too dodgy," said Steinbauer. When gloves began arriving in the United States, "nobody had any clue where these gloves were manufactured. They were coming from multiple factories in Thailand, so the gloves came in all different sizes and forms and what have you—and then they would go out the door with a Skymed label." Reportedly, Skymed's small staff in Bangkok would stand around a conference table stuffing used gloves into new packaging.

The two men began recording their phone calls and archiving the juiciest PPE videos they came across. In one video, an Australian man says he has just acquired thirty thousand boxes of Skymed gloves and is looking to resell them. He was unusually honest about the product. "The gloves are quality and all that, but are they all made in the same factory? We don't know. Are their certificates 100 percent legit? We don't know. It's up to you to decide whether you can pass on some certificates that are from another company." In another video Kampee tells potential buyers to make their nitrile glove inquiries directly to Sufficiency Economy City and avoid "outside parties" who are committing acts of "unlawful repackaging and fraudulent dealings."

---

2 When asked why he and Steinbauer stayed in touch with Skymed when they knew the company was defrauding buyers, Murtfeld said, "We thought it might be used in a documentary."

Murtfeld and Steinbauer knew, however, that dealing directly with Skymed hardly guaranteed that its deals would be legitimate. Quite the opposite, in fact.

Their final interaction with Skymed was the most hair-raising of all. In early 2021, their primary point of contact left the company. Murtfeld and Steinbauer decided to have one last call with her. About halfway through it, Murtfeld asked the question that had been on his mind for months. "Just out of curiosity, how much money do you think Skymed collected without delivering any goods?" he asked. After some hemming and hawing, she said it was probably around 200 million baht—which was then worth around $7 million.

"So what happened with the $7 million USD?" asked Steinbauer. "Did they send it back or did they keep it?"

"Everyone was almost in the same situation," she said. "They paid money but didn't get gloves."

———

One of the many people trying to make money in the PPE black market was Julius Nasso. He was in his late sixties and lived on a large rococo estate on Staten Island. Thirty years earlier, he had been Steven Seagal's business partner. The two men had met in 1987, and by 1998, Nasso had produced nine of Seagal's films, including *Above the Law*, *Hard to Kill*, and *Under Siege*. The relationship blew up in the 1990s, with each man accusing the other of financial improprieties.

Nasso never stopped producing movies, however, including documentaries about Harry Belafonte and Andrea Bocelli, as well as films full of car chases and gun battles. But he had plenty of other ventures as well. He cofounded a private-label vitamin company. During the Cabbage Patch craze, he opened a Cabbage Patch store in Manhattan.

His primary source of income, however, was a company he had started while still in college. It was called Universal Marine Medical Supply (UMMS), and it supplied cruise ships with the medical supplies they were required to have on board. (Nasso has a pharmacology degree.) By the time the pandemic arrived, his company was owned by a private equity firm, his son was running it, and it was supplying 95 percent of the world's cruise ships as well as thousands of smaller commercial ships. The pandemic had grounded every one of the 287 cruise ships his company supplied.

As Nasso tells the story, when the virus swept through the cruise ship industry, UMMS frantically met ships as they came into ports around the world to get supplies to them, primarily PPE, that were running low. Soon enough, though, the grounded cruise ships stopped needing PPE, and in any case Nasso was having as much difficulty finding supplies as everyone else. "There was all this bullshit going on," he recalled. "'We've got fifty million boxes in a warehouse in L.A.,'" he said, mimicking one of the hundreds of "joker-brokers" supposedly peddling PPE. "Then you go there, and the warehouse is empty."

Because he had been buying from Asian manufacturers for decades, Nasso thought he could do better than the joker-brokers. But with his first deal, he made a bad mistake, a mistake born of his overconfidence in his ability to take the measure of Asian manufacturers. He sent a 30 percent deposit—close to $1 million—to the AMY Group, a Vietnamese company that purportedly made nitrile gloves. And he sent $400,000 to another Vietnamese company, Vina Glove, for a smaller glove order. Talking to the companies' representatives, watching their videos, scouring their websites, Nasso was sure the two companies were legit. He was wrong.

When he received his shipment from Vina Glove, he opened the boxes to discover they were used gloves, many of them soiled and discolored.

As for the $1 million deposit he wired to the AMY Group, that company hadn't bothered to ship anything; it had simply pocketed the money and refused to discuss it when Nasso tried to get the owner on the phone.

Nasso had a friend, Philip Coleman, an Englishman who ran a distribution company that had been working to acquire PPE for hospitals and national health systems in Britain, Germany, and Sweden. "The whole planet was desperate to get nitrile gloves," Coleman said. "We could see that there was a whole network of people who were either pretending or were actually set up as distributors." But it was hard to tell the difference from afar. Having managed many successful orders for buyers worldwide, Coleman moved to Ho Chi Minh City in February 2021 with his family to get closer to the manufacturers, which would allow him to see, up close, the real factories he had been working with, and facilitate larger nitrile glove purchases.

Nasso and Coleman had done business together for years. The two men knew each other well. While in Vietnam, Coleman hoped to help Nasso track down the owners of Vina Glove and the AMY Group and get Nasso's money back for him. Coleman stayed in Vietnam for the better part of the year under a special visa that allowed foreign "experts" and their dependents into the country who had important skills that were useful during the pandemic. Vietnam let Coleman in because he had run global logistics companies for a quarter century.

What he discovered that year in Vietnam shocked him. As he later wrote in a document recounting his experiences: he had "stumbled into what was part of one of the largest and most deceitful scams on the planet."

There were, in fact, two different scams. In one, the seller shipped used gloves instead of the pristine gloves it promised buyers. In the other, the seller took a deposit but didn't send anything—because it didn't actually make nitrile gloves. Nasso had fallen victim to both scams.

Coleman first tried to get in touch with the head of the Vina Group in Ho Chi Minh City. The owner refused to speak with him, but he managed to get into the building and get a look around. "I walked into what seemed to be a quiet hall/room hidden away from the main offices and was absolutely shocked by what I saw . . . an entire 10,000 sq ft room full of dirty, stained and potently odorous blue and turquoise used medical gloves. There must have been millions of medical use single gloves all lining the entire floor in groups of colours."

Coleman sought help from the police. The head of the department's commercial fraud unit said she would be happy to help—if she got 20 percent of the missing funds. "This became a common scenario that I came across constantly thereafter," Coleman later wrote. "The Police take funds from foreigners on the pretense that they will go and make arrests and recover lost funds. They do not; they go directly to the factories and do a second deal with the scammers . . . in order to drop the claims."

In Ho Chi Minh City, Coleman was shown some fake-glove showrooms "that were used for scam videos." The videos were meant to show that the seller had lots of gloves, or even owned a factory that made gloves. "However, the stock in the background would be entirely empty boxes," he wrote. "Thousands of companies around the world fell for these videos and wider scams whilst they were distracted by the urgent nature of demand for Nitrile gloves for hospitals."

Having failed to make any progress with Vina Glove, Coleman traveled to Hanoi to confront the AMY Group, "the most feared glove company in Vietnam." He heard stories of AMY's reputation not only for victimizing buyers but for sometimes roughing up people who came looking for refunds. They were also said to have protection from organized crime, the government, and the police. Coleman's sources estimated that the AMY Group had stolen around $350 million from desperate nitrile glove buyers.

"They put up videos of warehouses and factories that simply didn't exist," said Coleman. "They had pictures of company officials posing with military guys and the local police force. And they made themselves look very honorable and ethical. And they just stole every penny that was sent to them."

As word got around that Coleman was trying to help Nasso recover his deposit, other victims of the AMY Group sought his help. The money they had lost ranged from $250,000 to $5 million. He also heard, though, that he should forget about trying to recoup the money; dealing with the AMY Group was just too dangerous. "If you know what's good for you," he heard more than once, "you'll stay away." He later recalled,

> Often I would hear that people had already hired locals to investigate or collect the debts and had in most cases been scammed for more money, or on some occasions their representatives had met with brutal violence. Stories were circulating about various people that had been physically hurt including a husband and wife that had obtained visas and travelled to Vietnam to demand funds from AMY Group. Following this they were both brutally stabbed as they entered their hotel in Hanoi. They barely survived.

He had a Vietnamese staff member whom he asked to approach the AMY Group, thinking that a local might have better luck making contact. But before the employee could even reach out to the AMY Group, he received a phone call from a friend on the police force. The friend said that the AMY Group was aware he was working with Coleman and warned him that it would be dangerous to get involved. He also said that they knew where Coleman lived. Coleman quickly sent his wife and child back to England. However, with Ho Chi Minh City in lockdown, he was unable to leave for another apartment; the penalty for being caught outside was a nine-month prison sentence. "I felt like a sitting duck," he wrote.

Finally, in October, Coleman was able to make his way to Hanoi hoping to confront the AMY Group and its thirtysomething CEO, Duong Duc Anh. Why was he willing to keep at it? Partly, he said, it was out of loyalty to "my friend and business partner," Nasso.

But it was also because he was angry: "These people cannot get away with this," he said. He had met with the highest level of the economic crime departments of the police and filed detailed claims on behalf of Nasso. Initially the police had promised they would recover the funds quickly. Once the police interviewed the factory owners, however, they came back and said that the company wasn't going to refund anything. So Coleman decided that despite everything he had heard, he would go himself.

He arrived at the AMY Group's offices unannounced, and though the receptionist was hostile, he was able to get a feel for the company. The AMY Group turned out to be a major construction and real estate company—with projects so sizable there was no way they could have been built without the involvement of the government. He also realized that the receptionist was someone whose name was on a number of documents relating to the scam. She told him that Duc Anh was rarely in the office; Coleman replied that he would return every day until he got a meeting.

Which he did, on his fourth visit. When it took place, Coleman made a strategic decision to downplay the money issue and engage Duc

Anh on subjects like travel and wealth, subjects he suspected the AMY Group CEO would enjoy talking about. Duc Anh enjoyed the conversation so much he invited Coleman to dinner. It was there that Coleman pressed him on the subject of the $1 million the company had stolen from Nasso. Angrily, Duc Anh told Coleman that "I should realize that he could have dealt with this any way he wanted as he put his hand to the side of his head and made a gun-firing motion."

"At this point," recalled Coleman, "I had to remind myself that this was still a dangerous situation."

The two men continued to meet, but whenever Coleman brought up Nasso's desire to be refunded his $1 million, Duc Anh would just say "no—like a spoiled child. He was very defiant."

Coleman made one last attempt to get the money back. He was put in touch with a wealthy businessman in Hai Phong, two hours from Hanoi. The man was said to have connections to the mafia. It was a cordial meeting in a fancy resort that the man owned, where Coleman showed him all of Nasso's documents and discussed what had happened and asked whether the man could help. "After spending two days going over these details," he later wrote, "I was informed that the recovery of the funds would happen should the owners of the funds in the US agree to pay back 50% of the received money as a collection fee. I thought this was completely ludicrous." And so did Nasso, who rejected it out of hand.

Coleman had one more moment in Vietnam that made him realize he needed to get home. Here is how he described it in his report:

I had increasingly become aware of people seemingly watching me over the previous few days. Of course, one can imagine these things however I had noticed several out of place looking men often standing around watching me enter and exit my building. As I walked towards my home that night the streets were very empty, and something seemed a little disconcerting. A car was approximately 200 metres from me, driving slowly. . . . As I walked towards my front door the car's full beam headlights went on which blinded me. It then accelerated at lightning speed towards me in a street that was not actually much wider than the car itself. I literally had a split second to throw myself through a closed front door of somebody's house. I landed in literally a living room with a family eating whilst the car, which I never saw properly at all drove at an extreme speed towards the exit of the alleyway. . . . I was pretty shaken by the fact that the door actually opened, had it not I am quite sure that the car would not have stopped. I decided it was time to take a break from Vietnam and join my family back in the UK.

Julius Nasso never did get his money back, but he did have one consolation. His friend's adventure was going to make a great documentary someday.

———

In the spring of 2022, Mike Bowen quit his job at Prestige Ameritech. All things considered, the company had come through the pandemic in far better shape than any of its competitors. Because of the long-term contracts it had negotiated with a handful of big hospitals, its big customers didn't bail when the Chinese dropped their prices. But after a career in the mask business, Bowen had had enough.

That June, Bowen flew to Hoboken, the New Jersey town across the Hudson River from Manhattan where Frank Sinatra grew up. He had always loved to sing, and decided he wanted to give it a try. He wanted to sing the songs of the Great American Songbook, the songs that Sinatra was so famous for singing. Every year, Hoboken holds a "Sinatra Sing-Off," and Bowen was one of the dozen men who had entered the contest. He sang the Jimmy Webb tune "Didn't We."

Bowen didn't win the contest, but he got enough encouragement to continue on his quixotic quest to be a singer. He found a pianist who wanted to work with him, and they landed some gigs in and around the Dallas–Fort Worth area. Eventually, they started playing at a steak house in Mansfield, Texas, a Fort Worth suburb. The diners liked them, and so did the owners. It became a weekly thing. Bowen was as happy as he'd ever been in his life.

"I'm so glad I don't have to think about masks anymore," he said.

12

Fever Dreams

E very mitigation measure that public health officials had urged since the start of the pandemic pointed toward one goal: keep people as far from each other as possible until an effective vaccine could be developed. Because the public health community viewed mitigation solely through the lens of COVID-19, they never really considered the potential negative consequences of measures like lockdowns or school closings. Someday, a vaccine would solve all those problems, wouldn't it? People of a certain age could remember getting a polio shot when they were children in the 1950s and what an important moment that was not just for them and their parents but for the whole country. Vaccines had vanquished polio, just as they vanquished measles, chicken pox, and a host of other diseases.

The problem had always been that vaccines took years to develop. Jonas Salk spent seven years developing his polio vaccine. John

Enders and Thomas Peebles needed nine years to develop the measles vaccine in the late 1950s and early 1960s. Baruch Blumberg took four years to develop a vaccine for the hepatitis B virus. And so on.

Vaccines also made very little money for pharmaceutical companies, which had become as obsessed with profits and "shareholder value" as the rest of American industry. Pharma companies were gun-shy because too often in the past they had scrambled to come up with vaccines for incipient viruses, only to discover that they weren't needed when the virus quickly died out. Companies had had to bear onerous litigation costs in the late 1970s and early 1980s, when people filed lawsuits claiming—with very little scientific backing—that some vaccines had seriously harmed them. Finally, the movement that began in the late 1990s alleging that vaccines led to autism in children put vaccine makers on the defensive, even though the claim was baseless.[1] As a result, according to Dr. Paul Offit, the director of the vaccine education center at the Children's Hospital of Philadelphia, the number of companies making vaccines dropped from twenty-six in 1967 to seventeen in 1980 to five in 2004.

And yet, despite this history, Dr. Anthony Fauci was claiming that he believed a COVID-19 vaccine could be developed in twelve to eighteen months. There was near-universal skepticism in the scientific community. Even though Fauci made it clear he thought Trump's estimate of three to four months—ahead of the election, of course—was absurd, his own timetable still drew scorn. "When Dr. Fauci said 12 to 18 months, I thought that was ridiculously optimistic," Offit told CNN. "And I'm sure he did, too." Another scientist, Amesh Adalja of

---

1 The 1998 paper that first made this claim was retracted in 2011 by *The Lancet*, the British scientific journal that had originally published it. In 2013, the *British Medical Journal* described the paper as "an elaborate fraud."

Johns Hopkins, concurred. "I don't think it's ever been done at an industrial scale in 18 months," he said.

What the skeptics failed to take into account was the existence of a new technology called messenger RNA. It had never been used to deliver vaccine doses before—in fact, it had never been used for *any* commercial purpose before—but in theory mRNA could make it both easier and quicker to develop a workable vaccine. There was another factor as well. The Trump administration not only helped companies jump-start the manufacturing process but guaranteed that if their vaccines worked, they were going to make an awful lot of money. For all the things government did wrong during the pandemic, developing the vaccines by working in tandem with private industry was something it got very right.

———

Scientists have known for a long time about the existence of messenger RNA. The story of its discovery is intertwined with the famous 1953 discovery of the structure of DNA by James Watson and Francis Crick. Four years after that discovery, Crick gave a famous lecture that expanded on his thinking, proposing what he called a "central dogma" about how genes function. One piece of Crick's dogma posited the existence of a molecule that served as a messenger of sorts, carrying out instructions for making the proteins that are responsible for nearly every task in our cellular life to our DNA. Then, in 1961, two teams of scientists published papers proving that Crick's theory was right. The molecule they discovered was labeled messenger RNA, or mRNA.

Theoretically, mRNA could be a key for curing an extraordinary number of diseases, because if mRNA could deliver the "right" instructions to a person's DNA, it could essentially instruct a misbehaving cell to behave. "To say this has been a goal of modern medicine is an understatement," says John Hempton, an investor with expertise in biology, who calls it the "holy grail." But practically speaking, that holy grail always seemed out of reach. mRNA wasn't cooperative. The scientists who first gave mRNA its name described it as an "unstable molecule," because it breaks down quickly. In addition, when our cells identify foreign pieces of DNA or mRNA, our immune system tends to treat them as viruses and seeks to destroy them, and the cells that contain them. In other words, mRNA was far from a magic elixir.

Because mRNA was so difficult to tame, mainstream biologists gave up experimenting with it, and sought other ways to fight disease. There were, however, a few dogged scientists who remained fascinated by its possibilities and refused to let go. One of them was Katalin Karikó, a Hungarian biochemist who in 1989 got a job as a researcher at the University of Pennsylvania Medical School. While that sounds like an august position, the reality is quite different: People like Karikó are often the worker bees of medical institutions. They're looked down upon by doctors and make very little money, particularly if, like Karikó, they're immigrants with few other options.

Unable to raise grant money, Karikó was demoted and moved to a dingy basement office. But she was nothing if not persistent. She continued her work with the support of a colleague named Drew Weissman, and the pair discovered at least part of a solution to the problems that bedeviled those working with mRNA. They found that by making certain chemical modifications to the mRNA, they could insert it into cells without activating an immune response. A number of leading scientific publications rejected their work, but in 2005 they were finally able to report their discovery in *Immunity*, a niche scientific journal. "One application of our findings is that scientists will be able to design better therapeutic RNAs . . . for treating diseases such as cancer and single-gene genetic diseases," Karikó said at the time.

That was a big, tantalizing promise. Yet no one seemed to care. "I told Kati our phones are going to ring off the hook," Weissman later told one reporter. "But nothing happened. We didn't get a single call."

The University of Pennsylvania kicked Karikó out of her office, relegating her to an even dingier space off campus. She had to fight even to get the university to file a patent for the discovery she and Weissman had made. Penn then sold the patent for an undisclosed sum.[2]

Karikó didn't seem to be bothered by the humiliation. "The bench is there, the science is good," she'd later tell *The New York Times*. "Who cares?"

Without Karikó's discovery, the company that would turn mRNA into a COVID-19 vaccine probably wouldn't exist. That company, of course, is Moderna, whose mission was so focused on developing mRNA into a useful tool that even its name was a play on the molecule. For all the ways in which the monomaniacal focus on money has been destructive to health care, Moderna's story shows that the solution isn't as simple as eradicating the profit motive, because it's the quest for profits that can spur medical innovation. Our system depends on how the rules are set—whether the incentives exist to create something new and better, rather than, say, gaming the system, or selling a story, or just getting rich. Moderna, for its part, was motivated to do some of each. It wasn't all good. But it's clear that without the potential riches that

2 In his book *Longshot: The Inside Story of the Race for a COVID-19 Vaccine*, the journalist David Heath reported that Karikó believes Penn sold exclusive rights to the patent for $300,000.

high-priced drugs can bring, venture capitalists would never have been willing to risk their money on a start-up like Moderna, which had plenty of promise but little hard evidence it could make mRNA work. There is a reason this all happened in the United States. As Akash Tewari, a biotechnology analyst with Jefferies, puts it, "If we didn't have the U.S. system, we wouldn't have the vaccines."

———

Moderna was founded in another laboratory some three hundred miles up Interstate 95 and run by a man who could not have been more different from Karikó. Derrick Rossi, a Canadian biologist, was ambitious not just to do groundbreaking science but to start a biotech company and make a great deal of money. In 2007, Rossi was working as a post-doc at Stanford University when he was recruited by an affiliate of Harvard to start his own lab. He brought with him a biologist named Luigi Warren, whom he'd met at Stanford. Warren was something of an iconoclast. A former software engineer, in his late thirties, he enrolled at Columbia University to get an undergraduate degree in biology. He went from Columbia to the doctoral program at CalTech, and eventually wound up at Stanford. He and Rossi, who was also in his forties, bonded over their shared love of David Bowie.

The two scientists were trying to come up with a new method for making so-called pluripotent stem cells: cells that can self-renew and become an entirely different type of cell. The inspiration came from Shinya Yamanaka, a doctor and researcher at Japan's Kyoto University who in 2006 published a paper that stunned the scientific world. He'd succeeded in taking mature stem cells and converting them back to embryonic stem cells by introducing new genes, which he called "factors." (In 2012, Yamanaka won the Nobel Prize for this work.) But his method posed problems for real-world applications, because it resulted in permanent changes to the DNA of the cell.

The race was on for a different method. Warren, perhaps because he came from outside the field and wasn't steeped in its long-held perceptions, proposed getting around some of the problems by using mRNA to deliver Yamanaka's factors. But he kept running into the same problem that had long bedeviled those who tried to work with the unstable molecule, namely that the body's defenses attacked it.

Later, in some forums Rossi would get the credit for stumbling upon Karikó and Weissman's modifications. But that was only true in the sense that it was his lab. In fact, Warren found the solution. In talking to other scientists, he was directed to Karikó and Weissman's work, as well as Karikó's solo work, which involved further modifications that bolstered the mRNA's ability to evade an immune reaction. Sure enough, in 2009, Warren, using Karikó's techniques, succeeded in creating stem cells from mRNA.

In 2010, Warren and Rossi published a paper in the journal *Cell Stem Cell* concluding that their discovery had "broad applicability for basic research, disease modeling, and regenerative medicine." Unlike Karikó and Weissman's earlier paper, the Warren and Rossi paper met with immediate acclaim. Everyone understood that reprogramming cells into pluripotent stem cells was a very big deal. Rossi was even named to *Time* magazine's "100 Most Influential People" list.

The publication of their work undermined both Warren and Rossi's working relationship and their friendship. The publication process is inherently stressful, and this was especially true for Warren, who was terrified about being scooped by another team of scientists, according to Greg Zuckerman's book *A Shot to Save the World: The Inside Story of the Life-or-Death Race for a COVID-19 Vaccine*. Rossi wanted a prestigious journal, whereas Warren was willing to go with one that was less prestigious in hopes of a quick publication. It exacerbated simmering tensions between the two men, and even before the article had been published, Warren had submitted his resignation. Within a year, he'd moved back to California.

Even before their paper was published, Rossi had begun to think about starting a company. Biotech was going through an extraordinarily fertile period, and he'd seen dozens of biologists turn their discoveries into well-funded start-ups. Rossi was introduced to Bob Langer, a chemical engineer at MIT whose pioneering work had led to more than thirteen hundred patents (both issued and pending) and had contributed to the founding of multiple companies. If you had to pick a name that would garner instant attention and credibility, it would be Langer's. That led to Rossi's introduction to Noubar Afeyan,[3] a charismatic Armenian chemical engineer who in 2000 had founded the venture capital firm Flagship Pioneering.

Afeyan is a scientist by training, but unlike many scientists he's also a brilliant salesman. Flagship's website boasts that it has helped underwrite the founding of more than one hundred companies, which have attracted more than $20 billion in funding. Twenty-five of its companies have gone public. He credits his status as an immigrant, along with the Armenian genocide, with giving him the ability to think differently as a means of survival. "If necessity is the mother of invention, then survival is the mother of opportunism," he says. "You tend to be open to risks others wouldn't consider reasonable."

Rossi pitched Afeyan and Langer on starting a company that would use mRNA to make stem cells. The two men were underwhelmed. But as they later told the story, they quickly saw that the idea could be

---

3 Apart from Afeyan, Moderna did not return multiple requests for input or comments.

much, much bigger. If mRNA could indeed be slipped into the body without creating an immune response, which now seemed possible, the human body could be turned into a factory for making its own medicines. The holy grail might finally be attainable.

Or at least that's how Afeyan and Langer have publicly recalled the conversations that led to Moderna's founding. Rossi has a very different version of events: In an interview with *The Boston Globe* in 2020, he called Afeyan and Langer's claim that he hadn't realized the potential of his idea "total malarkey." By 2014, he'd left Moderna. "I kind of felt like my baby had turned into some crazy monster," he told journalist Peter Loftus.[4]

But that dissension and sourness would come later. In late 2010, with all parties brimming with excitement, Moderna was founded. Rossi, Flagship, Langer, and Kenneth Chien, a Harvard scientist who had done a key proof-of-concept mRNA experiment, owned most of the shares. According to Loftus, the company launched with about $2 million in its coffers.

The following year, Afeyan, who was Moderna's board chairman, hired a French chemical engineer named Stéphane Bancel to be the CEO. Bancel, who had been running a diagnostic company, had no experience in drug development. But his skills as a salesman, and his charisma, rivaled Afeyan's. "He's resourceful, impatient and wants to achieve impact fast," Afeyan later said.

Very quickly, Bancel got a reputation for being an extraordinarily tough boss. "Everyone described the culture as fairly toxic," says Hempton. "Goddamn awful management team whose plans change daily, who talk all the time about the Moderna 'family' in our employee

4 Loftus's book is called *The Messenger: Moderna, the Vaccine, and the Business Gamble That Changed the World.*

meetings but then fire people on a whim," wrote one employee, anonymously, on the website Glassdoor.

The constant turnover, particularly among the scientists, raised eyebrows. EGO, AMBITION, AND TURMOIL was the headline of a very critical 2016 story in the health-care publication *Stat* about Moderna. The story recounted how in 2013, Moderna lured a high-profile scientist named Joseph Bolen to Moderna to be its chief scientific officer. Two years later, Bolen was gone, without explanation.

And yet, despite the turmoil, few would argue with Afeyan's decision to put Bancel in charge at Moderna. Bancel created a culture that pushed relentlessly to do big things, and do them quickly. "Anything you do may fail," says Afeyan. "So what you do is you act with a level of temporary certainty until you get data, and then you adjust what you're doing. . . . I believe he [Bancel] takes input on all issues, but he believes he needs to portray a level of confidence around certain things that allow us to make progress. It's foreign to people who assume that certainty is only possible when it's provable."

There may be no better measure of Bancel's ability to display certainty in the face of uncertainty than his decision, in 2016, to build a manufacturing plant in Norwood, Massachusetts. He hired Juan Andres, who'd spent thirty years in manufacturing at the drug giants Eli Lilly and Novartis, as Moderna's head of manufacturing. The company decided to invest about $125 million, or 10 percent of its cash, on the plant—even though it had no products to manufacture. "You need great conviction that your platform is going to be successful to make that kind of an investment with investor money," Andres told the authors of a Harvard Business School case study on Moderna. "It's not normal to invest so much into manufacturing rather than R&D when you're a young biotech."

Bancel had a simple, elegant way of describing mRNA's potential to investors, especially Silicon Valley venture capitalists. He'd say that mRNA was akin to software and that Moderna was a "technology company that happens to do biology." His pitch was that while most biotech companies are trying to develop one drug, the mRNA platform, once proven, could be used to develop multiple drugs. As a company presentation put it, "if mRNA works once, it will work many times," reaching "hundreds of previously undruggable targets."

For years, many investors believed in the fever dreams of riches that Moderna represented. Moderna was able to raise a stunning amount of money—billions—from venture capitalists, from development deals with big pharmaceutical and biotech companies, and from the federal government. The Defense Department's Defense Advanced Research Projects Agency, or DARPA, and the Biomedical Advanced Research and Development Authority, and the National Institutes of Health all helped fund the company. And Fauci was an important supporter of the company. This government help would later become an important sticking point, but at the time it was simply the kind of support the government often gives industries it views as priorities.

Despite all the money it had raised, and the scientific talent it had hired, a decade after its founding Moderna had yet to make a single revenue-producing drug, or even a drug that had made it as far as late-stage clinical trials. Products the company would highlight in investor presentations one year would disappear without explanation the following year.

Nor did the company publish much supporting data. This garnered it unflattering comparisons to Theranos, the disgraced blood-testing company whose claims of "trade secrets" turned out to be camouflage for fraud. Moderna, says another Boston-based venture capitalist, would "tout dozens of different development programs, and you'd have no idea what any of them did. They wouldn't give you timelines, and they'd kill stuff all the time while selectively disclosing the positive results."

To keep investor interest at a fever pitch, Moderna wasn't above resorting to mythmaking and hype. It's what companies too often do when they're trying to keep their stock price high without a revenue-producing product. And without that mythmaking Moderna might not have been able to raise the money it needed to keep going.

One example of its mythmaking was its claim that it had come up with innovations that obviated the need to rely on Karikó and Weissman's groundbreaking work. "Karikó and Weissman's patent posed a challenge for Moderna," wrote *Nature* in a 2015 article, citing an internal report from Flagship, which said that if the company couldn't find another methodology, "our company technology may be limited to licensing IP from UPenn." But never fear: Afeyan told the publication that a young staff scientist had indeed discovered a better way of modifying mRNA.

Perhaps Moderna's method was an improvement. But the facts would seem to show that what Moderna came up with still relied on Karikó and Weissman's work. That's because finally, in 2017, Moderna paid $76 million, along with additional royalties based on product sales, to get a sublicense from Cellscript, the company that had acquired the patent from the University of Pennsylvania.

"You wouldn't have realized that Moderna didn't have much in the way of IP that was particularly relevant or exclusive," says one scientist who was familiar with the company's early years. "They played it very cleverly."

As for hype, consider the press release Moderna sent out at the end of 2012, when it first introduced itself to the world. The company, it said grandly, was on the verge of "adding an entirely new drug category to the pharmaceutical arsenal in the fight against important diseases."

Not surprisingly, the release listed all the prominent names associated with the company, from Langer to Chien.

"It could be the biggest story since, well, probably the rise of Genentech and the entire [biotech] industry in the late '70s and early '80s," gushed a tech website.[5] Wrote *Science* magazine in 2017, "If you can hack the rules of mRNA, essentially the entire kingdom of life is available for you to play with."

The reality was more complicated, of course. That 2016 *Stat* article also outlined some of the questions that were arising about the company's actual achievements with mRNA. "Behind its obsession with secrecy, there are signs Moderna has run into roadblocks with its most ambitious projects," *Stat* wrote.

The biggest roadblock was the scientific one: the near-impossible task of getting the mRNA molecule to cooperate with the researchers trying to tame it. The Karikó modifications, as they came to be known, might get the mRNA past the body's defenses, but the more times you delivered an mRNA molecule into the body, the higher the risk of an immune response. Because many of the diseases scientists hoped to cure would likely need repeated doses, that was a problem. The mRNA molecule also needed to be protected from degradation before it reached the cells.

Part of the solution, scientists discovered, was to encase the mRNA in a tiny bubble of fat called a lipid nanoparticle, a technology that many scientists had worked on for decades.[6] But lipid nanoparticles came with their own set of difficulties. They tended to build up in the body and, with repeated dosing, could cause liver toxicity.

5 Cited in a 2013 article in *Boston* magazine titled "Does Moderna Therapeutics Have the NEXT Next Big Thing?"
6 A 2021 article in *Nature* called "The Tangled History of mRNA Vaccines" details how lipid technology came into being.

In typical Moderna fashion, the company claimed that its scientists had solved this problem. But that may have been an exaggeration. "I think they clearly overstated their ability to dose people over and over again without causing significant toxicities," says another biotech investor who has closely studied Moderna. "And when you're unable to dose people over and over again, that removes a ton of potential diseases from your target set."

Another intellectual property controversy started in 2018, when Moderna tried to persuade the U.S. Patent and Trademark Office (USPTO) to invalidate several lipid nanoparticle patents held by a Canadian company, Arbutus Biopharma. The outcome was mixed, but then, in 2022, after the USPTO had upheld some of the patents, Arbutus and a company it had helped launch called Genevant Sciences sued Moderna for patent infringement. As of June 2023, that suit was still ongoing. Should Moderna lose, it will have to pay Arbutus a royalty for use of the technology. (In a response to the suit, Moderna said it "denies the allegations" and that it had moved beyond the delivery technology owned by Arbutus.) But the question remains: Why would Moderna have started the fight if it didn't need the patents?

Was Moderna's larger thesis about the promise of mRNA another example of hype? Actually, it wasn't. One only had to look around and see that other biotech start-ups were chasing the same dream. One example was CureVac, a German company founded in 2000; it eventually raised $1.8 billion from investors including the Bill and Melinda Gates Foundation to further its work using mRNA to develop vaccines.

Another German company trying to harness mRNA's potential was BioNTech. It was founded in 2008 by the husband-and-wife oncologists Ugur Sahin and Ozlem Tureci. In 2013, Sahin and Tureci hired Katalin Karikó, the woman who'd started it all, to head its mRNA efforts.

BioNTech was the anti-Moderna. It published a slew of data, was regarded as a great place to do science, and didn't issue celebratory press releases every time it started a new project. It focused largely on cancer, but in 2018 it signed a deal that would turn out to be critical to its future, agreeing to a partnership worth up to $425 million with the pharmaceutical giant Pfizer. The goal of the partnership was to use mRNA technology to develop an influenza vaccine.

"It was always known that vaccines were the low-hanging fruit," says Hempton. Because the very purpose of a vaccine is to trigger a response by the body's immune system, mRNA's inherent weakness would become a strength. In addition, an mRNA vaccine was potentially both faster and easier than traditional vaccine making, which generally involves growing a pathogen and then putting it (or something derived from it) into the human body to stimulate an immune reaction. The process of growing the pathogen—for instance, influenza vaccines are grown in chicken embryos—is long, laborious, and fraught with potential problems. Merck's Ebola vaccine, one of the fastest ever to be approved in the company's history, still took about five years from start to finish. An mRNA vaccine, by contrast, could be created within weeks if not days.

Moderna had long resisted going all in on vaccine development. Low-margin vaccines were not what Moderna had promised investors; they expected the company to someday produce cancer or heart disease drugs—the kinds of drugs that can make investors rich. Vaccines had saved hundreds of millions of lives, sparing people from terrible diseases like smallpox, measles, and polio. But they were often given just once, and because they were purchased by governments, the pricing didn't excite investors, who much preferred companies that developed drugs that treated rare diseases that only a few thousand people needed but that could be priced in the hundreds of thousands of dollars. "To have a mega-blockbuster, what you want is a high-priced drug that you give somebody for the rest of their life," says Hempton.

Phil Dormitzer, a biochemist who would eventually help develop Pfizer's COVID-19 vaccine, which it developed in partnership with BioNTech, had worked at Novartis during the 2009 H1N1 pandemic. When H1N1 hit, Novartis essentially put the rest of its vaccines pipeline on hold to develop a vaccine. The company's scientists succeeded. But when the H1N1 virus turned out to be relatively mild, investors complained that Novartis had failed to meet its goals for the rest of its vaccines pipeline. Under pressure from shareholders, Novartis sold its vaccines and diagnostics business in chunks to smaller companies. "Even if you're successful, you may find that because other things haven't been done, you're now in trouble," says Dormitzer.

In a world obsessed with shareholder value, the vaccine business had no place. "Manufacturers are expressing concern about their ability to afford these costly disruptions to their profit-seeking operations," wrote *Stat* in 2018. "As a result, when the bat-signal next flares against the night sky, there may not be anyone to respond."

In December 2018, Moderna sold shares to the public, raising more than $600 million and valuing the company at a stunning $7.5 billion. It was the biotech industry's second-largest IPO ever, trailing only Genentech's public offering in 1980. Although the company had quietly begun working on a few vaccines, that part of the business was under the radar. In its pre-IPO presentations it spoke instead about the twenty drugs it was developing, six of which were in clinical trials. Its drug candidates, it said in one presentation, could generate anywhere between $17 and $37 billion in peak revenue. "We are at the beginning of a 20-year mRNA innovation cycle," Moderna claimed.

In the years prior to the IPO, Moderna had raised $2.6 billion from sophisticated, enthusiastic investors like venture capitalists. Yet in the immediate aftermath of the public offering, the reception it got was very different. The sunlight of the public market has a way of bringing questions to the fore, and the fever dreams were replaced with skepticism. In some quarters, there was outright disbelief that Moderna was for real. "Moderna has no approved products on the market and has consistently lost money as it ramps up its research and drug development efforts," noted Bloomberg News on the day of its public offering. Added *The Wall Street Journal*, "Moderna also has been dogged by doubts about whether it can realize its promise."

On the day of its IPO, its stock "broke," meaning that by the end of the trading session, it was selling for less than its offering price. It never really recovered. By late 2019—a year the company lost $500 million—the stock was still below its IPO price. Short sellers—investors who bet against companies—were swarming all over Moderna's stock, convinced it had further to fall. Many health-care investors thought Moderna was close to a scam. "All hat and no horse," said one skeptical investor. In other words, a whole lot of hype.

And then, of course, the world changed.

Dr. Kizzmekia Corbett, an immunologist at the NIH, remembers waking up on New Year's Eve around 6 a.m. to an email from her boss, Barney Graham, the deputy director of the NIH's Vaccine Research Center. He was following the news out of Wuhan. "Get ready for 2020," he wrote.

Like Fauci, Graham was a lion in the world of infectious diseases. He had been recruited by the NIH two decades earlier to help develop a vaccine for HIV. But as that effort failed, the center switched to infectious diseases, which were Graham's specialty. He'd been working on coronaviruses long before the pandemic hit. He'd essentially spent his life studying how viruses cause disease and how you can design a vaccine to stop them.

A coronavirus gets its name from the distinctive crown, or spike, that sits on its surface. When MERS hit in 2012, Graham and a colleague named Jason McLellan led a team of researchers, which included Corbett, that figured out how to engineer proteins in order to stabilize that spike before it fused with other cells. They published their work in August 2017. Two months later, the Department of Health and Human Services was granted a patent, which listed Graham, McLellan, and Corbett among the inventors. This was a critically important step for anyone trying to target that spike protein with a vaccine. "Had they not spent years already studying MERS, there is no way they could have turned around a vaccine so quickly," writes the journalist David Heath in his book about the race to develop the vaccines.

The NIH began to license the patent to vaccine developers on a nonexclusive basis. Although Moderna had begun working with NIH scientists on vaccines for a variety of viruses, the company declined to license the NIH patent. For a long time, no one much cared.

It wasn't immediately obvious, even to the NIH researchers, that the new virus that had been found in Wuhan was going to lead to a pandemic. Graham, however, thought that it offered the perfect opportunity to extend the NIH's work with Moderna to include efforts to develop a vaccine for this new coronavirus. As soon as the SARS-CoV-2 sequence was posted on virological.org, Graham, Corbett, and McLellan went to work with the Moderna scientists. They quickly decided that the spike protein was the most efficient way to target the new coronavirus. Then, using mRNA, they could introduce a molecule into the body that would briefly instruct human cells to produce the coronavirus's spike protein. The immune system would see the protein, recognize it as alien, and learn to attack the coronavirus.

"We even knew based on my lab notebook what doses would work in animals, what exact construct to design . . ." Corbett would later say in an interview. Adds Dormitzer, "There are a bunch of technology streams that have been in development over the past couple of decades, and they really came together for this."

From the point of view of the U.S. government, it was clear that this was a collaboration. Fauci would later say that the "vaccine was actually developed in my institute's Vaccine Research Center by a team of scientists led by Dr. Barney Graham and his close colleague, Dr. Kizzmekia Corbett." The NIH would subsequently refer to the vaccine as the "NIH-Moderna vaccine."

Not surprisingly, perhaps, Moderna's version of the story was different. "The vaccine technology was developed by Moderna," Bancel told an MIT publication in December 2020. "What we have done for a period of time is to send them [the NIH scientists] products to try with different viruses. . . . When the coronavirus sequence was put online in January, we had a meeting with them 48 hours later. And both teams, NIH and Moderna, had come to the same design."

But the wrangling over credit would come later. In those early months of 2020, there was only the work, which was intensified by the uncertainty.

On January 21, 2020, Bancel called Afeyan to ask how he felt about using the new virus as an opportunity to test Moderna's ability to move quickly. (Afeyan remembers the exact date because it's his daughter's birthday.) The need for the vaccine wasn't yet clear, because nobody yet knew how dangerous this virus was. But it was a test. "In the pharmaceutical business, moving fast is the last thing you actually value because you have to wait for regulators, wait for manufacturing, wait for trials," says Afeyan. "Nobody moves fast. It's like having a car that can go fast, except there's a speed limit. And suddenly the speed limit was off. We said, 'Let's do it for that reason.'"

Within days, Moderna announced that it had received funding from the Coalition for Epidemic Preparedness Innovations (CEPI)—a foundation established in 2016 to develop vaccines against emerging infectious illnesses—to come up with a vaccine against the novel coronavirus. The press release noted that the Vaccine Research Center at NIAID had "collaborated with Moderna to design the vaccine," and that NIAID would conduct the phase 1 clinical study, which determines if a prospective medicine is safe. Bancel was quoted as saying, "Advances in global public health require the collective effort of public-private partnerships— no organization can act alone. We are honored to be supporting NIH and CEPI."

Inside Moderna, some executives questioned whether working on this new vaccine was worth the diversion of resources it would necessitate. "All of the resources were already spoken for," says a former senior executive about that period. "It wasn't obvious what we should do, and there was potentially significant downside." Moderna had been among the companies that tried—unsuccessfully—to develop a Zika vaccine. That memory hadn't gone away. And Moderna's stock was struggling. It truly was a bet-the-company moment. "This is a pandemic response," Andres later told the Harvard Business School researchers. "If we decide to pursue this, it means we need to be all in. There's no exit."

Despite all the money it had raised over the years, Moderna lacked the funds to develop the vaccine. In February, the company succeeded in raising $500 million in a secondary stock offering, but at a price below the IPO. It wasn't enough. Investors didn't want their capital going toward a vaccine that might not produce any financial returns.

Bancel's magic seemed to run out, at the worst possible time. "I wasn't good enough to get it done," Bancel told the writer Greg Zuckerman.

The skepticism that Moderna could deliver on anything was widespread. "I would've bet against them all day long and twice on Sunday," says one longtime investor.

As the hedge fund manager Justin Simon put it, "There was a laziness that went on, a pattern recognition of, 'I've seen these guys before and they're full of shit. So they must be full of shit again.'"

For all its braggadocio, the only way Moderna was going to be able to produce a vaccine was if it got even more help from the federal government than it had already received. And help was on the way.

13

"There's Nowhere to Hide"

O n a chilly day in mid-April 2020, Moncef Slaoui, the retired head of the vaccine department at the pharmaceutical giant GlaxoSmith-Kline, was sitting by his unopened pool in Gladwyne, Pennsylvania, when his phone rang. The hopeful hint of spring in the air belied the dark desperation that suffused the world as the COVID-19 pandemic raged and the world's wealthiest country struggled to figure out a way forward.

The caller was Jim Greenwood, a former Republican congressman from Pennsylvania who, since 2004, had served as the CEO of the trade association BIO, short for the Biotechnology Innovation Organization. Greenwood was reaching out after getting a call from Alex Azar. He had an urgent question for Slaoui: "Do you think that if you had unlimited resources, money, and people that we could have a vaccine against COVID-19 widely available by the end of the year?"

On one level, Slaoui was an unlikely recipient of such a call. He was no fan of Donald Trump, and of course Trump had no use for anyone who didn't support him. Slaoui had never even been a Republican. He was an immigrant from Morocco, one of four siblings, all of whom got either their PhDs or their MDs, even though neither parent had gone to college. His childhood was a time of rampant repression; Slaoui's memories of high school in Casablanca included frequent student strikes followed by army clampdowns.

When he headed to the Free University of Brussels, in Belgium, he became part of the Moroccan Student Union, a Marxist group that wanted to make Morocco a more populist and democratic country. Slaoui, who is fluent in English, French, and Arabic, speaks in a measured and cosmopolitan manner that can mask strong passions. At that time, his passion was politics. For several years, he did little academic work, spending his time instead on political activism.

In 1981, he received a call telling him that he should return to Morocco because his mother was ill. He knew there were risks—the regime was not kind to dissidents—but he couldn't bear the thought of never seeing his mother again should she die. When his plane landed, an uncle with ties to the police met him at the airport. "I'm here to make sure you're not hurt," he said. Slaoui arrived home to see both his father and his mother crying. "Why are you destroying your life?" his father said. "If your uncle weren't connected to the government, you would be in jail, and you'd disappear. And if you want to change the world, condition number one is to be alive."

At that moment, Slaoui said to himself, "I will find another way to help change people's lives."

And so Slaoui embarked on a path that made him, politics aside, the best possible person to get Greenwood's call. He'd always been interested in medicine, and he began pouring his passion into immunology.

He was drawn to the creativity required to train the immune system to recognize and fight something that it had never seen before. "There are two human systems that are designed to predict the unpredictable and know the unknowable," he says. "That's the immune system and the nervous system."

After finishing his PhD in 1983, he spent two years as a postdoctoral fellow at Harvard and Tufts University. In 1985, he made his way back to Belgium when his first wife, an immunologist, was recruited by Glaxo Wellcome, which was trying to develop an HIV vaccine. Slaoui was still enough of a socialist to view the pharmaceutical industry with disdain. But as he watched his wife's work, he began to realize how world changing vaccines could be.

To Slaoui, vaccines held out more promise to help people than politics ever could. He'd often tell people that vaccines had saved more lives than any other tool in history.

In 1988, Slaoui began to work for what was then called SmithKline Beckman. (In 2000, Glaxo Wellcome merged with SmithKline Beckman to become GlaxoSmithKline. Today the company is called GSK.) Over the ensuing decades, he helped develop vaccines against genital herpes, human papillomavirus, rotavirus, pneumococcal bacteria, malaria, H1N1, Ebola, and more. In all, he supervised seven vaccines through development, an unrivaled accomplishment.

When the Ebola virus hit West Africa in 2014, Slaoui's division put everything else aside to make a vaccine quickly. It took only seven months to have vaccine ready for a phase 1 trial, in which the potential drug is tested for safety in otherwise healthy people. (This is the first of three phases needed to get a drug approved by the FDA.) But while the Ebola outbreak killed eleven thousand Africans, it had largely subsided by the time GSK's vaccine was developed.

Which meant, of course, that GlaxoSmithKline took a hit in the stock market. And the government officials who had been so adamant about the need to develop the vaccine suddenly had more important things to do. "Everybody who was talking to us every day, all the governments who were saying, 'Where are you? How can we help you?' just turned around and looked the other way," Slaoui says. Slaoui realized that the world needed a way to support the development and manufacture of vaccines that didn't depend on publicly traded companies trying to maximize shareholder value.

So Slaoui got GSK to agree to help create a nonprofit division it called the Biopreparedness Organization, or BPO. Its purpose was to design vaccines that could prevent pandemics and, just as important, a strong vaccine manufacturing capacity. Vaccine manufacturing is incredibly complex, particularly when done at large scale. To that end, Slaoui even persuaded GSK to buy an empty plant in Maryland. "Unfortunately, one of these days, one of these agents is going to be global and very lethal. It's going to be catastrophic," Slaoui told CNBC in 2016. "So we have to have a longer term commitment and solution that governments and a long-term institution should drive and fund."

GSK had always assumed that the government would help fund the BPO. But it turned out that the Obama administration wasn't interested. Wealthy foundations like the Gates Foundation also passed on the BPO. It never went anywhere. When Slaoui retired from GSK, he started dabbling as a venture capitalist while also joining a number of company boards. One of those boards was Moderna's.

What Slaoui calls his "aha moment" came in the fall of 2019, when Moderna reported the results of a phase 1 clinical trial for a vaccine against cytomegalovirus, a common virus that can cause severe problems for people with weakened immune systems. Since joining the board, he had become excited about mRNA's potential for developing vaccines. After the phase 1 trial, he *knew* mRNA would work.

By the time Greenwood asked Slaoui whether a coronavirus vaccine could be produced by the end of the year, he was convinced that mRNA might make it possible. At the end of the call, Greenwood said, "Listen, Moncef, I'm sorry, but you're going to get a call from the White House about this."

Two weeks later, he got an email from Robert Kadlec, the assistant secretary of HHS who was trying to help manage the Trump administration's early response to the pandemic. Kadlec invited Slaoui to come for an interview in Washington on May 7.

Greenwood's call to Slaoui marked a pivotal moment in the U.S. effort to subdue the pandemic. After months of government and industry being at odds, with Trump even tweeting out criticism of companies like General Motors and 3M that were trying to help, the two forces finally joined together. Pharmaceutical and biotech companies raced to develop a COVID-19 vaccine. The companies that developed vaccines were aided by the federal initiative Slaoui would soon head, which the administration called Operation Warp Speed. Without the government's involvement, some companies would no doubt have succeeded in developing COVID-19 vaccines. But it would likely have taken years. "I think history will remember this as an all-of-government and all-of-America approach to solving a societal problem," says a former senior civil servant. "We were able to cut through a lot of barriers, including bureaucratic barriers. It will be remembered as proof of concept that we can break down silos." Carlo de Notaristefani, a longtime pharmaceutical executive who joined Warp Speed to run manufacturing, says, "For me, the number one learning is that government alone cannot resolve a pandemic, and industry alone cannot. You need to bring the two together."

Trump announced the formation of Operation Warp Speed on May 15, 2020, laying out a goal of making 100 million vaccine doses available by November and 300 million by January 2021. He was flanked by Slaoui, who had been chosen over five other candidates to lead the project, and General Gustave Perna, the former head of the U.S. Army's Materiel Command, who would serve as the chief operating officer. Although most scientists remained doubtful that a safe vaccine could be produced that quickly, Slaoui said that he had seen some early trial data that gave him a measure of confidence. "We will do the best we can," he said.

That May 15 press conference marked one of the few times Trump had any significant involvement in Operation Warp Speed. That may help explain why it was the administration's one true COVID-19 success story—and ironically enough, as one person involved argues, that may also explain why Warp Speed could only have worked under Trump. Few other presidents would have been so hands-off. Warp Speed was devised by people who had been marginalized by the White House, and it was carried out, for the most part, by people like Slaoui, who thought the mission was so important they put aside their distaste for the president. "I think 99 percent of us voted Democratic," says one person who was involved.

The marginalized officials included the HHS secretary, Alex Azar, and his assistant secretary for preparedness and response, Robert Kadlec. Azar had made many enemies in the Trump administration even before the pandemic hit, and after Nancy Messonnier's briefing he was in Trump's doghouse. There was a steady stream of rumors that he would soon be fired.

As for Kadlec, he had served at the White House from 2002 to

2005 as the director for biodefense on the Homeland Security Council and had helped craft the bill that created BARDA. He completely understood that, given their past experience with vaccines, companies needed some assurance that there would be a market for a COVID-19 vaccine—assurance that could come only from the government.

But the pandemic gave Kadlec a visibility inside the administration that he hadn't had before, and that wasn't all to the good. Although he had his defenders—"Bob Kadlec is the right man in the right spot at the right time for our country," tweeted a former Obama administration official—others found him brusque and difficult to work with. Inside the White House, Kadlec had a reputation for "shoot first, aim later." And he was an Azar supporter.

Thus when Kadlec and an FDA official named Peter Marks first began discussing ways to shorten the time it took to develop a vaccine, no one else in government paid them much attention. Kadlec had looked into research done by Joseph DiMasi, the director of economic analysis at the Tufts Center for the Study of Drug Development, on how drug development times can be shortened; he and Marks brainstormed how they might put that research to use. To get a vaccine on the market quickly, the FDA would have to shortcut the normally lengthy process of drug approval by using an interim designation, Emergency Use Authorization, which permits expedited approval in an emergency. They also realized that any effort to speed up vaccine development would mean building the manufacturing capacity at the same time as the development effort, instead of waiting until the vaccine was ready. That was unprecedented.

Marks, who was a *Star Trek* fan, started calling their nascent plans Warp Speed. Kadlec, an amateur military historian, preferred MP2—Manhattan Project Two. They soon had the outline of a plan and drafted a memo to Azar.

Azar had already started to realize that things needed to change. At one point, he was asked to make a congratulatory call to Alex Gorsky, the CEO of Johnson & Johnson. BARDA, which is part of HHS, had agreed to give J&J $456 million to help accelerate the development of a vaccine. (BARDA also gave Moderna $483 million for the same purpose.) After Azar hung up the phone, he said, "That's the first I've heard of this."

During the call, Gorsky told Azar that phase 1 trials were scheduled to begin in September. That was six months away—far too long if the country hoped to have a working vaccine by the end of the year. There wasn't any sense of real urgency. And, Azar realized, BARDA hadn't done anything to instill urgency within J&J by, for instance, including incentives to accelerate development. Which caused Azar to ask himself a basic question: What, exactly, was the government getting for its money?

On April 10, Marks and Kadlec briefed Azar in his office. They agreed that "Manhattan Project" was not the image they were trying to convey, so they went with "Warp Speed." The central idea was to use the government's resources to accelerate the production of vaccines—and, importantly, to remove the financial risk to the vaccine makers by having the government agree to purchase a certain number of doses of any vaccine that gained FDA approval. Akash Tewari, the Jefferies analyst, says, "If Operation Warp Speed didn't create the market, none of this would have happened."

Azar wasn't worried about how much Warp Speed would cost. "We'd already spent $3 trillion [on the CARES Act]," he said. "So there is no amount of money that we shouldn't spend to get a vaccine faster. In business terms, there's an infinite return on investment."

In searching for someone to head up Warp Speed, Azar called Greenwood. He also called Art Levinson, the retired CEO of Genentech and a revered figure in the biotech world. "You don't have a discovery issue," Levinson told Azar. "So you don't need the world's greatest scientists. You have an execution issue, and you have a manufacturing issue."

Azar also needed to get the White House on board. During a meeting with Jared Kushner, Azar brought up Warp Speed for the first time. He told the president's son-in-law that if Russia or China had a vaccine before America, that would change the global strategic balance of power over the next several decades. The race to develop a vaccine would be akin to "the 1960s space race that pitted the Soviet Union against the U.S.," as *The Wall Street Journal* later put it.

Kushner quickly became Warp Speed's champion—and that mattered. Azar might be on Trump's blacklist, but Kushner was always going to have the president's ear. Kushner would also prove capable of protecting Operation Warp Speed from the infighting that plagued the Trump White House.

Greenwood soon called Azar back. "I've got your guy," he said. "His name is Moncef Slaoui." Greenwood also told Azar that he needed someone else, a man named Carlo de Notaristefani who had led manufacturing for Bristol Myers Squibb and then for the Israeli generic drug maker Teva. Greenwood described Notaristefani as an "unsung hero" because he'd been able to master the art of launching both one big product a year for Big Pharma and then a hundred new products a year for a generic drug maker.

Still, Warp Speed's future wasn't assured. Among some in Trump's inner circle, Azar was toxic. In Washington's corridors of power, one surefire way to undermine a colleague is through press leaks. Sure enough, Azar's team soon got wind that both *The Wall Street Journal* and *The New York Times* had stories in the works that would claim the HHS secretary's lack of leadership had resulted in a series of missteps, one of which was the lack of a vaccine plan.[1] Trump was also regarded as being particularly susceptible to what the media reported. If the media said the vaccine strategy was a mess, then the truth might not matter: Trump might hate the strategy.

The weekend of April 25, Azar woke to his staff telling him that his imminent firing was about to be reported in the press. Instead of ruminating, Azar decided to keep pushing forward. He went for a five-mile walk during which he called various administration officials including Secretary of Defense Mark Esper trying to enlist support for Warp Speed.

Azar would later say that he never knew for sure what the truth was, because Trump called him that Sunday to say he had never considered firing him. But others say that he was saved by Kushner and Adam Boehler, Kushner's former roommate who had joined the administration. They had concluded that the Trump administration had enough turmoil already; the president was in the process of firing officials who he believed had crossed him during his impeachment. Kushner and Boehler thought the administration would be better served if Azar were rehabilitated in the public eye, rather than let go. That Sunday, Azar went to Boehler's house, where they all agreed that one of the "wins" Azar could deliver was Warp Speed.

Those who wanted to see Warp Speed succeed had leaked word of it to Bloomberg News, hoping the reporters would break the story in time to help prove to the administration that Warp Speed was an initiative they should get behind. That would help shore up Azar too, although Azar wasn't supporting Warp Speed because it was a safe bet

---

1 *The Wall Street Journal* article, which ran on April 22, 2020, was headlined HEALTH CHIEF'S EARLY MISSTEPS SET BACK CORONAVIRUS RESPONSE. The key allegation was that he'd told the president that COVID-19 was under control.

for his own future: He'd been warned that if it failed, he'd go down with it.

Wednesday, April 29, turned out to be the key day. An early afternoon meeting was set for the Situation Room; this was where Azar and Peter Marks were going to present the Warp Speed plan to top officials like Chief of Staff Mark Meadows and the Coronavirus Task Force members Deborah Birx and Anthony Fauci. Or at least that's what some of those heading into the meeting thought was going to happen. One observer, savvier about how the Trump administration operated, described it as a "setup." If the meeting descended into chaos, as Azar's enemies hoped, then all they had to do was leak the details—perhaps *The New York Times* could add it to its still-unpublished Azar story— finish off Warp Speed, and maybe Azar too.

Marks began the meeting with a brief overview of Warp Speed. Almost immediately Birx unleashed on him. "Marks got killed," says a participant. She appeared to be particularly angry that BARDA hadn't been keeping anyone in the loop, and blamed Marks for that—even though he had no connection to BARDA. A participant says that she was also angry about the focus on mRNA vaccines, because they were unproven.[2]

Meadows was also firing off furious questions: Why, he demanded to know, wasn't the manufacturing capacity already up and running? Marks kept trying to explain that that was the exact purpose of Warp Speed. "This should have happened already," Meadows kept saying.

"This was one of the most unpleasant meetings I've ever had to witness in my career," Azar later told his team. "It was shoot first, aim second."

---

2 Birx did not return a message requesting comment.

But as everyone was walking out, Fauci put his arm around Azar. "Don't worry, Alex," he said. "mRNA is going to work."

And then, Operation Warp Speed—and Azar—caught a break. As the meeting was under way, Bloomberg News posted its story, with the headline TRUMP'S "OPERATION WARP SPEED" AIMS TO RUSH CORONAVIRUS VACCINE. It began, "The Trump administration is organizing a Manhattan Project–style effort to drastically cut the time needed to develop a coronavirus vaccine, with a goal of making enough doses for most Americans by year's end." The piece noted that Azar was in charge.

Later that night, the *New York Times* piece, which noted Azar's "difficult personality" and said he was on "thin ice," was published. What was important was what it didn't say: that the vaccine strategy was a mess.

Warp Speed had survived.

A few days later, Azar and Kadlec went to the Pentagon in search of their Leslie Groves. After all, the Manhattan Project had been led by two men: Robert Oppenheimer, who steered the science, and Groves, an Army Corps of Engineers officer whose team did virtually everything else, from constructing the site at Los Alamos to tracking Germany's nuclear efforts. "You need Gus Perna," Esper told them. (Azar would later credit Esper with mobilizing the entire Department of Defense in the service of public health.) Gustave Perna, a four-star general and former army deputy chief of staff, had spent his whole career managing procurement and logistics. For instance, when the army deployed to Iraq, how were they going to get food? Latrines? Equipment? If a detail goes wrong, the whole operation can go bust before it starts. "He's the kind of person whose mentality is that old proverb, 'For want of a nail, the kingdom was lost,'" Azar told his team after Perna agreed to join Operation Warp Speed.

When Slaoui had his job interview on May 11, he minced no words. "All I want to do is make a vaccine that helps our country and the world," he said. "I'm not going to be afraid to break things. I have no political ambition." If he had to hold meetings just to placate people, he was out. And if there was any political interference, he would resign on the spot. The other five candidates all expressed doubt about having a vaccine by the end of 2020. Slaoui alone said he could do it. He got the job. He resigned from Moderna's board and sold all his stock in the company, knowing that he was likely forfeiting a fortune. He also decided he wouldn't take a paycheck for overseeing Warp Speed. Three days later, when Trump unveiled Operation Warp Speed in the Rose Garden, Slaoui thought to himself, "There's nowhere to hide."

———

The Warp Speed team was given office space on the seventh floor of the Hubert H. Humphrey Building, a massive, almost Soviet-style block of concrete with tiny windows that had previously been used by the FDA. The team's first task was to decide which vaccines to support. A meeting to discuss the issue quickly bogged down in arguments, with Birx in particular continuing to raise objections about mRNA, according to several participants. Slaoui simply put an end to it. He announced that they were going to hedge their risks by supporting three different vaccine development platforms: mRNA; "viral vector" vaccines, which use a modified version of a different virus to deliver instructions to people's cells; and "protein subunit" vaccines, which contain pieces of the problematic virus along with another ingredient that helps the immune system respond to that virus. He then told the others which companies Warp Speed would be supporting: Moderna and Pfizer—which had cut a deal to partner with BioNTech—for the mRNA platform; Johnson & Johnson, Merck, and AstraZeneca for the viral vector vaccine; and Novavax and Sanofi for the spike protein platform. Slaoui was unapologetic about taking control. "This was the most important and most far-reaching decision we had to make," he says. "If the ones we selected weren't successful, it would be total failure."

The only vaccine candidate that wasn't fully Slaoui's choice was AstraZeneca's. Oxford University, which had a crack vaccine team at its Jenner Institute for Vaccine Research, had already begun a clinical trial for a vaccine it was developing; AstraZeneca was its distribution and manufacturing partner. And the press was already calling the Oxford-AstraZeneca vaccine a winner. That made Azar think about Birx's demands for a non-mRNA vaccine, so he put Kadlec and Marks in charge of negotiating a deal. On May 21, Operation Warp Speed gave AstraZeneca $1.2 billion in exchange for 300 million doses, so long as its vaccine got FDA approval. That came out to about $4 a dose. (The company insisted that it would not make a profit from the vaccine.)

When Azar called Trump to tell him about the deal, Trump was furious. "Boris Johnson is going to kill me," he said, according to someone who was in the room.

A few days earlier, Moderna had announced that its vaccine had generated neutralizing antibodies in eight volunteers. It was a tiny sample, and there was still plenty of skepticism. Nevertheless, Moderna's stock, which had sold for less than $30 a share back in April, shot up to $80. That evening, the company announced another stock sale. This time, it was able to raise more than $1.3 billion to help jump-start its manufacturing capabilities. In total, Moderna received about $10 billion from the federal government.

Each company got its own bespoke deal from Slaoui. Sanofi, which was collaborating with GSK, got $2.1 billion for 100 million doses. Johnson & Johnson got $1 billion for 100 million doses.

As for Pfizer, with 2019 revenue of nearly $52 billion, it didn't need or want to be part of Warp Speed. It feared that partnering with the government would slow it down. Inside Pfizer, the quest to develop a vaccine with its partner BioNTech was labeled "Project Light Speed." "You can have any resources you need, but you need to succeed," the company's CEO, Albert Bourla, told his vaccine team. "And by the way," he added, "my expectations on timeline are far faster than anything you think is actually possible, and you have no excuse not to deliver, because any resource you ask for, you're going to get."

But there was one thing Pfizer needed that only Warp Speed could supply: a guaranteed market. Even mighty Pfizer couldn't risk shareholders' wrath by making a huge investment that didn't pay off. Slaoui took care of that in July, making a deal to pay the company $1.95 billion for 100 million doses. Although Pfizer insists it was not thinking about profits when it began its vaccine work, this deal nonetheless set the price of a dose at close to $20. Moderna's U.S. price ended up being set around $16.

Where was Warp Speed's money coming from? Lacking its own congressionally mandated funds, the team had to scramble at first. The team pulled $10 billion from the CARES Act, which was there thanks to Mnuchin, who had added extra money to the Strategic National Stockpile in order to create a slush fund of sorts. They also pulled money from the hospital fund established by the CARES Act. "Thank God for Steven," Azar told a colleague. "If we had had to go to the Hill for a supplemental appropriation, Warp Speed would not have happened."

By late May, Slaoui held a virtual meeting with the companies to discuss the next step: the very large phase 3 clinical trials. "We are preparing to run what may turn out to be the largest and fastest field efficacy trials . . . in history," Slaoui wrote in the invitation to the meeting. The trials would require finding, preparing, vaccinating, and monitoring 120,000 people over six months—or more if Novavax and Sanofi got through their phase 2 trials. It was important that the group be diverse, given the disproportionate effect of COVID-19 on communities of color.

In normal times, phase 3 trials take years. Slaoui wanted them done in a matter of months. In addition to dramatically speeding up the process, Operation Warp Speed had to find and equip all the clinical trial sites with hard-to-obtain PPE so that everyone involved in the trials would be safe.

"We basically have to go from an early adolescent company to a full adult company, skipping all of late adolescence," Moderna's Juan Andres later told Harvard Business School. "It's like we are in the Champions League now and we have to play like we are going to win." Every moment mattered. Johnson & Johnson started its phase 3 trials in September, which was when it would normally have started its phase 1 trial. "I think it would be very difficult to claim that the vaccines would have been developed in this time frame without not just the money but the coordinating role that Warp Speed played," says Noubar Afeyan, the CEO of Flagship Pioneering, which helped found Moderna. "General Perna and Moncef Slaoui brought a level of expertise and experience and logistical capability and, I'd say, a soft hard touch. A velvet stick, such that people had to behave."

At the same time the vaccines were moving through their clinical trials, Operation Warp Speed was also building the capacity to manufacture them. Vaccine manufacturing capacity no longer existed in the United States, and the Trump administration was insisting that the vaccines be manufactured domestically. "There was zero excess capacity

to manufacture vaccines in March of 2020," says Carlo de Notaristefani, the former Teva executive who had signed on as Warp Speed's
manufacturing guru. "And since we didn't know which program could
be successful, we set up the supply chain to manufacture 300 million
doses of each of the six vaccines. That's very large numbers. That's 1.8
billion doses."

While giants like Pfizer assumed that they had the necessary manufacturing resources, a small company like Novavax, which had never
produced anything—and had just fired its manufacturing team because it was running out of money—needed all the help it could get.
"We had to stand up or expand twenty-three manufacturing facilities
across the country," says Notaristefani. That required ordering, install-
ing, and testing every last piece of equipment. "You need everything,"
he says. "Otherwise, you end up being in the situation where the small
screw means the 747 doesn't fly." Those facilities included a plant in
Baltimore run by a biotech company called Emergent BioSolutions that
had been funded by the U.S. government since 2006 and a Texas A&M
plant that was part of a partnership with Fuji, the Japanese company.

Nothing had ever been manufactured at either facility. "We had to
buy all the equipment, hire the people, train the people, install the
equipment, and qualify the equipment before we could start making
products," says Notaristefani. At Emergent alone, that meant hiring
some five hundred people. "Even when you have the shell, to do what
we did in six months normally takes three years."

The Moderna facility the company had built years before wasn't big
enough. Operation Warp Speed helped to expand it. Warp Speed officials also booked all the capacity for 2020 and 2021 at a handful of
contract manufacturers in order to ensure availability.

"We were lucky, because mRNA is a simpler process, given that it's
chemical rather than biological—you are not trying to grow living

things," says Slaoui. "But scaling it up is still an enormous challenge." Companies had to create the mRNA and then enclose it in that lipid nanoparticle. "It's a very sophisticated technology, very difficult to develop and control," says Slaoui. "But once you have the process, it's relatively simple and low risk to execute."

Because this was the first time mRNA had ever been used in a drug, Warp Speed and the companies had to figure out how the manufacturing process would work. "All of it started from zero," says Afeyan. "We were trying different processes to make it work, all of it on the fly," he says.

The logistical complexity was astounding. For every vaccine, Notaristefani says, there can be as many as two thousand components and hundreds of suppliers. "These are not things that you buy off the shelves," he says. "So you need to negotiate with multiple suppliers so that you can receive enough materials every week for years to keep the factories going." It didn't help that the pandemic, in addition to causing shortages of PPE, caused shortages of manufacturing components. Paul Mango, a former McKinsey consultant who served as Azar's deputy chief of staff, estimated that more than 50 percent of the raw material needed to manufacture vaccines comes from outside the United States—another unforeseen effect of globalization.[3]

As with so many other products, many of the key components were made in China. "Everything was missing or in short supply, from the plastic bags that would hold a finished vaccine before it was put into a vial to the vials themselves," says Mango. "This is an industrial mobilization story, not a vaccine development story."

To get the necessary supplies, Operation Warp Speed began using

---

3 Mango subsequently published his own book, which is titled *Warp Speed: Inside the Operation That Beat COVID, the Critics, and the Odds.*

the Defense Production Act (DPA), a law enacted during the Korean War that gives the government the power to order any company located in the United States to prioritize certain orders going to certain customers. In this case, it was used to get components to vaccine manufacturers. The glassmaker Corning, for instance, dedicated all its existing equipment to making the glass vials that would contain the vaccine.

"The lead time for plastic bags was forty-eight weeks," says Notaristefani, in what he says is just one of many examples. "We needed them in twelve weeks. So, the expert from the Department of Defense goes into the supplier and looks at the manufacturing plant and, basically, orders the supplier to re-prioritize their manufacturing and move the deliveries to the rated order ahead." Because these were all products used in the manufacture of drugs, this also involved another layer of coordination with the FDA, to make sure that Operation Warp Speed didn't inadvertently cause shortages of other medications.

Perna's team of army logistics experts, meanwhile, worked hand in hand with pharmaceutical experts. Notaristefani had set up small teams of people, usually led by army majors, inside most plants, to provide real-time information. "There was always some crisis somewhere, some material that was late, and that would risk delaying manufacturing at some of the factories," he says. It might be the plastics from China or the filling machine from Germany—a machine that was capable of filling three hundred to four hundred sterile vials a minute and required twenty engineers to install. "The army was calling FedEx and UPS and saying, 'Hey, this piece of machinery in Germany or Asia or wherever is going to take four weeks by boat,'" says Notaristefani. "'Can you get it on a plane and get it to us in forty-eight hours?' At that time, it could take three months to get a slot on a cargo plane. There was no capacity anywhere. So they were dispatching military cargo planes around the world to pick up transportable equipment."

Late one Saturday night, Notaristefani got a call informing him that there was a problem with trucks that were on their way to Moderna's Massachusetts factory carrying air handling units, which keep the air clean in the room where vaccines are being manufactured. The units are preassembled at the manufacturer and then loaded on a truck. Then they have to be lifted with special cranes into the buildings. Moderna had already hired construction cranes to lift the units into the building. But the units were stuck in New Jersey because they didn't have the necessary permits to carry oversize cargo over the weekend. So military colonels leaned on state officials, who in turn sent the state police to escort the units across state lines, sirens blaring, so Moderna wouldn't lose a week and have to lease the construction cranes a second time.

"There are tens of thousands of choices and decisions and actions that normally take place over years," says Slaoui. "Here, they needed to take place within hours."

The team adopted the routines and lingo of the army. "Battle ready" meant adherence to the calendar, including a daily meeting at 8:00 a.m. "We would go through all the new issues and the things that needed to be done to make sure nothing was overlooked," Slaoui says. "It created a discipline of execution. You can't have a meeting on Monday and say 'I'll do this' and the next day say you haven't done it. It makes it impossible for you to drop the ball because you're going to be held accountable the next morning."

There was more. "NSTR," for instance, means "nothing significant to report." "I had a cheat sheet with all of the acronyms and terms the army uses, some of which are incredibly effective," says Notaristefani. "We all struggle with teleconferences where you have twenty people on the line and people tend to talk over each other, right? But when you put twenty people from the army on, that never happens, because they communicate the same way they do on radios. So if I'm talking, I say 'break' if I pause, but I'm going to continue talking, so don't interrupt me. Only at the end do I say 'over,' so someone else can talk. It's simple, strange, and very effective." He continues, "If I ask someone to do something, that person will always answer, 'Acknowledged.'" That way, everyone knew the task had been assigned and the assignment had been accepted.

For those who came from the private sector, working with the army was a revelation. "It was honestly my best work experience," says Slaoui. "The army doesn't know anything about vaccines, but they know everything about logistics." He adds, "I had a very different view of the army coming in. That completely changed." Notaristefani, for his part, says he plans to use some of the lessons he learned in his private sector work.

Of course, it wasn't all roses and champagne. Trump's erratic press conferences were a distraction. The unwillingness of the FDA commissioner, Stephen Hahn, to condemn the use of the antimalaria drug hydroxychloroquine, which the president was promoting as a COVID-19 cure, infuriated many FDA officials. Trump's complaint, which he voiced often, that the FDA was purposely delaying the approval of vaccines until after Election Day was an even bigger problem. In early August, Trump told Geraldo Rivera that a vaccine might be available before Election Day, which would help his chances. It was the worst thing he could possibly have said. If it were to appear that the pharmaceutical companies were rushing their vaccine development for political reasons, it would do enormous damage. People wouldn't trust the very medicine that was supposed to immunize them from the coronavirus.

In response, the CEOs of the vaccine manufacturers drafted a joint statement in early September: They would apply for FDA authorization of a vaccine only if it demonstrated safety and efficacy in a phase 3 clinical trial. "We believe this pledge will help ensure public confidence in the rigorous scientific and regulatory process," the pledge read. Slaoui told *Science* magazine that he would quit if anyone in the administration pressured him to rush a vaccine to market before its efficacy was proven.

The FDA, for its part, increased the time it wanted to wait after the phase 3 volunteers were given their second shot to at least sixty days. That made it clear the FDA would not be in a position to authorize a vaccine until after the election. The delay appeared to be an effort to prove to the public that the vaccine process was not going to be influenced by politics.

Through all of this, Warp Speed itself remained remarkably immune from political pressure. "I was surprised that we didn't get a lot of political interference," says Notaristefani. "That was my major concern. So frankly, it was good for me that we were left alone and almost forgotten to a certain extent." He adds, "I think it was mostly Alex [Azar] acting as a shield for the organization." Slaoui says that he would get calls from people pushing vaccines and therapeutics that they "knew" were going to work. "Jared would say, please listen to them, so I'd listen to them and call him and say, crap *no*," he says. "And that would be the end of it." About Kushner, he says, "The guy is fact based and straightforward. He'd say, 'If this is what the science says, what the data says, then that's what we're going to do.' He gained my respect."

Of course, the big question was never far from anyone's mind: Would the vaccines work? And if they did, how well would they work? Phil Dormitzer, who at the time was the chief viral scientist at Pfizer, notes that forty-four thousand people were enrolled in the company's phase 3 trial. A number that big illustrated how large the doubts were about the vaccine's efficacy. "The higher the anticipated efficacy, the smaller the trial you need," he says. "We designed our trial based on an assumption of a 60 percent efficacy, which we picked because that's the efficacy of a well-matched flu vaccine."

Dormitzer had rented a little apartment near the facility in Pearl River, New York, where Pfizer's vaccines research and development is based. One evening, he received a phone call from Kathrin Jansen, who at the time led Pfizer's vaccine research and development. "You cannot tell anyone else because this is material nonpublic information," she said. "But the trials showed that the vaccine is at 95 percent efficacy." Dormitzer was stunned. "It was an absolutely overwhelming moment," he says. "From the moment I got that news, I knew that although things might get a lot worse before they got better, they were going to get better."

Slaoui was in his hotel in Washington, D.C., when Bourla called him with the news. "I was expecting high efficacy, but it was an unbelievable joy," he later told *Science* magazine. "It may have been 5 a.m., and I remember telling myself, 'I'm not going to scream.' When I think about this now, it gets emotional. I just realized, 'Oh my God, we're going to control this pandemic.'"

Pfizer announced the good news on November 9, 2020—a week after the presidential election. The following Sunday afternoon, November 15, Moderna learned that the efficacy of its vaccine was nearly identical to Pfizer's.

For a brief moment, the country was euphoric at the news. Dr. Barney Graham later told *The Washington Post* that he started sobbing. Dr. Fauci called the results "just extraordinary." *The New York Times* called it a "historic turning point." And *The Washington Post* called it a "pharmaceutical industry fairy tale."

The markets reacted joyously. The S&P had its best November since 1928. Both Pfizer's and Moderna's stocks soared. "I'm an ornery cynic," says one Wall Street trader who had previously bet against Moderna's stock. "But thank God for the believers, the people who are willing to fund companies like this."

Alas, it wasn't long before people were fighting over the vaccine. The earliest fights were over which groups should get the first doses. In those early days, vaccine availability was limited. Progressives wanted people of color to be first in line because they had suffered disproportionately from the pandemic. Public school teachers believed that *they* should go first; if teachers weren't vaccinated, they would continue to teach remotely, said many union leaders. The CDC recommended that health-care workers and the elderly get priority, which for the most part they did.

There were, of course, some failures and setbacks. Both Johnson & Johnson and AstraZeneca had to pause their clinical trials when several participants came down with rare blood-clotting disorders. While both vaccines were eventually approved, the news about blood clots steered most people away from those two companies.[4] As for Novavax and Sanofi, scientific glitches outside Warp Speed's control caused the companies to delay their request for Emergency Use Authorization until 2022. For the most part, their vaccines are being used abroad.

There were plenty of people who recognized Warp Speed's historic accomplishment and celebrated it. "This will go down in history as

---

4 In mid-2022, the FDA ruled that J&J's vaccine should be administered only in rare situations.

one of science and medical research's greatest achievements," wrote Dr. Eric Topol, a scientific "rock star,"[5] on Twitter. He put together a time line to demonstrate how incredibly compressed the schedule had been.[6]

The initial distribution of the vaccine went less smoothly than its production had. Part of the problem was that Operation Warp Speed decided it had to delegate the distribution to the states. After all, the Warp Speed officials weren't supposed to be involved in the fraught decisions about who should get vaccinated first. There was also an unusual glitch by Perna's team, when more than ten states discovered that their allocation of Pfizer's vaccine was much lower than they had been led to believe. Perna didn't duck. "It was a planning error," he said. "I am responsible."

Another part of the problem, Mango later wrote, was that Pfizer delivered only half of the doses it had promised in December. Because Pfizer initially had refused to work with Warp Speed, it didn't get access to the Defense Production Act and couldn't get the raw materials it needed. Ultimately, in December, Pfizer signed a new deal with the government, in which it got access to the DPA and promised to deliver 200 million doses by the first half of 2021.[7]

There was also criticism of the fact that Warp Speed didn't meet its goal of delivering 100 million doses by year's end. Its leaders say that it was more aspirational than anything else. Azar, borrowing from the management expert Jim Collins, called it a BHAG—"a big hairy auda-

---

5 According to *GQ* magazine and the Geoffrey Beene Foundation in 2009.
6 https://twitter.com/erictopol/status/1332771238771630080?lang=en.
7 Pfizer notes that "scaling up a vaccine at this pace was unprecedented," and says that "after 2021 we delivered more than 2.5 billion whereas no other manufacturer had manufactured 500 million. Today, we've delivered more than 4.5 billion doses to 181 countries."

cious goal" meant to motivate people. "How do you define success?" says one of Warp Speed's senior leaders. "I knew we would never be able to get all the doses we wanted, but I was absolutely convinced that we would have enough doses for everyone in the U.S. by mid-2021." Which they did.

The vaccine rollout also offered a striking contrast between the United States and Europe. It took Europe months longer before it had widely available vaccines. That's because European countries had contracted to purchase doses but hadn't done anything to spur manufacturing. "They didn't put up their sleeves to localize manufacturing in Europe," says Slaoui. "So they didn't get their doses."

For its part, the incoming Biden administration said it would retire the name Warp Speed, citing the "urgent need to address the failures of the Trump team approach to vaccine distribution." To those who had worked so hard to get the vaccines out quickly, the move was both dismissive and inappropriately political.[8] "The biggest lesson for politicians in public health is: Never politicize," Slaoui later told *Science*. "Just let people do the work, and if there are things that are wrong, let's fix them versus make a whole story out of it because that freaks out people."

If only we had been capable of that.

———

Katalin Karikó and Drew Weissman were vaccinated on December 18 at the University of Pennsylvania. Her inoculation was a press event,

---

8 Moncef Slaoui was soon accused of sexual harassment for an affair that had taken place a decade earlier at GSK. He believes the affair was dredged up to discredit him and, by extension, Operation Warp Speed.

because the world finally understood the importance of her pioneering work. Even with Moderna's and Pfizer's efforts, even with Warp Speed, if it hadn't been for Karikó's dedication, it would have taken much, much longer to develop a COVID-19 vaccine. Meaning that tens, if not hundreds, of thousands more people would likely have died.[9]

9 In his book, Mango cites an NIH study showing that by August 2021 the Warp Speed vaccines had saved about 140,000 lives in their first six months of use.

14

To Vax or Not to Vax

There were always going to be people who refused to take the vaccine. There has been an anti-vax movement in the United States since at least the late nineteenth century, when the Anti-Vaccination Society of America was founded to protest the smallpox vaccine. In more recent times, an anti-vax movement sprang up when a British doctor, Andrew Wakefield, published a paper in 1998 claiming to have found a link between autism and the so-called MMR vaccine[1] that children routinely get when they're about a year old. Wakefield's paper was fraudulent—there is no such link—and he was stripped of his medical license. In 2001, he moved to Texas and devoted himself to exposing the supposed dangers of vaccines. His first disciples were the parents of autistic children desperate to find a reason for their offspring's

---

1 The initials MMR stand for measles, mumps, and rubella.

disorder.[2] By the mid-aughts, the actor Jenny McCarthy and Robert F. Kennedy Jr., the son of the late senator, had joined Wakefield's crusade. Over the years, the influence of the anti-vax movement only grew; by 2018, some 20 percent of Americans believed that vaccines were harmful, according to a survey by Zogby Analytics.

There were other issues that were going to make people distrust the COVID-19 vaccines. Black Americans could recall times in the past when they'd been cruelly deceived about medical treatments.[3] Although disparities in vaccination rates narrowed over time, even by early 2023, immunization among Blacks continued to lag whites, according to the Kaiser Family Foundation. The manifold problems with America's healthcare system also played a role. In response to a tweet noting that the gap in death rates between rural and urban Americans had tripled over the past two decades, Jennifer Nuzzo wrote, "My conversations with hundreds of people who weren't convinced of the benefits of vaccination very much matched these trends: almost all did not have regular access to healthcare. Let's not call it anti science, when it may be a trust deficit due to lack of sufficient access."

Add the fact that some people experienced COVID-19 as nothing more than a mild flu, which helped create the perception in some quarters that protecting against it wasn't worth the trouble—and it was clear that persuading everyone to get vaccinated with these brand-new mRNA vaccines was never going to be easy.

And yet persuading everyone to get vaccinated was precisely the

---

2 It's worth recalling that for decades most experts blamed childhood autism on bad mothering.

3 Perhaps the most appalling example was the Tuskegee syphilis study, in which white doctors injected hundreds of Black men with syphilis and then watched the results without medical intervention. It went on for forty years, not ending until 1972.

goal of the public health community. It wasn't just that the vaccines saved individual lives. It was also that many public health officials believed that vaccination might bring about the ultimate goal: herd immunity. If enough Americans got vaccinated, wouldn't that finally halt COVID-19 in its tracks? Nobody could say for sure what percentage of the population needed to be inoculated to reach that goal, except: the more the better.

For this one brief moment, the vaccine was seen as the silver bullet everyone had been hoping for. After all, hadn't Anthony Fauci been saying for months that when a COVID-19 vaccine finally became available, it would be a "game changer"? And didn't California's governor, Gavin Newsom, tell his constituents that "we could put this behind us in a month" if enough Californians were immunized?

Nor was it just blue state officials urging inoculations. Despite his anti-lockdown stance—indeed, despite peddling merchandise with the insulting phrase "Don't Fauci My Florida"—Governor Ron DeSantis urged Floridians to get vaccinated. "If you are vaccinated, fully vaccinated, the chance of you getting seriously ill or dying from COVID is effectively zero," he said at a press conference. "These vaccines are saving lives." The same was true of another vocal critic of COVID-19 mitigation measures, the Texas governor, Greg Abbott. "Texans can help bolster the state's effort to combat the virus by getting vaccinated," he said in a press release. "The COVID-19 vaccine is safe and effective, and it is our best defense against the virus."

The federal government went all in. "Our data from the CDC today suggests that vaccinated people do not carry the virus, don't get sick, and that it's not just in the clinical trials but it's also in real-world data," President Joe Biden's new CDC director, Rochelle Walensky, told Rachel Maddow in March 2021. In late February, CBS aired a special titled *A Shot of Hope: Vaccine Questions Answered*. It featured Fauci, who now had an additional title: chief medical adviser to the president. "As soon as the vaccine becomes available to you, please take the vaccine because . . . the data that we have so far says that the vaccines that we have in use at least prevent very well severe disease that leads to hospitalization and death," he said. On the CBS Sunday morning show *Face the Nation*, he went further. He said that when vaccinated people become infected—which, unlike Walensky, he acknowledged would sometimes happen—"the level of the virus is so low, it makes it extremely unlikely . . . they will transmit it." He added that vaccinations not only helped the vaccinated but also contributed "to the public health by preventing the spread of the virus throughout the community."

Even Donald Trump urged Americans to get vaccinated—at least at first. Appearing before the Conservative Political Action Conference in February, he boasted that his administration "took care of a lot of people" by developing the vaccine. "Everybody go get your shot," he said.

That was in late February. Six months later, Trump spoke at a rally in Cullman, Alabama. "I believe totally in your freedoms," he said, knowing that that had become a rallying cry for the anti-vaxxers. "But," he added, "I recommend taking the vaccine. I did it, it's good, take the vaccines." Trump had been holding these rallies before, during, and after his presidency. His supporters had always cheered him, no matter how outlandish his statements. But when he told the crowd in Cullman to get vaccinated, they booed and jeered. Trump got the message. That was the last time he would ever suggest that vaccinations saved lives.

What had happened in the interim, of course, is that the vaccine had become politicized. Distrusting the vaccine had become a marker of one's status as a Trump supporter, even though Sarah Huckabee

Sanders, the Trump administration's former press secretary, initially called them the "Trump vaccines" and even though in a rational world a decision to be vaccinated would not amount to a political statement. Instead of being an example of America at its best, the vaccines had become an example of America at its worst.

———

The political story is usually framed as an example of Trump supporters acting irrationally, and there is truth to that. Time and again, the media found examples of someone dying of COVID-19 because they refused to take the vaccine that would likely have saved their life.

For some Trump supporters, the vaccine became part of the same continuum that included the Deep State, the "stolen election," and the January 6 insurrection. The mRNA vaccine's side effects, they claimed, were more dangerous than the virus itself. (There were, in fact, instances when the vaccine was linked to serious illnesses like the immune disorder Guillain-Barré syndrome, but they were very rare.) It was also linked to cases of myocarditis in young men, which, while also rare, would turn out to be a thornier issue. Vaccine critics complained that the few doctors who were brave enough to point this out were being canceled by social media and the public health establishment. Conspiracy theories ran rampant: Bill Gates, said to be one of the vaccine masterminds, had put a tiny microchip inside the vaccine to make population surveillance possible. Anytime a well-known person died unexpectedly, the vaccine's side effects were blamed.[4] And so on.

---

4 When Buffalo Bills safety Damar Hamlin suffered a cardiac arrest after a hard hit during a game against the Cincinnati Bengals, vaccine critics blamed his collapse on the vaccine—even though it wasn't known whether he had been vaccinated.

But there's more to the story of vaccine distrust than conspiracy theories. It's worth remembering that questions about the safety of the vaccines started early, and it wasn't because of Republican fearmongering. Vinay Prasad, a doctor and epidemiologist at the University of California, San Francisco, wrote that the theme that we were "rushing a vaccine" was common in media coverage throughout 2020.[5] Not surprisingly, by that September, Pew research showed that trust in vaccines had plummeted, with 78 percent of respondents feeling that the greater risk was moving too fast with vaccination, rather than too slow, and 77 percent feeling that a vaccine would be approved before its safety and efficacy were fully understood.

In fact, it was the Democrats, not the Republicans, who first politicized the vaccine. In September 2020, for instance, Andrew Cuomo said that New York State was going to conduct its own review of the vaccines once they became available. "We can no longer trust the federal government," he said, meaning the Trump administration. And the vice presidential candidate Kamala Harris said this on the campaign trail: "If the public health professionals . . . tell us to take it, I'll be the first in line to take it. Absolutely. But if Donald Trump tells us we should take it, I'm not taking it."

Once Trump lost the election—and the Biden administration started pushing the vaccine—it flipped. Trump's supporters became the vanguard of vaccine opposition. In a CBS poll conducted in mid-March 2021, one-third of Republican respondents said they wouldn't take the vaccine, with another 20 percent unsure about whether they would. Some of the holdouts told the pollsters they were afraid the vaccines

5 "COVID-19 Vaccines: History of the Pandemic's Great Scientific Success and Flawed Policy Implementation."

had been developed too quickly. Others said they had had COVID-19, and thus had the antibodies already. Mostly, though, they said they wouldn't get vaccinated because they didn't trust the government.

It was quickly clear that the cost of not being vaccinated could be high. In the spring of 2021, when the vaccines were widely available, an ABC News analysis of federal data found that the excess death rates in states that voted for Trump were more than 38 percent higher than in states that voted for Biden. By the spring of 2022, the ten states with the highest vaccination rates all voted for Biden, while nine of the ten states with the lowest vaccination rates voted for Trump, according to numbers compiled by the CDC. (The exception was Georgia.)

And so, early on, the story seemed easy. No one remembered the things that complicated the narrative. Everything that was still going wrong was plainly the fault of those who were too selfish and stupid to get vaccinated, and those selfish and stupid people were Trump Republicans. (Most commentators ignored the Black holdouts.) On NPR in mid-July 2021, Walensky said it out loud: "This is becoming a pandemic of the unvaccinated." Some commentators even began to say that those who were not vaccinated should be denied medical care. This was expressed most pungently by the radio personality Howard Stern. "When are we gonna stop putting up with the idiots in this country and just say it's mandatory to get vaccinated? Fuck 'em. Fuck their freedom," he said. "If you didn't get vaccinated and you got COVID, you don't get into a hospital. You had the cure and you wouldn't take it."

Most vaccine supporters wouldn't go that far. But vaccine passports were something they did support. Once the vaccines became widely available, many cities and states began requiring people to show proof of vaccination to get into sporting events, restaurants, offices, and much else—which meant that the unvaccinated were locked out of much of society.[6]

Sadly, the Biden administration, and the public health establishment overall, also sowed distrust in the vaccines. How? In their understandable desire to see everyone get vaccinated, they oversold the vaccines. Quite simply, while the vaccines prevented many deaths, they were not the silver bullet they had been portrayed to be. Take the outbreak of the delta variant that occurred in Provincetown, Massachusetts, in July 2021. Three-quarters of those infected had been vaccinated. Only 4 of the 469 cases required hospitalization, and all 4 had underlying medical conditions. On the one hand, the low number of hospitalized COVID-19 patients meant the vaccines were still a miracle. On the other hand, the fact that vaccinated people had gotten infected at all—which the CDC labeled "breakthrough infections"—suddenly cast doubt on much that Walensky, Fauci, and others had been saying.

Paul Offit, the University of Pennsylvania infectious disease expert[7] who also sits on the FDA's vaccine advisory committee, has long argued that the government's messaging was wrongheaded. But, he says, "I think they thought they were doing the right thing." The less charitable view is the data never supported the promises the government made and the wiser course would have been to acknowledge not only what the vaccines could do but also what they couldn't do. Back in November 2020, when the results of the phase 3 trials were announced, the focus was naturally on the good news that the vaccines had achieved

---

6 This was true in much of the world, of course. One of the most publicized incidents came in January 2022, when the Australian government refused to allow Novak Djokovic, the defending Australian Open champion, to play in the tournament. When Djokovic arrived in Australia expecting to play, he was deported.

7 Offit is also the author of multiple books, including *Deadly Choices: How the Antivaccine Movement Threatens Us All.*

95 percent efficacy. That was supposed to mean that 95 percent of the vaccinated didn't get COVID-19. But the study's volunteers were tested for COVID-19 *only* if they showed symptoms. So the trial didn't tell anything about asymptomatic infections. Nor did the trial measure whether the vaccines prevented transmission, and if so, for how long.

Without question, the vaccines did the most important thing: they prevented most (though not all) hospitalizations and deaths, and for the most part they did so without serious side effects. But when Walensky told Rachel Maddow that people who were vaccinated didn't carry the virus, she couldn't possibly know whether that was true. And when Fauci said vaccinations help prevent the spread of the virus in a community, there was no way he knew that to be true either.[8] "The vaccines were entirely oversold," said Jay Bhattacharya. "The evidence did not examine transmission at all."

Offit, for his part, argues that public health officials should simply have stressed that the vaccines minimized the risk of hospitalization and death. There was no need to call cases where vaccinated people got COVID-19 "breakthrough infections," as if something terrible and unforeseen had happened. "Even if the entire world were vaccinated and this virus never mutated to the point of creating variants, the virus would still circulate and it would still cause mild disease in some people and severe disease in others," he said. What the vaccines actually did was wonderful. Wasn't it enough?

"They [public health officials] decided that the problem was that it was the unvaccinated who were transmitting," says Bhattacharya. "In fact, it was everybody, the vaccinated and unvaccinated alike." He

8 As the World Health Organization director, Tedros Adhanom Ghebreyesus, acknowledged in the fall of 2022, "While vaccines have saved countless lives, they have not substantially reduced transmission."

added, "To blame any single person or any single group demonizes that group without any public health benefit whatsoever."

In the words of Prasad, "The COVID-19 vaccine has been both a story of the success of science and the failure of policy."

There came a point when it became quite obvious this was definitely not "the pandemic of the unvaccinated." The omicron variant, which first arose in South Africa and was the dominant strain in the United States by the end of 2021, was vastly more transmissible than either the original coronavirus or the delta variant that had preceded it. As omicron spread like wildfire, infecting vaccinated and unvaccinated alike, it was the elderly who bore the brunt of it, even though more than 90 percent of Americans over sixty-five had been immunized. As the *New York Times* opinion writer David Wallace-Wells pointed out, "the unvaccinated share of mortality" fell from 77 percent in September 2021 to 38 percent in May 2022. Meanwhile, the percentage of the inoculated who died from COVID-19 grew from 12 percent in January 2022 to 36 percent in April.

Did this mean the vaccines weren't effective? No. But with so many more people getting COVID-19 via the omicron variant, there was inevitably going to be a higher incidence of cases and of hospitalization and death. In addition, what was true of almost any treatment that marshaled the immune system was true of the mRNA vaccines. They didn't work as well for people eighty or older, whose immune systems are, almost by definition, weaker. "Vaccinated people in their late 80s have a similar risk of Covid death as never-vaccinated 70-year-olds," wrote Wallace-Wells. "If it was ever comfortable to say that the unconscionable levels of American deaths were a pandemic of the unvaccinated, it is surely now accurate to describe the ongoing toll as a pandemic of the old."

In 2020, 350,000 Americans died of COVID-19. In 2021, that number rose to 475,000. In 2022, it was a still significant 267,000, according to preliminary data from Johns Hopkins.

———

In a way, Moderna's trajectory mirrored that of the vaccines. At first, Moderna was the pandemic's golden child, generating billions of dollars in revenue after never having made a penny in the previous decade. The company's market value, around $50 billion in early January 2021, stood at more than $200 billion by August. Four of Moderna's founders and executives—the CEO, Stéphane Bancel, the Harvard professor Timothy Springer, the Flagship head, Noubar Afeyan, and the famous chemical engineer Bob Langer—became billionaires.

True, Pfizer's emergency FDA approval had beaten Moderna's by a week, and its mRNA vaccine revenue was roughly double that of the biotech upstart. But Pfizer was the country's dominant pharmaceutical company; Moderna couldn't hope to approach its manufacturing heft.[9] Then again, Moderna became something that was unheard of for young biotech companies: a household name.

Both Pfizer and Moderna immediately set out trying to expand their markets. That's what companies do. One obvious way was to make shots available for younger populations. And many parents, long convinced that even their healthy children faced serious risk of COVID-19, were desperate to have the vaccines made available for them. By the end

9 Pfizer also announced in early November 2021 that it had developed a COVID pill called Paxlovid that significantly reduced hospitalizations and deaths; it generated sales of $19 billion from that drug alone in 2022.

of 2021 the companies had conducted clinical trials to extend the potential vaccine population to children from five to seventeen; by July 2022 parents could vaccinate infants as young as six months.

What is less understandable, especially once it was clear that the vaccines did not prevent transmission, is the way in which the public health authorities pushed the vaccines for children. "The risk is too high and too devastating to our children, and far higher than for many other diseases for which we vaccinate children," Walensky told the agency's advisory panel in advocating for children to be vaccinated.

"I'm still shocked," says Bhattacharya, who argues that because severe COVID-19 is so rare in that age-group, the clinical trials needed to be enormous to show any benefit. And unlike the original vaccine trials, where the end point was the prevention of symptomatic infection, the end point of these trials was simply to measure antibody production. "That is not a sufficient basis to make a recommendation to the population at large," Bhattacharya says.

That wasn't the only questionable way the government promoted the vaccines—and helped Pfizer and Moderna make money. As it became clear that the immunity conferred by the vaccines did wane (although the protection from serious illness did not seem to do so), Pfizer and Moderna announced that they would seek authorization for booster shots.

In August 2021—before the FDA advisory committee had weighed in on whether booster shots would be beneficial—the Biden administration announced that they would be rolled out in a month for everyone over sixteen. In effect, the White House was acting as if the FDA's authorization didn't matter. In late August, two senior officials, Marion Gruber and Philip Krause, resigned to express their dismay about the way the process was being handled, says one source familiar with events. "They [the Biden administration] did exactly what Trump was doing, which was meddle in scientific decisions," says one former senior FDA employee. "I've never heard anyone affix a date and time to a decision that the FDA was supposed to make." It was "the administration's booster plan; it wasn't the FDA's booster plan," Offit told *Politico.*

On September 17, the advisory committee on which Offit sat voted that booster shots should be recommended for only the most vulnerable groups—the elderly and the immunocompromised. A CDC advisory panel issued a similar recommendation. Two months later, sidestepping its own advisory panels, the FDA approved the boosters for anyone over eighteen, thus aligning itself with the administration's desire.

Offit is among the experts who think that the way a healthy person's body defends against a virus—long-lasting T cells can fend off the serious effects long after the antibodies have faded—meant that the importance of boosters was exaggerated. "I think [the booster's benefit] has held up to be true for those who are over 65," Offit told an American Medical Association interviewer in the spring of 2022. A year later, Offit said in an email that "the most recent evidence suggests three doses of an mRNA containing vaccine or two doses plus natural infection likely gives long-lived protection against severe disease for young (<75) healthy people."[10]

Offit's case is all the stronger because, as he points out, any medicine comes with the risk of side effects. The vaccines are no exception.

---

10 A paper looking at data from New York and California showed that the risk of hospitalization among those who had not had a previous COVID-19 diagnosis and were not vaccinated was 11.5 per 1,000, while the risk of hospitalization for those who had a prior infection, regardless of vaccination, was 0.3 per 1,000.

There have been enough reports of myocarditis in young men to make one ask whether, for healthy young people, the risks outweigh the benefit. A parent didn't have to be a Trump supporter to question whether their teenage son should get immunized.

In the fall of 2022, Moderna and Pfizer rolled out yet another vaccine product, the so-called bivalent boosters. These jabs were supposed to help protect against the omicron variant as well as the original strain of COVID-19. Bhattacharya points out Moderna's booster was at least approved based on antibody production in humans; Pfizer's was approved based on antibody production in . . . eight mice. "They presented to our committee on June 28, and the data were completely underwhelming," says Offit, who also notes that the virus had already mutated yet again, rendering the data even less valuable. And yet, the very next day, the administration put out an announcement that they were going to spend billions of dollars buying 170 million doses from Pfizer and Moderna. By the fall, the CDC was recommending the booster for everyone over five, even though human data showed that the effect of the boosters was short-lived at best. Because the original vaccine (plus, says Offit, a third dose six months later) still likely provides protection against severe disease thanks to the T cell response, what is the point in constantly chasing new strains of the virus with boosters that offer too little, too late?

The CDC tried to ignore the questions about the boosters by announcing in late December that adults eighteen and over who'd received a bivalent booster shot had had 31 percent fewer emergency room or urgent care visits than those who had gotten the original series of three shots. But the data was not from a randomized clinical trial, meaning that other factors could help explain the seeming success. Nor do we know whether healthy young people, particularly those at risk for myocarditis, should continue to be boosted at all, or what the optimal path would be for those who have recovered from a COVID infection. "The way to answer these questions with highest scientific accuracy is to demand Pfizer and Moderna conduct a randomized controlled trial for each question," wrote Prasad. "The bottom line is that 'following the science' doesn't always tell us what to do when the science is messy," added the website *Vox*. "Even simple questions like 'were the booster updates worth it' can evade easy answers."

"The CDC risks eroding the public's trust by overselling the new shot," Offit wrote in *The Wall Street Journal*. Actually, the trust had already eroded; in the month after their approval, less than 2 percent of those eligible got the new jab.

Offit's biggest fear is that the government's flawed push to keep vaccinating people against COVID-19 risks eroding confidence in vaccines overall, with potentially deadly consequences.

———

The boosters raised another important question: Was this the best use of the vaccine? Wouldn't the world have been better served had those jabs been used to inoculate people in other parts of the world who had no access at all to vaccines? In August 2021, Tedros Adhanom Ghebreyesus, the head of the WHO, called for a moratorium on booster shots so that all available vaccines could be used to vaccinate at least 40 percent of the rest of the world. "We do not want to see widespread use of boosters for healthy people who are fully vaccinated," he said. He described the practice of giving booster shots to healthy people as "immoral."

Like most Western countries, the United States didn't view it that way. Americans were dying, and the first order of business was always going to be to make sure Americans had access to vaccines. In fact, the contracts the Trump administration signed with the vaccine

manufacturers explicitly prohibited the government from sharing sur-
plus doses with the rest of the world, according to documents obtained
by *Vanity Fair*.[11] "In the beginning, Europe, the U.S., every country
was working for itself and against the others," says a former member of
Warp Speed. "And the industry was caught in the middle." In his book,
Jared Kushner writes that he strong-armed Pfizer into keeping doses in
the country in exchange for access to the Defense Production Act. "We
will not let those doses leave the country," he says he told Pfizer CEO
Albert Bourla. "Why are you playing God," Bourla asked. "Because I
represent America," Kushner says he responded.

But that certainly wasn't the whole story, because there was a second issue that prevented most U.S.-made vaccines from leaving the
country. In 2005, Congress passed a law that granted sweeping protection from liability to the developers of vaccines and therapeutics during
public health emergencies. But that liability protection did not extend
to other nations. "If you are a pharmaceutical executive who sent vaccines to the rest of the world, they could then use that to put you in
jail," said the former Warp Speed executive. "I'd be shocked if a CEO
would agree to do it without protection from liability."

There was a way to help less developed countries attain vaccines—
at least theoretically. Pfizer and Moderna could waive their intellectual
property rights, thus allowing countries to make their own vaccine without having to pay an exorbitant fee. This idea went back to the AIDS
epidemic when Africans were dying in terrible numbers and African
countries couldn't afford antiretrovirals. In 1997, South Africa passed
a law giving the country the right to import the drug from a generic

11 "'We Are Hoarding': Why the U.S. Still Can't Donate COVID-19 Vaccines to
Countries in Need," by Katherine Eban, April 6, 2021.

manufacturer in India that was blatantly violating the patent of the brand-name manufacturers. The pharmaceutical industry sued and was backed by the U.S. government. But the onslaught of negative publicity caused the industry to fold on the trial's first day in 2001. Antiretroviral manufacturers wound up protecting their patents in an unusual way—by giving the drugs away for free.

In the fall of 2020, as the FDA came closer to authorizing Pfizer's and Moderna's vaccines, South Africa once again took the lead in calling for vaccine makers to waive their patent rights. Along with India, it sponsored a proposal at the WHO to force such a move. By early 2021, Ghebreyesus had thrown the organization's weight behind the proposal. Failing to deliver equitable access to vaccines "will be paid with lives and livelihoods in the world's poorest countries," he said in a press briefing. He cited a report from the International Labour Organization that found that some 8.8 percent of global working hours were lost to COVID-19 in 2020, resulting in a decline in global labor income of $3.7 trillion. Another study, this one commissioned by the International Chamber of Commerce Research Foundation, found that "vaccine nationalism" could cost the global economy up to $9.2 trillion, with at least half of that loss affecting the wealthiest economies, as the global supply chain shut down.

"Vaccine nationalism might serve short-term political goals," said Ghebreyesus. "But it's in every nation's own medium and long-term economic interest to support vaccine equity."

Instead of dealing with the inevitable lawsuits that would result from trying to force major pharmaceutical companies to hand over their patent right, a group of NGOs attempted a work-around. Gavi, a group founded to vaccinate children against deadly diseases, along with the Coalition for Epidemic Preparedness Innovations and the WHO, formed an organization called COVAX, with a goal of creating its own vaccine portfolio by purchasing prospective doses from various manufacturers. Its funding would come from the wealthier nations, and it would act, in effect, like an international version of Warp Speed.

COVAX set a goal of delivering two billion doses to the world's poorer countries. That would still leave billions unvaccinated, but it was a start. Dr. Seth Berkley, Gavi's CEO, said that because COVAX was the purchaser, it would bear the liability risk, rather than the vaccine manufacturers. "We put in place for the first time a global, no-fault compensation scheme for every dose of vaccine." He added, "Now, should that have been necessary is a different question."

The companies that were supposed to supply vaccines to COVAX included the Serum Institute of India (SII), the world's largest vaccine manufacturer. Gavi provided the funds to permit the technology transfer and scale up of two vaccines, the AstraZeneca vaccine and the Novavax vaccine. Up to 50 percent of those vaccines were supposed to be for India, and the rest for other developing nations. Gavi agreed to deliver 200 million doses of whatever vaccine was approved, as soon as possible. When the deal with SII was announced in the fall of 2020, Berkley called it "vaccine manufacturing for the Global South, by the Global South, helping us to ensure no country is left behind when it comes to the race for a COVID-19 vaccine." India's prime minister, Narendra Modi, boasted at Davos that India had beaten the pandemic and would save other countries with its vaccine exports.

But then a second wave of the pandemic hit India, and Modi's government responded by halting all vaccine exports.[12] "India is suffering

---

12 This was reported by the *Financial Times* on March 26, 2021; *The New York Times* reported that it was not until September that the country's health minister said it would resume exports of the vaccines.

immensely under the weight of Covid," wrote Dinesh Thakur, a public health activist, in an article for *Stat* in May 2021. "Now its failures are threatening much of the world." COVAX had to delay its deliveries to low-income countries. COVAX ultimately ended up shipping out a little more than 900 million doses to 144 countries in 2021, less than half of its original 2-billion-dose goal. "By the way, Modi never said afterwards, 'Thank you, COVAX,'" Berkley noted. "He was, 'I got the vaccines for India.' He didn't say, 'I took them from the supply that was set up for the rest of the world.'"

————

By late spring 2021, so much vaccine was being manufactured in the United States that the country risked throwing away doses that had expired. "I know companies asked the U.S. for permission to reroute some of the products to other parts of the world, Europe first, then the rest of the world," said a former Warp Speed official. "And I don't believe that negotiation went very well."

In fact, the Biden administration didn't act any differently than the Indian government as the case count in the United States began rising that spring: it panicked. On March 30, CDC head Walensky teared up in a press conference. Expressing her fear of "impending doom," she said, "We are not powerless. We can change the trajectory of this pandemic." She added, "But right now I'm scared."

Two days later, according to *Vanity Fair*, there was a meeting at the White House during which it was decided that America needed to keep its vaccine supply in the country. The domestic situation was "so severe," an unnamed official told the magazine, "that every federal entity that might work on overseas donations had instead been tasked with vaccinating more Americans. The rest of the world would have to wait."

That March, a joint report released by the drug industry and the Coalition for Epidemic Preparedness Innovations reported that of the potential ten billion to fourteen billion vaccine doses the industry planned to produce in 2021, more than two-thirds were claimed by wealthy and middle-income countries.

With so little vaccine getting to the world's poorer countries, the issue of vaccine patent rights gained new momentum. Pope Francis, for instance, sent a video message to a huge concert, Vax Live, aimed at raising money and awareness about the need for vaccine equity. The pope called for "universal access to the vaccine and the temporary suspension of intellectual property rights." Prince Harry and Meghan Markle were involved in the effort, as was David Letterman and many other celebrities. Jennifer Lopez and the Foo Fighters performed at the concert, which was streamed worldwide.

Moderna was a particular source of ire. After all, hadn't the government helped design the vaccine? Hadn't Moderna's vaccine, like the other mRNA vaccines, relied on the work—and the patent—of Dr. Barney Graham and his team at the National Institutes of Health's Vaccine Research Center? Pfizer had licensed the NIH patent from the government, but Moderna had ignored it. Wasn't the government in a position to pressure Moderna to share its technology? Plus the government had given Moderna billions of dollars in federal funding, both in grants and in vaccine purchases. Surely, the billions Moderna was now earning were due, at least in part, to the work of government scientists like Graham.

Graham himself certainly thought the government had the moral authority to pressure Moderna. In late April 2021, he gave a rare interview to the *Financial Times*, telling the paper that the NIH patent gave the Biden administration "leverage" over manufacturers—leverage it had so far been unwilling to use. "That's one of the reasons [I joined the NIH]: it's to be able to use the leverage of the public funding to solve public health issues," he said.

Given America's long-standing support for patent rights, it came as a shock when, in the spring of 2021, the Biden administration abruptly reversed course and said it supported the worldwide waiver of patent rights the WHO had been calling for. Pharmaceutical stocks in the United States and Europe plunged on the news.

Longtime advocates for drug access saw it as a win that would have enormous long-term benefits. Advocates had been "hoping that this day would come," Tahir Amin, the cofounder of the Initiative for Medicines, Access & Knowledge, told *Stat*. "That [intellectual property], including patents, has received so much attention during Covid . . . that it has been a teaching and learning moment for many unfamiliar with this system."

Maybe.

In the end, the proposal to waive patent rights didn't accomplish anything. Even with the Biden administration backing the proposal, it had to be approved by the other member countries of the World Trade Organization. And the U.K., Canada, Japan, Germany, and the European Union were strongly opposed. The proposal was soon forgotten.

Even if it had gone forward, however, it might have been meaningless. COVID-19 wasn't HIV. Vaccines are not antiretrovirals. If the patent rights were lifted, a manufacturer could make an antiretroviral without a great deal of difficulty. But an mRNA vaccine required superior manufacturing know-how, substantial capacity, and access to raw materials. "The problem was the AIDS activists, who said, 'This is all about IP,'" says Berkley. "I have gone blue in the face trying to explain this." It was, he said, like eating the best chicken of your life in a three-star Michelin restaurant—and then getting the recipe from the chef. "If you go home, that chicken will not be the same as it is in that restaurant. The skill in making it is what matters."[13]

Back in the fall of 2020, Moderna had offered to waive its patents. But those knowledgeable about the mRNA vaccines always understood there was less to that offer than met the eye. "Something as complex as a COVID-19 vaccine cannot be easily reverse-engineered," wrote the economist Mihir Swarup Sharma. "Simply telling companies they're free to try won't do much." As that fact became clearer, the clamor for Moderna to share grew louder. And at that point, of course, Moderna effectively said no. "Our patent pledge stated that, while the pandemic persists, Moderna will not use its patents to block others from making a coronavirus vaccine intended to combat the pandemic," said a Moderna spokesperson in March 2021. "There was no mention of a commitment to transfer our know-how beyond our chosen partners."

Nor did the U.S. government succeed in extracting concessions from Moderna. Not only did Moderna refuse to license the patent developed by Graham's team, but when the company filed for its own patent on the vaccine design in July 2020, it did not include the NIH scientists who had developed it with Moderna. In the filing, Moderna said it had "reached the good-faith determination that these individuals did not co-invent" the relevant parts of the vaccine.

Moderna was also involved in a second patent dispute with Arbutus, the company that had patented the use of lipid nanoparticles that encase the mRNA. As part of its response to Arbutus's lawsuit, Mo-

13 Even after COVAX was able to get shots to poorer countries, the problem became distribution. Poor countries lacked the infrastructure to get the shots into arms. "Initially, the problem was 100 percent the supply of vaccines," says Berkley. "By year two, it was 80–90 percent a delivery issue."

derna invoked what's known as the government contractor defense. In effect, Moderna argued that if it were found to have infringed on the Arbutus patent, the government, rather than Moderna, should have to pay the royalties on the company's vaccine sales. In other words, government scientists didn't deserve to share the patent for the vaccine, and taxpayers deserved no share of the revenue, but taxpayers were on the hook for patents Moderna might have violated along the way. "It's consistent with how they've gone about things since the very beginning," says one knowledgeable party.

"What is the Biden administration doing to sort of lean on this company?" a reporter asked during a press briefing. The White House spokesperson Jen Psaki replied, "The process of technology transfers, as you know, involves teaching other—another company how to make a vaccine that takes specialized scientists and transferring intellectual property. We absolutely want that to happen, but my understanding is also that the U.S. government does not have the ability to compel Moderna to take certain actions."

The New York Times pointed out that Moderna had shipped a greater share of its doses to wealthy countries than any other vaccine maker. According to Airfinity, which provides analytics for infectious diseases, by the fall of 2021, Moderna had provided roughly 1 million vaccine doses to countries classified by the World Bank as low income. Meanwhile, Pfizer had supplied 8.4 million, and Johnson & Johnson had supplied approximately 25 million doses of its single-shot vaccine. "Moderna has become the world's vaccine boogeyman," wrote the online news website *Axios*.

(In December 2022, Moderna finally agreed to license some of NIAID's patent rights, resulting in a payment of $400 million in the fourth quarter. Moderna also agreed to pay NIAID a small percentage of its vaccine sales as a royalty—but of course, the deal came only after Moderna's vaccine sales had slowed to a crawl.)

By the end of 2021, residents of wealthy and middle-income countries had received about 90 percent of the nearly 400 million vaccines delivered, according to the Our World in Data project at the University of Oxford. "We distributed the vaccines extremely unfairly," says Bhattacharya. "Vaccines should have been given to every old person on earth, or at least offered to every old person on earth before it was offered to anyone else. That would have prevented a tremendous amount of acute disease and death. The fact that we hoarded them is a shame on rich countries."

Berkley estimates that in high-income countries during the first few years, the wastage—meaning the doses that expired without being used—may have been as high as 40 percent. What did it say about capitalism that in that first year after the vaccines were available, doses were hoarded and wasted in rich countries, while people elsewhere were dying? "This isn't about inequality, which we always knew capitalism could create," wrote Sharma. "It's about inefficiency, which capitalism is supposed to avoid."

———

In August 2022, Moderna took another nasty—and yet unsurprising—step. It sued Pfizer and BioNTech. Moderna claimed that the only reason it hadn't filed it earlier was "so as not to distract from efforts to bring the pandemic to an end as quickly as possible." The key claim was that the Pfizer-BioNTech vaccine relied on Moderna's method for modifying mRNA so that it didn't provoke that unwanted immune response. Recall that in 2017, after years of trying to evade the Karikó-Weissman patent, which laid out the recipe for making that modification, Moderna had finally been forced to pay $76 million to license it. In the arcane, complex world of intellectual property law, it is entirely possible that it is both true that Moderna had to use the Karikó-Weissman patent to invent its own modification and that Pfizer and BioNTech then copied Moderna's innovation. But in practical terms, it's another irony that Moderna was suing BioNTech, where Karikó works, and without whose dogged work Moderna itself probably would not exist.

Indeed, in a countersuit filed that fall, Pfizer and BioNTech wrote that Moderna was trying to "claim credit for others' work" and put itself in the "single, starring role" by ignoring the contributions of others, from Karikó to the NIH.

During the U.S. Tennis Open that fall in New York, fans could see the Moderna logo plastered along center court at Arthur Ashe Stadium, right up there with American Express, Chubb, and J.P.Morgan. As a sponsor of one of sport's most prestigious events, Moderna was announcing that it was taking its place in the pantheon of great American companies. Or so it hoped. But by that time, much of the glow had come off. Its stock price had plunged from its peak of $425 to just over $100, not because of the controversy about vaccine equity, but rather because the demand for its COVID vaccine was declining faster than anyone had predicted. In the second quarter of 2022, Moderna had to write down $500 million of inventory, due to a "substantial reduction of our expected deliveries to COVAX and deferral of deliveries to other customers, particularly to the European Union," as its financial filings noted. In September, Switzerland's health officials said that the country would destroy more than 620,000 expired doses of the Moderna vaccine because there was no longer much demand for the shots. That was followed by the Serum Institute of India announcing that it would halt production, because it too had millions of unused doses.

Still, if you believed Moderna, vaccines were just the beginning. mRNA was the medical platform of the future—and that is certainly true. One silver lining of the pandemic was that mRNA, biology's molecular problem child, was now a proven lifesaver. Now the task was to use it to make drugs that went well beyond the COVID-19 vaccines, from treatments for rare diseases to personalized cancer vaccines. "Out of the horror of COVID will come remarkable advances," said Wellcome's director, Jeremy Farrar. It might well be true. John Hempton, who runs a hedge fund that invests in biotech stocks among other things, says that the speed with which COVID-19 vaccines needed to be made resulted in huge improvements in the manufacturing process. Those improvements dramatically decrease the toxicity, meaning that scientists might be able to use mRNA to treat a whole range of diseases they couldn't treat before.

At a J.P.Morgan conference in January 2021, Stéphane Bancel rhapsodized about the possibilities—both for mRNA and for Moderna. "In 2019 the worldwide vaccine revenue was $35 billion," he said. "How big do you think that market could be five to ten years from now if one was able to develop a lot of infectious disease vaccines?" Not only was Moderna in phase 3 clinical trials for CMV, a latent virus that can be passed from pregnant women to their babies, but the company was also working on vaccines for RSV, a childhood influenza that can be deadly. "I believe this is just the beginning," Bancel said. "All of our vaccines are the same technology. If you were safe once, and it works, it will be safe again and work again."

For much of 2022, as vaccine sales slowed down and it found itself embroiled in one controversy after another, Moderna's stock had been battered. Bancel's net worth had fallen by some $3 billion. All the new products he was touting didn't yet exist, and who could say if they ever would? And the market for mRNA therapies had become very crowded. Indeed, a company did get FDA approval for its RSV vaccine in the spring of 2023—but it was GSK, not Moderna. But difficulties had never stopped Bancel before. As Wall Street well knew, nobody could sell a story better than Stéphane Bancel and Moderna.

PART IV

"The Pandemic Is Over"

15

"The Free State of Florida"

In December 2021, as the omicron variant became dominant in New York City, Mayor Bill de Blasio decided to toughen the city's already tough vaccine mandates. In addition to the usual blue state rules that people had to show proof of immunization when entering a restaurant, shop, or sports arena, city hall directed that all children twelve and above had to be vaccinated. (That was later reduced to children five and up.) And, the city said, employees "who perform in-person work or interact with the public in the course of business" also had to show proof of vaccination. This held for both private sector and public sector workers. Companies that failed to comply could be fined $1,000 or more per incident. City employees who declined to be vaccinated could be fired. As, in fact, many were, including one thousand city workers and close to two thousand education department employees.

There were, however, some carve outs. They included "non-NYC resident performing artists, college or professional athletes, and anyone who accompanies them." Artists or athletes who resided in New York were *not* exempt, however. How it made sense to exempt visitors but not city dwellers was difficult to discern, and few examples illustrated that better than the case of Kyrie Irving of the Brooklyn Nets.

The National Basketball Association had been the first professional league to shut down in March 2020, a move that had drawn wide praise. Three months later, it was also the first league to start up again, when twenty-two of the league's thirty teams[1] were relocated to Disney World in Orlando, where players, coaches, officials, trainers, and anyone else affiliated with the league lived in a kind of bubble, from which they were not supposed to stray. Everyone in the bubble was tested regularly for COVID-19; remarkably, when the season ended in October, there hadn't been a single positive case.

Although the NBA abandoned the bubble the following season, it was a disjointed effort, a shortened season with games canceled, often at the last minute, because too many players had COVID-19 (invariably mild). In Brooklyn, the Nets had an additional issue: its star guard, one of the best players in the NBA, was refusing to be vaccinated.[2]

In truth, Irving had this in common with any number of professional athletes, but most of the others avoided controversy by staying mum about their vaccine status. Because of Irving's importance to the

---

1 The eight teams that were left behind had already been eliminated from the playoffs. Other professional leagues soon adopted the NBA's bubble strategy.

2 Irving was involved in several other off-the-court controversies. He once said that he believed the earth was flat. He also endorsed an anti-Semitic film. In February 2023, Irving was traded to the Dallas Mavericks.

Nets—and because he played in such a competitive media market—that wasn't possible. In mid-October 2021, hounded by reporters about whether he was immunized,[3] Irving finally said that "nobody should be forced to do anything with their bodies." He added, "I know the consequences here, and if it means I'm judged and demonized for that, that's just what it is."

The NBA did not have a vaccine mandate, but it did require players to abide by local regulations, and New York clearly required Irving to be vaccinated to play basketball. Under New York's rules, visiting teams didn't have to be vaccinated, but Nets players did. At first Nets management took the position that Irving could not be part of the team so long as he wasn't vaccinated. But by mid-December, as it became obvious that Irving wasn't going to fold, even though it was costing him millions of dollars in compensation, the Nets decided that he could play the team's away games. Or most of them: he couldn't play in Toronto either, because all noncitizens coming into Canada had to be vaccinated (though Canadian citizens did not). In San Francisco, fans had to show proof of vaccination to enter the Chase Center, where the Golden State Warriors played, but the players on the visiting team didn't. So Irving could play there. In fact, under New York's rules, the unvaccinated Irving could *attend* Nets home games; he just couldn't play in them. As the writer Ross Barkan put it in a Substack post, "What *is* the science behind the unvaccinated Irving sitting in the stands to watch unvaccinated players from the 76ers or Heat shoot baskets while he's barred from play? Well, there is none."

---

3 The two other athletes whose anti-vax stances received similar publicity—and condemnation—were the tennis star Novak Djokovic and Aaron Rodgers, the quarterback for the Green Bay Packers.

———

The ubiquity of the omicron variant, which arrived on U.S. shores in November 2021 and soon became the dominant strain, marked a turning point in the way many people thought about the virus—as well as their willingness to accept the non-pharmaceutical interventions that had been part of their lives for two years. Omicron was said to be four times as infectious as its predecessor, the delta variant—which, in turn, had been at least twice as infectious as the original strain of COVID-19 that had come from Wuhan. But it wasn't as dangerous. Omicron confirmed to many Americans that the coronavirus could, in fact, be transmitted to people who had been immunized.

By mid-January 2022, some 91 percent of Democrats, 76 percent of independents, and 63 percent of Republicans had been vaccinated, according to data compiled by the Kaiser Family Foundation. Yet there was an enormous spike in infections, peaking at more than 800,000 cases per day across the country. This peak was significantly higher than any previous one. But thanks in part to vaccinations and in part to omicron's reduced potency, the percentage of people who were dying was far lower than during previous peaks. In January 2021, for instance, when new cases topped out at 250,000 per day, the daily COVID-19 death toll stood at around thirty-four hundred. In January 2022, despite more than three times as many cases, a thousand fewer people per day died. And from that peak, the number of deaths declined rapidly.

Lots of people who had been wearing masks since March 2020, had been avoiding large crowds, and had been working from home and following other COVID-19 protocols found themselves coming down with COVID-19. The elderly and those with weak immune systems still needed to be protected, but for many other people COVID-19 no longer struck fear as it once had. Yet from the White House to statehouses to city halls across the nation, government officials continued to call for people to keep using many of the same measures to stay safe. And millions of people were no longer willing to listen.

After two years during which the pandemic was at the center of American life, plenty of people were ready to move on, even if that meant accepting some risk—which, with omicron, was now manageable for most of the non-elderly. But a second reason they were ready to move on is that as government entities slowly lifted mitigation measures, they created situations that were almost laughable—like Kyrie Irving forbidden to play in Nets home games but allowed to sit in the stands. Novak Djokovic, the tennis great, offered another example. He too refused to be vaccinated and had had COVID-19 at least twice, which meant he surely had antibodies. In 2021, he was allowed into the United States to play in the U.S. Open. In 2022, however, he could not enter the country because President Joe Biden had signed an order preventing unvaccinated foreigners from entering the country.

In New York, many subway riders stopped wearing masks long before September 2022, when the state made mask wearing optional on subways. "On a C train from the Jay Street station in Brooklyn," wrote James Barron of *The New York Times*, "14 of the 51 people in the car I was in had masks on—27 percent, about the same as on a later A train." In 2020, anyone who got onto a subway car unmasked would have been scolded by fellow straphangers. Now? No one seemed to care.

Healthy university students were among the least likely to become seriously ill due to COVID-19. Yet most universities continued to insist that they be vaccinated to return to campus, and some continued to have mask mandates. New York City lifted its vaccine mandate for private employers in November 2022. Yet it remained on the books for city employees until February 2023.

Mask mandates were just as illogical. For most of the pandemic, the private schools that conducted in-person classes insisted that students wear masks, even though they were the least likely to get COVID-19 or become seriously ill from it. Why? School officials invariably pointed out that they were following the CDC's recommended protocols, which called for schoolchildren to be masked. But by the spring of 2022, the CDC had dropped its mask recommendation—except, incredibly, for children five and under, who, again, were the least likely to be infected.

Once again, it was the Brown University economist Emily Oster who pointed out how foolish this policy was. In February 2022, she wrote an article for *The Atlantic* titled "Kids-Last COVID Policy Makes No Sense." Her point—one that Martin Kulldorff and the other authors of the Great Barrington Declaration had also made—was that children should have fewer restrictions than adults, not more. The reason that wasn't so, she believed, was that parents were still irrationally fearful—the result of "alarmist messaging." "The CDC and the American Academy of Pediatrics have chosen to emphasize risks to children in a way that is at odds with the choices made by their European counterparts," she wrote. "After two years of telling parents to be afraid for their children, policy makers can't simply turn around and tell them that kids are low risk and everything's fine."

Oster followed up that article with one in March that was specifically about masks. The headline was blunt: MASKING POLICY IS INCREDIBLY IRRATIONAL RIGHT NOW. In this article she noted that even as the CDC has dropped its indoor mask recommendations for kids six and older, it continued to maintain the policy for younger children. "Some parents of young kids have been driven insane by this policy," Oster wrote. "I sympathize—because the policy is completely insane."

Even the World Health Organization, a bastion of conservative pandemic advice, said that younger children didn't need to wear masks. Oster also cited a study from Spain that "found no difference" between unmasked five-year-olds and masked six-year-olds. Children younger than five had even lower virus spread. Finally, she pointed out that "any negative effects are likely to be concentrated in younger children, who are learning to speak and interpret emotional cues. The possible costs of continued mask wearing may be the largest for the very cohort still subject to mandates." As usual, her critics jumped all over her. As usual, she was right.

———

In Florida, despite Governor Ron DeSantis's enthusiastic support of vaccines, he never felt the same way about vaccine mandates. They were embraced, of course, by most blue state governors, but DeSantis's distaste for them was not political, at least not at first. "The data is showing us that you are much less likely to be hospitalized or die if you are vaccinated," he said in July 2021. "However, the vaccinations have not created herd immunity. If the idea is that if you force everyone to do this, you'll have herd immunity, that has not happened. It's still spreading." DeSantis claimed, falsely, that Anthony Fauci had said that if 50 percent of the population were immunized, COVID-19 surges would end. (At the time, about 70 percent of Floridians had had at least one jab.) "That isn't true," said DeSantis. "We just have to be honest about what [vaccination] is doing, and what it's not doing."

Four months later, when the federal government tried to impose a nationwide vaccine mandate, DeSantis became much more aggressive in his opposition. This time politics was very much a part of it. The Occupational Safety and Health Administration, which oversees workplace safety, issued a rule in early November 2021 requiring all large employers to ensure that their workers were vaccinated. It also required all federal employees to be vaccinated. Immediately, twenty-six business organizations and twenty-seven states, including Florida, filed suit.[4] DeSantis went further. He quickly called the state's legislators into a special session, and within a matter of days they passed a bill he had asked for, outlawing most vaccine mandates in Florida. Under this law, no government agency could order an employee to be immunized. Schools could not order students to be vaccinated, nor could they impose mask mandates. And while the bill still allowed companies to enforce vaccine mandates, it created so many loopholes that any employee could easily evade vaccination. Companies that were caught trying to force employees to be immunized could be fined $50,000 per incident. Indeed, the state had already fined Leon County $3.57 million for what it said were repeated attempts to impose a vaccine mandate on county employees.

What made this announcement especially noteworthy is that it marked the first time DeSantis cast his opposition to vaccine mandates as a matter not just of science or common sense but of conservative principle. At a bill signing ceremony in Brandon, Florida,[5] DeSantis said, "We're going to be saving a lot of jobs in the State of Florida. We're going to be striking a blow for freedom. We're going to be standing up against the Biden mandates, and we're going to be better as a result of it." He continued: "The states are the primary vehicles to protect people's freedoms, their health, their safety, their welfare, in our constitutional system. What Biden is doing is not constitutional. There has

---

4 The suit was successful. In January 2022, the Supreme Court decided 6–3 to void the rule. Health-care workers and noncitizens coming into the country were still required to be vaccinated.

5 The phrase "Let's Go Brandon" had become by then a Republican meme. It meant "Fuck Joe Biden." When DeSantis was asked why he was holding the bill signing in Brandon, he said, "Brandon, Florida, is a great American city."

never been a federal vaccine mandate imposed on the general public." This central idea—that he was a governor standing up for freedom— would soon become his mantra.

In November 2021, DeSantis signed a bill that invalidated any lockdown, mask mandate, or vaccine mandate imposed by any Florida city and county. (In a press release, he described this measure as "stemming the tide of . . . government overreach.") That same law also forbade any restaurant or store to ask a customer for proof of vaccination. In blue states, people had to show proof of vaccination to get into most restaurants, gyms, sports arenas, and the like. In Florida, vaccine passports were forbidden.

The state clemency board, on which DeSantis sat, pardoned any Floridian who had been arrested or fined by a municipality for violating COVID-19 restrictions. He won a lawsuit against the CDC, which was preventing cruise ships from operating unless 95 percent of their passengers had been vaccinated—and even though 80 percent of potential cruise ship passengers said they would feel safer with a vaccination mandate.

As time went on, and as DeSantis became ever more convinced that he was right, he also became more unyielding to anyone who disagreed. In the early part of the pandemic, DeSantis appeared to be driven by a genuine belief that he was making the right choices for Floridians. By the latter part of the pandemic, his motivation seemed to be purely an expression of power—and how he could wield it against anyone who dared to cross him. Early in the pandemic, for instance, he had allowed Florida counties to impose their own mitigation measures if they believed the measures were warranted. Not anymore. When thirteen school districts defied him and instituted mask mandates, the governor responded by docking the salaries of the school board members who had voted for the mandates. More than a year later, the DeSantis administration targeted fifteen school board members for defeat in the 2024 elections. Eleven of them had voted for school mask mandates.

He became a regular on the Fox prime-time shows, like *Tucker Carlson Tonight* and especially *The Ingraham Angle*, hosted by Laura Ingraham, where he would bash the Biden administration and talk up Florida's success during the pandemic and beyond. Certainly, there was much to talk up: The Florida economy was humming. By May 2021, the unemployment rate was 4.7 percent compared with New York's 8.5 percent and California's 8.3 percent. DeSantis's insistence that businesses remain open meant that Florida saw far fewer closings than New York and California—and more start-ups. (Floridians filed more than 600,000 new business applications in 2021, double that of New York.) The restaurants and bars were full; tourists were flocking to Disney World and Miami Beach; and except for health-care workers almost no one wore masks. DeSantis began describing the state as "the free state of Florida." When he set out the state's 2022–23 budget, he called it "the freedom first budget."

DeSantis's approach to dealing with the pandemic had made him extremely popular in Florida. It also catapulted him to national prominence. He was being seriously talked about as a potential Republican presidential nominee, especially after he breezed to reelection in 2022. Clearly responding to that chatter, DeSantis undertook a series of high-profile policy moves—detractors called them publicity stunts—designed to solidify his reputation among the Republican base. He pushed for passage of a bill banning instruction or discussion of LGBTQ issues through third grade—the infamous "Don't Say Gay" law. (In May 2023, the Florida legislature expanded the "Don't Say Gay" rules through twelfth grade.) When Bob Chapek, then the CEO of the Walt Disney Company, spoke out against it, DeSantis had the legislature punish the company—the largest employer and biggest taxpayer in the state—by stripping Disney of a self-governing district it had controlled for more than fifty years. When critical race theory became a hot topic, DeSantis forbade its teaching in Florida public schools. He removed the board of a small progressive university and replaced it with cronies whose mandate was to strip the school of its progressive values. To show he was tough on "voting fraud," he had several dozen former felons arrested for supposedly casting illegal votes in the presidential election—even though they had been told they could vote by election authorities. He had some fifty newly arrived migrants rounded up in San Antonio, put them on two chartered planes, and sent them to Martha's Vineyard, a summer retreat for the wealthy off the coast of Massachusetts.

These stunts did not reflect well on DeSantis, to say the least. They displayed an astonishing heartlessness, a willingness to use human beings as pawns to his ambition. His bullying became his dominant public posture. He also showed that he had no compunction about changing positions if it could further his rise to the top. Even when his earlier position had been rooted in something he claimed to hold dear: data.

The shift, which shocked many of the experts who had supported DeSantis during the pandemic, was clear by October 2021. A month earlier, the governor had appointed a new state surgeon general, Dr. Joseph Ladapo, a health policy researcher who had recently joined the University of Florida as a full professor. Ladapo had written a series of columns in *The Wall Street Journal* objecting to the established wisdom about pandemic mitigation. In addition to being anti-lockdown, he promoted hydroxychloroquine, the same treatment that former president Trump had long touted. And he claimed to have treated COVID-19 patients, something former colleagues said was untrue. DeSantis had read the columns and been impressed.

A month after he took office, Ladapo claimed that a study conducted by the Florida health department had shown that men between eighteen and thirty-nine had an "abnormally high risk of cardio-related death" from mRNA vaccines. Therefore, he concluded, they should avoid getting vaccinated. The study cited by Ladapo was unsigned and hadn't been peer-reviewed or published, and its findings were "preliminary." (It was later discovered that Ladapo had doctored the data to make the cardiac risk appear worse than it actually was.) "Putting out half-baked reports from a department of health is a dangerous thing to do," Daniel Salmon, who leads the Institute for Vaccine Safety at the Johns Hopkins Bloomberg School of Public Health, told *The Washington Post*.

DeSantis had to know that Ladapo had overreached with his conclusion, given the weakness of the data. He may have even known that his surgeon general had fudged the data. Subsequent studies did in fact show that the mRNA vaccines brought an increased risk of myocarditis in young men, but not nearly to the extent of the Florida study. But, as one study put it in *The Journal of the American Medical Association*, patients who got myocarditis via COVID-19 "typically experienced symptomatic recovery after receiving only pain management." The notion that the vaccines were generating a high number of COVID-19 deaths among healthy men simply wasn't true. Yet as controversy raged around Ladapo's continued insistence that men under thirty-nine should not be vaccinated, DeSantis said nothing to contradict his surgeon general.

On the contrary. By 2022, DeSantis had completely switched his position on the efficacy of the mRNA vaccines. An early supporter of vaccines, he became their fiercest opponent. The right was demonizing them, and now, so was he. And he used his powerful platform to once again make the kind of antiestablishment noise that the Republican base would notice. He petitioned the state supreme court to impanel a grand jury to investigate "any and all wrongdoing" by the manufacturers of the mRNA vaccines. There was no doubt about what he hoped to find: documents that would show Pfizer and Moderna had known about the myocarditis side effect but had said nothing. In announcing his request to the supreme court, DeSantis talked about the pharmaceutical industry's "history of misleading the public for financial gain."

"There are good and sufficient reasons to deem it to be in the public interest to impanel a statewide grand jury to investigate criminal or wrongful activity in Florida relating to the development, promotion, and distribution of vaccines purported to prevent COVID-19 infection, symptoms, and transmission" read the request to the court. It was an appalling act given what had gone into creating and distributing the vaccines—and, more important, given all the lives they had saved.

Nine days after DeSantis filed his petition, the state supreme court granted it. The grand jury would have a year to dig into Pfizer's and Moderna's files, searching for damaging documents. Would DeSantis be running for president by then? Yes, as it turns out. In late May 2023, he made it official: he was running.

In a DeSantis profile the *Miami Herald* published just prior to the announcement of his candidacy, a Kentucky congressman named Thomas Massie recounted a phone call he had with the governor in the summer of 2020, a time when he was being widely criticized for ending lockdowns and mask mandates.

"I know my position is unpopular right now, and I'm getting hammered in the media," DeSantis told Massie. "But I'm going to lean into it because in a year or two they're going to realize we were right. And I think we'll be in a good position in a couple of years from now."

———

The report that the New York attorney general, Letitia James, issued in late January 2021—the one that found that New York had undercounted nursing home deaths by as much as 50 percent—was the beginning of the end for Governor Andrew Cuomo. The pandemic had built him up, and the pandemic would help bring him down.

The next blow came in February, when Cuomo's top aide, Melissa DeRosa, told a group of state legislators that the administration had withheld the true nursing home numbers after the state was ordered by the Trump Justice Department to turn them over. "We froze," she said, adding that she and Cuomo feared that the data was "going to be used against us and we weren't sure if there was going to be an investigation." It was a shocking admission, which was soon leaked to the *New York Post*. Amid the uproar that DeRosa's admission triggered, several legislators called for Cuomo to resign. And the Crown Publishing Group, the division of Penguin Random House that had bought Cuomo's book, canceled a second printing and the paperback. It also stopped promoting it. Crown's president, Gillian Blake, told *The New York Times* that the firm did so because of "the ongoing investigation into [New York State's] reporting of Covid-related fatalities in nursing homes."

The scandal damaged Cuomo significantly. The days of the Cuomosexuals were long gone. The legislature no longer feared him, as they had for most of his time in office. And when he was hit with a new scandal before the old one was even in the rearview mirror, well, at that point, it was only a matter of time.

The second scandal was the sort that powerful men rarely survive anymore: allegations of sexual harassment. Since December, Lindsey Boylan, a former aide, had been claiming that Cuomo had sexually harassed her. In late February she wrote an article for the online platform Medium, describing his behavior in great detail: how Cuomo would find excuses to touch her lower back, arms, and legs; how he kissed her on the lips after a one-on-one meeting; and how, during a flight on a private jet, he suggested that they play strip poker. "I hope that sharing my story will clear the path for other women to do the same," she wrote.

It did. By the end of March, nine women had aired similar allegations, everything from an unsolicited intimate embrace to reaching under a woman's dress and fondling her, to inappropriate comments about an aide's looks and clothes. (Cuomo generally responded to the allegations by either denying them or saying his behavior was not meant to make the women feel uncomfortable.)

Once again, Letitia James launched an investigation. New York's two Democratic senators, Chuck Schumer and Kirsten Gillibrand, called on Cuomo to resign. The legislature began proceedings that would likely lead to impeachment.

In August, James issued her report. It was devastating. She concluded that Cuomo had "sexually harassed multiple women, and in doing so violated federal and state law." The legislature gave Cuomo a week to submit his defense as it prepared to impeach him. All through the spring and summer, Cuomo insisted that he had done nothing wrong and would not resign. But on August 10, he bowed to the inevitable and left office in disgrace.

Upon taking office, the new governor, Kathy Hochul, made it clear that COVID-19 was her top priority. The delta variant was sweeping through New York, causing case counts—and deaths—to rise. Hochul imposed a mask mandate on schools. In December 2021, she broadened the mask mandate to include all public venues that did not require vaccines. She also imposed a vaccine mandate for hospital and nursing home workers. Unlike the spring of 2020, when New Yorkers felt duty-bound to comply, this time many New Yorkers resisted. "With the city struggling to reopen fully, Hochul just put another nail in its coffin," wrote the *New York Post* editorial board. Nearly a quarter of New York's counties said they planned to ignore her mandates.

Hochul did one other COVID-related thing when she first took office. She added twelve thousand deaths to the roll of those who had died of COVID-19 in nursing homes.

———

Since the start of the pandemic, California had prided itself on being the first in the nation to impose non-pharmaceutical interventions. Newsom had ordered a statewide lockdown before any other state, and it was also the first to order state workers and health-care workers to be vaccinated.[6] But as the days turned into months and the months to years, there was pushback even in this bluest of blue states. Several state legislators proposed a bill that would force every employee in the state, whether private or public, to be vaccinated. (The bill would have also allowed children twelve and above to be vaccinated without their parents' consent.) The bill was shelved after the police and firefighters' unions objected. (Los Angeles nonetheless pushed through a vaccine mandate on city workers despite the heated objection of the California firefighters' union.) Although Newsom lifted restrictions on restaurants and arenas, a vaccine passport was still required for any event over five thousand people. And a vaccine mandate for schoolchildren was only lifted in February 2023, though it had been paused the previous April. "This is long overdue," Jonathan Zachreson, a father of three, told the *Los Angeles Times*. Zachreson's outspoken opposition to most of Cali-

6 Anyone who wasn't vaccinated had to be tested for COVID-19 on a weekly basis.

fornia's pandemic policies had catapulted him to a seat on his local school board.

Still, there are twice as many Democrats in California as there are Republicans. The failed recall notwithstanding, most of those Democrats never stopped believing that masks for schoolchildren, and lockdowns, and rigorously following the recommendations of the CDC had been the right way to fight the pandemic. It was how one followed the science. It was how liberals, especially, could show they were better than the Trump supporters who scoffed at mitigation measures and vaccines. Yes, more stores had permanently closed in California than anyplace else in the country, but surely that was worth it if lives were saved. Wasn't it?

But what if you were a liberal and had stopped believing that establishment scientists were offering sound advice? What if you had come around to thinking that closing schools had been a terrible mistake, and that the inequality fostered by lockdowns was unconscionable? Then you were likely to be viewed as a heretic—like Jennifer Sey.

Sey, the chief marketing officer at Levi Strauss, was a longtime San Francisco resident. The school closures—and the harm that policy was likely to do to schoolchildren—troubled her, so much so that she began to tweet about her concerns—"as a parent, not as a Levi's executive," she says. When the city's schools didn't reopen in September 2020 she became more involved, writing articles and attending rallies. That's also when she received her first call from someone in corporate communications, who told Sey that her outspoken opposition to school closings did not reflect well on Levi's and that she was hurting her chances of someday replacing the current CEO, Chip Bergh.

She didn't stop. And neither did the phone calls, which came at two-week intervals. In her interactions with Bergh, he began calling her a "Trumper"—which she wasn't. "San Francisco is almost exclusively left, and I consider myself part of that cohort for the thirty years I lived there," she said. "The mindset that was adopted by the left was that you couldn't question any dictates, whether it was closed playgrounds or triple masking. And if you did question any of it, you must be a horrible person." When her own CEO labeled her a Trumper, she said, it was because there was no one in his world who was questioning any of the actions by Newsom or the federal government. "It was beyond the pale that someone could suggest that maybe kids were better off in school," she added.

By the middle of 2021, Sey had more than 100,000 followers on Twitter. She had become an important voice among the dissenters. With the company's employees working from home, she took the opportunity to move to Denver, which was more hospitable to a wider range of views. Shortly after the move, however, she did something that made her persona non grata at her own company. She had appeared on Laura Ingraham's show on Fox News.

Employees, most of them progressives, were outraged, with many demanding that she be fired. She was accused of being antiscience, anti-LGBTQ, and a racist.[7] She received an email from a mid-level executive in the corporate communications department, someone she had considered a friend. The email summed up the issues her colleagues had with her appearance. It read,

Jen, I have been thinking about this, and my sense is that there are people who just don't like what you're saying or where you said it.

7 Many progressives took the position that calling for schools to be opened was an act of racism because you were implicitly saying that it was okay for the Black kids who went to public schools to die of COVID-19. That the data said otherwise was something they never accounted for.

It's in conflict with the good/bad world we're living in, where Fox is Bad and MSNBC is Good. Was going on Fox (and that show in particular) an endorsement of what they stand for? Are you "one of us" or "one of them"? Perhaps an oversimplification, but that's what it feels like. I think explaining why Fox is important.

I don't think you actually need to address each of those, but I'm guessing that the following is pretty close to the list:

1. Why did you choose Fox/Laura Ingraham's show?

2. Do you endorse the views of Fox News and Laura Ingraham?

3. Are you anti-mask?

4. Are you anti-vax?

5. Are you into conspiracy theories?

6. Are you anti-union?

7. Is advocating for school reopenings perpetuating systemic racism? (mostly white moms, etc. etc.)

8. Is there a conflict of interest between your role as Levi's brand president and what you're saying on your personal Twitter?

In June, Sey went on what she jokingly calls an "apology tour." "I didn't apologize, but I did try to explain my advocacy to employees," she said. In response, she says, she received many complimentary emails and thanks from her colleagues. But when it became clear that she intended to keep tweeting, her position inside the company became untenable. In January 2023, she resigned.

After she left, Ancel Martínez, director of business and financial communications at Levi's, put out a statement taking issue with Sey's narrative. "This is not a case of Levi's stifling dissent," it read. "However, Jen went far beyond calling for school reopenings, frequently using her platform to criticize public health guidelines and denounce elected officials and government scientists. As a top executive, her words and actions effectively undermined the company's health and safety policies, creating confusion and concern amongst employees." In other words, calling for schools to reopen was okay, but pointing out that the public health guidelines had often been wrong, that caused "confusion and concern." Questioning the various mandates and mitigation measures was not appreciated in blue state America.

The important question worth asking now is, did the lockdowns and mandates make a difference? The obvious comparison is anti-mandate Florida versus mandate-friendly California. In May 2022, the *Bloomberg* columnist Justin Fox published an analysis of the COVID-19 outcomes in the two states. By the simplest and most important measure—COVID-19 deaths per population—California came out ahead, with 241 deaths per 100,000 compared with Florida's 322 per 100,000. The two states ranked twelfth and twenty-eighth, respectively, in that category.

Fox then dug a little deeper. Floridians over the age of sixty-five account for 21.3 percent of its population, compared with 15.2 percent in California. And of course the elderly are by far the most vulnerable to the virus. When adjusted for age distribution, Florida's rate dropped to 275, while California's rose to 267—a pretty small difference. "The 'DeSantis doctrine' on Covid has been defined as protecting the elderly while letting the young take risks and that's pretty much what the state's policies delivered," he wrote.

"It turns out they're roughly the same," said Jay Bhattacharya. But, he noted, Florida didn't have a lot of the other harms from lockdowns.

They kept their schools open. They didn't have the unemployment California did. Or the business closures.

Within California, there was one city that did better than any other—indeed, better than any big city in the country. That was San Francisco. By the spring of 2023, 22 percent of the population of San Francisco County had been infected, but only 0.13 percent had died. In Los Angeles County, which had lockdowns and vaccine mandates the equal of San Francisco's, 34 percent of the population got COVID-19, but 0.35 percent died. That's a huge difference.

What explains it? Jay Caspian Kang, a writer for *The New Yorker* who lives in the Bay Area, attempted to find out. His article was published early in 2021, by which time only 189 San Franciscans had died of COVID-19, an astonishingly low number. "You have to look for the virus," one physician told him—meaning you must find the people who are most likely to get seriously ill from the virus. "Health officials must find and communicate with vulnerable, hard-to-reach people," Kang wrote, "those individuals, in turn, must be aided in taking steps to protect themselves." Unlike virtually every other city in the United States, San Francisco was in a position to do that. Because of the AIDS crisis, the city had an infrastructure and protocols that allowed it to find and help such people. Seeing that most of the early patients were Latinos, for instance, the city set up testing sites in Latino neighborhoods and actively sought out people to get them tested. It was able to draw on "a tightly interwoven network of public health initiatives, including a city-run quarantine hotel program and contact-tracing system, and a community-led drive for food and cleaning supplies." The city's experience with AIDS gave it an enormous advantage.

The second reason is that the largest skilled nursing facility in the country, Laguna Honda, is in San Francisco, and it's owned not by a private equity firm but by the city's public health department. It can house 720 residents and employs seventeen hundred staff, the same as eight for-profit nursing homes in a typical midsize city. The staff is decently paid, and the care is better than average. When COVID-19 arrived, the city quarantined Laguna Honda's residents, created a crisis team to help the staff deal with the inevitable cases, and managed its nursing staff effectively. At the time of Kang's article, only two residents had died of COVID-19. As of March 2023, that number had risen to eleven—still remarkably low.

Finally, there was "an infrastructure of trust and communication connecting the city's government, universities, and marginalized communities," wrote Kang. Again, that trust had been built during the AIDS crisis. "This network has been invaluable during the coronavirus pandemic. In places such as Texas's Rio Grande Valley, where poor and minority communities are more alienated from their local governments, it has been nearly impossible for health officials to mount a humane and targeted intervention, and cases have surged."

The San Francisco experience should cause us to reflect on the Great Barrington Declaration. Its primary message was that the most important thing to do in a pandemic is protect the most vulnerable. That's what San Francisco did. Would the city have had the same result if it hadn't also insisted on lockdowns and mask mandates? We'll never know for sure. Still, it's more than a little ironic that the city with the least tolerance for pandemic dissent wound up following the path put forth by the dissidents' most vilified document. But that's what it did. And it worked.

16

"This Is a Business"

As the pandemic ground into its third year, there was still so much that was unclear about the virus itself, from what caused surges in particular locations, to why the symptoms could be so varied, to what the long-term health consequences were. At the same time, however, COVID-19 brought great clarity to certain other things. Among them: the rotten state of health care in America.

Consider: By the spring of 2022, the CDC had recorded one million deaths in the United States from or with COVID-19. The arguments about how to count such deaths may never be put to rest, but what's clear is that excess deaths per capita in the United States were far larger than in comparable countries. In a study of twenty-nine high-income countries, the United States experienced the largest decline in life expectancy in 2020, and unlike European countries the United States did not recover in 2021. America was also the only country whose lowered life span was driven mainly by deaths among people under sixty. Whether deaths were caused by COVID-19 or the effects of the response to COVID-19 (such as increased suicides or untreated illnesses), America was far less resilient than comparable countries.

This was so even though, as everyone knows, the United States spends far more on health care than any other industrialized country— an average of almost $13,000 per person per year, according to CMS, over $5,000 more than any other high-income nation. Not surprisingly, the United States also spent far more on treating COVID-19. The average nightly cost of caring for a COVID-19 patient in intensive care was more than $20,000 in an American hospital, almost double that of number two Norway ($11,950 per night).[1]

Another painful truth: health care is increasingly unaffordable for many Americans. Covering a family of four through an employer-based plan now costs as much as buying a new car every year, according to the news website *Axios*. A 2021 study by the Stanford economist Neale Mahoney reported that Americans had $140 billion in outstanding medical debt. Medical debt was the number one source of debt collection, surpassing collection of credit card debt, utilities, auto loans, and all other sources *combined*. Seventy-nine percent of those with debt said they skipped or delayed care or medications due to cost.

Recall that more than half a century earlier Tommy Frist Sr., the cofounder of HCA, expressed his belief that "private enterprise can build and operate hospitals with an efficiency which will combat the spiraling cost of hospitalization." Rarely has a belief been so wrong. Instead, the system became increasingly inefficient, maybe even detrimental, to the health of America as a whole, even as it put tens of bil-

---

1 This study was done by virtual care company Bridge Patient Portal in partnership with Medical Web Experts.

lions of dollars into the pockets of shareholders—which, at least if you believe in old-fashioned capitalism, wasn't supposed to happen. Despite the dramatic reduction in hospital beds, the rate of growth in hospital spending over the last sixty years has eclipsed the rest of health care. According to the Health Care Cost Institute, in the last decade one big factor in that increase was emergency room costs. Spending per person on emergency room visits increased 51 percent from 2012 to 2019. Where did all the money go?

During the pandemic, it was the emergency room doctors and nurses who manned the front lines. As the first wave of the virus gave way to the delta variant and then the omicron variant, doctors and nurses went from shock and horror to exhaustion. Non-COVID patients began piling into emergency rooms alongside COVID-19 patients. "During the first surge, COVID was the only thing we saw in our ERs," Dr. Craig Spencer, the director of global health in emergency medicine at Columbia University Medical Center, tweeted in early 2022. "Now record-number COVID cases are hitting at a time when our ERs are already seeing extremely high numbers of non-COVID patients too. Thankfully the Covid patients aren't as sick. BUT there's SO many of them."

Some nurses say that 2021 and 2022 were worse than 2020. "We'd experienced so much death and we'd already burned through so much," says @shesinscrubs. "We were hemorrhaging nurses, and then we had to take care of extremely sick patients in numbers we'd never seen before." She said that at her hospital (which she doesn't want to divulge for fear of losing her job), one of the many hidden icebergs were COVID-19 patients who suffered from underlying conditions that were more dangerous than the virus—patients who needed dialysis, for instance, but who couldn't find a time slot because everything was so backed up. Mental health professionals also found themselves overwhelmed helping patients who were suffering from psychological problems in the wake of COVID-19.

Hospital staff—most obviously nurses, but also certified nursing assistants, respiratory therapists, lab technicians, and so on—were quitting in droves: the pandemic drilled home the fact that patient care mattered less than profits. "There is a tipping point where people realize they are disposable," said @shesinscrubs. "High-quality nursing care doesn't happen unless every layer of the system is compensated and supported. If the pharmacy techs can't keep up with the demands for meds, if the linens can't be turned, then we can't adequately care for patients. We're all experiencing the same crisis. We're underpaid and overexploited—and leaving." Between February 2020 and October 2021, a staggering 30 percent of health-care workers had either been laid off (12 percent) or quit (18 percent), a survey by the research firm Morning Consult showed. This meant, of course, that the staff left behind was forced to shoulder more and more work, thereby increasing the burnout. Another survey, this one by *Becker's Hospital Review*, found that a shocking 90 percent of nurses were considering leaving their profession in the next year. "The operational flaws and staffing coordination issues that have been building up over time have reached a breaking point due to the stresses of Covid," it reported.

Kelley Cabrera, the Jacobi nurse whose job had been her longtime dream, was one of the many who left the ER, in her case to take a job in a school. "It feels like the system is breaking down and I just didn't want to be part of that anymore," she says.

As nurses quit, hospitals had to bolster their staff with so-called travel nurses, who work for staffing agencies rather than hospitals. Given the shortage of nurses, they were able to command much higher salaries than the nurses they were replacing. By the winter of 2021, one hospital CEO told HHS that the cost for a travel nurse had gone from around $60 an hour to $200 an hour. "To get them in here to help has become an impossibility," he said.

Seeing the travel nurses commanding so much money destroyed the morale of those who had remained. It also began to wreak havoc on already unstable hospital finances. U.S. HOSPITALS PUSHED TO FINAN-CIAL RUIN AS NURSES QUIT EN MASSE was the bleak headline of a December 2021 *Bloomberg* story. "COVID exacerbated the economic fragility of hospitals," says John McCracken, a professor of health-care management at the University of Texas at Dallas.

———

Of course, as with all things COVID-19, the burden was not borne equally. The "have" hospitals like HCA continued to have plenty. In fact, it looked as though HCA would come out of the pandemic stronger than ever. Its 2020 profits of $3.8 billion were actually greater than in 2019, only to be exceeded in 2021, when it made nearly $7 billion.[2] The company, which had spent more than $29 billion on share repurchases and dividends since 2010, according to calculations by the Service Employees International Union, announced that it would buy back another $8 billion worth of stock in 2022. In the discussion of 2021's superlative earnings, the CEO, Samuel Hazen, cited as factors the company's tight control of costs and a 10.5 percent increase in revenues per hospitalized patient.

Even as the pandemic raged, there was evidence that HCA still found perfectly legal ways to exploit the loopholes in the way the United

2 These profits included a onetime gain of $1.6 billion from the sale of some facilities.

States pays for health care. Perhaps the most compelling example was Mission Health in Asheville, North Carolina, a not-for-profit chain that HCA bought in 2019. Mission specialized in rural health, operating free primary care clinics in impoverished communities. "A lot of the working poor, people who would otherwise fall in that crack between Medicaid and the health-care exchanges, used them," says a former Mission doctor.

Prior to the sale, North Carolina's attorney general, Josh Stein, negotiated conditions to which HCA was supposed to adhere, including maintaining the same level of charity care until January 2029 and building a replacement hospital for Angel Medical Center in Franklin, about sixty-five miles from Asheville. The then mayor of Franklin, Bob Scott, says he was suspicious from the beginning.

With good reason. Almost immediately, the complaints began piling up. HCA scrapped a worthy Mission experiment in which it was reimbursed for outcomes, returning instead to the long-standing (and more profitable) fee-for-service model. It closed two of the primary care offices. Dr. Timothy Plaut, who had been a primary care doctor at one of the closed offices, told the local ABC affiliate that more than seven thousand patients, many without insurance, had been treated at the two clinics.

A disillusioned Scott says Franklin was stripped of services. Under HCA's new plan, patients who needed more than bare-bones care would have to go to the mothership in Asheville. "It's the worst thing that has ever happened to health care in our town," he said. "It's for profit and nothing else."

Hundreds of nurses and doctors quit. By the spring of 2022, the *Asheville Watchdog*, a local news service, had identified 223 doctors who had left Mission. "Everybody who cares about quality has left because it's awful," said a former doctor. Overall, the Service Employees International Union says that staffing levels at HCA's hospitals lag the national average by about 30 percent.

In 2020 and 2021, three lawsuits were filed against HCA over its acquisition of Mission. They all claimed that HCA was trying to monopolize the health-care market in western North Carolina, thereby artificially inflating prices. The initial lawsuit, which was filed by six Asheville residents, charged that one of HCA's corporate practices was to divert patients to HCA's flagship facility in order to consolidate hospitals and raise prices. Mission Hospital–Asheville had become one of HCA's most profitable institutions, the lawsuit said. Its rates for commercial insurers had increased, on average, to 372 percent above Medicare, and after HCA's purchase Mission Hospital–Asheville ranked eighty-eighth out of eighty-nine hospitals in North Carolina for unnecessary procedures. It was also in the top 2 percent nationwide for performing unnecessary procedures, according to the Lown Institute. (HCA disputes all the allegations in the lawsuits and says that it has spent more than $100 million upgrading Mission facilities. HCA also notes that a "substantial portion" of the claims in the first suit were dismissed—although a portion of it was allowed to proceed.)

In a way, though, what happens in the courts is almost beside the point. As Keckley wrote in his newsletter, the fight between Mission and HCA is a "bigger and wider" story. "Most in the Asheville community and beyond are inclined to believe the balance between profit and purpose in healthcare is disappearing," he wrote.

There are also allegations that HCA was resorting to an old trick: gaming Medicare. In early 2022, the Service Employees International Union released a report titled "HCA: Higher Healthcare Costs for America," and alleging among other things that HCA was admitting more patients to its emergency rooms than was necessary. Why would HCA do such a thing? Because Medicare pays far more per patient when they are admitted to an ER instead of being treated on an outpatient basis. By the SEIU estimates, HCA had received excess Medicare payments of nearly $2 billion since 2008. It's unclear if the SEIU would argue that this behavior continued during the pandemic, because the data wasn't yet available. But forcing already overburdened ER nurses to care for yet more patients, and to have those patients risk exposure to COVID-19, would be "a much bigger problem than it would be in any other time," said Joseph Lyons, who led an investigation of HCA's emergency room practices for the SEIU.

HCA says that it "remains confident in our compliance with regulatory requirements" and that "our admissions decisions are based solely on professional medical judgment." The company also points out that the SEIU is not an unbiased researcher. The pandemic brought the simmering issues around unionization in health care to the fore, just as it did in other industries, and it's certainly true that the fight between HCA and the SEIU has gotten very bitter. HCA says that it believes that "labor unions do not benefit our patients, hospitals, or colleagues," and that SEIU "launched a smear campaign" that included "spreading misinformation and pushing for media coverage of their unfounded claims" during the pandemic. HCA calls the effort "shameful."

But when speaking to investors, HCA has been only too happy to brag about its prowess at moving emergency room visits into admissions, noting in various investor presentations that they rose from 60 percent of admissions in 2011 to 70 percent six years later, according to the SEIU.[3]

---

3 In 2022, *Fortune* magazine published an in-depth piece about the allegations titled "A Labor Union Is Accusing America's Biggest Hospital Chain of Medicare Fraud—and Stoking a Debate Over For-Profit Medicine and Soaring Health Care Costs."

Even as HCA thrived, have-not hospitals never stopped struggling. That was especially true of America's rural hospitals. "I don't know how we don't see a surge of rural hospital closures in the first half of next year [2023]," says Alan Morgan, the head of the National Rural Health Association. "The numbers simply don't add up." Given all the sobering statistics about rural health, from the increased risk of death from COVID-19 to the increased mortality rate when local hospitals closed, he added, "At some point in the future, we'll just need to slap a warning label on the welcome signs of small towns: 'Living here may be hazardous to your health.'"

Sometimes, rural hospitals close because of the warped economics of hospitals. But sometimes, the closures get a helping hand from the accumulated damage done by decades of what can only be called private market profiteering—financial engineering that strips hospitals of their ability to withstand an emergency like, well, a pandemic.

In December 2021, for instance, Watsonville Community Hospital, which serves a less affluent agricultural region near Santa Cruz, filed for bankruptcy. It is one of only two hospitals in Santa Cruz County. The bankruptcy was precipitated by the rising cost of staff compensation, but really, that was just the final blow. For years, Watsonville had been part of Quorum Health, a string of mostly rural hospitals. During the years Quorum owned it, Watsonville "faced substantial operating difficulties and negative cash flow," as the bankruptcy filing put it.[4]

---

4 Quorum, which was spun out of the for-profit hospital chain Community Health Systems in 2016 with a hefty debt load, in part due to CHS's previous ownership by a private equity firm, declared bankruptcy in 2020.

In 2019, Halsen Healthcare, a newly created limited liability company run by a controversial man named Daniel Brothman, bought Watsonville. In classic fashion, it financed the deal by selling the underlying real estate to Medical Properties Trust. Which meant Watsonville now owed $4 million in annual rent, on top of its other expenses. By the time Watsonville filed for bankruptcy, it owed MPT more than $40 million.

The community had to save the hospital. "There are two emergency rooms in this county," DeAndre James, the executive director of a local foundation, the Community Health Trust of Pajaro Valley, told local publication *Lookout Santa Cruz*. "If [Watsonville] hospital closes, and that emergency department closes, you have one emergency department for over 200,000 people. Not a good idea."

The foundation set about trying to save the hospital. The bankruptcy court set a high purchase price of about $65 million—a chunk of which went to MPT—but the local group was able to raise the money through donations, including $25 million from the State of California. Think about that: local citizens and the state government had to save a hospital that had been sucked dry by the supposedly efficient private market.[5]

Investors had come to see that hospitals are no different from the big banks: when times are good, investors make money, and when times are bad, taxpayers have to come to the rescue. In a 2022 report, a team of Credit Suisse analysts urged investors to put their money in hospital REITs like MPT, arguing that the pandemic showed that if hospitals are failing, the government, whether federal or local, will have no

5 MPT has previously argued that its actions kept Watsonville alive during the pandemic. It has called its business "strong and sustainable" and has filed a lawsuit against a short seller for publishing what it calls "baseless allegations."

choice but to rescue at least some of them and pay off the investors. The pandemic "has made investors realize that the U.S. government may indeed be giving 'implicit' credit support to the U.S. hospital industry," wrote the Credit Suisse analysts. Maybe. But the market is no longer so sure what this means for MPT. As interest rates began to rise, putting even more pressure on hospitals' ability to pay MPT, and *The Wall Street Journal* published an investigative article about the company, its stock began to crater, falling from almost $25 in early 2022 to below $10 by the spring of 2023.

———

The good news is that, thanks in no small part to the pandemic, both the elite media and the body politic began to wake up to the excesses and distortions brought about by the business model HCA had helped pioneer. In May 2021, for instance, a congressional subcommittee held a rare hearing on hospital consolidations during which legislators listened to a series of witnesses urge increased competition to help bring costs down. By July 2022, the Federal Trade Commission under its wunderkind commissioner, the then thirty-three-year-old Lina Khan, had filed objections to four proposed hospital company mergers, arguing that the combined hospitals would lead to higher costs and reduced quality of care. The mergers were abandoned. "The FTC will be health care's biggest headache until 2025," when President Joe Biden's term ends, said the health-care expert Paul Keckley. On the other hand, with the top ten companies controlling 25 percent of the nation's hospital markets, there was only so much the FTC—or any other government agency—could do to rein in costs. But doing something was better than doing nothing.

Nursing homes were a different story. With so many COVID-19

deaths having taken place in facilities for the elderly, the industry found itself, deservedly, under a microscope. *The New York Times, The Washington Post*, the *Star Tribune* of Minneapolis, and many other major media outlets conducted investigations into the damage done to nursing homes—and nursing home residents—by private equity firms. The connection between private equity's asset stripping and the high number of COVID-19 deaths in nursing homes was much easier to understand than the more complex problems with hospitals. And the articles making that connection were more likely to spark outrage among readers.

A classic example was a story published in August 2022 in *The New Yorker*. Titled "When Private Equity Takes Over a Nursing Home," it focused on a facility in Richmond, Virginia, St. Joseph's Home for the Aged, that was so renowned for its superb level of care that there was a three-year waiting list to get a room there. But in June 2021, the Little Sisters of the Poor, who had owned it for 147 years, sold it to a private equity firm, the Portopiccolo Group, that specialized in buying up nursing homes.

What ensued was what always ensues when a private equity firm buys a nursing home. Major staff cuts dramatically reduced patient care, which, among other things, meant leaving bedridden residents unattended at night so that by morning their briefs were "so saturated with urine they'd turned brown." The magazine described several instances in which preventable injuries and illnesses led to deaths. (In the article, Portopiccolo denied that its practices brought about unnecessary deaths.) When challenged about the cuts by a staff administrator, a Portopiccolo executive replied, "This isn't about nurses and residents. This is a business."

At the beginning of the pandemic, hoping to keep COVID-19 at bay, the Little Sisters had decided not to accept any new residents. It worked. Under their management, the facility had suffered only four cases and no deaths. Once Portopiccolo took over, the nursing home began accepting new residents again. And as longtime nurses quit, it began relying more heavily on travel nurses. Sure enough, in September 2021, one of the travel nurses tested positive, and soon the virus was sweeping through the ranks of residents and staff. "In just four months under Portopiccolo, there had been seventeen infections and six deaths due to COVID," wrote Yasmin Rafiei, the author of the *New Yorker* article. "My analysis of federal nursing-home data revealed that the home's COVID casualties, in terms of infection and death rates, placed [it] among the worst one percentile in the U.S. In the same four-month period, Portopiccolo's fleet of nursing homes across the country contended with some seven hundred infections and more than sixty deaths due to COVID."

One person who was paying close attention to the failings of private-equity-owned nursing homes was Elizabeth Warren, the Democratic senator from Massachusetts, and a fierce critic of corporate behavior. She was outraged, for instance, to learn that the former Genesis CEO George Hager had left the company barely two months after receiving a $5.2 million retention bonus. In a letter to the company, Warren demanded that it "provide more information on how much federal and state aid it has received to date, how much executive compensation it has doled out since early 2020, and the timelines and decisions of the board to provide these exorbitant bonuses to its top executives."

Genesis responded two weeks later. The company had received $417 million in state and federal grants, much of which came from the CARES Act, as well as another $248 million in government loans, it acknowledged. But the company insisted that the pandemic up to that point had cost Genesis $460 million in COVID-19-related expenses and that protecting patients and staff had always been its top priority. As for Hager's retention bonus, the company explained he had decided to leave because his role had suddenly changed and that the bonus he had received a few months earlier essentially replaced his severance, which had been set at $5.1 million.

And why had Hager's role changed? Because Genesis was in terrible financial straits and bankruptcy lawyers would soon be calling the shots. In a federal filing it made in November 2020, the company said its COVID-19 costs had outstripped its government stimulus money by $60 million in the third quarter. It did avoid bankruptcy—barely. In March 2021, just a few months after Hager resigned, the company announced a complex agreement with Welltower, the company that owned its real estate, as well as an infusion of capital from a private equity firm, to bolster its balance sheet. It also admitted that it wasn't just COVID-19 expenses that caused the bankruptcy; it was also "the pressures of our long-term, lease-related debt obligations."

Warren was hardly satisfied. On March 16, 2021, she sent the company a follow-up letter. "In short," she concluded,

> it appears that Mr. Hager walked away with an extraordinarily rich compensation package, leaving behind thousands of dead and sick nursing home residents and staff and a company in financial ruin despite being bailed out by hundreds of millions of dollars in taxpayer funds. Your residents, your shareholders, and the American public deserve an explanation for this greed and the tragedy that preceded it.

The next day, the Senate Finance Committee, on which Warren serves, held a hearing to investigate the extraordinary number of COVID-19 deaths in the nation's nursing homes. One witness was Adelina Ramos, a certified nursing assistant who worked at a Genesis nursing home in Rhode Island. Under questioning from Warren, she explained that her facility was so chronically short-staffed that it often had to decide which of two patients needing help would get it; they didn't have enough personnel to help them both.

Even President Joe Biden joined the chorus. In February 2022, his administration released a series of reforms to improve nursing home care, including minimum staffing requirements, and a crackdown on operators with poor track records. During his State of the Union address, Biden included this sentence: "As Wall Street firms take over more nursing homes, quality in those homes has gone down and costs have gone up." He then added, "That ends on my watch."

Well, maybe. For one thing, most of his proposed reforms would require new laws, and congressional Republicans are unlikely to go along. For another, it seemed more and more like a case of closing the barn door after the horse has left. According to the American Health Care Association, nursing homes lost 200,000 workers during the pandemic, bringing workforce levels to the lowest they'd been in more than a quarter century. Having extracted their billions from the industry, private equity appears to be moving on. In a *Forbes* column in late April 2022, Howard Gleckman, an expert on aging at the Urban Institute, noted that increasingly, big investors were leaving nursing homes behind in favor of the far more lucrative home health-care business. And *Fortune* magazine reported in May 2022 that private equity had found a new corner of health care to invade: the fast-growing autism therapy business.

As for Genesis HealthCare, it remains a large company, with some 250 nursing homes in twenty-two states and a rehab division that supplies services to some seventeen hundred health-care facilities. Its board chairman, David Harrington, is a former health-care turnaround specialist and a partner in Pinta Capital Partners, a private equity firm. Another director is Arnold Whitman, the CEO of Formation Capital, the private equity firm that bought Genesis for $2 billion back in 2007 and then sold its real estate four years later for $2.4 billion. A third director, John Randazzo, is a health-care entrepreneur who "served as a senior advisor to [a] global private equity firm, Warburg Pincus, for over 20 years." Try as they might, these financiers have been unable to boost the company's share price. As of the spring of 2023, Genesis's stock is worth a fraction of a penny.

———

In March 2020, in the midst of the first pandemic surge, headlines blared that TeamHealth had fired Ming Lin, an emergency room doctor who had spent seventeen years at PeaceHealth St. Joseph Medical Center in Washington State. TeamHealth was one of the two major ER staffing companies. It was owned by the private equity behemoth Blackstone. Lin had been speaking out in the press and on social media about the lack of PPE and other protective measures as he and the other ER doctors tried to treat the first wave of COVID-19 patients. Team-Health says that any claim that it fired Lin is "categorically false," and that they tried to find him a position in another TeamHealth-run ER. But whatever the reason for his termination, it nevertheless became a flash point for all the fears about private equity's influence in health care.

Mark Reiter, the past president of the American Academy of Emergency Medicine, says that Lin's firing was a very visible reminder of how corporate medicine can be harmful both to physicians and their patients. During the pandemic, Reiter watched other emergency room doctors who worked for corporate-owned staffing companies, and who were already under enormous stress in the pandemic, also having to deal with "incredibly difficult things at work," he says. "They were being terminated, sometimes for advocating for appropriate protections for patients and doctors. It was a difficult situation." He also said that even when normal patient volumes began returning, the corporate-owned practices were slower to resume normal staffing levels, which he thinks has had a negative effect on patient care. "We've certainly had conversations with the Department of Justice, the U.S. Attorney's office, with HHS, with the Office of the Inspector General, with members of Congress," he said.

Lin has added momentum to a group called Take Medicine Back; its goal is to get private equity firms out of health care. There are laws on the books that prohibit a nonphysician from interfering with the professional judgment of a physician. There are also laws—laxly enforced—prohibiting corporations from practicing medicine. Lin, Reiter, and others began rallying doctors to complain to regulators that Team-Health and Envision (EmCare's parent company) violate those laws. In late 2021, the American Academy of Emergency Medicine helped bring a lawsuit against Envision alleging that its corporate structure violated California prohibitions on the corporate control of medical practices.[6]

It's unclear what will happen on the legal front, but both Team-Health and Envision were also struggling financially. Envision had initially averted bankruptcy in part thanks to the federal government—a combination of money from the CARES Act and the ultralow interest rates provided by the Federal Reserve, which helped both companies refinance their debt. Even so, by the fall of 2022, the credit rating agency Moody's had downgraded Envision to its lowest rating, citing its "aggressive financial strategy, characterized by high financial leverage, shareholder-friendly policies, and the pursuit of acquisitive growth. This is largely due to its private equity ownership by KKR." As this book

6 Envision says its operating structure is "common across the health-care sector" and that "legal challenges to that structure have proved meritless."

was being completed, Envision was filing for bankruptcy. As for Team-Health, its bonds were rated junk by rating agency Fitch Ratings, which also noted its high leverage.[7]

It's hard not to look back at private equity's forays into health care with a kind of grudging awe. Through a combination of gaming the reimbursement system, financial engineering, and taxpayer bailouts during the pandemic, private equity firms managed collectively to make hundreds of millions of dollars from health-care companies that they then left on the brink of failure. "I think the PE firms were very, very savvy about exploiting all the loopholes," says Mortell. He's surprised that they've gotten away with it, given the broader implications for America's health care. "It's beyond a local market losing a hospital," he says. "There's the wider impact that private equity has played in making everyone's health-care premiums even more unaffordable than they already are."

Despite everything, most observers were betting that nothing will change; in fact, the smart money said that private equity's presence in the health-care sector will become ever bigger. It was already happening. Private equity was moving into autism therapy. Home health care. Travel nursing companies. According to the health-care news site *Stat*, since the beginning of 2021 through early 2022, at least eight private equity firms had bought at least seven staffing agencies.

———

In addition, venture capitalists and private equity firms were pouring billions of dollars into mental health facilities as people struggled to

7 KKR blames Envision's financial difficulties on United Healthcare, which it says forced Envision's providers out of network and routinely denied claims.

deal with pandemic-related challenges, according to *The Wall Street Journal*. All in all, the amount of private equity money going into health care continues to grow. In 2021, there was a record $151 billion of private equity health-care deals, according to the consulting firm Bain. There was so much *opportunity* in health care—opportunity that had mostly been squeezed out of other industries. "They are now targeting those sectors that have maintained some insulation from the decades of shareholder primacy because everybody else involved agrees there are some other values at play," said Oren Cass, the founder of American Compass, an organization that fights against the financialization of the American economy.

Still, pointing a finger at private equity misses an important point. "None of the players have done anything other than operate within laws and policies that allowed it to happen," says Keckley. "We allowed it."

All the players did was take advantage of the codified American belief that markets bring efficiency. It's the same belief that allowed HCA to flourish without any questions as to whether its success was good or bad for the overall system, and the same belief that has led to the reduction of beds in areas where beds were needed.

Despite the billions upon billions of dollars that have flowed to financial players—billions that could have gone to providing better care—no one ever seems to get angry enough to change anything. As Keckley points out, there is no Occupy Health Care movement.

And yet the hope among critics of the current system is that the pandemic, as awful as it has been, will continue to serve as a wake-up call. "The folks that are protecting this system at all costs are taking a big risk," says Keckley. "The next generations are not going to want what we have." In New York, Mount Sinai abandoned its plans to replace its often overwhelmed 683-bed Beth Israel hospital with a new 70-bed facility. Instead, it says it's going to modernize the existing facility. "The COVID-19 pandemic brought unprecedented challenges to our city, regional healthcare providers and the Mount Sinai Health System," the health system said. "These changes forced us to assess and rethink many aspects of how we can provide and improve care, including reenvisioning the future of Mount Sinai Beth Israel."

At the other end of the world from New York City, in Riverton, Wyoming, a group founded by two women raised the money to replace their hospital, which had been sucked dry by private equity ownership—Apollo, in this case.[8] "If a county that voted for Donald Trump by a 36-point margin can commit to a socialist project like a nonprofit community hospital, it's probably a sign of something," wrote *The American Prospect*, which noted that since the pandemic began, "major community movements have sprung up, from Riverton to Asheville, North Carolina, Yuma, Arizona, and Bradford, Pennsylvania, around the notion of restoring community control to hospitals that have been, or are in the process of being, converted into dingy ATMs for wealthy financiers."

It's a start.

---

8 Riverton was part of a rural hospital chain called LifePoint, which was bought by private equity firm Apollo in 2018. The land was then sold to MPT. Apollo then sold LifePoint for $2.6 billion from one of its funds to another, thereby netting about $1.6 billion, according to a piece by Appelbaum and Batt titled "The Role of Public REITs in Financialization and Industry Restructuring." LifePoint received $1.64 billion in COVID stimulus grants, they report.

17

Supply Chain Blues

On March 23, 2021, the *Ever Given*, a 220,000-ton, thirteen-hundred-foot container ship, ran aground in one of the narrowest stretches of the Suez Canal. It took six days of around-the-clock work to free the massive ship, during which time the line of ships waiting for their own chance to pass through the canal grew to more than three hundred. According to *Lloyd's List*, each day the *Ever Given* blocked ship traffic, almost $10 billion worth of products were prevented from getting to their destinations.

The breakdown of the PPE supply chain should have made plain the fragility of the global supply chains. If anyone missed the point, the *Ever Given*'s accident offered another example. Modern supply chains assumed that there would be no mistakes, no sudden issues, no emergencies like a pandemic or a grounded container ship. Resilience had been abandoned, and now we were paying the price.

It was as if PPE were the butterfly that flapped its wings, bringing on a crescendo of supply chain problems all across the globe. Many of the shortages were exacerbated by the crunch in the global shipping market, which sent the spot rate for a single container from Asia to the United States to a high of $20,000, up from less than $2,000 pre-pandemic. Labor shortages at the ports, plus constraints on the trucks that haul the merchandise to the rail yards, meant that ships couldn't be unloaded, and waited for weeks—and even months—anchored offshore. By the fall of 2021, some sixty ships, with billions of dollars' worth of clothing, electronics, and furniture, were waiting in the harbors outside the twin ports of Los Angeles and Long Beach. (The two ports receive 40 percent of shipborne imports to the United States.) Retail prices began to rise. The head of the Port of Los Angeles, Gene Seroka, told the *American Journal of Transportation* that the logjams would likely last through 2022. "Containergeddon," the shipping industry began calling it.

As the pandemic ground on, each week brought fresh news of a previously easy-to-obtain item that had disappeared. The IV contrast dye liquid injected into patients' veins before imaging procedures. Sriracha. Tampons. Garage doors. Baby formula. (Baby formula!) Potatoes. Chlorine. Ketchup packages. Each shortage was due to various unique factors, but they all stemmed from the same basic issue: just-in-time supply chains that lacked resilience.

"It is a huge enigma," says one CEO of the shipping market. "We've completely lost the signal." Pre-pandemic, it took thirteen days for his company's items to get from China to L.A. By the spring of 2022, it took seventy days.

Marc Schessel, who had spent the entire pandemic searching for PPE he could get to hospitals, was now being asked by these same hospitals to search for all kinds of medical devices that were no longer readily available thanks to the supply chain breakdown. Although he had only completed one significant PPE deal in all that time, he was having a fair amount of success in acquiring these other medical supplies for his hospital clients. That's because during the three years he worked to get PPE, he had gotten to know manufacturers and distributors all around the globe. Those relationships were now allowing him to become a kind of one-man distributor. What Schessel was doing hardly resembled modern just-in-time globalization—it was more a throwback to an era when relationships were what mattered. In times of stress, that still mattered.

It turns out that synchronizing a globalized economy is a lot more fraught than most economists ever realized.[1]

———

The shortage that weighed most heavily was semiconductors, those tiny chips that are to the modern economy what water is to life, powering everything from phones to cars to computers. Thirty years ago, more than one-third of all microchips were made by American companies. By 2020, that number had slipped to 12 percent, according to the 2020 Industrial Capabilities Report to Congress. High-end manufacturing had moved to Taiwan, the Pentagon noted, and lower-end manufacturing to China. Most Americans viewed the semiconductor shortages as a key reason for frustrating delays in buying, say, a new car. But it had serious national security implications as well. Given China's stance

---

1 The war in Ukraine is beyond the scope of this book, but the recognition of how critical Ukraine was to the supply of food was a shock to many. Even semiconductors were dependent on Ukraine's economy, given that the country produces half the world's neon.

toward Taiwan—a stance that grew increasingly menacing in 2022 and 2023—it was, in fact, dangerous.

"Beijing is already in a position, through its geographic and political position, to threaten virtually our entire supply chain through theft, corruption of microelectronic products, disruption of supply, coercion, and other measures even short of military action," the Pentagon report warned, adding that "a U.S. business climate that has favored short-term shareholder earnings (versus long-term capital investment), deindustrialization, and an abstract, radical vision of 'free trade,' without fair trade enforcement, have severely damaged America's ability to arm itself today and in the future."

It was Taiwan, not China, that had first made a decision to become an exporter of semiconductors. In 1974, the Taiwanese government began investing in technology and putting up what amounted to venture capital to start companies. Just over a decade later, Morris Chang, born in China and educated in the United States—and who had worked for various U.S. semiconductor companies—moved to Taiwan, where he founded Taiwan Semiconductor Manufacturing Company, or TSMC.[2] In the ensuing decades, as semiconductor manufacturing became more and more capital intensive—a new "fab" can cost upwards of $15 billion—one American company after another stopped investing in it, leaving the field to TSMC. (A fab takes raw silicon wafers and turns them into integrated circuits.) Today, TSMC's major customers include most of the big American chip designers, from Qualcomm to NVIDIA to even Intel, which once dominated the business. TSMC's market share for manufacturing advanced microchips is approaching 90 per-

---

2 The history of Taiwan's semiconductor industry is detailed in a 2003 book published by the National Academies Press titled *Securing the Future: Regional and National Programs to Support the Semiconductor Industry.*

cent, and its market value is over $400 billion—over three times that of Intel.

China went after the lower end of the market and almost all of the back-end work, like assembly and testing. With the majority of the world's electronics already assembled in Southeast Asia, the dictates of globalization practically demanded that American companies rush to China. But that wasn't all. Companies also began building chip research and development due to the low cost of the talent coming out of all of China's colleges. "Ten years ago, I would have said that you're on the outside looking in if you weren't building a China team," an executive at one semiconductor company says.

But companies found that China was its own version of Hotel California: once they were in, it was impossible to get out. "We all got snookered," says the executive. "We trained all these people, and they are really good engineers—and now they're there. When you dig deeper, so much of the basic materials are also in China. You think, 'Holy shit, it's all in China.' And we can't leave." A *Bloomberg Intelligence* article, for instance, estimated that it would take eight years for Apple to move just 10 percent of its production capacity out of China, where 98 percent of its iPhones were made.

Did American companies understand that they had handed China at least some of the keys to the kingdom? "They knew," says a longtime semiconductor analyst. "But absolutely nothing happened. The view was, 'If we treat them right, they'll be our friends.'" But it wasn't until the then president, Donald Trump, began speaking out about the Chinese absorption of so many U.S. industries that the body politic started paying attention.

It was the pandemic, along with China's COVID-19 strategy of imposing lengthy lockdowns—which included shutting down manufacturing plants for months at a time—that suddenly made people realize that while the United States still designed most chips better than anyone else, America's manufacturing ability was mostly gone. Apple said it lost $6 billion in sales due to chip shortages in 2021. In the spring of 2022, NVIDIA said that lockdowns affecting its Chinese facilities had cost it $500 million in revenue. The auto companies estimated that they would manufacture three million fewer cars in 2022 for lack of semiconductors. And then China began to make louder noises about Taiwan. "Yes, the United States supports Taiwan because of democracy, freedom and human rights; the biggest reason why that support may one day entail aircraft carriers is because of chips and TSMC," wrote Ben Thompson, a Taipei-based analyst who runs a highly respected publication called *Stratechery*.

In 2021, Pat Gelsinger, a manufacturing guru who had left Intel twelve years earlier, was brought back as CEO. Gelsinger announced that Intel would try to reclaim the manufacturing crown it had thrown away, and he lobbied hard for a bill designed to get American semiconductor makers back in the game, the so-called Chips and Science Act, which passed Congress in July 2022. The $280 billion bill includes $52 billion in subsidies designed to boost domestic chip manufacturing. Intel, TSMC, and Samsung have all announced plans to build new fabs in the United States.

On the one hand, it's a good thing that the United States is finally starting to take seriously the threat from China and the importance of making crucial products domestically. *Stratechery*'s Thompson wrote that he, for one, was in support of the Chips Act. "The goal should be to counteract the fundamental forces pushing manufacturing to geopolitically risky regions, and Intel is the only real conduit available to do that," he wrote.

On the other hand, for a country that claims to believe in free-market capitalism, it raises some uncomfortable questions. During the pandemic the United States had to bail out our hospitals. Now America was handing money to semiconductor companies to make them competitive again. Why is this different from the bank bailout in 2008, which caused so much rage? And if taxpayers are subsidizing a for-profit corporation, what does that say about that corporation's responsibilities to society, as opposed to its shareholders?

It's also unclear whether it will work. "It is more economically viable to build a new wafer fab in southeast Asia, even Europe, than the United States," the semiconductor executive says, due to the restrictions around Chips Act funding and the higher costs of labor in the United States. He says a precision manufacturing worker in Arizona, where TSMC is building a fab, may cost fifteen to twenty times per hour what that person would in Taiwan. "There is a huge risk that the consumer will not want to pay," he says. And while Intel may be talking a big game about catching up, most industry observers don't think it's possible. Even the $52 billion in federal subsidies is barely more than the almost $40 billion in capital expenditure that TSMC invested in 2022 alone.

By the start of 2023, the shortages of semiconductor chips had turned into a glut as consumers pulled back on purchases of items like phones and PCs. You might think that this would make Intel's manufacturing plan easier, but that was not the case. The slowdown was particularly punishing for the company. Its 2022 revenue fell below TSMC's for the first time ever, and the company forecast that in subsequent quarters revenue might even dip below the 2010 level.

Perhaps if Intel could reinvest some of the $130 billion it spent buying back its own stock from 2001 to 2020, it would have a better shot at reclaiming its former glory—and strengthening the country.

———

Another reason for the supply chain breakdowns was a serious shortage of truck drivers. Truckers move almost three-quarters of America's goods, according to the American Trucking Associations, which meant they were labeled "essential workers" during the pandemic. And like so many other essential workers—meatpackers and Amazon warehouse employees, nurses and nursing home attendants—there came a point when they had simply had enough. The federal pandemic stipends made it possible for millions of them to say they were no longer willing to put up with the combination of inadequate pay and impossible working conditions that the pandemic, once again, had highlighted. Many of them quit.

Why did goods often sit for months at the Port of L.A.? The truckers stopped showing up. By the start of 2022, fully 30 percent of the port's twelve thousand drivers no longer came in on weekdays. That percentage rose to 50 percent on weekends, the port's head, Seroka, told the journalist Harold Meyerson.

That's because they weren't paid to show up. Truckers are excluded from the federal Fair Labor Standards Act of 1938, so they don't get overtime pay if they work more than forty hours a week. Once the pandemic hit, they were forced to wait in line for hours—on their own dime—to get a shipment. "Bar none, that's the worst segment of trucking," says a longtime trucker named Mike Nichols, who adds that the waiting time would disappear if truckers had to be compensated. He adds, "The only conceivable reason for that exemption is that shippers and mega carriers have better lobbyists than drivers and unions."

Another trucker, Desiree Wood, says that any job that involves a big retailer is just as bad. "They have no respect for your time whatsoever," she says. "They have a very strict appointment for you to get there [to one of their distribution centers], but then they say, 'Oh, we don't have the product ready. Go park over there and we'll call you.' Well, when will it be? I don't know. The longest I've ever been a place is four-teen hours. We don't get paid for that time. And then you might say, 'Well, I haven't eaten today, and I need to go to the bathroom. Can I use your restroom and your snack machine?' They'll say, 'No, we don't let truck drivers use our bathrooms.'" In Las Vegas, she says, trucks are piled up on the streets surrounding an Amazon warehouse because Amazon doesn't provide anywhere for them to park.

This is not what was supposed to happen when Jimmy Carter de-regulated the trucking industry back in 1980. It was supposed to be about cutting through red tape and saving consumers money. And that did happen. But a lot of new entrants flooded the market and paid driv-ers far less. As the years went by, their cavalier attitude toward drivers only got worse. "The companies are operating under the assumption that drivers will wash out in six months, so they don't need to do any-thing to make the conditions better," says Wood.

And wash out they do. A 2019 study[3] found that the annual turn-over rate of long-haul truckers is a stunning 94 percent. To address that, the big trucking companies started schools, but the schools might be worse than nothing. "They churn out rookies who go out on the road with people who have been on the road for barely longer than they have," Nichols says. "It would be so much better and safer for everyone if they just paid better, had better equipment, and charged better rates."

In the pandemic, the demand for goods shot up, and so did the need for truckers. Ever more poorly trained people piled into the indus-try. Perennial problems like parking—Nichols and Wood say there are

3 The study was authored by Stephen Burks, a University of Minnesota economist, and Kristen Monaco of the Bureau of Labor Statistics.

not enough spaces for truckers to park when they need to sleep—got even worse. The government has passed bills that include money for parking, but Wood says the biggest obstacle is convincing communities at a local level that it's important—they want to bring industry, but they don't understand the accompanying need for parking.

Nichols, who started trucking in 1986 at eighteen, still loves the business. But he says that prior to deregulation "trucking had a lot more honor." With deregulation, he says, "it became a race to the bottom—whoever could haul it cheaper."

The American Trucking Associations estimates that the nation needs 80,000 more long-haul truckers to move its goods in a timely fashion and that by 2030 that shortfall may double to 160,000. "It's a self-inflicted wound that they have created for themselves," says Wood.

———

Did big business learn anything from the pandemic? If so, it would be hard to say what that might be. Six months before the virus took hold in the United States, the Business Roundtable, which represents many of the nation's largest companies, announced that its members were moving to a new model of capitalism. Instead of a monomaniacal focus on shareholders, they were going to practice what they called "stakeholder capitalism." Shareholders still mattered, of course, but this new credo was also supposed to give equal weight to customers, employees, and communities. Among other things, all the companies that signed the Business Roundtable's statement promised to pay their workers "fairly."

You might think that a pandemic would give companies a powerful rationale to put this new ethos into practice. Many companies had to shut their doors, at least temporarily. At other companies, the white-collar employees could work from home, but the assistants, janitors, food staff, and the like had no work. Many companies promised to give their frontline workers extra pay for braving the coronavirus.

But a lot of "stakeholder capitalism" and the "share the wealth" sentiment seemed to be more words than actions. On some level, that's inevitable. Under the law, corporate directors have a fiduciary duty to a company's shareholders. As long as executives can argue that good social practices are a proverbial win-win, there's no issue. The problem is when the social good comes in conflict with the bottom line. Thus it was that of the forty-eight companies that signed the Business Round-table pledge, only one said it was approved by the company's board, which would be a necessary measure for any real change in corporate purpose. "The most plausible explanation for the lack of board approval is that CEOs didn't regard the statement as a commitment to make a major change in how their companies treat stakeholders," wrote Lucian Bebchuk and Roberto Tallarita, the director and associate director, respectively, of the Harvard Law School Program on Corporate Governance, in a 2020 *Wall Street Journal* op-ed.

Still, paying workers during a pandemic—even if they had little to do—would hardly qualify as ignoring shareholders. And yet in the spring of 2022, the Brookings Institution took a close look at twenty-two big companies, including Walmart, McDonald's, Dollar General, and Amazon, which together employ more than seven million front-line workers, more than half of whom are non-white.[4] (Those four companies are also among the top five U.S. employers with the most

4 "Profits and the Pandemic: As Shareholder Wealth Soared, Workers Were Left Behind," April 21, 2022.

workers receiving federally funded safety net benefits in nine states analyzed by the General Accounting Office, which pointed out that millions of full-time workers rely on these benefits.) Brookings wanted to know whether the companies had kept the promises they had made to take care of their employees during the pandemic. They found that workers' pay did increase, particularly as labor shortages became acute. But the increases were what Brookings called "modest." "Paltry" might be a better word: an average of a 2 to 5 percent real increase in wages through October 2021. By the spring of 2022, only seven of the twenty-two companies were paying at least half of their workers enough money to cover their basic expenses.

Meanwhile, the shareholders of those same companies grew $1.5 trillion richer. The $27 billion in additional compensation that workers got was less than 2 percent of the increased wealth that went to share-holders. The twenty-two companies spent five times more on dividends and stock buybacks than on all additional pay for workers. In his book *Ages of American Capitalism*, the economic historian Jonathan Levy de-scribes four stages of American capitalism. He calls the current stage "capitalism based on asset price appreciation." Maybe the pandemic marked the last frenzy of this particular stage. But workers could lose either way: if asset prices stopped appreciating, that didn't mean work-ers would do better.

———

Although big business came through the pandemic in fine shape—often in better shape than before it began—small business was another story entirely. In New York, more than six thousand stores and restau-rants permanently closed, according to data collected by the online rec-ommendation company Yelp. California's most populous county, Los

Angeles County, accounted for a stunning fifteen thousand business closures, more than any other county in the United States. The hardest-hit businesses were restaurants, retail stores, bars, beauty salons, and gyms. "I think it's hard to cut someone's hair digitally," Bill Allen, the CEO of the Los Angeles County Economic Development Corporation, dryly noted. He added that businesses owned by women and minorities were the most vulnerable because they had less capital and less access to the banks that were doling out the PPP money.

Legislators like to proclaim that small business people are the backbone of the country, and while they did set up the PPP to help them, the major corporations still had unbeatable advantages. For instance, despite the supply chain problems, manufacturers intent on getting their goods to big retailers like Walmart and Amazon were usually able to do so, while mom-and-pop stores could do nothing but wait. "After lockdowns, everything transitioned to supply chain disruptions," says Holly Wade, a top executive at the National Federation of Independent Business. "We haven't seen any relief for a lot of small firms, and we're hearing lots of stories about the larger companies figuring out ways to access their products more easily than small firms. They have economies of scale, resources, that small firms would never have. For small business, their issues are likely to be resolved last."

Restaurants, in particular, were left to their own devices. Big cities like New York and Chicago allowed restaurants to sell take-out liquor and build outdoor seating areas (which were of limited use during the winter, of course). But they also took the brunt of the on-again, off-again nature of most blue state lockdowns. They would often be allowed to open at 25 percent capacity, and then 50 percent, but just as they hoped to open completely, the COVID-19 numbers would rise and they would have to shut down again.

Since early in the pandemic, independent restaurants had been lobbying Congress for financial help. Their idea was to base each restaurant's aid on their 2019 revenue. The amount the restaurants sought was $125 billion. Such a provision had been in the relief package that passed toward the end of the Trump presidency, but Senate Republicans removed it before the bill went to the White House for the president's signature.

In March 2021, restaurants finally got some relief when Congress created the Restaurant Revitalization Fund. The good news is that it gave grants, not loans. The bad news is that it was for $28.6 billion, not $125 billion. Which also meant that of the more than 278,000 applicants, only about a third of the restaurants and bars that applied received any money. "It was a fiasco," says Chicago's Rick Bayless. "When the money ran out, it just ran out."

Bayless got money, but Gabriel Stulman in New York did not, for no reason other than the randomness of a program with high demand and not enough money. As a result, says Stulman, he was put in the unfortunate position of having to compete with other restaurants that did get federal grants. Especially given the limited labor force, being able to pay workers more was a big advantage.

Stulman was bitter for another reason. As he saw it, the Paycheck Protection Program was set up as a backdoor bailout of the banks. He points out that banks got the 5 percent fee on the PPP loans they made.[5] Because the total amount of the PPP was $660 billion, he calculates that more than $30 billion went into the pockets of the banks just for processing loans. On top of that, the money Stulman paid his landlords went straight to the banks that owned their mortgages. "It's

---

5 The fee was a sliding scale of 5 percent for loans under $350,000 and 1 percent for loans larger than $2 million.

a circle," he says. "The money went right back to the banks. It's disgusting, and it was designed that way."

———

The government's PPP loan program ended in May 2021. Some $800 million had been doled out to businesses, according to the General Accounting Office, though most had been disbursed in the early part of the pandemic. Originally intended to allow small business people to pay their employees' wages, the program's rules evolved over time, with more money allowed for the business itself and less for employee wages. The PPP money sustained thousands of businesses—a worthy effort, even if that wasn't the original intention.

Because the program was put together so quickly, with few guardrails, it was inevitable that some of the money would wind up in the hands of fraudsters. The Federal Reserve and the Treasury Department had argued about this early, with the Fed pushing to get money out the door as quickly as possible, knowing full well that because it was abandoning the usual due diligence—which would slow things down—the incidence of fraud was likely to be high. Treasury wanted to act more carefully, but the politics of the situation—the need to get the money out quickly—meant that the Fed's argument carried the day. Indeed, much of the $5 trillion the Trump and Biden administrations dispensed overall had little oversight and few strings attached.

As early as the summer of 2020, federal investigators were attempting to root out fraud and prosecute those who had scammed the government. As time went on, that effort grew dramatically. *The New York Times* reported that by August 2022 there were five hundred federal investigators working on fraud cases, including personnel from the FBI, the IRS, the Secret Service, and the U.S. Postal Service. The Labor Department alone had thirty-nine thousand (!) investigations going. The Justice Department named a director of COVID-19 Fraud Enforcement. To help the investigators, Congress extended the statute of limitations for some pandemic fraud from five to ten years.

By September 2022, the government had seized $1.2 billion in stolen funds and had charged some fifteen hundred people with fraud, according to the Justice Department. But that was just a drop in the bucket. An estimated $80 billion in PPP funds went to people who might have inflated the number of employees they had, or invented a business that then applied for PPP money or for a free hotel room after claiming they needed to self-isolate because they were infected and then rented out the room and pocketed the money. There were all kinds of ways to get one's hands on the government's pandemic funds illegally. It was clear that prosecutors would be bringing cases against COVID-19 fraudsters long after COVID-19 itself was no longer a health emergency. Both political parties would later complain that the rampant fraud in pandemic relief programs—*The Christian Science Monitor* called it the "biggest fraud in US history"—was due to the failure of the other party to monitor the disbursements.

⸺

And then there was the Federal Reserve. Supersmart economists— some of whom worked at the Fed—appear to have embraced a saying that has never caused investors anything but trouble: "This time it's different." The old rules of economics no longer applied. You could pump $5 trillion into the economy to deal with COVID-19 ($3.1 trillion in the CARES Act, and $1.9 trillion in President Biden's American Rescue Plan); you could keep interest rates lower than they'd ever been; you could pile up federal debt—and it wouldn't cause inflation! Inflation was a relic.

House Speaker Nancy Pelosi told reporters that in the early days of the pandemic, as Congress formulated the CARES Act, Powell encouraged her to "think big" because "interest rates are as low as they'll ever be."

In fact, the Fed had become so sanguine about inflation that on August 27, 2020, its chairman, Jerome Powell, formally unveiled a new mandate in a speech at the Fed's annual symposium, which had always been held in Jackson Hole, Wyoming, but was held virtually because of the pandemic. Instead of reining in the economy when it feared inflation might exceed 2 percent—as the Fed had historically done—the central bank said it would let inflation run higher than that "for some time" if it had been lower than that previously. This was called "flexible inflation targeting."

"They set down the old rule book and said inflation can whack us over the head three times before we'll do anything about it," says one observer.

It seemed as though everyone were on the team. "I think the price of doing too little is much higher than the price of doing something big," said Biden's new Treasury secretary, Janet Yellen, in a February 2021 CNBC interview. "We think the benefits will far outweigh the costs in the longer run."

Was *anyone* worried about inflation? Well, yes. Many traders saw inflation coming—but the Fed had stopped listening to Wall Street. Larry Summers called Biden's $1.9 trillion American Rescue Plan "the least responsible macroeconomic policy we've had in the last forty years," and criticized the Fed for not putting on the breaks. "The Fed's idea used to be that it removed the punch bowl before the party got good," he told *Bloomberg*'s Joe Weisenthal. "Now the Fed's doctrine is that it will only remove the punch bowl after it sees some people staggering around drunk." But even Summers was dismissed.

If the pandemic first revealed the limits of the expertise at the once-revered CDC, now it was revealing the limitations of the expertise at the Federal Reserve. Both were exacerbated by the same problem that had gripped so much of America: an unwillingness to hear outside voices that expressed disagreement.

But what would happen if inflation did start to rise significantly? Powell said he wasn't worried. "Is there a risk that inflation will be higher than we think?" he asked rhetorically. "Yes. We don't have any certainty about the timing or the extent of these effects from reopening. We think it's unlikely they would materially affect the underlying inflation dynamics that the economy has had for a quarter of a century. The underlying forces that have created those dynamics are intact."

Powell told *The New York Times* that in June 2021. Four months later, inflation topped 6 percent, the highest level in more than three decades. And *still* the Fed continued to describe it as "transitory," and stubbornly kept rates low. There was such faith in the Fed's mastery that in November, when President Biden nominated Powell—a Trump appointee, recall—for another term as chairman, both Democrats and Republicans praised the decision. The market shot up on the news.

Was this the final throes of a Fed-driven bull market in everything? The signals were all there. You could see it in Wall Street's profits. In 2021, J.P.Morgan, the country's biggest bank by assets, made almost $50 billion, which was roughly one-third more than it had made in pre-pandemic 2019. Goldman Sachs made so much money that it planned to give its senior executives an extra round of bonuses, which the *New Yorker* magazine described as a "one-time COVID bonus, or, more accurately, a COVID–Federal Reserve bonus."

You could see it in the stock-trading frenzy, which spread to novice retail investors, as it always does at the peak of a bull market. Many of these investors were convinced it was easy to get rich in the market—and besides, they were trapped at home by lockdowns. What else did they have to do? By the second quarter of 2021, Robinhood, the online trading app aimed at individual investors, had more than twenty-one million active users. A group of Robinhood traders used their collective buying power to push GameStop, a failing video game retailer, from $1.15 in March 2020 to $53 a share in November 2021. A major hedge fund that was shorting GameStop went bankrupt betting against the novices.

You could see it in debt markets. Big private equity firms continued their debt-fueled buyout spree using so-called leveraged loans, which often were sliced and diced into securities, much as subprime mortgages had been back in the early years of the twenty-first century. It was unclear who owned all of that debt, but increasingly, the big private equity firms, which set up additional funds to buy these leveraged loans, themselves owned it. It looked like a virtuous circle, in which private equity firms could create the demand to finance their own deals.

And you could see it in home prices. Not only did the Fed continue its program of quantitative easing, but it specifically continued to buy mortgage-backed securities, helping to drive the price of a thirty-year fixed-rate mortgage to a record low of 2.68 percent by the end of 2020. You might think this would be good for people who wanted to buy homes, and to a certain extent it was. But it was even better for investors, especially private equity firms, who started to snap up houses they could then rent to people who couldn't afford to buy a home (in part because investors were buying so many of them and pushing prices up).

The Fed said there was no reason to worry because this wasn't like the housing bubble that led to the 2008 financial crisis. The credit of home buyers was strong, and there wasn't a proliferation of risky mortgages.

But that didn't mean it was healthy. In May 2022, *The Wall Street Journal* published an article about A. J. Steigman, whom the paper noted was the number one broker in the metro Atlanta region, responsible for more than $86 million of sales or leases the previous year. Steigman lived not in Georgia but in Florida, where he sold homes to institutional investors over the internet, with neither buyer nor seller ever seeing the house.

By the first quarter of 2022, Redfin reported that investors were purchasing a record 20 percent of homes that were sold. "We have had a huge transfer of wealth from taxpayers and renters to those who bought houses with the Fed's borrowed money," noted Pantera Capital, an investment firm.

Did Washington's policies to mitigate the consequences of COVID-19 offer any benefit to the public at large? Yes. It turned out the government policy—fiscal policy, it's called—could be extraordinarily effective, much more effective than leaving it all up to the Fed.

According to official government data, by the fall of 2021 the pandemic stimulus checks lifted nearly twelve million Americans out of poverty. The unemployment rate across all demographics fell to previously unimaginable levels—which meant there was suddenly a serious labor shortage, with more jobs than willing workers. The collective wealth of the bottom 50 percent of households nearly doubled in the two years from the start of 2020 to the start of 2022, according to Federal Reserve data cited by *Bloomberg*. Notwithstanding all the small businesses that closed, others opened, because entrepreneurs were finally able to take a chance on their own ideas, maybe because of government money, or maybe because they'd sold a house for a lot of money or made money speculating in cryptocurrencies. As people left the workforce, a management professor named Anthony Klotz coined the phrase "the Great Resignation." It's not clear that that was ever real, but what was true was that suddenly power was in the hands of labor, not employers. Wages began to rise. Research by the Cleveland Fed published in early 2023 found that those who had lost their jobs during the pandemic recession experienced virtually no wage losses at all, a startling outcome.

The problem is that the sheer amount of the medicine that had been administered came with a serious side effect. In this case, despite the assurances of so many officials, the side effect was inflation.

In addition to Summers, another contrarian who had always feared that prospect was Mohamed El-Erian. As the inflation signals began to flash red, he worried about who would get hurt most. It wasn't the wealthy. What would inflation do to all those gains that the less well-off had achieved? "The Fed's inflation miscalculations risk hurting the poor" was the headline of a piece he wrote in November 2021. He went on to point out that when staples like gasoline and food rise in price, lower-income households, which spend more of their budget on such things, face far more pain than do higher-income households. Inflation, which is far higher than the headline number for these households, could nullify any wage gains. He added that the Fed's lack of action also would "bolster the view that the Fed is captive to financial markets . . . and insensitive to the continuous worsening of inequality."

By March 2022, when the consumer price index hit almost 8 percent, El-Erian noted, in shock, that the Fed was still pursuing quantitative easing. "The Fed has consistently and repeatedly mischaracterized inflation as 'transitory,'" he wrote.

Kevin Warsh, a former Fed governor, wrote in *The Wall Street Journal*, "A central lesson is already clear: Nothing is as expensive as free money." He added, "The Federal Reserve's zero-rate policy ranks among the most significant economic policy errors in nearly half a century."

That March, the Fed finally did begin to hike interest rates. But there would be no quick or easy fix. By June, inflation topped 9 percent. "The worst mistake we could make would be to fail. It's not an option," Powell said. "We have to restore price stability. We really do. It's the bedrock of the economy."

As food prices soared, the lines at food banks began to grow again. Bloomberg reported that by the spring of 2022, the line at the food bank in Odessa, Texas, was as long as it had been during the worst of COVID-19. Brookings reported that at those twenty-two companies it had researched, inflation erased at least half of the average wage gains for frontline workers.

And, of course, as the Fed raised rates, asset prices began to plunge. The first half of 2022 was the worst six months for stocks since 1970, with the S&P 500 falling 21 percent. Spreads on junk bonds widened; suddenly risky companies couldn't sell debt. Pandemic superstars like Zoom and Peloton crashed back to earth. Robinhood, which lost $295 million in the second quarter of 2022, laid off almost one-third of its staff. By the summer of 2022, its stock was down 90 percent from its high.

What *Bloomberg* called the "Covid billionaires," a group that including Jeff Bezos, Elon Musk, and Stéphane Bancel, saw their personal pandemic era wealth dissipate. It became clear that cryptocurrencies, once hyped as the revolution that would redefine the very concept of money, were simply a byproduct of the very traditional monetary regime they thought they'd replace. One after another, they imploded. THE FED PRICKED THE EVERYTHING BUBBLE was the headline in *The Wall Street Journal* on June 14, 2022.

At least some of those who had previously believed that their success was due to their own smarts had a moment of reckoning. "We've actually had a massive tailwind because we had a zero interest rate environment that allowed us to raise unbelievable amounts of money from investors who frankly had few other alternatives because interest rates were zero," said Chamath Palihapitiya, a venture capitalist turned promoter of SPACs—the risky investment vehicles that also flourished in the mania. SPACs he had backed fell some 90 percent from their peaks, although because he had already cashed out by selling most of his shares early, his contrition didn't have much of a cost.

You might say, no harm, no foul. What the Fed gave to the rich, it took away. But that's an overly simplistic reading. If it hadn't been for the decade of distortion following the financial crisis, the Fed would have had more room to maneuver in the pandemic, and both headline inflation and the inflation in asset prices might have been less dramatic.

Instead, both the collapse in asset prices and the inflation that the Fed had refused to acknowledge for too long exacerbated the sense that everything was out of control, that no one knew what they were doing, that those who were supposed to be experts were lurching haplessly. It was yet another reason not to trust the government.

The decade plus of easy money had also left an enormous pile of debt behind. By the end of 2022, *Bloomberg* reported that globally almost $650 billion of bonds and loans were "distressed," meaning that the borrowers might not be able to pay their creditors.

There were other asset bubbles that would crush not the rich but the middle class and the poor if they popped. Lev Menand, the Columbia University Law School professor, is particularly worried about housing. "There was a huge run-up in the cost of real estate," he says. "It doesn't show up in inflation in the conventional sense, but it's asset price inflation. And a by-product of reversing the accommodation the Fed provided is going to be a reversal in that dynamic." He also asks what will happen as the wealth Americans thought they had in their homes begins to disappear with the increase in interest rates. "A huge portion of society has all of their savings tied up in their homes," says Menand. "You can address an economic downturn by increasing the value of those assets, but trying to respond to a boom by reducing the value is going to be very disruptive."

As the market rout continued, it added to the crisis facing the many pension funds that don't have enough money to pay their beneficiaries. The miracle that private equity had promised pension plans also started to fall apart. Cheap debt made the private equity honchos incredibly wealthy. A downturn wouldn't touch them, but it would destroy the retirees who had come to depend on them. In 2022, pension funds reported their worst year since 2009. And that was before the losses from private equity.

Companies taken private by these firms aren't valued in any public forum, but if, say, publicly traded oil companies are down 50 percent, then similar companies owned by private equity firms have lost value too. There's no way to know for sure, because the firms don't have to report their results to the public, and they can and often do avoid recognizing losses as long as possible. But in early 2023, a pension research group called the Equable Institute noted that although 2022 numbers still included overstated private equity valuations, the losses were going to have to start showing up. "Private equity returns are a major threat to pension plans' ability to pay retirees," wrote PitchBook, which covers the industry.

At least through the start of 2023, the job market continued to defy all the inviolable precepts of economic theory, which held that rising rates were supposed to increase unemployment. Instead, the job market remained exceptionally strong. "It kind of shows you why we think this will be a process that takes a significant period of time," Powell told the Economic Club of Washington. The fear was that the recession that could follow interest rate increases would wipe out what remained, post inflation, of the gains of the very workers pandemic fiscal policy had most helped.

Longtime skeptics of Fed policy also worried about the prosaic, but very profound, effect of rising interest rates on the federal budget. "If interest rates increase, the debt reckoning comes due," Cochrane says. "The government is like a borrower in the early 2000s who bought a home with a teaser rate."

Nor had the structural problems in the market, the ones that had led to the repo market malfunction in the fall of 2019 and which had played out on a far larger scale with the onset of COVID-19, been fixed. Maybe there wouldn't be another pandemic, at least not anytime soon, but might rising interest rates also cause a shock to the system as investors began pulling money from riskier assets? "Substitute any economic shock that might cause people to reevaluate the price of financial assets," says Menand. "We enjoyed a decade of benign market conditions without any significant shocks that would destabilize this inherently unstable system. The pandemic just happened to be the cause. It may not be the last one."

Menand wasn't the only one with a warning. "The Fed will keep hiking until something breaks, and clearly the cracks are forming," wrote Scott Minerd, the head of risk management at Guggenheim Partners, in 2022. It turned out that Menand and Minerd were right: the system was inherently unstable, the pandemic wasn't the last shock, and things did start to break. But it wasn't the shadow banking sector, at least not initially—it was the banks. As interest rates rose, the value of bonds shrank. Banks that held bonds suddenly had paper losses—though if they had to sell the bonds, the losses would become real.

Sure enough, in March 2023, Silicon Valley Bank (SVB), once the country's sixteenth-largest bank, which catered to the venture capital industry, had to sell, because its customers, mainly start-up companies, began to pull their deposits. Once the run started, it didn't stop.

Although deposits were supposed to be guaranteed only up to $250,000, there was an instant outcry from the venture capital community about all the jobs that would be lost if start-ups couldn't recoup their uninsured deposits. Within a few days, the banking agencies had announced a government guarantee of all deposits at both Silicon Valley Bank and Signature Bank, a New York bank where a run had also begun. Once again, the government was bailing out things that were supposed to be outside the safety net.

By May 2023, three of the largest bank failures in U.S. history had occurred in just the past two months. It was unclear what else the government might have to do to shore up the system. What *was* clear was that the whole mess was a by-product of government policy with a dollop of management incompetence on top. Government policy flooded the banks with money that they had to invest—and no one in charge was on top of the risks that would ensue. "The entire concern is that very easy money and high liquidity over a long period creates perverse incentives and perverse structures that become fragile when you reverse everything," wrote Raghuram Rajan, the former IMF chief economist and former governor of the Bank of India. What was also clear is that once again, it was smaller banks and the small businesses that were their customers that were most at risk. Who would keep their money at a small bank that might face a run if they could put it at J.P.Morgan Chase instead? But why would a J.P.Morgan Chase ever bother with a tiny loan to a small-town business? It was a potential problem that flew in the face of America's supposed support for the small.

There were many more unresolved questions. "Over the past 13 years, the Federal Reserve has consistently solved problems—whether they were partly or entirely of its own creation—by becoming larger and more involved in the financial system," wrote Bill Nelson, who was a deputy director of the Division of Monetary Affairs at the Fed and is now the chief economist at the Bank Policy Institute, on his blog. "That greater size and involvement has led in turn to still more problems, which the Fed has again sought to fix by expanding its reach into markets. This process has transformed the Fed from an efficiently scaled institution conducting policy with a small imprint on financial markets to a behemoth."

And a behemoth that was likely to be subject to a new kind of political pressure. "Now that people have seen that we have these powers, future administrations will be under pressure to appoint people to the board who will use those powers in particular ways," says Quarles. In his view, it is uncomfortably analogous to what happened to the Supreme Court in the 1960s, when people began to realize that a technocratic institution that was designed to resolve questions of law actually had the power to set the direction of the country. "The fights for control of this institution [meaning the Fed] may rise to become as vitriolic as the fights over the Supreme Court," he said.

18

The Pandemic Next Time

T he pandemic is over," President Joe Biden told the CBS news show *60 Minutes* in September 2022, two and a half years after the coronavirus first wreaked havoc on New York and the Northeast and then spread across the country.

In one sense, Biden's announcement was a belated acknowledgment of the obvious. Most mandates had already been lifted, as had most capacity limits on restaurants and stores. Proof of vaccination was no longer needed to get into a sporting event. Most people had stopped wearing masks, and some companies—though not all—were telling employees that they needed to start coming to the office again. COVID-19 testing sites were still on street corners, but they were mostly empty. Life had returned to normal—or at least a close approximation.

On the other hand, Americans were still dying of COVID-19, as were people all around the globe. The week after Biden's statement, the

United States averaged more than fifty-seven thousand new cases—and more than four hundred deaths—a day, adding to the one million plus Americans who had lost their lives to the virus. Not surprisingly, the epidemiological establishment was horrified by Biden's statement. Michael Osterholm, the University of Minnesota infectious disease expert, said he feared Biden's comments had "wounded" the government's ability to persuade people to get the latest COVID-19 booster, which had been approved for all adults a few weeks earlier. And of course, Anthony Fauci, three months from retiring at the age of eighty-two, was hardly ready to declare the pandemic over. Having previously predicted that there would be a spike in cases in the winter, he told a gathering after the president's remarks, "We are not where we need to be if we are going to be able to live with the virus, because we are not going to be able to eradicate it." (At a fundraiser in New York a few days later, a chastened Biden told the audience that "if you haven't gotten your boosters, get them.")

Osterholm's fear came true: the bivalent booster was a complete bust. But it's unlikely the reason was Biden's proclamation. No, the reason was that many Americans no longer trusted their own government's health recommendations. The CDC, the FDA, Anthony Fauci: they had all lost a great deal of credibility with their misrepresentations and with a series of recommendations—like school closings—that were now widely accepted as having done far more harm than good.

In the summer of 2022, the CDC director, Rochelle Walensky, was handed the findings of an internal examination she had ordered the previous spring. "To be frank, we are responsible for some pretty dramatic, pretty public mistakes, from testing to data to communications," she said in a video distributed to the agency's roughly eleven thousand employees. She never uttered those words to the American public, though.

Maybe modern communications, with its need for sound bites that oversimplified complex issues, just wasn't suited to getting people through a pandemic. But when "maybe" or "we don't know" isn't allowed; when reputable scientists who hold dissenting views are banned from social media and described as "fringe"; when error is never acknowledged; and when the lived experience of people is ignored—it is inevitable that people will lose faith in experts telling them how to behave. When mitigation practices that are supposedly based on scientific facts turn out not to be so, is it any surprise that people will feel betrayed?

A study by the communications giant Edelman showed a direct correlation between the trust of a country's citizens in its health-care system and the overall health of its population. "Citizens expect democratic governments to be responsive to their health concerns," Orkun Saka, an economist at the University of London, told *The Washington Post*, "and where the public-sector response is not sufficient to head off the epidemic, they revise their views in unfavorable ways."

Saka coauthored a study that examined the effects of epidemics on political trust. The study concluded, "One can envisage a scenario where low levels of trust allow an epidemic to spread, and where the spread of the epidemic reduces trust in government still further, hindering the ability of the authorities to contain future epidemics and address other social problems." In other words, a lack of trust can lead to an even greater lack of trust. One wonders what percentage of Americans will be willing to be vaccinated when the next pandemic arrives.

What was also distressing was how little had changed as a result of the pandemic. COVID-19 had put a harsh spotlight on conditions in the nation's nursing homes, but there had been no effort at the federal level to make them any better by, say, passing a law that would mandate minimum staffing levels. Private equity firms continued to move into health-care businesses, despite the harm they had caused with their ownership of nursing homes and emergency room staffing companies. The hospital system was as bifurcated as ever, with the safety net and rural hospitals on one side and the for-profit hospital chains on the other. If San Francisco offered a model for how to fight a pandemic in the future, most other cities didn't seem to notice. *Fortune* magazine, in an article about private equity's incursion into the autism business, asked, "Can the culture of private equity, with its focus on cost-cutting and profit maximization, coexist with a community whose needs are highly varied, individualized, and sometimes lifelong?" Thanks to the pandemic, the answer to that question was obvious.

For all the country had been through, the United States had seemingly learned next to nothing about how to deal with a pandemic. Did the United States have a national contact tracing strategy ready to go? No. Had the government refilled the PPE stockpile? No. Were public health agencies across the country coming up with protocols to protect the most vulnerable and thus minimize deaths? No. "The way we deal with epidemics is panic, neglect, panic, neglect," said Seth Berkley, the head of Gavi. "This was a $12 trillion hit on the global economy. Not only was it a $12 trillion hit, but there are the lives lost. We don't know what the death rate is exactly but assume right now that somewhere between fifteen and twenty million people died. It disrupted the entire world. We need to remember that." But Berkley is skeptical that we will. He remembers raising money for an Ebola vaccine when Ebola hit. "Money is not the issue," officials around the world told him. "'Whatever it takes, whatever you need,' they said. Then, three months later, you go to some summit, and they're like, 'Ebola, that was yesterday's problem. We don't have any money for that.' How do you get people to understand that this is about global health security?"

Berkley believes that for all we talk about risk, people simply don't know how to measure it. "America has three layers of nuclear deterrents," he says. "We have land-based missiles, but if they fail, we have air-based missiles. If those fail, we have submarines. Nobody questions that massive expenditure, because they think the consequences are so bad." But, he said, another pandemic is more likely than a nuclear war.

In October 2022, the Biden administration published the National Biodefense Strategy, its blueprint to defend against both man-made threats and naturally occurring pathogens. Despite numerous references to COVID-19, and how the coronavirus had given the world a lesson in the damage a pandemic can do, the plan was little more than an $88 billion wish list. Just like every previous pandemic plan, going back to George W. Bush's original plan in 2007, it offered no explanation for how its goals would be accomplished. It called for the country to generate more PPE and alternative PPE supply chains. Have a vaccine ready to go within 130 days. Facilitate recovery to restore the community and the economy. All well and good, but something the pandemic had also taught the world is that vague and sweeping pronouncements, by themselves, didn't do anybody any good.

———

The pandemic did nothing to nudge corporate executives away from their obsession with shareholder value. A record amount was spent on stock buybacks in 2022, with Apple, Google, Microsoft, and Facebook leading the way. Aside from Apple, most of the big tech companies announced significant layoffs; after all, customers were no longer as dependent on the virtual world as they'd been during the lockdowns. CEO compensation also set a record—as did the pay gap between the chief executive and the rank and file.

In 2022, with its vaccine revenue over $18 billion[1] and $4.8 billion in profits, Moderna announced a $3 billion stock buyback. It followed that up with the classic pharma tactic to maximize profits: it said it was considering a fourfold increase in the price of its vaccine, infuriating the Biden administration. *Politico* reported that the relationship between the company and the administration had "deteriorated dramatically." White House officials "openly complained about Moderna's hardball tactics" and called the company "highly arrogant," *Politico* wrote. On Capitol Hill, Senator Bernie Sanders demanded that Moderna's CEO, Stéphane Bancel, testify at a hearing bluntly titled "Taxpayers Paid Billions for It: So Why Would Moderna Consider Quadrupling the Price of the COVID Vaccine?"

"Maximizing shareholder value" during the pandemic did have one unexpected consequence: it caused millions of workers to rethink the value of their work. Working during the pandemic prompted some Amazon warehouse workers to organize union drives, including a successful one on Staten Island, New York. Starbucks workers also made numerous attempts to form unions in individual stores. Some were successful. Millions of workers who quit or were laid off during the pandemic simply didn't bother to rejoin the workforce; as of the spring of 2023, the workforce had some two million fewer workers than in 2019. There were labor shortages all across the economy, forcing companies to raise wages to lure employees. This was particularly noticeable in the health-care industry. With so many nurses having left the profession, hospitals were being forced to pay a premium for the travel nurses who were now a critical component of hospital staffing. Saving money by

---

1 Both Moderna and Pfizer told Wall Street that their 2023 vaccine sales would decline significantly as people stopped getting boosters.

cutting back on necessary staff wound up costing hospitals more in the long run.

Hospitals, in fact, were in trouble. The consulting firm Kaufman Hall estimated that a stunning 53 percent to 68 percent of the nation's hospitals ended 2022 with significant losses, largely due to the increased cost of labor. Jack Lynch, the president and CEO of Main Line Health, a five-hospital nonprofit system serving Philadelphia and its western suburbs, summed it up. "In my 35 years as a healthcare leader, this is the most fragile I've ever seen the American healthcare system," he told the publication *Fierce Healthcare*.

Even for financially healthy hospitals like HCA, questions were growing about how they achieved those profits. The Service Employees International Union continued to fire broadsides at HCA, alleging that nurse understaffing was chronic. In North Carolina, the state treasurer, Dale Folwell, asked HCA to sell Mission Hospital in Asheville back to the community after watching costs rise and discovering that Mission charged privately insured patients up to 300 percent more than Medicare patients.[2] According to a survey by Jarrad, a consulting firm, 53 percent of the people surveyed believe that hospitals put profits over patients. Hospitals were becoming yet another institution Americans were doubting.

———

As for globalization, it was still the reigning ethos, though you could see cracks in the edifice. The pandemic had caused people—including

2 Folwell's analysis was cited in a 2023 NBC News piece titled "Some Workers at U.S. Hospital Giant HCA Say It Puts Profits Above Patient Care." HCA denied the allegations.

the country's academic experts and business leaders—to finally talk openly about its drawbacks. The supply chain woes that started with PPE and then rippled through the rest of the economy had woken up many economists, journalists, academics, and government officials to the danger inherent in the constant search for the efficiency that globalization enabled. "Resilience"—meaning having goods in reserve for emergencies, and alternate supply chains, and reliance on goods that were homegrown rather than imported from China—was suddenly a buzzword in New York and Washington.

The Biden administration not only continued the Trump tariffs on Chinese goods but instituted export controls to prevent U.S. companies from sending advanced semiconductor technology to China. The U.S. trade representative, Katherine Tai, gave a speech in which she called for an industrial policy that would be designed to protect the country's national interests. Free trade, she said, "cannot come at the expense of further weakening our supply chains [and] further exacerbating high-risk reliances." Canada's deputy prime minister, Chrystia Freeland, spoke at the Brookings Institution, where she called for the world's democracies, both in the West and in Asia, to reorient their trading toward one another. "Friendshoring," she called it.

Russia's invasion of Ukraine—and its efforts to blackmail Europe, which depended on Russian oil and gas—were certainly factors in this new thinking. But it was also spurred by a handful of thinkers whose belief that the economy needed to work better for the less well-off was suddenly given new prominence. Dani Rodrik, the Harvard economist who had long questioned conventional free trade theory, was suddenly in demand as a speaker. The *New York Times* columnist Paul Krugman, who for years had sneered at those who objected to globalization, was now writing columns with headlines like THE WORLD IS GETTING LESS FLAT. The *Financial Times* columnist Rana Foroohar was among the chief proselytizers for this new way of thinking about trade; her book *Homecoming: The Path to Prosperity in a Post-Global World* offered examples of companies that were building resilience into their business models, and it suggested how the movement could grow.

At a conference Foroohar organized in October 2022, one of her allies, the economic historian Gary Gerstle, said, "I find this an incredibly hopeful moment." Nobody could say yet what the future of trade would look like—and whether it would truly give working-class Americans a better deal and create economic resilience. For all the talk, reshaping the supply chain was no easy task, as James Crabtree, the executive director of the International Institute for Strategic Studies Asia, pointed out in the *Financial Times*. With the exception of semiconductors, "decoupling has barely begun to happen," he wrote. He also noted that in theory, it sounds great for the United States to source products from, say, Vietnam instead of China—but if Vietnam in turn was still sourcing underlying components from China, that didn't exactly solve the problem. Nor was that the only issue, Yes, the pandemic did crystallize how badly we needed something better. But on top of the decades of refusals to solve the problems, it also created a new risk—the possibility of a turn toward a strident nationalism that would sweep with it the good things about globalization too and leave in its wake a far more dangerous world.

———

The polarization over the methods used to fight the pandemic had not abated and was not likely to anytime soon. The right believed that most of the non-pharmaceutical interventions were a form of pointless Kabuki theater and that mandates infringed on personal freedoms. The left contended that the mandates had saved millions of lives and that those who refused to wear masks or get vaccinated were putting their own selfish desires over the community's well-being.

In March 2023, *The Wall Street Journal* got ahold of a classified Department of Energy report that concluded with "low confidence" that the coronavirus might well have originated from a leak at the Wuhan Institute of Virology. This had been a source of contention since the earliest days of the pandemic, with most officials insisting that the pandemic was the result of the virus passing from an animal, most likely a bat, to a human. Although the Energy Department's report was far from conclusive, and other U.S. agencies were divided as to the origin of the virus, the right was practically giddy over the news. Twitter was ablaze with reminders that those who had espoused the lab leak theory had been accused of misinformation and censored. Once again, they said, the elite consensus had been wrong.

In fact, the former CDC director Dr. Robert Redfield complained to Congress after he left office that Fauci had "sidelined" him from debates about the origin of the virus, because Redfield supported the lab leak theory and that was contrary to the party line. "This was an *a priori* decision that there's one point of view that we're going to put out there, and anyone who doesn't agree with it is going to be sidelined," he said, "which I will argue is antithetical to science."

The more important issue, as David Wallace-Wells pointed out in *The New York Times*, was whether experiments using rare viruses—so-called gain-of-function research—should prompt "a global reckoning over lab safety procedures" and the wisdom of doing such research in the first place. But the partisans on both sides didn't seem terribly interested in that question.

In Florida, Governor Ron DeSantis began championing something he called "medical freedom"—a campaign that "proposes permanently limiting Covid-19 vaccination and mask requirements and giving cover to physicians whose medical views depart from scientific consensus. He also plans to set up a panel to review recommendations from the Centers for Disease Control and Prevention," according to *Politico*.

A few months earlier in California, Governor Gavin Newsom signed a bill that was backed by the California Medical Association intended to do just the opposite: discipline doctors who spread COVID-19 "misinformation." The San Jose *Mercury News* described potential offenses as "promoting untested or ineffective treatments and cures and questioning the effectiveness of face masks and vaccines."

Yet hadn't we learned by now that yesterday's misinformation might well be tomorrow's truth? Even now, there's so much about COVID-19 we still don't know, from why some people were afflicted with "long COVID" to what caused surges in certain places at certain times. And then there was this: Excess deaths, which had originally been thought of as a consequence of the pandemic, had remained surprisingly high even though COVID-19 deaths were way down. Throughout the second half of 2022 and into the early part of 2023, there continued to be high rates of excess deaths. The same was true in other Western countries, across all age-groups. Between June 2022 and January 2023, for instance, there were thirty thousand excess deaths in England alone.

There is a clear precedent in living memory for immense social and economic shocks leading to surges in heart disease. And there were plenty of other potential causes: increased opioid use, a surge of alcoholism, a higher murder rate, and deaths related to the difficulty of getting hospital care for anything other than COVID-19. Ultimately, the causes of the excess deaths are probably varied and involve a combination of factors. We may never be able to answer the question as to causation definitively—but we certainly won't if we don't take a hard look.

———

If there is one area where a consensus seems to have formed, it was over the issue of school closings. In February 2023, the National Assessment of Educational Progress released its first national "report card" since the beginning of the pandemic. It confirmed what earlier studies had already shown: Student achievement plummeted during COVID-19. The math test scores for fourth and eighth graders fell in nearly every state. No state showed significant improvements in reading. The lowest-performing students saw the largest declines in achievement.

A 2022 paper published by the National Center for Analysis of Longitudinal Data in Education Research (CALDER) concluded that the shift to remote or hybrid school during the pandemic "had profound consequences for student achievement." Using testing data from more than two million students in ten thousand schools across the country, a team of researchers from CALDER, the Northwest Evaluation Association, Harvard, and Dartmouth College found that learning gaps in math "did not widen in areas that remained in-person." But they found that, especially in high-poverty areas, students lost more ground the longer they were remote. "If the achievement losses become permanent," they wrote in their conclusion, "there will be major implications for future earnings, racial equity and income inequality."

What was also clear was that the pandemic had caused a certain percentage of students to simply give up on school. The New York *Daily News* reported that in 2022, 350,000 public school students "repeatedly missed school," and that among children living in poverty, chronic absenteeism was 45 percent, nearly double what it was before the pandemic.

On Twitter, the head of the American Federation of Teachers, Randi Weingarten, kept up a steady stream of tweets claiming that her union had pushed hard to get schools reopened during the pandemic. Given how hard her union had fought to keep schools closed in 2020 and much of 2021, her tweets were practically the definition of gaslighting.

School closing also played a role in the mental health crisis affecting thousands of children. Three medical groups, including the American Academy of Pediatrics, declared a national state of emergency in children's mental health, citing "dramatic increases in emergency department visits for all mental health emergencies."

But of course, that had been obvious from the beginning, or at least it should have been. One doctor, who describes herself as an ardent progressive (she asked that her name be withheld), eventually signed the Great Barrington Declaration—the document so many mainstream scientists had savaged when Martin Kulldorff, Jay Bhattacharya, and Sunetra Gupta first posted it in October 2020. This doctor had been among those who had originally viewed the declaration as apostasy. But her experience as a psychiatrist who works with underprivileged autistic kids had changed her mind. She saw firsthand how, for the children she counseled, the consequences of lockdowns far outweighed the consequences of COVID-19.

"What really drove me was my clinical experience," she said. "What happens to a child when every single support is removed from them? What's the impact on their family and siblings? What I was seeing was complete regression. It was devastating, and the downsides of lockdowns and school closures were not being openly discussed in the mainstream media. I was horrified. Why aren't we talking about this?" She described the situation she saw as 2022 wore on as a "sickening mental health crisis."

———

Finally, there was the policy of locking down citizens to consider. Remember when Richard Hatchett, one of the authors of Bush's original pandemic plan, told Michael Lewis that if you locked everyone up, you would not have any disease? The question, he added, was whether you could do that in the real world.

We now had the answer to those questions. Even if you locked up everyone, you would merely be delaying the disease, not eliminating it. And no, you couldn't lock everyone up in the real world. China offered the ultimate proof.

During the pandemic's early months, Chinese citizens had accepted the severe lockdowns imposed on them as their patriotic duty. But when the government shut down Shanghai, a city of twenty-five million, during a February 2022 outbreak, the reaction was very different. China's version of a lockdown was far more severe than anything imposed on Americans; people were not allowed to leave their homes—period. *The Guardian* described it as a "ruthlessly enforced lockdown that has caused income loss, stress and despair for millions struggling to access food or emergency healthcare."

People went out on their balconies to bang pans and scream in protest. Defying the censors, they wrote bitter criticisms online. There were some widely publicized suicides. In May, when the lockdown was lifted for about half the city, the people who could leave their apartments took to the streets to protest. In one case, according to *The Wall Street Journal*, locals "found a government storage site full of vegetables that had rotted rather than being delivered to hungry families and smashed them in the street." Even the Chinese had had enough. In November 2022, a building caught fire, and some of the residents died because, thanks to China's lockdown, their apartments were locked from the outside. A video showing fire trucks unable to get close enough to put it out—while residents screamed, "Someone save us!"—went viral. People expressed their outrage on social media, and in areas that were not locked down, protests became violent.

Finally, in December, the central government abandoned its "zero-COVID" policy, ended all lockdowns, and pushed the issue down to local governments. What happened next was no surprise: China, which had done a poor job of vaccinating its citizens, was suddenly awash in COVID-19 cases. It was like New York in March 2020, with hospitals turning away patients and crematories overwhelmed with bodies. *The New York Times* quoted a group of academics who estimated that between one million and one and a half million people had died in the space of just two months.

By then, Australia and New Zealand, two island nations that had had some of the tightest mitigation measures in the world, had also given up trying to keep COVID-19 away from their shores. Australia ended most of its restrictions in the fall of 2021, realizing that its tough lockdown was unable to stop an omicron surge. But with 96 percent of the population vaccinated, deaths were minimal despite the large number of cases. A few months later, New Zealand, with an 89 percent vaccination rate, followed suit. In Denmark, officials lifted all COVID-19 restrictions in February 2022—even though it had, at that moment, the second-highest infection rate in the world. COVID-19 was "no longer a threat to the critical functions of society," the Danish researcher Michael Bang Petersen told *The Atlantic*. He added that while from a purely epidemic point of view a decision to continue restrictions might have made sense, "that decision would have come with costs too."

Maybe—*maybe*—the social and economic disasters that lockdowns created would have been worth it if they had saved lives. But they hadn't. Imposed without any prior evidence of their efficacy, lockdowns helped "flatten the curve" in the short term, which was certainly beneficial for beleaguered hospitals, but their long-term utility was negligible. To look at a list of countries and their death tolls, you would scarcely be able to guess which ones used lockdowns as a mitigation strategy and which ones didn't.

"Every restriction we place may slow viral spread, but may carry dozens of unforeseen countervailing consequences," said Vinay Prasad. "Scientists can help define these trade-offs, but scientists have no special ability to speak about values on behalf of all citizens. In other words, science is necessary but not sufficient to deal with COVID-19. Thinking otherwise is a dangerous view that steals political power from people and gives it to scientists under false pretenses."

Exhibit A was Japan, a country in which people were careful about their behavior: they wore masks, practiced social distancing, and so on. But Japan did not lock down its major cities or close its schools, restaurants, and stores. In a nation of 125 million, fewer than 50,000 people died—or 36 people per 100,000. The United States by contrast saw more than 300 people per 100,000 die.

"In medicine," said Jay Bhattacharya, "when a patient dies and it appears to have been preventable, the doctors in the hospital and the caregivers will have something called an M&M conference—a morbidity and mortality conference. And the idea is you openly and honestly discuss what went wrong without pointing fingers. And then let's never make those mistakes again. That," he added, "is what needs to happen with the pandemic."

He's right of course. There were important—and instructive—fact-finding efforts after the crash of 1929, the *Challenger* explosion in 1986, and the financial crisis of 2008. A truly bipartisan COVID-19 fact-finding commission could explore how America's pandemic response went astray and how to avoid making the same mistakes next time. It could point out the changes the CDC and the FDA need to make to regain their positions as trusted sources of health information. It could examine why the public health establishment worked so hard to discredit dissident scientists like Bhattacharya and Martin Kulldorff, instead of engaging them in scientific debate and research. It could try to bring light to unacceptable conditions in too many nursing homes and safety net hospitals. It could work to break through the ideological fights over masks and lockdowns and mandates so that there was finally an understanding of what worked and what didn't. And it could show the country how to establish medical supply chains with resilience.

As of the spring of 2023, however, there was no move to establish such a commission. Both sides were too entrenched in their beliefs. The Republicans controlling the House of Representatives established a select subcommittee on the coronavirus pandemic. But the only thing it seemed interested in was showing that the virus was the result of a leak from the Wuhan lab. It was a completely partisan inquiry. Under Rochelle Walensky, the CDC issued a stinging rebuke of its own performance in the pandemic after Walensky received the results of an examination she'd ordered. "This is our watershed moment," she said, citing the loss of trust in the agency. "We must pivot." As of the spring of 2023, the details of the underlying investigation had not been made public, and Walensky herself had resigned. Public trust in the CDC, which was also facing lawsuits for overstepping its authority in the pandemic, had eroded. It was unclear whether Americans would be willing to listen next time. The FDA also launched an independent investigation of its performance, but neither the Trump administration nor the Biden administration followed up on the recommendations.

In the words of Winston Churchill: "Those that fail to learn from history are condemned to repeat it." The silver lining of the pandemic is the harsh spotlight it shines on our failings. We can look backward in order to move forward, or remain mired in our dogmas.

Acknowledgments

Twenty-three years is a long time for any relationship, but in book publishing, it's an eternity. We are blessed to have been working that long with our editor Adrian Zackheim and our beloved agent, Liz Darhansoff. Starting with *The Smartest Guys in the Room*, which Bethany coauthored and Joe helped edit, through *All the Devils Are Here*, and now *The Big Fail*, their counsel, their support, and their friendship have been a constant in our writing lives. We are grateful.

At Portfolio, we would also like to thank Trish Daly, who went above and beyond, Megan McCormack, Amanda Lang, Linda Friedner, and Ingrid Sterner. At Darhansoff and Verrill, we'd like to thank Eric Amling. We had a crew of excellent researchers, including Maggie Boitano, Cecilia Newell, Clara McMichael, and Benjamin Sherman.

The Big Fail could not have been written without the willingness of many of the participants to talk to us. The on-the-record sources we especially relied on include Lev Menand, Marc Schessel, Paul Offit, Jay Bhattacharya, Mohamed El-Erian, Moncef Slaoui, Mike Bowen, Clyde Prestowitz, Tara O'Toole, Carlo de Notaristefani, and Karen Petrou.

Authors need family and friends to help them get to the finish line in one piece. Bethany first:

My daughters, Laine and Calla Berkowitz, are my greatest joy. They've been understanding of my need to work, curious about the progress and process of the book, and remarkably self-sufficient through it all. They've even, on occasion, fetched me lattes. I'd also like to thank my dear friends—you know who you are—for hand-holding, wine, and love over the last three difficult years, and endless conversations about the book. In particular, I'd like to thank the talented Deborah Roth for reading early drafts and the final manuscript and providing invaluable feedback. I'd also like to thank Anat Admati at Stanford, whose work on society and business have helped shape my thinking. Gratitude to Melissa Marquino and Matthew Kuntz, who have been here through the entire process of this book and helped keep my world working. And I'd like to thank my parents, who are always game for a challenging intellectual discussion, and my sister, Claire McLean, who has offered insight and many late-night talks. Without the love and help from the wonderful Maggie Tag, none of this would have been possible.

Joe's thank-yous:

Kimberly Jung and Poppy Damon at Blanchard House, my podcast home, began as colleagues and became friends; their support was invaluable. Andrew Ross Sorkin helped me regain my footing at a particularly bad time. My mentor, Charlie Peters, is ninety-six; he remains an inspiration. My sister-in-law, Andrea Neuville, never failed to raise provocative questions about pandemic mitigation. Pam Blackburn made sure I was fed after a long day of writing. Wendy Heilbut, Ken Auletta,

Peter Elkind, Alex Songolo, Peter Rose, and Will Burns all lent support at various times in various ways.

My family expanded greatly during the writing of this book and that was a source of enormous joy. My daughter, Kate, and her husband, Mike, had a daughter, Mari, and my son Nick and his wife, Ellie, also had a daughter, Rosalie. They are an absolute delight. My son Amato and his wife, Paula, became foster parents to two wonderful children, Kayleigh and Bella. In the space of a year, I went from having no grandchildren to having four. I'm a lucky man. I'm so proud of my grown children I can hardly stand it. I love them all.

I also have a twelve-year-old, Macklin. His attitude toward this book was that he had better things to worry about. A wise kid. His frequent interruptions were always welcome, and his very presence constantly lifted my spirits. Someday, he'll be old enough to read *The Big Fail*. But I'm not holding my breath.

This book could not have been written without the love and support of my wife, Dawn. Our life together is inspiring, joyful, intellectually challenging, adventurous, and full of love. What more can a guy ask for?

A Note on Sources

This book is the product of well over one hundred interviews, along with contemporaneous news accounts, scientific and academic papers, and work published by Wall Street research firms. In particular, we drew upon work in *The Wall Street Journal*, *The New York Times*, the *Miami Herald*, the *Los Angeles Times*, *Bloomberg*, and the health-care publication *Stat*. We'd also like to cite the detailed work on private equity's influence on health care done by Eileen Appelbaum and Rosemary Batt, along with Eileen O'Grady and others at the Private Equity Stakeholder Project.

Several of the books we drew upon deserve special mention. They include *The Lords of Easy Money: How the Federal Reserve Broke the American Economy* by Christopher Leonard, *The Prince: Andrew Cuomo, Coronavirus, and the Fall of New York* by Ross Barkan, *A Shot to Save the World: The Inside Story of the Life-or-Death Race for a COVID-19*

Vaccine by Gregory Zuckerman, *Shutdown: How Covid Shook the World's Economy* by Adam Tooze, and *Uncontrolled Spread: Why COVID-19 Crushed Us and How We Can Defeat the Next Pandemic* by Scott Gottlieb.

We have tried to be rigorous in identifying the sources of both anecdotes and data in the text itself. To the extent possible, we also identified in the text many of the people who sat for interviews. However, a number of sources insisted on anonymity to talk to us frankly about what they saw in the White House and elsewhere during the pandemic. We are grateful to all our sources—whether named or anonymous—for their willingness to speak to us, many at great length.